Inside Outside

A Retiree's Peace Corps Journal from South Africa

by Sydney Kling
gogoskling@yahoo.com

ISBN-13:978-0-9794257-1-4

DHOT, Inc.
100 South Spring Street
Springfield, IL 62704

Cover Design by Melissa Downin

Library of Congress Cataloging-in-Publication Data

Dedicated to Don Fuchik
Without whose sincere interest
my journal would not have
been published.

ACKNOWLEDGMENTS

I wish to express my sincerest love for the wonderful friends I made while living in South Africa and for the family and friends to whom I returned in the United States.

This book is a journal of experiences during my Peace Corps assignment in South Africa. Although the locations and agencies are accurate, some names of the people have been changed to protect their privacy. I apologize and take full responsibility for any errors that may have been made when describing certain behaviors and traditions.

I am extremely grateful for the commitment and dedicated support provided to me by Linda Fuchik, Mindy Kling, and Andrea Butler Miller. Their tedious reading, editing and encouragement made the completion of this book possible. To my family and friends, a special thank you for your sustained support that allows the continuation of this project.

All proceeds of this publication will be given to the volunteers who continue to provide home-based care and support to those families in Siyabuswa who are affected by the HIV and AIDS epidemic.

Sydney Kling

Chapter One

Peace Corps the Toughest
Job You'll Ever Love
How far am I willing to go
to make a difference and
can I make a difference?

"Today's Peace Corps is comprised of men and women from across the United States who share a common set of values—a commitment to service, a belief in cross-cultural understanding and the hope of making the world a better place."

(Peace Corps Publication)

CHAPTER ONE

JANUARY, 2000

Yes, I did retire! And now I felt like a pre-teen once again. The first three months were odd. I kept myself busy, busy, and then even busier. But how could this be, when I had always thought living multiple lives was so hectic? And this "busyness" certainly was not anything like caring for children, attending school, and working regularly. I was right, the first few months were just that, busy but not constructive. Oh, I was doing everything and having lots of fun, but without personal satisfaction (what do those words mean in this context?). If I needed responsibilities to achieve satisfaction, then it was up to me to do something about it. Dived head first into several volunteer positions and each, be it the Red Cross Disaster Team, Hospice, Crisis Nursery, or even manning the first aid station at the State Capitol meant something intensely personal to me. These types of activities carried me through several months. Even so, I continued spending hours and hours and more hours thinking. What could I do at my age that I may have wanted to do but didn't know how to go about it? Could I ever leave my family, could I ever leave my friends, could I ever leave my country, could I ever travel by myself? Should I do any of the above? No, I guess not. And that was the word that did it. I guessed not, not could not. Okay, now what!? Should I take a driving trip around the states? This would provide me with the opportunities to visit all the people I have known through the years. But do I want to do this by myself and who do I know that could make this kind of commitment? No one. And wouldn't I just be giving myself more time to think and be in the same quandary next year? Yes. Okay, cut this out, what is one accomplishing with this mish-mash of thoughts and dreams? What do I do next? Who do I ask? Is there anyone? NO. That's right, no one is exactly at the same time, place or experience in one's life as you, yourself.

SEPTEMBER 2000

I had many dreams, and every dream brought question after question and all during the first summer of my retirement. I had asked God, Jesus, my own Angel (?), the same questions for years and years but now I decided to listen. It worked! A very short notice appeared in the local paper that stated that anyone interested in the Peace Corps should call the 800 number and request further information. I had seen, without it making an impact on me, the message before. Had thought about the Peace Corps many, many times over the years but just knew I would never be the one to try for the opportunity. But this time, the thought did not leave my mind and after several days of thinking about little else, I did make the call and someone somewhere said the information would be sent right out. It was not. I forgot about it for a short time, maybe a couple of weeks and then something propelled me to call again. I had not thrown away the number. This time the information and the application were sent right out.

Now should I or should I not? Over and over and over, the thoughts interrupted whatever I was doing. Should I or shouldn't I and who could I ask?

No one, because no one could feel exactly as I did. I did fill out the application and waited to see where it would take me...nowhere for several long weeks. But finally, the recruiter through the University of Illinois, Champaign, notified me that a time would be set for the introductory interview.

DECEMBER 2000

It was now the time that I needed to sound out my children and I decided to do this on a one-on-one basis over our individual Christmas celebrations. Susie, my eldest, and her husband, Rick were the first responses. "That's great! It is something we would like to do." John, my older son: "That's wonderful, something I have always thought about." Mindy, my daughter, and her husband Sam: "That's cool." David, my youngest child, and his wife Sangita: "We are proud; we wrote for information years ago and still want to do it." I had worked out the details on how I could leave for such a long time. John was to stay in my home and take care of it, Mindy was to pay my bills and handle any financial problems, Susie was to okay any maintenance such as new furnace, air conditioner, windows, etc., and David, who lived several hours away, was to troubleshoot for the other three. All agreed.

Was this too easy? Are they trying to get rid of me? Many friends were quick to tell me that their families would never let them leave for more than two years. David responded to my questions, "No, this was not an easy way to get rid of you, Mother, but instead each of us is happy that you are happy and still in control of your own destiny." This is not true. Remember, I had turned my destiny over to God and am learning how to listen when help arrives.

It is Christmas time of 2000 and I have been retired for almost a year. I am ready to take a two-week trip to India with the idea that this could give me a little insight on what I might be facing. I had not been accepted into the Peace Corps as yet and had no inkling, if accepted, where I might be sent.

I did go on the trip to India and during the first few days, I thought, "No way!" But it was also during this trip that I knew it (the Peace Corps) was something I really did want to do and it was here that, again, I left it in God's hands. From this time on, the road was paved and all the bends were straightened.

JANUARY 2001

By now it was the end of January of 2001 and the initial interview had come and gone. I had told the interviewer that I would like to be based in Thailand, Nepal or even the Czech Republic, but that I had no real preference. It could no longer be kept a quiet quest (totally) because I needed to have references from my old boss, the volunteer coordinator for Hospice, and a good friend. Hopefully, they also would be supportive. And of course, they were (who asks for references from those who won't give the best)? The references were turned into the Chicago office and it was time to wait and see if I would be nominated. This waiting seemed to go on and on and on. But that's because it was all I seemed to be able to think about!

MARCH-JUNE 2001

Little by little, I was sounding out my friends. Have to admit this only added more fun and games (with wine) to my retirement. After the first response: "Are you really going to do this?" All were more than helpful. Seemed like forever but finally the nomination was placed by someone in Chicago and after a few weeks, an extensive medical packet arrived. Now once again, I did have a full-time job: to certify that I was healthy. I truly doubted if I could remain in a healthy state for the length of time it would take me to finalize all the appointments, tests, exams and to complete the excessive paper work! I knew I felt good but so do an awfully lot of people before they find they have something dreadfully wrong. But no, my health did not stand in the way. All the tests came back normal but they (medical powers) could not leave it at "normal". Must, just must, have the actual pathologist and laboratory results! Finally everything was completed, copies were made and the whole shebang was shipped off to whomever. Now I waited once again. It got to the point where I wanted to scrap the whole idea or at least not tell anyone or answer any more questions, because I simply did not know any of the answers.

Time does go by and all the papers were A-OK, and the Medical Office in Washington DC gave me a clean bill of health. Now WAIT and WAIT I did, but finally received the INVITATION! Shortly after, a young lady from the national office told me that I might be off to South Africa! Whoever said I wanted to go THERE!!! This country had never even been in my thoughts at any given time during this process. Although I still could not be sure that this was where I was going, I did start to read about the country. In fact, I had almost finished reading Mandela's Long Walk to Freedom and my excitement was growing, when the Big Mail came: the packet telling about South Africa and giving me a little more information.

> *"In many areas of the world, access to basic health care is limited. In some communities, the lack of clean water and adequate sanitation exposes children to serious but preventable illnesses. The rapid spread of HIV and AIDS poses a serious threat to the future of many developing countries. Health and nutrition volunteers help at the grassroots level, working with local governments, clinics, non-governmental organizations, and communities where the needs are most urgent and the impact can be the greatest. Their efforts are concentrated on outreach, awareness, and prevention programs that teach public health, hygiene, and sanitation."*
>
> (Peace Corps Publication)

I CAN DO ANY OF THE ABOVE!

I started reading in earnest and becoming seriously nervous, apprehensive, scared, petrified, and ecstatic, but never sick to my stomach (that is when I know something is not right with whatever course I have chosen). Was slowly heading past the point of no return. Too many people are rooting and betting on me and I am not sure I can pass my own family's or my friends' expectations. Why did I ever, ever start this process in the first place?! And it has been a full time 24/7 process.

JUNE, 2001

Today is June the 14th and I can tell it is a day to remember. I put on the music, start cleaning the china cabinet (yes, the china cabinet that no one, I mean no one, is going to notice on Saturday) and the same china cabinet that John isn't going to care whether it gets cleaned or not for the two years I am away. Somewhere in the middle of this project, the impact hits like a thud. Tears roll down my cheeks and I am not even thinking about the Peace Corps. But then I do. And I am scared, scared, scared for all of the reasons I have thought of and dealt with for almost a year. So I call Betty (friend from Collinsville) and ask her to please, oh please, stay over on Sunday night and she said I was really nuts because she has already told me she would!

Later on the same day, I went to lunch with Susan, a friend from Hospice, and that was nice but I thought all the time that I should tell her I was going to call Peace Corps and back out. This was the very first time that that thought had entered my mind. Just told myself that I had kept quiet when I was checking all this out so perhaps I should keep quiet now. And did! I came back home and kept on with the china cabinet, thinking that I still had the kitchen and back porch to do. Put the music back on and the first song I heard was Bobby Vinton's "Born Free." Yes, the tears came again but this time, it was because I was feeling very fortunate that I would be able to go and I forgot how I had felt just a few hours ago. This moment is when I decided to keep a journal in earnest. These mixed feelings cannot be described unless it's the moment, or very soon after, that they are occurring. Makes sense to me. Now I will head into the kitchen. Everyone, just everyone, will look under my kitchen sink (because I will tell them to do this!).

Okay, the party is over and it was more than anyone could have expected. I know without a shadow of a doubt that I do not deserve all the accolades given to me. After all, my departure has not even taken place. I also know that it is very difficult to hear such powerful statements when inside of me, I am trembling uncontrollably and am apprehensive that in no way can I live up to what is expected. My expectations have never been to change the world, only my little tiny space in it. Now, I am not even sure of that.

Will get back to the party but now am going to backtrack for a moment and remind myself a little about what this process has really been. Obtaining the references was in itself no big deal. The three people were the first outside of my family that had been told of my interest in the Peace Corps. After their responses were received, I did meet on January 21, 2001, with the recruiter in Champaign, IL. This meant driving over there and finding my way around campus on a very cold winter night. At first, I tried to meet with a friend and she would have given me directions but we missed connections. Parking is atrocious but did make it and was only a few minutes late.

The young lady who interviewed me was very pretty, articulate and was quite professional. I told her that my biggest fear was learning a new language. Also told her, I was interested in Thailand, Nepal, or the Czech Republic. Never mentioned or omitted for that matter, Africa. Did tell her I wanted to do something in the health arena. The interview was approximately one and ? hours and seemed to go quite well. She had been in the Peace Corps and was not only knowledgeable but willing to share with me some of her experiences. She also gave me more forms to fill out as soon as possible (key words here because these forms seemed to go on and on and on again). Remember I am backtracking here.

FEBRUARY 2001

February 2, 2001

Fingerprints: first to the Department of Motor Vehicles (where I had gone for the Red Cross). No, they could not do it and an appointment had to be made to have these taken at the City Police Department. I ended up making several re-appointments because the policeman who was to take the prints kept getting called out on a case. However, this did not faze me because he was very nice and said he enjoyed taking prints for a good cause.

February 27, 2001

"Congratulations on your nomination! Our Placement team recently received your file from the Peace Corps recruiter. We are charged with assisting you through your review processes. Your application will be reviewed by Placement, Legal and Medical personnel prior to consideration for invitation."

(Excert from letter confirming nomination)

I took time away from this process to stay with Devan and Divia (grandchildren) for a week while their parents had a little rest and relaxation in Los Angeles. When I returned to Springfield, the medical packet was waiting for me. What an exercise in patience: to make, remake all the appointments and tell all the pertinent parties why I couldn't wait three months for any appointment. Mind you, it is now toward the end of February and I have no idea when I will be going (more importantly I have no idea IF I will even be accepted).

MARCH 2001

My primary physician did my physical and filled out pages of forms. He was very precise and extremely patient. "Yikes, nitty gritty details!" He also saw that the definitive results were on both the pathologist and laboratory reports and made copies of the EKG strips. I met during this week with the dentist, who gave me copies for submission of all my previous work (back at least 15 years) in detail, no less. Later I was asked to return to him and request the original x-rays. Yeah, never does one do anything right the first time. Good thing it is not brain surgery or rocket science for which I am applying! It is now the eye doctor's turn and he also has to write the prescription a couple of times as did the technician who fit me with new lens. Both are patient and most helpful but even with new glasses, I cannot read the prescription. Next came the OB/GYN ordeal. The Pap smear and mammogram are completed as well as HIV screening and the bone density tests. Once again, I have to get the okay for the laboratory to send me the actual reports, not just NORMAL. Now I ask myself: am I healthy or am I trying to find something wrong? It's a cinch that, by now, the whole city is raring to get me out of it! After six weeks, everything is completed, copied, and submitted to the proper place. Now, sit, sit, and sit. I went to Florida with a friend for a week's short vacation. I called it a vacation from a vacation! But when I return people are asking, because EVERYONE KNOWS!! No, I haven't heard and yes, I am still interested. After all, I am too healthy to stay home and don't want to have to go through another physical examination. It is obvious that these does do not want to see me again. I am invited to attend a Peace Corps Reception at the University (this must mean that I am going). No, it doesn't. The two young women, representatives of the Peace Corps, are just being nice. But this time, I did not have trouble getting around the campus and met a few nice, informative returned volunteers. They gave my morale a shot because each said that entry was a long, tedious process for everyone.

APRIL 2001

April 25, 2001

I was going to call the recruiter on the 26th when a staff person from the Medical Office called and reported that, yes, I had passed the physical and now it was up to the Placement Office. It has now become a habit to sit and wait as, at the same time, more and more people are trying to get me out of here. Finally, someone in the Placement Office does call and asks if I am seriously interested in going to South Africa. I could honestly answer that I never had, even in fun, considered it. I responded with YES, YES. Please note, by now every single piece of information, response or activity had become second nature to do in duplicate or even in triplicate. I respond with this quick yes probably to save face, but at least now I can answer local questions...and also start boning up on a real place! A different set of fears set in. Can I? Will I? Do I? Should I? Is it possible that all of this has been a force set in motion and over which I had no control? Part of me is ready and has been and another part asks, "Just exactly what do you think you can do?" Now is the time to place my whole being into God's hands once again (had it ever left)? I am sleeping once again: the Peace Corps is definitely the thing to do for whatever the reasons. Perhaps I will never be told just why...just that it must be done.

MAY 2001

May 8, 2001

"Congratulations! It is with great pleasure that we invite you to begin training for Peace Corps service. You will be joining thousands of Americans who are building stronger communities around the world. This call to action gives you the opportunity to learn new skills and to find the best in yourself."

(Excerpt from letter of invitation)

JUNE 2001

June 7, 2001

"Welcome to Peace Corps! You have been invited to join the dynamic, new NGO Capacity Building HIV/AIDS project. The project represents an exciting challenge for Peace Corps South Africa. Additionally, the project enables you to make meaningful contributions both in the fight against HIV and AIDS and also, in the creation of sustainable Non-Governmental Organizations (NGOs)."

(Excerpt from letter of acceptance)

June 26, 2001

This past week has been a good one! I have to remember that I am excited now and still not sick to my stomach. Actually, (love that word too!) am ready to get this show on the road. Every solitary day, there is something about South Africa in the news and I am thinking as I read, "I wish I could be of use to some big, big problem." Perhaps now I can.

This saying gooooood-bye to everyone is not easy. I get mixed emotions, and feel as if I am at a wake (mine). Have eaten out every day for more than two weeks and many times twice a day. The wine still tastes good but am hungry not at all. Well, maybe for a hot dog and a slice of watermelon. Oh yes and pizza and a chocolate milk shake. Am saving these for the last final final. Always wondered how a person chooses a last meal and this must be a little like it. Also, the phone calls are hard to make because it's as if I am never coming back. Haven't heard from my old classmates except at Christmas for years and now several call...as do other friends across the country. Again, I hope to be able to live up to whatever all these people expect of me. If truth be known, I really want to live up to my OWN expectations. This is more difficult because I do not know just exactly what these are. But now have been given another chance to find out. Time will tell. There are too many things I tried to do and didn't make it and now I am praying that this isn't one of them.

CHAPTER ONE

JULY 2001

July 1, 2001

I am now into my last few days at home. Have everything done that I can think of and things, things, things are lying all over. Still haven't decided just what to take. Is this procrastination? Yes. Have met with everyone I can and, as always, there seems to be loose ends. One daughter is redoing her kitchen and the other daughter is struggling with a wrecked racer of her husband's. My son, who is to stay at my house, is torn between staying here or with his significant other. But these events are taking place and these children of mine would be making whatever life decisions are necessary for them regardless of my presence and/or interference.

Chapter Two

Dear Grandma,
First off, I would like to thank you. You have taught and shared so much with me. I have long considered you a role model and hero. You have proven these characteristics in more ways than one, this trip being one of them. I have no doubt in my mind that you will succeed in your goals overseas. It makes me very proud and happy to see others will be fortunate enough to have you as their new hero. I will miss you very much! Good luck to you and please remember to keep high spirits and have fun.
Love Always, Miranda

Written by my granddaughter, age 20, on the first page of the journal she gave me two days before leaving for South Africa.

CHAPTER TWO

JULY 2001

July 1, 2001

I was fortunate and able to go out privately with each of my older grand-daughters and this was a positive farewell. One could not have asked for a more special hour. Am not going to take the time to write all the wonderful farewell gatherings I did have, did not miss many restaurants or special foods. Will just hope that we start all over again when I do return. My last day, I did try to have that hot dog and corn on the cob and watermelon and ice cream cone and potato chips and coke. That did it! Isn't this country great? My journal will continue when I reach South Africa. I'll use the journal that my eldest granddaughter gave me. It is, without a doubt, the very best gift that she could have presented to me.

I lie in bed the last night. I reread,

"There is no teacher like experience...doing what others can only imagine, leading where others follow, taking dreams and making them a reality. The Peace Corps is just such an experience. It's a job that allows you to learn while you teach, encourages you to challenge yourself and your expectations, and gives you the opportunity to improve yourself while helping others.

For many of the more than 160,000 people who have joined the Peace Corps since its founding in 1961, their two-year service has been the chance to re-examine their perceptions and redefine their goals and aspirations. It has immersed them in a new language, a different culture, and an exotic location. All of which makes volunteering in the Peace Corps the chance of a lifetime.

But it is also bracingly real. This is hard and demanding work. It requires commitment, ingenuity, patience, flexibility, and caring. But for the people you work with and the community that you leave behind, you will make an immeasurable difference

Although the Peace Corps traces its roots and its mission to the early '60s, when John F. Kennedy challenged students at the University of Michigan to serve their country in the cause of peace by living and work-ing in the developing world, it is very much an organization of today. In everything from AIDS education to emerging technologies and new market economies, Peace Corps volunteers help address the issues that affect the human condition throughout the world."

(Peace Corps Publication)

Perhaps I have read this cover page hundreds of times. Now I only have this last night to rethink my own motivation for joining and ponder/wonder if I truly wanted to know another completely different and strange culture. I told myself that through the years I had resided in several areas of the United States from Iowa, to Idaho, to California, to Louisiana and back to several areas in the Midwest. Because of this mobility, I had held many different nursing positions.

The most significant of these positions might have been the one I held within the State Public Health Department, in which, among other programs, I was the administrator of the Genetics Section. This brought me into direct contact with families of different races, ethnicities and cultures. Many of my colleagues throughout the nation were of different backgrounds from my own.

Telling this to my self helped, but still I had serious apprehensions about my abilities to take off by myself, to an unfamiliar country and do what, only God could know. I also reread the invitation telling me I would be working with non-governmental organizations or "NGOs." What are they? "Helping them build capacity and become sustainable." What does this mean? Woe is me!

July 5, 2001
> *"Man is a man through other people."*
>
> (South African Proverb)

Very first real day! I am really leaving Springfield, Illinois, United States of America...for somewhere in South Africa. Arise at 3:00AM, although I had never really gone to sleep. Susie, my daughter, came by at 5:00AM on the dot to transport me to the airport...the shortest lap of a very long trip. Mindy, my daughter, and her daughter Mallory, and John, my son, meet us at the airport. I am giddy...love them so much.

Flight to Chicago was fine and I feel just fine. Went straight to the gate for departure to Philadelphia where indoctrination is to take place. No problems; 20 minute wait until boarding time. A window seat is available and I settle down...who am I kidding? It (What is this "it?") hits me with a smack! What am I doing and how can I possibly be away 27 months? I cannot. And now my heart is pounding and racing and skipping...tears are coming and already I really, really want to go home. I have a seat by myself so just cave in. I know it will pass but "it" doesn't and now I am in the motel room stilled and calm...NOT. Again, all went well from the departure to the arrival in Philadelphia. The flight was smooth, luggage was waiting for me, shuttle to the Holiday Inn arrived within two minutes and the room was ready for early check-in. I am by myself.

July 6, 2001
STAGING: This is similar to the legion of workshops I have attended throughout the past years and it's to start in the period directly after lunch. Now it is the late morning and I am no longer by myself. My first roommate is Karon, 26 years of age, very pretty, friendly and a breath of fresh air as she sits across from me on the other bed. We share our excitement and also a few of our fears. She has youth on her side but I have experience on mine. I am envious that she has her life before her and is embarking on experiences that will surely make a difference in the rest of her life decisions. She is envious that I have made choices and still have what she called a "zest" for more adventures. I was not thinking of this as an adventure, but rather as something I "had" to do. (Later, we will

recall this conversation and comment on the mutual respect that came into being during this, our very first meeting).

Afternoon orientation has its up and downs. Excited...lots of nice people and a good mix...I am not the only one over 60 years of age and for me, that is a relief. There are 27 of us and only 3 men...one couple. Of course, we have the Welcome and Introductory speeches followed by Policies in Practice. We are then to discover what will happen to us upon our first few days after arrival in country. I do not believe that the reactions of any of us were at all similar. Several were a little sick, whether from apprehension or a bug, I never did know. A couple were taken back to find living conditions would not be what they expected, and others, like me, have no clue even after staging, what to expect. Tonight four of us go to dinner at an eclectic restaurant: Greek, Thai, and Indian. But nothing South African. We didn't have any idea what this kind of food would be. All in all, it was a good first day. Tomorrow we are off to South Africa.

July 7, 2001

Immunizations-and there were several. Later I walked to the Federal Building on a sight-seeing jaunt but did not stay gone for long. We had to leave for the airport at 11:00AM for a 3 hour bus ride. This trip went fast and I watched every single thing out the window on this last day in the United States. My emotions were kept in check now because I could see that everyone, regardless of circumstances, was feeling very much as I was.

We boarded the plane at 5:15PM New York time and stopped to refuel but didn't leave the plane. We arrived in Johannesburg at 3:00PM South African time. I am very fortunate that I love to fly, can sleep on a plane, and that the flight was non-eventful. Now we board a bus for a long ride from the airport to the outskirts of Pretoria where we will be staying at the Roode Valle Country Lodge for three days. It is very nice and my roommate for this go-around is Mary Jo. After the long trip, we all know each other by at least a first name. Each has been pleasant and easy to meet and all are exhausted. Peace Corps personnel welcomed us. They were also all very nice and recognized our exhaustion. This first night it was early to bed, but sleep...sleep...sleep? No way. The hotel was way too cold and had no heater. This is South Africa??? Finally Mary Jo falls to sleep reading and after I wrap up in a towel, I fall asleep too. We are up at 5:30AM, take a hot bath (YES) and are off for whatever the days may bring. Today, this is a tour of the general area, including Soweto. Tomorrow we are to have several hours of classes to prepare us for our initial host families.

July 9, 2001

Very first thing we are to learn is a new language: "Setswana" for now...HA! Then, those of us with the HIV/AIDS NGO assignment will be learning yet another. Another HA! First word is, "dumela" or hello. I am a dunce! But will learn. Did learn a good bit about living with families. We live with one family while in training and another when we are given our long term assignment. So far, everyone's spirits are up. We had several very good speakers, one of whom was Fanya Mazibuko, the Executive Director of TEASA, (something to do with teachers). He told us a little of the history of South Africa and apartheid. He was very moving and inspiring. Later the Peace Corps gave us a welcoming lunch with the leaders of the different areas. I was most impressed with Yvonne, the Country Director. But for me, and I tell myself, for most of us, we were too overwhelmed with the newness, strangeness, and loneliness of our own feelings to absorb anything concrete and of help to us. Tonight my initial interview for placement took place. How could this be? Another interview and what are they going to do with me if I don't answer properly? Return me over 10,000 miles back to home? They would not do this. But after the interview with Cam, the person who will become my immediate supervisor, I felt that I just might be the exception and HOME I just might go. However, I left this interview anticipating that I would be working with agencies to set up a large network of home-care services. We shall see (little did I know what the word "flexibility" would turn out to encompass in the long run).

July 10, 2001

Will have to write in my journal often because every day is new and long and sleep just hasn't been easy to come by. Worry about the stupid things...what to wear, for instance...no choice, only brought a few items, relatively speaking, that is.

Today we went on a tour of Soweto, a township outside of Johannesburg. Soweto, although it has some of the wealthiest inhabitants of South Africa, is jammed with more people in a small area than would be thought possible. And most of these are living in devastating, abject poverty. We did get out of our bus and visited (?) with some of the people. Most homes were of cardboard and covered with either newspaper or oilcloth. Others were of corrugated tin with no roofs or doors. Most had very little light and no furniture. BUT the faces of the children were bright with delight that visitors would want to talk with them, even though neither group understood the other.

We later saw the photography exhibit of the Soweto uprising.

"On June 16, 1976, students in Soweto organized a demonstration against the use of Afrikaans as the language of instruction in schools. When police shot and killed some of the protesters, a series of riots and demonstrations began nation-wide. As news spread over the world, Soweto became a tragic symbol of the struggle against apartheid."

(Description of a photograph)

The sequencing and tedious detail of this exhibit brought us all to our knees. Later we came back to the hotel to process the day...and could not.

Late in the afternoon, we rode past Nelson Mandela's home in Johannesburg and then visited Winnie's home (his first wife). Both have led unbelievable lives and both are courageous leaders of and for their people.

We had to repack (again) for our trip to the training center tomorrow. Oh, yes, we also toured the Peace Corps Office in Pretoria. We were fitted for bicycles and helmets! Is this for real?

July 11, 2001
> *"Someone who never eats a meal outside of his own home may think that only his mother can cook."*

> (Author Unknown)

Off from Pretoria. Hardly marching! Bus ride to Sandfontein is approximately one and one/half hours. We are, or I am, sick with joyous anticipation and at the same time, I have a horrible nagging fear. Not only am I among strangers of my own ilk but now will be entering a new realm of the completely unknown. We do arrive all intact, tumble off the bus and are met by a large crowd of noisy, rambunctious, and yes, dancing children. We are greeted by the chief of the village and even by TV cameras (never did see our 10 seconds of fame). Again tears of sheer beauty could not be held back.

Finally the moment! We are introduced to our families. It was overpowering and a great relief. They are welcoming us with sincere exuberance. All of them except mine, that is. The father, Frans, who came by himself to meet me, is approximately 60 years old and did not say one word to me. We stare at each other, neither speaking, and I feel my legs about to give out and I want to go HOME. Around me, there is noise, laughing, cheering and talking. Near me there is silence. Finally, his granddaughter, in whose home another volunteer will be staying, comes to his rescue (mine) and introduces us. She rejoins her volunteer and Frans and I remain in silence for what seems like hours but is only about fifteen minutes.

We are offered a huge meal, food of which some I recognize, and some I do not. There was a porridge (yes, porridge) of some type. It had the consistency of a cross between paste (not pasta) and grits. But it was not white, yellow or brown. Instead it was purple and tasted sour. I thought it was because it was rancid or old, but no, this was its own unique, delicate flavor and many of the others developed a taste for what would become a staple. Whenever I am nervous, I can eat and the time did pass. We did have chicken, beef and many other cooked, cooked and cooked again vegetables. While we are eating, the children continued to perform several dances and it is truly a wonderful welcome.

Frans does have a car (this is rare and it is even rarer when he actually drives it). But now Frans and I are alone in his car and we travel several miles to his home in Sandfontein. For some reason, I do not have fear but am uncomfortable because he is so quiet. I find out during this short trip that he does speak English, but only when directly asked a question.

We arrive at his home and surprisingly, I find that I will be staying with the largest of all the families who are to be our hosts. My family is father, mother, granddaughter, daughters, sons-in-law (two each) and several little children...fourteen in all. In no time, I can name each of them because their English names are easy. We live in a village called Sandfontein. Can you believe this?

They have a wonderful home...large and very nice and I am on the inside and they are sleeping in separate quarters on the outside in little bungalows. I have all the comforts...I don't know how to handle these arrangements but will figure it out tomorrow. I am sooooo tired and I want to go to bed. Will I sleep in this big house all by myself, my very first night in Sandfontein? There is no phone. Where is everyone else? It is dark and very, very quiet. But I do sleep and am awakened at 5:00AM by the patter of slippered feet and a soft knock at my bedroom door. Actually, I had been awakened by the turn of the key in the door but it did not frighten me. Little Frans (age 6) is greeting the morning (his words) and me. This will be the norm for the 10 weeks that I stay with them.

Chapter Three

A Person Is A Person
Because Of People
> *Umuntu, umuntu ngabantu*
> *Umuntu*
> *umuntu umuntu*
> *nga bantu*
> *HI E E - HE - HE - E – E*
>> (Sung by Brenda Fazi, young South African singer)

CHAPTER THREE

JULY 2001

Okay, all is well. The adult members of this family do have the little buildings (there are three) outside. But the parents are also out there now. It takes several days before this arrangement has been explained to me. When Frans, the grandfather or patriarch of this family, was öffered the opportunity to build his new home, he took it. But the little one-room houses that his family had shared remained. This was true all through the villages. Frans and his wife Meriam had cared for their children in these little homes with no amenities. Now the big house was strange and not satisfying in terms of safety. Doors were bolted, bars were on windows, and still "the crooks" could hide there! He had already had a car hijacked from his back yard and the only way to deal with this was to live close to the car and outside the house. They did come in for meals and to watch the television, but dressed and slept outside in three very small one-room concrete buildings. Frans and Meriam were in one, their daughter, Paulina and her baby, Kagiso, in the next, and Aggie and Ruth, two teen-age girls, in the third. Little Frans, also Paulina's son and Ledia, whose mother, Hermione, did not live here, took turns sleeping in first one little house and then the next.

Me, I am in the "big house"...and it IS a big house. My bedroom, which usually is the guest room for whichever other family member shows up on the weekend, has a large bed with a red velvet bedspread, a dressing table and a large wardrobe. Very much like home. There is also a master bedroom with even nicer furniture that no one uses and a large living room with davenport, chairs, and TV/stereo. Everyone congregates here usually about 5:00PM until 8:00PM.

The meal in the evening is eaten at the dining room table, with Frans served first, then me, then the rest of the adults who are home and finally the children. I thought, "This is because I am new in the home," but no, this is the way it always is and would continue to be. We do not have a kitchen sink so dishes are done by bringing water from the bathroom (inside) tub and heating it on the stove. Meriam will not allow me to help with the cleaning and that is not only to show respect for a guest in her home but also because of my age. But when they find I can bake cookies and make potato salad or spaghetti, she does let me into the kitchen on weekends.

But I am ahead of myself. Have been in this country 4 days now and am learning so much, my mind is in a whirl. We had our first technical session today and it is true, young people should be given their chance. They are much quicker on the draw and more articulate with today's jargon. I'll just try to go with the flow and start in on the Isindebele language.

And start in we do. We are to have a language class in the morning and Technical sessions during the afternoons. We had to draft a mission statement as a group with input from each of us. Now all are tired...so tired that personalities begin to emerge. Interesting! It does not take long to realize that although each of us is to have input (another piece of jargon we soon tire of), only a few are comfortable enough to take advantage of this free spirit of give-and-take.

Tonight, more family came in and I was questioned at great length about America. This is the part I like except they see us as "Days of Our Lives" characters. I am more comfortable with this large family and they are becoming used to me, too. I think!

July 14, 2001
My Birthday!
In South Africa!

No birthday cards or any mail yesterday on mail call. Why did I say that? What is mail call? We have not received any mail as yet. Just to make sure I wouldn't cry on THE day, I told this family at supper last night. Today, of course Frans (little) greeted me with a birthday wish early, early...even before 5:00AM. They had told me that they celebrate birthdays with little fanfare here so his good-morning wish was especially loving.

Today is Saturday and yes, our group will have classes on Saturdays. Several people wished me well and that was nice. I had thought not to tell anyone...for about two seconds. But of course I did. Actually they had already had us write down the dates of everyone's birthdays. Break time came and several of us took a little jaunt to the bathroom. Up the hill, down again and back behind the bushes! Yes, there is a building but behind the bush was better. We decided this was the use of the building, but we were never ever quite sure which other critters would also be putting it to use at the same time. Came back, took my seat and had forgotten about the DAY. Then everyone hollered to those of us inside to come out (Cat in the Hat) and we did (we are learning to follow directions). AND there on papers on the dirt were soft drinks, cookies and a card made from scratch that is beautiful and signed by everyone. Those tears are welling in my eyes, after all. I do know, if you cry on your birthday, you will cry every day for a year afterward. I may be doing this anyway so couldn't take any chances. But not the end of the story...they also had my mail...which they had kept yesterday so I would receive it exactly on my birthday. And yes, there were cards from Miranda, Judy, and Mary, and letters from Stroudie and my cousin Barbara (all friends from America).

Okay...enough you say. No, No! This afternoon Wilhemina (Meriam's daughter) and her husband Pete took me to Sun City, the gambling resort. We left about 5:30PM and they took me by the airport...size of Springfield's but no planes. It is beautiful. Architecture so different, it is hard to describe but just one thing. Imagine the Springfield Airport (that size if not larger) with high vaulted ceilings, only entirely thatched! This was a special side trip because they had no idea how much I love the sky or anything to do with space and flying. Do not mind saying, though, that I was apprehensive, because by this time of evening it is very dark; there are no lights anywhere in the surrounding countryside and the airport was deserted. I thought maybe these strangers had brought me out here to kidnap me and steal my American gambling money, of which I had none. But, of course this was not the case at all. But I did realize that if one is at an airport without personnel (we even went up into the control tower alone), or even planes, I was destined to be in this country because there was no way out.

After another long ride across from nowhere and heading for what looked like nowhere, we arrived in Sun City and Pete literally took me on a grand tour...as much as we could take. Huge, unbelievably beautiful and gaudy to the extreme, it is truly an oasis in the middle of somewhere. Would be great to stay at the motel(s). Similar to Las Vegas with the vast amount of people, but not like it at all. All were gambling at machine after machine and yet were visiting constantly with each other. Almost as if everyone knew each other and this was a social event. I asked about this atmosphere and Peter told me that this is not a well-known attraction like Monte Carlo or Las Vegas or even the riverboat casinos therefore everyone probably does know at least a few of the people here each night. We gambled for only 10 minutes and about 10:00PM headed for home.

End of a beautiful day! No, No! We arrive home and the house is dark...everyone goes to bed early here. Wilhemina and Pete walk me in because the nights are dark and there is NO light anywhere if the moon is not out. "Happy Birthday!" was shouted out and four of the teenagers (12, 13, 16, and 18) had the table set and a beautiful cake, chips and Sprite. Told me they knew I was missing everyone (I had already shown my family pictures and told about everything I could think of) and they wanted to spoil me. See?! It does pay to advertise your birthday and I don't think it is selfish to want to feel good. And I do! It's been a glorious day from start to finish.

July 19, 2001
> *I see you with my heart*

> (South African Proverb)

It has only been two weeks and it feels like forever! We are so busy every day that each just falls into the next. My host family is wonderful and trying very hard to spoil and fatten me up. But I really miss not having a confidante. We meet for our training on Mondays with the whole group (27) and the other five days with only the NGO group (13). Three of us, Kevin, Cecelia and me, have been assigned to Siyabuswa (where is that?). We must learn Isindebele and naturally Kevin and Cecilia stay way ahead of me. So the first days are miserable but once again this utter frustration passes and I WILL learn! But TWO languages! Come on! Anyway, every day we are to have 1-2 hours with the language trainer. Judas is very patient and very nice. He only has the three of us so it could be worse. How? I just have to get over being so self-conscious when practicing.

After language, we walk a mile to the classes for technical training. I do not realize it for a few days but this walk to and from will become the highlight of my day. We hike down a hard, sandy, rutted road, (sometimes no bigger than a path) and the cars that do pass are the only moving thing that can move this sand...and this sand finds a final home in our hair, toes and all parts in between. But the children along the way are skipping, laughing, playing and they greet us over and over. My way to practice: " Dumela" and they do not laugh.

A typical day is to go very much like this. The first speaker may share with us communication skills (lots of games and ice-breakers), followed by a lesson of South Africa and stories of the different cultures. Every day there is a morning and afternoon tea break as well as a lunch break. We are often to meet in small groups to practice facilitating, planning, processing, organizing, teaching, and networking with those with whom we will ultimately be in daily contact. These sessions go on and on and on. I retired from this, didn't I? But now I am becoming allied with Mary Jo, my first roommate in this country, and we wish we were going to the same place. But no...we are even learning different languages and we are absolutely no help to each other. These classes last till 4:00PM and then sometimes language for another hour (this happens rarely); then the walk home. I am cold both ways, actually am cold all day and do not warm up until at night under very heavy blankets. This village, Sandfontein, in the Northwest Province, is very poor. But the people are generous in what they do have and are willing to share with anyone. It is the norm for someone to visit exactly at the time the family meets for a meal and this person will be asked to join the table. And they do. Later, I find that this person had no food on this particular day or days and visits different families on the road until invited to eat. When he/she does have food, the favor is returned. We have class in the sparsely-furnished classrooms at the grade school. The toilets are outside and if a seat is present, it is so low to the ground that it feels like a pit toilet to those of us who are adults. There is no electricity and water is from a communal pump. The children are the neatest in their uniforms and very white shirts. They laugh and squeal every morning as we arrive and have given most of us African names or call us by the name our family has given us. Mine is "Larado" which means love. It is even now, in these first few weeks, that I realize they speak openly with their hearts. We do not speak like this in the United States...with such unconscious warmth. These children do it beautifully and we are gratefully responding. There is no heat in the classrooms so most of us are bundled up in sweatshirts and long pants. My family does have a space heater that they have given me but they only have one and many of the families have none. I don't know how they do it, except maybe it's genetic. They do not complain of the chilliness (downright cold for me) but instead hate the summer heat (which will be just right for me).

July 20, 2001

Today, visitors from Moqawsi AIDS Council visited our class. In many ways they are like an American nonprofit agency and yet there are many deep and disconcerting contrasts. They have very little capital with which to operate and manage, for the most part, with the services of volunteers. They recognize the need for early testing and identification but have not defined a plan on how to manage this. For the first time I feel more comfortable with what I might be doing. After all, did I not spend years and years trying to defend early screening for genetic diseases and counseling for those in need? But tonight, I studied with Kevin and Cecilia, came home exhausted and the momentum of the day was totally lost.

Ruth (18), granddaughter of Meriam and Frans, came in late this afternoon to visit with me by herself. She told me her mother had died several years ago and that she does not trust hospitals or anyone in the medical field. Seems her mom had surgery in the hospital and died a few days after...without returning home. Ruth has finished high school and received her certificate but cannot find a job. She would like to go to Pretoria but her grandmother will not allow this. We are interrupted at this point and I think this interruption is good and a reprieve for me. I do not know how to advise her because I do not know the cultural mores behind her desires...along with the reality of their new governmental freedom. She also told me today that she wants to write Miranda (my granddaughter). Great...they will like each other. Even though there is electricity, the lights are dim...my eyes are tired.

July 21, 2001

Kagiso (5 months) had immunizations yesterday and a nurse shot him in the hip and today it is really red, hard and swollen. Meriam (grandmother) massaged it very hard and rubbed a little whiskey on it. Hopefully, he will be better tomorrow. In this family, there are members of all ages and on weekends even more of them will be in and out. But guess it will make the transition easier when I move on to another strange family (dream on). Amazing that back home, I live by myself and here I am...thrown in with an extended family of fourteen, with ages ranging from 5 months to 67 years. I would never choose to live this way. Why am I?

July 22, 2001

This weekend has been very nice. Saturday, Aggie (16) and Philipine (12) went with me to class. They made me very proud because they took the lead in a mapping exercise. It was fun and they were most helpful. After we walked back home, we made peanut butter cookies without baking soda, which were very tough but the taste was okay. So much happens every day that I cannot even remember. But a group of Peace Corps volunteers went out to relax and for what they called a little R and R. Believe it or not, I did not go. Guess I am getting older. Fact is, I have had one glass of wine (this is the truth) since the 4th of July! And don't miss it at all (that is a fib).

July 23, 2001

Today was also pleasant. Up at 7:00AM and had the place to myself till 8:00AM. Studied my language and today I feel good about it. But know that tomorrow I will be behind again. Paulina, one of the adult daughters of Meriam and Frans, has been helping me and if I make it through, it will be because of her. Spent a couple of hours at the shop this afternoon and tonight will try to study again.

The shop is a Tuck store (a convenience store by American terms) managed by Meriam and way out in the middle of a wasteland. It is a large building with essential household supplies for sale. Meriam leaves in the morning about 7:30AM and does not arrive home until 6 or 6:30PM. Frans takes her and also picks her up. She is there s even days a week except for church on Saturday and emergencies. Only a few people buy from her each day and there are hours that she spends almost in total isolation. I don't know what she thinks about or how she spends her time. She reads very little and there is no TV out there. Perhaps I will find out more about this and situations like it later.

I need to put this down NOW. Have been so frustrated and downright sad because I haven't talked to my children and finally found the phone (not many here) and reached both Susie and Mindy. I felt so good but of course, I cried and again it hit me right in the heart that I could only chat with them and won't see them for a long time. Guess this is why the PC (Peace Corps) keeps us so busy and exhausted. We cannot use our time being homesick. Enough! Tomorrow we start HIV and AIDS technical training.

July 24, 2001 (I think)

Today was not a good day: I'm slower than the rest with the language, did terrible on the HIV/AIDS pre-test and have decided to make up my own words for language training. No one understands me anyhow. But tomorrow will be better! I was cold all day and didn't warm up until Paulina set me in front of the heater. Guess the cold is the main reason I feel so lousy tonight. We did start our HIV training today. I feel a little more confident about what I will be doing. This confidence is because I have absolutely no idea what I will be doing so how do I know that I cannot do it? And in this case, although I know very little about HIV per se, I did know more than some in our group. That, of course, leaves this whole group knowing very little. However, we still have our brain cells intact and can retain most of the information. We also found out a little more about what our specific roles will be...but this we have found to change from day to day so it was really no help at all! Although Siyabuswa has been mentioned as a place where we might be sent, we still do not know for sure nor do we know the needs of the area in which we may be working. It hasn't even been a month yet and it is quite an endurance test on so many levels (age not the least of it) and yet there are enough perks to keep one going (host family, letters from home and Mary Jo).

July 25, 2001

New day and more information is given to us regarding HIV/AIDS. Enough to have us quaking in our boots! We were told that during the year 2000, it was estimated that more than 34 million people in the world have AIDS and of these almost 25 million are in sub-Saharan Africa! We were also told that approximately 10% of South Africa has AIDS. In some villages, this number can be as high as 40-50% of the local population testing HIV positive. In South Africa alone, there are an estimated 1500 new infections every day. These numbers are very difficult to obtain because people will not be tested and if tested, results are not accurately reported. I found out this data, by myself, after being in the area only a short time and visiting with Meriam's son, Berhold, who comes from Pretoria on the weekends. Everyone is a little frayed...no, a whole lot! We now know the general areas that we will be going to, but not the villages or our exact assignment. Does this sound confusing? You better believe it. The others are chomping at the bit and I'm anxious, too! But...no matter where we'll be assigned, there is not anything we can do now, today.

This family is becoming my rock. Ruthie (18) wants to go to Pretoria and get a job but wants to have her Grandma's permission to do this. So when tonight Meriam comes into my room, shuts the door tight and sits on the bed I thought, "Oh, Oh, Ruthie's dropped the bomb." But instead, she wanted me to pick half of the lotto numbers! Yes, they have no money but still it is fun to play games and pretend that one will become an instant millionaire. I laughed, she laughed and we fell back on the bed. First, honest, unthinking laughter since I left the States! Will remember it for a long time.

July 27, 2001

Today was quiet. A few of the other group went into Rustenburg and were accosted on the street. Very scary for them and a learning lesson for us who will go to Rustenburg tomorrow. Yes, we finally have an outing to go shopping. I must find a warmer jacket because I have been borrowing Pearl's (PCV) and we are heading into cooler weather (what, is this not Africa)?

We also found out where we will go to shadow another volunteer. Alice (PCV), is going with me so I will not be alone. Very few of us will be...and this is good. Alice (teacher group) and I will be shadowing another teacher. Therefore, I will not be going to the place of whatever assignment I receive, but to a school and still will have no idea what my particular job may be. But we are to receive our real assignments the week after we get home (HOME!!).

We have learned a lot more about AIDS this week. People are dying...more than we could possibly have realized. Every single day and not just one a day...but sometimes many...and not somewhere else, but here. Much too fast, much too young.

Kevin and Cecilia asked me to go for a beer later tonight but I'm beginning to relish my hour before bed and this family does not drink, period. They might not let me back in. How could they keep me out? I have the place to myself. I decide to go but do not stay long and do not drink any beer.

July 28, 2001

Today, a very good day...we went to Rustenburg on a shopping spree and I now have a warm jacket and gloves! We went to the mall and it was similar to the malls in the States, except one of the anchor stores was a giant grocery store. I had a chocolate sundae with pecans and took a half hour to eat it. It was soooooo gooooood! Tonight I cooked spaghetti for the family, from scratch (how else). But by this, I mean fresh tomatoes and no tomato sauce or paste. They all liked it. Could only think of Devan and Divia (my grandchildren) and tried to call them but did not get through. This was the only downer of the day. Have to get ready to "shadow."

July 29, 2001

Philipine (12) cooked breakfast...good dishes...very nice. Frans (6) made my bed so guess the spaghetti was okay! They say they will miss me and I'll only be gone a week. Phil and I went for a long walk and she will write Mallory (my granddaughter) soon. Tonight I pack for next week. I am excited about our upcoming visit one-on-one with a seasoned PCV but have kind of settled in here and am also a little apprehensive. Once again, don't know if I'll ever get the hang of all these changes. Each and every day there are new and different experiences. I ask the question, " If I am not going to be working with teachers and will be working with NGOs, why am I not shadowing with a PCV already working with an NGO?" I am told, "There are none in the area where you are going." The word "flexible" is being used more and more often. Why?

My Week Away from "Home"

Monday

We traveled today from Sandfontein to Kameelrivier A. We left Sandfontein for Pretoria in a Peace Corps van and then we were on and off a combi several times until we finally reached a pick-up spot. A combi is a van and we have been told it will be the mode of transportation for most of us for the rest of our sojourn. The combi is always very, very crowded. In this case, there were 16 of us and our back pack, bedding etc. in one vehicle designed to carry 12. But everyone stayed cheerful.

Joyce, our PCV with whom we will be shadowing, met Alice and me at the Kwaggafontein taxi rank (combi) and she was very nice. We rode to her village in a combi filled with local people.

Joyce, a teacher, is my age and has been here for thirteen months. Both of us are delighted to meet her and will bombard her with questions. Mine will be different questions because we found out very early that she went bungee jumping last week at Victoria Falls. I want to do this, too.

She answers hundreds of our question, (number not exaggerated by much). Her place is a separate dwelling of two rooms and located in the back of the main house. She has no inside toilet or running water. But she does have electricity and she has both rooms fixed very nicely. I am also questioning her about trips to take when visitors come (they will, too).

Today and this week, we will get the feel of this Peace Corps. Joyce is the only white person in this village but she is within biking distance of a couple of other PCVs.

Tuesday

We visited two teaching facilities this morning. One is a primary school, grades (standards) 1-7 and the other is a medical clinic. Both are far behind in so many ways. I am torn. Would like to work in this area (I think) but am not too sure if I can handle two years at the pace things get done here. There are so many struggles going on at the same time: new freedom from governmen-

tal control, but needing control because of lack of knowledge on how to handle unemployment and still pay one's own way; all are to be sent to school but those with money are sent to better systems and others fall way, way behind; medical access is not acceptable in many areas but in others is as good as any in the world. Certainly least desirable is the HIV/AIDS crisis, soon-to-be pandemic. Will talk more about this later when I know more.

This afternoon we are going to reschedule a workshop. Joyce tells us this is an everyday occurrence (rescheduling). She can set up a workshop and no one shows up, or she can set the time for 10:00AM and no one comes until they feel like it...which could be any time.

Wednesday

Happy Birthday Mindy (August 1)! I tried to buy a cell phone, had it all picked out but the shop could not take my credit card. Therefore, I could not call Miranda or Mindy. That makes me a little homesick (a lot). We went to the 7th standard today which I think corresponds to our 8th grade in the United States. We helped them act out seven short skits re: AIDS and relationships. They did exceptionally well and provided a spark to me that made me think that just maybe I can help these families. But the thought kept going through my mind: "Who is in this group?" And I knew there could be many. Each young person was so bright and at this moment, I can't go on. One young girl told me, " Your heart is so big it shows on the outside." Is this a "Peace Corps Moment"?

Thursday

A good day! Alice and I helped Joyce with a workshop for the teachers re: HIV/AIDS at Rethabile School. They asked many questions and later asked us to visit a family. Think I may have a job yet. We shall see.

Friday

Went into Siyabuswa with Mary (from local School Board) today. Bought a cell phone and the sons in Joyce's host family, Leonard and Jack, helped me program it. Visited the Health Department; no one was there and now I hope I do not end up there.

After visiting the village, I change my mind once again and think I would really like to work with the families here. Later we went back to the school and the kids all wanted us to stay. I hoped to, too.

Tonight we are going to a celebration for the girls who have returned from "school." This is a school that young women attend in isolation for several weeks. They are to be taught by slightly older peers on the art of being a woman. But times have changed even in this small village: NO longer are young women circumcised.

It is just past 1:00AM and I am writing this because I don't want to forget. We did go across the village, accompanied again by Leonard and Jack, to a house in which the yard was filled with people. Older women are sitting on the ground to the side of the house or are in the back cooking and making biscuits (cookies). Older men are in the front yard. The men are in a very large circle and *laughing, drinking, shrieking, and generally having a good time. Both the men and the women look too old to be the parents of the young people and we are told that most are the grandparents.*

We are paraded around and the three of us, Joyce, Alice and myself, are uncomfortable because we are not a part of any group. Where are the parents? Where are the young men? Where are the young women? It is very dark and the only light is the huge fire for the old men and cooking fires in back for the women. The girls are to come out and dance for all of the people at 11:00PM and no one is allowed to see them until they present. We, because we are AMER-ICAN, are allowed to peek inside the door. My glances show me a large stark room full of young...and I mean young...girls: bare from the waist up but with neck and arm jewelry. Then we are shooed away and find a place on the ground to sit and await the performance. All this time, the men continue to shout, drink and laugh. The girls do not come and it is getting very late. Finally, the girls come out of the house and start to dance around the circle of men. This, of course, draws their attention and all is quiet for about 30 seconds and then the shouting and laughing starts again. By this time, the younger people (mothers, fathers, sisters and brothers) have arrived and the party is truly a glorious cele-bration for the young girls. It is awesome. We watch for a short time and then, because it is very late and it is obvious that the party is to continue until some-time tomorrow, we ask the boys to take us home. They do.

<u>Saturday</u>

The girls came to Joyce's host family about 11:00AM in full dress which meant they remained bare from the waist up. Beautiful hair cut...very, very short. Thousands of beads are banded around their necks, arms, wrists and legs as well as beaded aprons. Today, the men served the girls; killed and roasted a goat while the women cooked an enormous black kettle full of porridge (ugh...a blob of white sticky corn meal) but actually tasted quite good.

The girls (12 celebrating at this home) were very somber and serious. None did any talking or even smiling until after the meal. Each was painted a deep shade of red and this dye covered almost her entire body. Do not as yet understand this traditional rite of passage but will read up on it before writing any more. I could not tell if the girls were scared, proud, stoic, or just worn out. Do know it was extremely unsettling to see fathers and grandfathers sitting around a fire after midnight just waiting for these young girls to come out and perform. But, today as the afternoon progressed, the girls were obvious in their delight at having passed whatever this test was. The men, and now the women, gave gifts and praises to whichever young lady belonged within their family. At this point, the three of us relaxed and actually enjoyed the festivities.

Tonight, we attended a dinner party given by Mary, a local friend of Joyce's. There were ten people who were served around a huge dining table on fine china and with real silver. Mary herself had cooked most of the food and there was a lot. We listened to American jazz and country western music. Visited, laughed and felt the most at home since leaving the USA. This was due, in part, to the fact that Mary's home is in every way very much like our own homes and each person there spoke English very well. Now I have a cell phone and called Susie (daughter). All is well in this piece of the world for the moment.

<u>Sunday</u>

Attended the Methodist Church with Mary and it was very much like any Methodist church, except there was much more music...and the men sit on one side and the women on the other. Everyone sang loud and didn't care if he/she was on or off the tune. The minister spoke of Moses providing water for his people and of Jesus feeding the multitudes. Do not know which language the sermon was in but the minister explained directly to me the passages he would be discussing.

This week has been an experience in sharing information about the Peace Corps, the traditions of South Africa, and a little about ourselves. Alice was a Christian and has now converted to Islam. The three of us had several conversations about our respective religions. Think I even found out more about myself and my own spiritual beliefs. In some ways, I find myself questioning even some of the Americans that are here. I guess we all come with pre-conceived ideas and our own histories...and then internalize and draw in our vision to very minute dimensions. It is times like these that I wish I were younger. This week also served the purposes for which Peace Corps was designed. The three of us, by sharing the unique experiences of an entire week, became staunch allies and friends.

<u>Early Monday</u>

Unbelievable! Am anxious to get back home! That's right, anxious to get back home to my own host family. And at the same time, I am very nervous that they will not want me back!

<u>Later Monday</u>

They all seemed and acted like they were glad to see me, from Kagiso on up to Frans. Tonight I rode with Frans to pick up Meriam and should have taken my camera. The sun faded as a red mass behind a mountain. The horizon was to the side and the sun went down half behind the mountain and half on the horizon. The colors were indescribable, except if one were Taylor Caldwell.

I am exhausted. Am going to read my novel. No studying, no letter writing, just the novel and sleep. This will be the very first time since I left home that I have done this.

CHAPTER THREE

Chapter Four

"Okay," "yes," "of course," "that's right," "why not?"

(Phrases often used at the same time by the local people to prove they know many English words)

CHAPTER FOUR

AUGUST 2001

August 7, 2001
<u>Tuesday</u>

We debriefed today about the shadowing and it seemed an exceptionally long day. By now, the group has been together long enough that most of us are voicing opinions, a few quite vehemently. It is amazing to me that, although we are each adults, each educated in a specific field and each far away from our families, we rarely agree 100% on any single issue about which we are to offer consultation and assistance. How in the world does anyone expect to effect change for a myriad of people when no two of us from the same culture can agree? <u>But</u> I did receive <u>12</u> letters from home and I saved them till bedtime. So maybe that was why it became such a long day!

<u>Wednesday</u>

Back into the swing of it and "it" feels good! A wonderful day and finally feel at ease with this group. Think I have found my own style and it is comfortable. Today, Judas told me I might end up surpassing Cecelia and Kevin with the language struggle. This, of course, is not true but it was nice of him to say it. He also said he could see the "real" Sydney emerging and that this was good. I think so, too! I have no idea just what he means by this but since he is young enough to be my grandson, I think it is that we are becoming friends. And I am spacing out time once again to read my Bible and know this is why I feel better. Of course, the letters from America play a huge part. We are now spending more time in technical training and trying to learn a little about just exactly what we will be doing. This has become a futile exercise but does give us a topic of conversation. I feel much more energized. I think everyone does.

Sing! Sing? You must be joking! This was NEVER EVER even so much as mentioned as a prerequisite for succeeding. "Okay, of course, that's right, why not?" Judas (language teacher) wants us to sing at our swearing-in and that means that Kevin and I would be singing a duet. I do not use ANY of the previous phrases.

<u>Thursday</u>

I can tell you today was a day! Woke up at 3:30AM...no big deal...always do...but before I could get back to sleep, the outside door was unlocked and two people came into the kitchen. Now I know that if I am ever frightened, I will not die of a heart attack because I proved it this morning. Instead, my heart goes to my toes while the blood that it is supposed to pump is in no way producing the fight-or-flight phenomenon. Instead, I lie there and decide it must be Meriam and Frans, for whatever the reason. After about 10 minutes (probably 30 seconds) of soft talking, my bedroom door opens and the light is turned on. I don't have my glasses on and as this apparition appears, I could tell it was not Frans. He said he was so sorry, so sorry, so sorry...but just stood there. Me? I did not scream, just said "Yes?" and then "It's all right." Who is frightening whom here? He called for Paulina and here she comes in her night-ie and says, "Oh, Sydney, this is Funny Face (whoooo?) and he thought he was going into Aggie's room" (she is away at boarding school). They leave and go I know not where but my adrenaline has now kicked in and I am ready to take flight, but where? Finally the morning comes and lo and behold, my (yes, my) phone rings at 7:30AM and my heart takes off somewhere, again to a point unknown. But it is Mary from Kameelrivier A. She wanted to check up on me and to reassure herself that we returned safely. Will wait and see just what Paulina has to say about her introduction to me of little Kagiso's father (Funny Face).

Tonight all the kids are home for the weekend. Philippine came in and visited a long time with me. You know, I seriously wondered how any of us could last with these ten weeks of togetherness, living with strangers of all ages. Now I wonder how those who didn't land in such an extended host family are managing? These kids (all of them) are doing their very, very best to help me. Even "gonna" make me sing…now come on!   We are moving ever closer to our "real" assignments. I am telling myself that it will go "Kuhle (well)."

August 10, 2001
Friday
Happy Birthday
Devan (my grandson in Indiana)!

Really frustrated tonight. Looked forward all day to calling him and today we didn't get back till after 6:00PM. The public phone was closed. Yes, the public phone. Did call on the cell phone, got the answering machine and left the number. Now it is 10:00PM here and no call as yet from the Birthday Boy!

Good day, though very long. Starley (PCV) is sick (?) and in the hospital. No one can say what is wrong and we hope she will be back on Monday. She's been gone since Tuesday. Several are down with colds or the flu. Cecelia stayed home today with a headache and generally feeling lousy. Everyone in this family is ill, even the baby. Probably I'll be next.

Phillippine is going to write Mallory (my granddaughter) and Aggie is going to write Cassie (another granddaughter).

More lectures on AIDS, NGOs and our jobs today. We are to receive our assignments Monday after lunch. It is now August and by Labor Day, I will have been in this process a full year. For some, it has been much longer. But I'm excited now and feel deep inside that this is a "real" job…not just a token gesture to make America look good.   I have not told anyone about my "night visitors" because today, rationally, I know exactly why they came into the big house from the one-room house. But I am so thankful that the AIDS lecture of today was today and not last week. Last night, I did not even think about being raped and truly did not even consider being killed. But today, the young man who gave us more information about AIDS in South Africa put a new fear in me. He told us many myths about the cure for AIDS and the one that leaped straight at me was: old women are raped and this rape will cure the AIDS in the man.

<u>Saturday</u>

Felt like an American today...except for the combi negotiations. All of us, teachers and NGOs, (yes, we now have a title for the rest of us) went to Rustenburg. We left Sandfontein at 9:15AM, arrived in Rustenburg at 11:45AM, left for home at 3:00PM and arrived home at 4:30PM. This sounds fairly easy, but one must know that the village is only 30 to 40 miles from the city. We have learned the hard way that it is nigh on impossible to just enter a vehicle and drive nonstop to your destination. Obtaining transportation has become a science to be studied by us and it means developing skills that might be daunting to even two-year-olds who are American computer experts. We all shopped till we dropped (only buying odds and ends). Catilla (PCV) told me which CDs to give to Ruthie and Aggie as host gifts: "Mama's Gun," "epyKahbadu," and "Indiaar Ie." More about this later.

Last night, several PC volunteers met at the VIP Bar across the fence and road from my host family. Ruthie and Aggie insisted that they take me and then I could have a glass of wine. I realize by now that I never should have told them that I do like wine. They are determined. We did go but did not stay because no wine was available. Later, the two of them returned to the bar and surprised me by bringing me sparkling apple cider. A Peace Corps moment!

Now back to Saturday. We were all invited to Kevin's host family for a "brie" (barbeque) tonight. I did not plan to go and went ahead and cooked spaghetti for this family. But Cecelia and Catilla came over and the cat was out! After we ate, everyone insisted that Ruthie and Aggie walk me down and back. Very, very dark and Aggie told me to "just trip, fall down and get used to it." Then she barely lets me move! We did have a very nice time and came back with no mishaps. And they saw to it that I got my "wine." I ended up giving the CDs to them and the shrieks were an American moment. These are good times but make me miss all my family even more. But it's much better than being lonesome. No, the better word is lonely.

<u>Sunday</u>

"Yes, okay, of course, that's right, why not!" Today, Philippine, Frans, and Ledia each wrote letters to Mallory, Devan, and Divia respectfully. They did an unforgettable job. We walked down to mail the letters (this was a first for all three). Then Frans gave me a tiny pillow with his own inscription of "I love you." Once again I'm outdone by little people.

Now a little about the culture in Sandfontein. As we walked, I could not help but go back in time, when the world was free and before so many countries became so technical and sophisticated. Children are scampering all up and down the road, yards, and pathways: laughing, squealing, running, skipping. Women and men are walking and calling out to each other. Yes, it was like this for me, growing up in small town USA in the 1940s. And yes today, I am pleased to watch and to own a television set. But now I feel we perhaps have gone too far too fast and kids are not able to complain and yet enjoy the long, hazy, boring days that go on and on through the seasons.

Changes are happening, albeit slowly, here in Sandfontein and I am witnessing some of them firsthand within this family. The difference is that, as a child and for me, these changes were happening rapidly and without the realization of how the whole world would be affected. I was living with new technology as it was being developed and never wished it to slow down. I am trying to tell these teenagers in this home that "You have the best, you really do," and to take advantage of this. Women can now leave their homes and young people want "out." For us, this is "normal" and small towns are growing even smaller. But here in Sandfontein, this is a significant change that those over 35 years of age cannot understand. The young believe that America has always been free, women independent, and no one poor. Those older may not even realize there is any other place than South Africa and Sandfontein. No one, regardless of age, can conceptualize that this country is quite similar to the States of fifty years ago. In reality, TV and technology are turning the continent "western," and perhaps no more vividly than in their cities.

It is surprising the respect these young people show me, more so than the younger PC trainees. And yet I can see that, although they are also respectful of Meriam and Frans (grandparents), this respect does not come as naturally for the adolescents as it did for those of their parents' generation. I think that culture in its essence may not be able to maintain this respect as time and communication technology move these young people into closer alliances with their peers throughout the world.

August 13, 2001

"Cooperation is doing with a smile what you have to do anyway"

(Will Rogers)

Monday

Today is the day! We receive our assignments, locations and other details. Needless to say, the morning dragged on...on...on.

We returned from lunch and then we found out. I don't know what I expected.but it was NOT what I got. The goals and aspirations of the different organizations were attached on the walls around the room. We paraded around and read each of them. There was a hospital (might go there), two orphanages (or one of these), a home-based care group, (hopefully there). There was also a group that focused on the awareness and prevention of HIV/AIDS (I did not consider this worth my time reading because as a nurse, I would be going to one of the the the others). The envelope puleeze!!! Oh, there must be a mistake! There is not. I am going to Siyabuswa and with an organization (NGO) called AIDS, Sexuality, and Health Youth Organization or ASHYO. "Yes, that's right, okay, of course, why not?"

I was noticeably upset and asked if there was a mistake. I was told that this is a group of young men and they had requested an older person (not as old as me or a woman, I am sure). My first thought to this response was, "Had I come halfway around the world to make and serve coffee?" We had our break and Mary Jo is going to an orphanage and doesn't want to do this, either. We thought perhaps we could exchange sites. No way...this, for some reason, is not an option. I was told, quote, "Sydney, you said you can be flexible." Obviously, another word to add to my "word hate list." After break and talking with the rest of the group, I gave myself a handslap a few times and decided to make the best of it. And then...I am told that I will be staying with an older couple...inside...no privacy. Now I was ready to cry. But truly didn't. I was a little sick to my stomach and then gave myself what my mother would say was an "attitude adjustment." After all, I had not known to which country I would be sent and I have learned to like South Africa. Just maybe (doubtful), I'll take to Siyabuswa and the job. At this point, I really do not know if I will like or dislike either the job, the town, the home, the family or all of the above. But this whole PC experience has been left in God's hands and this must be case...now more than ever.

Tonight Frans (little) made me a card from Kagiso (the baby). Ledia and Mary made me cards which all give me "love" with no attached strings. Ruthie confided in me about her desire to move to Pretoria, become a model, and study in America. I think this tells me that I am at a good place in my life and probably at first even the princess on the glass mountain didn't appreciate her stay there. Isn't it amazing that we are able to discuss problems with ourselves? I'm better tonight and I can do this. Will do it!

Tuesday

Okay, Okay, Okay. As much as I can understand from reading the proposal of ASHYO is that the young men(all are 20-30 years of age) are to train the trainers (does not say who the trainers are to be). I see that I may be able to guide these young people or members (starting with the Board) in methods of teaching and facilitating small and large groups. The target population is more than 300,000 (how many?) people in four districts. The goal of the organization is to empower the youth (whaaaat?), with regard to their responsibilities to the community. Sounds confusing to me and absolutely no clarification is provided within the written proposal. "To help raise awareness, educate, and mobilize young people to action regarding HIV/AIDS, STDs and child abuse; network with other fraternal structures with similar objectives at the national, provincial, regional and local levels." Believe me, this is word-for-word from the proposal and as far as I can tell, does not say anything about how or what will actually be accomplished? There are many more words, including "facilitating, guiding, directing" (never being flexible) but I get the picture. To me, it echoes of the Newborn Screening and Genetic Counseling programs back in the early 80's. But now I am excited. I see the words "home care" and "hospice" (the words are only mentioned anecdotally) and this means I can help. How, I do not have a clue.

Wednesday

Quiet day. Language class, and now there are just Kevin and I. Cecelia is going to be sent to a different location (wish that I were). We attended lengthy and compelling lectures on HIV/AIDS. Two young people who do indeed have the disease, and a physician dedicated to the care of those infected, presented. We are planning a song and dance routine (in Seswanee not Isindebele) for a talent show the other group is hosting. Yes, me, who can't carry a tune and have two left feet. Oh well, no one will see me (pulled my age and insisted on the back row).

Had our first evaluation today (did not even know we were to receive one) and mine was just fine. All positive, even from Judas, the language instructor. The last statement, "Sydney is a happy and positive soul who will most likely work well with people at post." Don't have any idea who said this out but I'll keep it just for the record. And of course I'm glad I keep my daily "attitude adjustments" to myself.

August 17-21, 2001

"A man is always cautious when passing a place where he once saw a snake"

(South African proverb)

<u>Thursday</u>

We spent a busy, busy two days and it will be difficult to remember all that happened. Someday I <u>will</u> take the time to talk about this family in depth. We were to be picked up at 8:30AM (time changed three times and none of us knew any of this...a SA trick it seems). We were picked up at 9:10AM...loaded literally, all 15 of us with back packs, food etc. into one combi, and headed for Pretoria and the Peace Corps office. Of course we arrived late, our debriefing was very quick and we were off for the Township AIDS Project (TAP). This project operates on a minuscule budget and a huge heart full of passion. Many people of all ages were milling around and anxious to visit with us. Apparently, especially the young people are committed to educating, counseling, and testing anyone and everyone they can get to listen.

We moved right along...skipped lunch and rode to Johannesburg and the National Office of NAPWA. This is the National Association for People Living with AIDS. We met with two delightful young ladies. Both are HIV positive and both are committed to living full, productive lives and urging others to do the same. Did stop for a sausage roll (awful) and then on to the AIDS Consortium. A vast amount of written information is available and this agency serves as a resource center for the Mpumalanga and several other provinces.

We returned to Pretoria and settled into a backpackers hostel to stay overnight. Several of us took a cab (not a combi) to the mall and had dinner at an elegant Thai restaurant. For me, spicy and delicious. Anyway, back to the hostel and a night to forget. There were eleven of us sharing two dorm-type rooms. This meant that one or more of us, man or woman, was up roaming around or giving massages all night long. The night was very long because at 3:00AM, there were seven of us out on the patio drinking coffee. A couple of us did not even return to bed.

<u>Friday</u>

Just as hectic. Over to the PC office by 7:15AM to wait and than rode to the AIDS Training Information and Counseling Center. Very nice setup. The speaker told us that she counsels more than 150 people every Monday. I can not believe this number and doubt anyone else does. We rode to the University of Pretoria and visited the Center for the Study of AIDS. Very impressive and another very good resource center. Oh yes, we stopped today for bagels and coffee...another plus. On to Love Life in Rosebank, which does have a huge budget and is doing fantastic, unbelievable work. They focus on changing behaviors and mindsets re: AIDS and giving young people a chance instead of hammering out the ABC (abstain, be faithful, use condoms) credo. Most young people are now aware that AIDS is a crisis and now must do something productive with this knowledge. We finished at the AIDS Law Project and even saw the offices of Nelson Mandela when he was working in Pretoria as a lawyer.

We headed home. Because I was the last to be dropped off, I did not arrive until 8:45PM. This family was very worried. All in all, it was a great "field trip." But now I have many more unanswered questions. If all this money, time, expertise, and effort is available, why, oh why, are people not receiving help? The numbers of those infected are increasing rapidly, the numbers of those dying are increasing just as rapidly. And if we count into the hundreds those that are willing to help, there remain millions who will not. When this is equated throughout the country, the percentage of those receiving quality care is so low that it is barely, if at all, measurable. I am telling myself tonight that perhaps the answer to this devastating crisis may be revealed when I reach Siyabuswa.

<u>Saturday</u>

Later, we went to another village, Mobodisa. The teacher-half of our big group hosted a big Arts and Talent show. It was great! Our NGO group did do our little song and dance routine which was also successful. Everyone participated: old, young and in-between. First, everyone sang the South African National Anthem, followed by a prayer, and a short speech describing Peace Corps and the objectives of the festival. The local AIDS Council led us in a candle-lighting ceremony (our first). All this was followed by the students performing by singing, dancing and presenting a drama depicting AIDS from diagnosis to the burial scene. These presentations were uplifting and inspiring, despite the subject. We closed with our own National Anthem and tears ran down my cheeks. Never had it sounded so beautiful. It was a wonderful day and this evening, I talked to Mindy for longer than usual and that made the day complete. But now I have joined the ranks and do not feel well. Will be in bed by 8:00PM and can hardly wait.

<u>Sunday</u>

Quiet day...am catching cold so thought it was a perfect day to study. I can hardly wait to get in bed. Did fix a tuna and macaroni dish (kind of blah) and potato salad (which everyone said they liked). Wrote three letters and tried to work on the language. But procrastinated big time and am now going to bed and read. Did not study at all.

Monday

Okay...give in...don't give in! Am sick, by 2:00 PM really felt zonked. Thought to myself...bet by tonight I will really be homesick...I want my own bed...I want Miranda's soup...I want Susie telling me what to do! So what happens? I make it home, very dizzy, tired, sore throat, etc. Ruthie and Paulina take one look at me and allow me to go to bed. Meriam comes home and I am spoiled like a three-year-old. First some pill, (there is no saying NO). Then cough medicine (Jamaican) which is the best, then salve (Vicks but a little different) on my back, chest, neck and bottoms of my feet. Then supper (in bed), a large glass of orange juice and lights out. I did sleep all night and felt much better from then on. Meriam is a whiz and I never got past the homesick thoughts. Or rather never had the chance to get to them.

Tuesday-Thursday

We have spent these days learning about, not only our own, but each other's organizations. Do not know enough about my own assignment let alone any of the others to make any concrete observations. So I am going to describe this family instead, now that I have been here several weeks.

First there is Frans (67) and the head of the family. He is a retired mine worker. Very quiet around me, although now he always speaks and we do talk a little more. He is the one that taught me to say the greetings properly. Evidently he is and was a very hard worker because the family (every single one) treat him as #1. Even with this nice house, he still lives in the old one with none of the indoor conveniences, except a very small television set and smaller heater (which he gave to me). I don't know how he spends most of his hours during the day. He does visit Meriam at her shoppe and sits for long periods in his yard, talking with one friend or another. At times I think he is depressed but don't know if they have that word in this culture. He eats very little but does eat when I cook...possibly to be polite...cannot tell. He is quite thin, has nose bleeds (too often) and I fear that his blood pressure is high. He seldom joins the family in this house to watch TV but often takes the little ones with him and is playful with the baby. I would like to know his history. And perhaps we will really talk one day...but more than likely I will learn to know him through Meriam and Paulina.

Meriam (61) is the matriarch of this family and commands a deep respect from everyone. I don't know how she does it. I don't see how she can work so hard (she denies she does) but she goes to her shoppe, from 7:30AM until 6:30PM every single day. Comes home and manages to see that all goes well here. She is beautiful through my eyes and we are becoming good friends. Each day our conversations are becoming more substantial and we are sharing more of ourselves. She has told me of her hopes for the younger children and even her own daughters and sons. They are truly no different than those hopes of most mothers or grandmothers. She is proud of each but worries because the girls cannot find jobs. She prides herself that she is aware that the world of Sandfontein, as she knows it, is changing. And not always for the best. She considers the family "poor" and prays every day for the well-being of each of her loved ones. The ambivalence of her thoughts is stressful to her. She uses these terms but perhaps in her case, does not recognize the depth of their meaning. I think she is trying to say that she recognizes that although she is happy that her children are advancing and doing well in this modern day, she is also fearful of where this will lead them in the future.

August 23, 2001
Isiphaphamjhini (airplane)
> *Gogo dwells in the living room of risk,*
> *Rumbling through sandstorms of Sandfontein, South Africa*
> *Switching words from English to Setswana to Ndebele slowly*
> *She sits quietly, calm Gogo mind drifting thinking,*
> *"I like the word phaphanami"*
> *"How can I use the word phaphanami/"*
> *She sighs, thinks, ok- rhythmic of hymns*
> *influence her thoughts*
> *Thinking ok*
> *The phaphanami put it plugger in the park-nonsense*
> *The pink and purple phaphanami...crazy*
> *Gogo becomes the plane-*
> *phaphanami, thinking, thinking*
> *"Can I fly?' My thoughts*
> *can fly... and... and I... all for the*
> *sake of using the word phaphanami*
> (Poem written for me by PCV, Catilla, rYzn 2001)

Seven weeks have gone by since I left home. How do I feel? Still more than two weeks to go, I mean two years...what kind of slip is that? Certainly do wish I could write with the humor of J.Viorst or the beauty and detail of T. Caldwell, or with the depth of J. Steinbeck. But will just have to do with notes to remind me of these times. And of course, I will always have Catilla's poem that she wrote for me.

<u>Thursday, Friday and Saturday.</u>
Very long, long days. Lots of interaction in our classes and it is apparent we need to work on our own organizational behavior. Surprisingly, this is not age-related as one might expect. Am not too sure that any of us remember just why we came. Think we must be ready to move on...or is it just that we are downright petrified of the unknown and we are having a "group" reaction?
Friday night and we went to Kevin's (PCV) 30th Birthday party. It went unbelievably well and everyone was in a party mood. Thank God for small

favors. Must have been close to 75 people with all PC trainees, many families and other friends. Lots and lots of food, etc. I made potato salad (what else?): a 5 # bag of potatoes, 18 eggs, and the rest and it was all gone. "Best ever"…still don't know why it is such a hit. Have requests to make it for our family good-bye party. With spaghetti???

On to Saturday. My fear now is that once I get to my site, I'll be there a few days and THEY will decide they do not want me. As far as training, I'm just thankful that PC is devoting this much time to us. Seems we are the first group to be doing this kind of development and taking on the AIDS crisis at the same time as South Africa is struggling with its new-found democracy.

Went to Rustenburg today bought new tennis shoes and Wilhemina (35) a birthday present. Also had a glass of wine and a chocolate pecan sundae. Yes, at the same time. Nice day but Wilhemina (daughter of Meriam and mother of Philipine and Mary) had gone home by the time I returned. Hope to catch her tomorrow.

<u>Sunday</u>

And this they tell me is a SA typical occurrence. It is the first day that I did not have to be up at 5:30AM to race the kids to the bathroom! Knock at the outside door at 6:00AM: some guy wants the keys to the gate (autogate). I was sure I had seen him so I gave them to him. Came back to bed but decided to be ahead of the kids for sure and wash my hair. No hot water but took a bath in lukewarm and of course survived. Back in my room and here come Mary and little Frans. We wrote, talked and played till everyone else comes in.

Hermione (Ledia's mother) and Paulina start cleaning and I end up with Kagiso. He falls asleep with me rocking him. I listen to the TV gospel music and everyone one is busy, busy. I start to cry…homesick, stressed and with that hor-rible feeling that there is "no reason" to feel this way. But I do…the baby wakes up and in comes Philipine (12). She wants just the two of us to fix a really nice lunch. I say okay, what does she want? She wants spaghetti, tossed salad, car-rot salad, rice, vanilla pudding, and POTATO SALAD. I say yes to all but the potato salad. So we start chopping, chopping; she has carrots all over the place. Hermione, Paulina and Aggie have just scrubbed and waxed all the floors.

Right in the middle of all this commotion, in come Pete and Wilhemina. I think "Good, now I can give Wilhemina her birthday present and make this a birthday lunch." No, they fix cheese sandwiches (11:00AM) and she leaves to be back at 5:00PM. At 1:00PM, Pete asks us, "When will we eat?" I say "Do you want to eat now?" Everyone says yes. Then when I go in to say," Five min-utes 'till food is on the table," Hermione and Paulina leave for a wedding! Aggie leaves and Pete goes in the other bedroom for a nap! I do, too.

Thirty minutes later, music is blaring. Aggie is back with Naughty Boy (another grandson) and his friend. Hermione is back and everyone wants to eat. We wake Pete and the six of us eat…not Paulina, not Wilhemina and not even Philipine. The littlest had gone to the shoppe with Meriam so I am eating with the group in this family that I do not know. They are laughing and talking in a language that of course I do not understand (not even in Isindebele). Actually, they are doing a mix of Setswanee, Zulu and English. They stop long enough to ask me questions about AIDS and the United States but luckily, not long enough for me to answer. The spaghetti is good and now I have been so busy with the whole family that my homesickness has passed. Naughty Boy and his friend did the dishes…a first for me in this male-dominated culture. Does this not sound exactly like a number of days back when my own family was growing up? Now it is almost 4:00PM, have done no studying and won't. Will write some letters though. I'm scared to death that they will stop coming (the letters). Tomorrow we continue to prep for OST (on-site training).

Monday
    Atmosphere at training is much better today. Yvonne, the Country Director of Peace Corps, came and spoke to us once again about rules…she definitely eased some of the stresses many of us are showing. Cam, our Associate Peace Corps Director, also spoke with us about what is expected of us for next week. Had more talks on safety at site, ethics and mental health. Received another shot (some type of meningitis), easiest so far and suffered no side effects.

Tuesday
    Language this morning and now we have some hard words and should be using all that we have learned in sentences. Sooner or later, I hope to understand conversations. This afternoon we have more on AIDS and then are free to pack for tomorrow. Paulina was also going to help me with pronunciation. However, she did not. Instead, we had a very nice dinner with way too much food. Meriam and I also had a long, interesting conversation. She told me about having very little money, sending Aggie to private school, hoping Ruthie is safe and her worries about the others. It took Hermina six years to finish nursing school and her pay is minimal. Meriam talked about God and how he sees all, does all, and we must believe to survive. I am sure I agree. She sincerely worries about me and voices her gratitude that Peace Corps is helping her family. I, too, wish we could help out in this village perhaps the next group can.

Wednesday
    It is now 8:15PM and I'm on my 2nd glass of wine. It's been a very, very long day. Should I even start? Did not sleep last night…had many, many dreams (so I did sleep!). One was about an argument I had with Dorothy (friend from home), about cleaning house. Now come on! But morning finally did come with its usual hubbub of everyone getting ready for the day. Meriam was in a little tizzy, telling Sophie (cleaning lady, nonpaid) to make sure my clothes (yes, mine) were ironed and ready. Before she left for the shoppe, she knelt on my floor and prayed for my safety. I prayed for Ruthie's. I did eat breakfast. Had packed my books, raincoat, and bedding in two boxes. Plus I had my back-

pack, with the plan in mind that a bus was to take us to Middleburg. Kevin and I went to language class and we just talked. Judas released us after an hour to go home and pack. Home we go.

Wilhemina and Pete are there to wish me a safe trip and to visit (what???). Later Cecelia came over and we do visit, and visit and then visit some more. From 9:30AM until 12:15PM, we visit. Supposed to have left at 10:00AM. "Come on" again! Now comes the combi (no bus), can't take boxes can take boxes. We drive by Mary Jo's area I say we should pick her up. I think I see her but no one listens and I'm not sure if she has gone on with Ed, Bev and Jennifer. Say again we should drive by and again, no one listens. We drive to the college and no Mary Jo. Everyone blames the driver but everyone is so concerned about boxes that no one is listening to anyone. "No, you can't take boxes." There is only one combi for the 13 of us. "Yes, you can, we will get another combi." "No, you can't" and on and on and on. Back the driver goes to get Mary Jo. She is distraught, thinking she has been stranded. But she gets over being upset, as does everyone else and finally Kevin has us all laughing. Boxes WILL stay at the college and we are on our way at 1:15PM.

The driver gets lost in Pretoria; we stop for ice cream, and make it to our destination by 6:00PM. A meeting with Cam goes well, a glass of wine goes better, and talking with Mary Jo, a breath of fresh air, goes the best.

Tomorrow is the day! We meet our Directors and prepare to spend a week with our new host families and the Show will be on the Road.

Chapter Five

"I just wanted to tell you I think what you're doing in Joining the Peace Corps is a wonderful, brave thing, to do. I have to admit, after reading the family handbook, I'm more scared for you than I thought. I like the way they get straight to the point, but I don't always like what they're saying. Your leaving was meant to be, or it wouldn't have gotten this far, so I know God will look out for you, and keep you safe. Please be assured we will take good care of your 'life' in the U.S., and will anxiously await your return home. I love you Mom"

(Farewell note from daughter, Mindy)

CHAPTER FIVE

AUGUST 2001

August 30, 2001
<u>Thursday</u>

Today was a day never, ever to be forgotten. Do finally have to face facts. I have bitten off more than I can chew, let alone swallow. We met our NCO Directors; mine is named David. He is about 26 or 27 years old. Very nice and very much the gentleman, but others met a director more within their own age range and also anticipate jobs more up their individual alleys. David has a bad cold and stayed very quiet, but at least he came, even sick. I appreciate that and respect him for it. I think he will use me somehow, but am quite sure he did not realize my actual age. As the day progressed, he and I both felt more comfortable with each other, (I think!). However, we did not have a ride to Siyabuswa. Cam, our PC Assoc. Director in charge of the NGO group, had to deliver us via a PC driver and vehicle.

After an almost two-hour ride, with everyone very tired and nervous, ("everyone" meaning David, the driver, Cam and me) we arrive. It is close to sundown. We drive in what to me is a back way, but actually just one of many ways, one more deeply rutted than the next. Finally we arrive and everyone comes out to meet me. There must be at least fifty neighbors or whomever (probably only five or six) and everyone is laughing and talking at once. Cam and David came into the house with me (Thank God for small favors), but it does not take long for me to think that this family DOES NOT speak English much better than I speak Ndebele. I am very sad and close to tears, feel adrift and want to scream "Help." But I tell myself that Christine and Rabie have opened their hearts (and home) to me and that we will each learn.

About this time, as Cam and David leave me and I am desperate and frightened, Thobi (9 yrs.) comes in. She also lives here. She does speak English much better than I speak Ndebele and is willing to help me with everything (again Thank God, this time for huge favors). The three of them agreed that I would feed myself, sometimes eat with them, and sometimes cook for them. This situation is much more like what I anticipated so will continue to tell myself that each day will be better. My homesickness once again passes.

I do have an inside room, (I think for this week), inside toilet (and outside toilet), running but not hot water. There is electricity, though food is prepared on an old wood- burning cook stove (I do not even know how to build a fire). We are each self-conscious at first, of course, and because we cannot converse decently, I escape to my room as soon as possible (by 7:00PM).

Long, long, night. Up and down, both physically and mentally, totally heartsick. And then as it must be, I remember to place myself in God's hands. This first morning, there is no hot water so I boil some in a very small pan on a hot plate that has one working burner. There is also no food so Christine fixes "fat cakes" which are fantastically good. At first it seemed different than life in Sandfontein. No, not so very different EXCEPT for the chickens, geese, pigeons, ducks and sand on every single inch of ground. As I go looking for her, Christine is outside sweeping the sandy concrete area and shooing the fowl this way and that. The sun is stunning at 5:30AM. I don't know if I'll get used to it but it has only been 14 hours since I arrived.

Happy Birthday Susie (daughter in America)
  David and Lucas (one of the young men working within ASHYO) were here early to pick me up and show me the way to the ASHYO office. Met so many people this morning, I can't begin to pronounce their African names, let alone remember them all. The office is tiny but David has allotted a corner of a desk, a shelf, and a drawer to me. There are three more young men who greet me and they appear glad to see me. Then he took me on a walking tour…post office, shopping area, taxi rank, clinic, etc. Won't remember all this either. David is sick. After seeing that his AIDS Campaign in the complex is to his liking, he sent me home. Hopefully, he went home to bed.
  I'm home now with Rabie and feel more than a little discombobulated. Think I'll read and take a nap. Have a headache, maybe closing my mind down will help.
  2:00PM. Thobi home from school and to the grocery we go. Believe it or not, ran into two of the men I met this morning. Came back home and then left immediately to go to the market. No, the grocery and the market are not the same but are in the same location.
  Rabie tells me to call him Mkulu (means grandfather), although I am older. He tells me," Your mind is moving entirely too fast for an old lady" (I think, or this is what Thobi tells me). Do believe I know why older people (me) purposely tune out an anticipated chaos (as good a reason as any).
  Will explain about ASHYO as well as these new people later, after I describe the others…Ha!

Saturday
  Slept better last night. My door opened and the light was turned on at 6:00AM! It was Christina with coffee for me. Big surprise…said she would do this every day because she does it for Rabie.We shall see. Anyway, the day did go by in spurts. Walked to the shops with Christina and Thobi; then back again two more times with Thobi. Different way each time…all areas look alike and I don't understand what anyone is saying. I am meeting people…more people…and more…am becoming exhausted with activity going on and much of it directed straight at me. Went with Thobi to pick up pictures…more people. She (Thobi) is helping me (constantly) to learn everything. <u>Right Now</u>! Hopefully, this will ease up soon.
  Meg (14 months as a PCV) came over to visit this afternoon…great to see her and she answered many questions. She is all of 23 years of age but at least there is another body from the United States in the vicinity. And she is within biking distance.
  Tonight Mkulu (Rabie), Christine and Thobi went to church. Think they must be very active in the Apostolic church because they were in white

robes, blue belts or sashes and white hats. Seems Mkulu is a Pastor. They did not come home until 9:15AM. Elizabeth and Martha (teen-aged cousins of Thobi) spent the night here so I would not be alone. Never mind that I had never seen them before or had any idea who they were. But both were up at 6:00AM, scrubbed all the floors and left when finished. I got up at 6:45AM and washed my hair, had coffee and a pleasant hour to myself. Salome (next door) came to visit at 8:30AM and it pays to be nice to everyone because she is going to ride with me by bus to Pretoria and see that I get on the right combi to Rustenburg. But jeepers, I am so tired.

Last night did not end until I got the call from Mindy. Now I want to go home and want to go home now! And for the first time I wonder why, oh why, I ever ever started this process...I hate, hate that word! Right up there with objectives and evaluation. I want to be there for Mindy. She,of course, would say no-no to that but she needs my support. Mindy is strong, but no one is as strong as they want others to believe.

Sunday

Thobi, Mary (her best friend) and I went to the"shoppes" once again. Tonight I will cook spaghetti and hopefully this afternoon, Thobi will rest. Rather doubt it though. They did and so did I. Then the three of us went for a long walk to wake up. I cooked and David came by to check on me. And best of all, Mary Jo called and we chatted. If she were closer, this would be less of an ordeal. But tonight I do feel better after David came by. Tomorrow, I am to go to the office at 8:00AM to help write a business plan!? Me? Are not business plans one of the reasons that I retired?

Monday

To David's office. Met several of his staff, and also a few of the home health staff, eight or nine, all young and most are men but are very nice and each a gentleman or a lady. They tried to made me feel wanted, needed, and as much at home as possible. But must say, although each man was dressed very nicely,I was a little taken back when one showed up with dreadlocks, another with an ear-ring, and you get the picture. If I had seen this group on the street in Chicago, I would have turned and headed another direction.

After the introductions, David and I went on a whirlwind walking tour...must have walked 6 miles (here it would be 10 kilometers) on sandy and rutted roads. I truly am physically, as well as mentally exhausted. Went to the bank to obtain a loan for a business plan (whaaat agriculture??). Did not succeed for this trip...something to do with wrong account number. Walked up to Siyabuswa B to the District or Circuit offices. Met many, many different people. Back to the office and then on to the local health clinic, which by the way is very nice. They were ready to put me to work on the spot.

Feel much better today and of course, this family and I are becoming more comfortable with each other. Late this afternoon I watched Thobi and her friend play a game with yarn strung between two points. They each took turns jumping across one or the other piece at different levels until one missed. Whoever can jump and not touch at the highest level is the winner.

Top: Thobi's Birthday (Left to Right- Christine, Thobi, and Rabie)

Tuesday

Orientation Day: remembered a few more people and met many more! But a good day because the young men, Njongo, Vusi, Lucas, Oupa, all said they would use my knowledge and so did the women working as home-care volunteers: Rachel, Linah, Evelina, and Kari.

Now I can start writing a little about the life here in this part of South Africa. For instance, the Post Office is a physical plant similar to that we see in the US. But they are much busier all hours of the day and the line has no rhyme or reason. If the clerk sees you have been waiting, she/he will call you to the front, but people just move in and out, up and down, from back to front, or even sit on the floor and wait. No one seems to get upset. Cannot tell for sure, but I think many people are not only picking up mail, but are also collecting a pension and/or government living checks. More on this later.

Today is Thobi's Birthday and we had cake and coke. Now she acts like every other nine-year-old and overeats. Went to bed with a stomach ache which she is quick to say was totally my fault. Seems they do not have cake and coke for birthdays (except for very special years or for those who have lots of money) but never every year, as we do.

Tomorrow I make the trip back to Sandfontein...by bus and combi and through Pretoria and Rustenburg. This will make me one step closer to the life of a PC volunteer. I am to leave here at 5:00AM or maybe 4:45AM. Man, we do put our lives in the hands of strangers!

<u>Wednesday</u>

Up at 3:30AM...no water at all. Christine does make sure I have enough from a barrel outside for a cup of coffee. I brushed my teeth using the coffee! Salome fetched me (her word, not mine) at 5:00AM sharp and we walked to the complex to catch the bus to Pretoria.

I did travel back to Sandfontein by myself but <u>not</u> without help all the way along. Salome rode to Pretoria with me (she goes to college), walked me to the combi rank that would take me to the Bosman rank (at least a hundred combies there) and a lady there told me which combi to take to Rustenburg. She sat beside me and saw to it that I got off at the right place and someone there showed me which combi to climb into for Sandfontein. And then two women saved my seat and told me where to go to the public bathroom. Another woman would not let me go by myself, nor would she let me even enter the place without her. Now come on, never have I been able to go in front of someone but this became the first of many exceptions to that rule. I made it, and thank them with all my heart, bladder and kidneys because it was another 1 ? hours till I was back here in Sandfontein. Even longer before I would be within proximity of any facility that would ease the above organs.

I had left Siyabuswa at 5:00AM, arrived straight up noon and it can't be that far in mileage. I have no idea which part of this world I would have ended up in <u>if</u> I had not put my trust (life) with each of these strangers.

Should write about these combies: a combi (taxi) is a small van that should carry 10-12 passengers but does carry 18 passengers and all the wares, groceries, luggage, babies and anything else that is necessary. The driver does <u>not</u> leave for <u>any</u> place until completely filled (packed). So one might wait 1 or 2 or even 3 or 4 hours before the combi moves. And <u>then</u> they stop for gas. At all the ranks, there are open markets: hundreds and hundreds of stands and vendors. To me, it is utter chaos to find your way to any one of them, let alone the right one.

Back to the combi: the money for the fare is paid from the back forward so everyone digs for rands which means lifting, shifting, unloading, repackaging and then passing the rands seat over seat up to the driver! This only after it is loaded to his satisfaction and he is on the road! Lord only knows how or if it is the correct amount but everyone seems to help everyone else and no one gets impatient. (hmm)! Wouldn't do any good. It is best to be the last one on because the time you must wait to leave is less, but then you're the one who must get on and off to let others with (all their packages) off. And for this frail (am becoming so) old lady with a loaded backpack, I really didn't have the strength.

But made it here in one piece and the backpack remained intact. Paulina and Wilhemina were here to greet me with hot coffee, a peanut butter (with lettuce) sandwich so it was worth coming back, even if for only a week. My room is spotless and a beautiful spread is on the bed. And the kids are lapping up the gummy bears that I bought in Pretoria (shades of Devan and Divia!).

<u>Thursday</u>

Class all day today at the college...almost everyone was satisfied with their placements and even those who voiced concerns are happy to be assigned to a "real" place. After all my fretting, I believe my arrangements will be better and more comfortable than anticipated. Some of the others will be living in very small one-room, concrete block buildings with no amenities at all. Now that I know where I'll be for two years, that, in itself, feels really good.

<u>Friday</u>

We are winding down the training NOW! Last language class today. I wrote the speech for "Swearing In" and Kevin has agreed to give it. Thank God for another huge favor!

Isindebele Version

Sithanda ukuveza amazizo wethu wokuthokoza u/wazi lobandulo. Siyhokoza amavolantiya, abe bangani bethu, kumndeni esamukele emakhaya wabo, kumphakothi osirhelebhe bona, sizwisise amasiko kunye namalimi wesewula Afrika, Kubaberegi bakwa Peace Corps abasise kele esikhathini les. Sigale phambili emnyakeni emibili ezako, ubudlekwano lobu bunagele phambile, kunye nobudlelwano obutiha kunhlangano zomphakathi, kunye nomphakathi. Asenze umehluke, ekulweni nomulwana wentumbantongo kunye nentumbanton-ga. Izandla ziyagezana , the hands wash each other (proverb). Siyathokoza.

English Version

We would like to express our gratitude for an amazing training experi-ence. Thank you to the volunteers that have become close friends, to our host families who have fully accepted us into their homes, to the communities that have helped us to understand South African culture and language, and to the Peace Corps staff for supporting us through this time. We are looking forward to the next two years, making these bonds/relationships stronger and building new relationships in our NGOs and communities. Let's make a sustainable dif-ference in the fight against HIV and AIDS.

This of course, is not the literal translation into English but is made workable for the speech by our language instructor, Judas. And believe me, when you listen to first Kevin, then Judas, and finally me orate it, no one would realize that each of us was not saying our own speech! Judas also gave us his evaluation of our language skills and this is mine: "Sydney is able to participate in simple conversations about survival needs. She can give correct meanings to words." I, of course, knew that his evaluation was based on my urgent need to speak with my hands and the fact that he understood my spoken words. After all, he put them there. This is to say that no one else understood anything I was say-ing!

Saturday

Today is or was another South African day to rember (can't spell in English anymore). We had class from 8:30AM until 12:30PM. Mary Jo and I had decided to go into Rustenburg for R and R, but I needed to be back by 5:00PM. More about this. Today Leah (teacher) has just exactly what I need re: assessment, etc. on my new job. For everyone else, too! No way will we be out early. She talks in slow motion and takes time for questions but it is helpful. She, of course, made up for the delay by giving Mary Jo and I a ride to the combi stand. Now it is 12:25PM. Many combis come and go on by. Mary Jo and I walk to another isolated rank, first combi is full, second is going to Northam (wrong town), third is OK and we take it to Moqwasi. We wait and wait and finally leave, but the gas station where we stop for gas has no gas. The driver backtracks to get gas and then must take the long way in to Rustenburg. Mary Jo tells me to follow her and we cut through long lines of combis only to find we have gone exactly the opposite and wrong way. Back we go through the maze, ask many people and forget to greet first and are ignored. Small things such as asking "Where?" before greeting a person, even a stranger is absolutely unacceptable (in any culture come to think of it). Finally, we find the right line just as a full one moves out. Wait...wait...and get to the mall at 2:45PM. We must leave by 4:00PM in time to get back for the party. We are starved so pizza must come first...no time for ice cream. I had to get more "Beautiful"for my women at home. Do get to the store and they are completely out. No one else in this mall sells Estee Lauder so I am back to square one. Do find a gift for Meriam, and we head to the grocery store for food (for Mary Jo, not me). Lo! or Hark! who do we meet but PCVs, Bev and Ed. Their task was to shop for our party tomorrow. "Oh, you ride back with us for free." We did and arrived home at 6:30PM. Party was for Cecilia, Kevin and me by our host families who are neighbors (within walking distance). Luckily we had met Kevin and Cecelia along the way so we were all late. Party was very nice and everyone quite chipper, although I was tired. Came home by 9:45PM and went directly to bed but did not sleep well once again. Don't know exactly why!

September 9, 2001

Dear Father in Heaven. Thank you for bringing us to this country where we have lived with these beautiful people. Help us, as we move forward, to appreciate all these families have done for us. Guide us now that we may bring strength to those who are weak, wellness to those who are sick, knowledge to those who need education, beauty to those who see ugliness and hope to those who despair. We ask this, Oh Lord, as we join together today. Amen

(The prayer offered at the luncheon given by PCVs to our host families)

Sunday

Off to a good start! Woke up for good at 4:30AM. Up at 5:00AM and started heating water; by 6:00AM had the potatoes on to boil and I am on a roll.

By 8:00AM I am ready to wash my hair and the nice <u>hot</u> water runs right down the drain never to be seen again (plug in upside down!) By now kids are up, in and out, out and in. Frans makes my bed, and arranges all my dresser space. Ledia is playing and Philippine is in control. I write a letter, walk down with the kids to mail it, come back, eat breakfast and all is well.

Thirty minutes later, I decide to wash my slippers and go to hang them on the line. Big Frans is sitting with his head down and gushing blood like a geyser from his nose. I get ice and tell him what to do and he does the opposite as soon as my back is turned. This, of course, throws everyone's plans awry and we are all in a panic. Meriam is at her shoppe. Fortunately, Wilhemina can drive (she is a combi driver) and I tell her we MUST get him to the doctor. We do go to the hospital in the next village. They keep him because his blood pressure is off the roof. Wilhemina brings me back to our farewell party hosted by the PCVs for the village host families.

We do have our dinner. I was so proud of my host family, because everyone came except Meriam and Frans. There were 13 of the family represented. And I gave the opening prayer and the closing benediction. This was a first for me and made me every bit as self-conscious as the song and dance routine!

Later, Wilhemina and Pete asked if I wanted to ride along to visit Big Frans and I did. He looked awfully tired and had no answers as yet. Doctor will be in to see him in the AM. Said he did have high blood pressure. Blood had been running from his nose like a faucet. Am certain he could use a transfusion...at least in the old days this would be the course of action. Not so today, especially here, with the HIV problem.

The hospital was very depressing. We went to the male medical ward and it was almost full. Only place I've seen wards like this is NEVER. Walls an odd color green and row upon row of cots with filled with very sick men. No technology at all: no IV pumps, no wall call lights, no monitors and only a few bedside tables. I only saw one or maybe two people who may have been staff. The place was very bleak and stark. The nurses must have been many hours behind in dosing out medicine. The grounds, however, were beautiful and security was present (whatever for?). It truly appeared to be, what I can only imagine the old TB sanitariums (hospitals) to have been like.

Told Philippine and Aggie good-bye tonight because they had to return to boarding school in Rustenburg. We almost cried and Philippine did. For me, it was like leaving family all over again...and still have the rest to go. It is hard to come and much harder to leave. As we all know "every time we do, we never thought we would."

Later tonight a man is drunk and at my front door hollering to come in. But the doors to this house are locked and the family out back is well aware he is here. I'm not scared, just one more stress on a weekend that has worn me out.

Hark! Light! Susie and Miranda called. It was wonderful to talk with them. Rick, Susie's husband, is winding down and the two of them are going traveling...more power to them while they have their health. Enough for one day...except Miranda really sounds like she has her work cut out for her. Hard,

hard classes. Small world when your granddaughter has the same college professor as you did.

After they called, Sam (teacher) called to remind me that we have a self-defense class tomorrow and to wear jeans. Thought it would be Mindy or John so was really disappointed. Today will go on!

<u>Monday</u>

Guess this will be another day's journey into night! After 11:00PM last night, this older man knocked on everyone's door. Tried to open this one (thanks for the iron security doors and I had the keys). He hollered and hollered, high as he could be. I was only a little scared because I knew who it was. Finally after making the rounds a few times, he was quiet. Later Paulina comes to my bedroom window and asks for the keys. Surprisingly I wasn't frightened when her voice woke me for the second time. Did return to sleep, (where else could I go?). I was up by 3:30AM to put water on and back up at 4:00AM because I thought it was 5:00AM. Water ran straight down the drain again, but did heat enough to wash face, etc. Glanced at the clock and it was only 5:15AM. Thought, okay, will take a little nap but no, Meriam comes in to cook rice for kids' lunch because there is no bread. In fact, there is very little food at all. So this one morning when I do decide to eat to help pass time, the food is low. But Philippine had brought me a cake yesterday and there was a little left. Aha, every excuse to eat and study my language for the test tomorrow. Aha again, no cake left.

September 11, 2001

Oh, say, can you see, by the dawn's early light,
What so proudly we hailed at the twilight's last gleaming,
Whose broad stripes and bright stars through the perilous fight,
O'er the ramparts we watched were so gallantly streaming?
And the rocket's red glare, the bombs bursting in air,
Gave proof thro' the night that our flag was still there.
Oh, say, does that star-spangled banner yet wave
O'er the land of the free, and the home of the brave!

(Our very own National Anthem)

If I don't write every day, I forget what happens from one day to the next. But not this day! It was busy and very full and extremely emotional for every one of us. We had the last language and technical classes. We (Kevin and I) practiced both short speeches. We all had a short 2 hour session on safety and Dara (PCV) was a big help to me. She already knew the moves and told me to think AGGRESSIVE! She's right. She could easily have thrown me and will be able to protect herself. Hope I never am in such a position.

Leah (Technical Trainer) had a beautiful class as her last with us...probably the best. We had just finished with Leah and were ready to celebrate with ice cream and cake and then.........**Everyone's whole world, as we know it, shattered and collapsed. The two towers of the Trade Center were blown to**

pieces when two planes piloted by maniacal suicidal terrorists made direct attacks. It is impossible for me to write further. I want to go Home...to America...as does every single one of us. America is our country.

We did go through the motions of leave-taking with our host families. Gifts were exchanged and the tears flowed. It was very, very difficult because of the devastating catastrophe that is on all of our minds. Even the people in this little village of Sandfontein know that this horrific act will reverberate throughout the world and will affect their lives as well as ours. We were told to stay put until further notice. We want our real families. Absolutely the whole world is stopped...not a single plane in the air. Both David and Susie called. My family is intact at this time but I know there will be sons, daughters and loved ones of friends who were lost. No one, throughout every country, will remain untouched by this nightmare. We are at war and don't even know for sure with whom. But we will know soon and then even more will be killed. The infamy is unfathomable and all of us are sick and want to be at home in America.

Wednesday

Very long, long day. We were released to go shopping for our new home stays but no one really wanted to do this. Packed to leave tomorrow. Tomorrow is the day we will be sworn into the Peace Corps. We will no longer be trainees but instead will be bona fide volunteers.

September 13, 2001

We were picked up at 7:00AM and waited until almost 11:30AM for the ceremony. It was truly beautiful but the tears were for America and not because of the beauty of the ceremony. We left and drove to Middleburg and did have a delightful dinner which Cam (our Associate Director) planned and it was truly a memorable day and evening. But never would we lay aside the thoughts of the horrible and insane actions that have left the American people very sad. But President Bush promises that America will persevere and rise above this evil. We will find and punish the crazy minds behind the monumental tragedy.

Friday

David (my NGO Director) and his uncle (driver) picked me up and we traveled to Siyabuswa and my new host family has graciously welcomed me back. Christine and Thobi had changed my room around, provided fresh flowers, and cleaned top to bottom (this must be done because of the critters in the rafters). Had a big dinner and unpacked. Thought I would be asleep by 7:00PM but it is now 9:00PM and am still wired due to excitement, nervousness, homesickness, and all the words that describe miserable. Have never felt so very far away from everyone I hold dear.

Chapter Six

Nkosi Sikelel I-Africa
Maluphakanys' u Phondo lwayo
Yizwa imithandazo yethu
Nkosi Sikelela Thina Lusapo Lwayo
Sound the Call to come together
And United we shall stand
Let us Live and Strive for Freedom
In South Africa our Land

(South Africa National Anthem)

SEPTEMBER, 2001

September 13, 2001
<u>Saturday</u>

First full day at my new home away from home! Christine and Thobi went with me to buy a table for my room. David came by to see how I was doing. I understand much more what my role may be and do believe I can help...even if only by loving the people. I recognize the differences in our cultures but have learned that there are also many, many similarities (albeit 50 years ago). An example of this would be that fifty years ago in the United States, for the most part, men did the outside work and what they considered the hard labor jobs while women did the inside housework and cooking. Today in South Africa, this is still most often the case.

I took a real nap and later settled my monthly expenses with the family. They gave me my African name which is amazing: "Nomhlakambo". Cannot spell, say or even hum it as yet and am quite sure I have misunderstood the meaning. Went to bed early and was greeted with coffee at 6:00AM which Christine again promises she will do every day. Can't complain about that, now can I?

<u>Sunday</u>

Probably the first day that can be compared to that of a normal day back home. Did my own laundry, everything by hand and by carrying water to the bathtub. Believe me, jeans are not easy for this lady. Christine smiled and Thobi laughed but then left me alone. Hung the clothes out to dry in full view of every living thing in close proximity. Walked to the shop to get a paper (did not get) and back again for a birthday card (did get). Visited, played cards (game?) with Thobi, Mary, and Martha. Organized my room (what is there to organize?) We bought a yellow enamel kitchen table (shades of the US in my childhood) and that along with a bed, two of the kitchen chairs and a wardrobe make up the room.

Mindy called and told me how horrible and catastrophic events are at home. Again I want to <u>be there.</u> She is being strong about her own situation and so I must be too!

Now to continue on with my host family back in Sandfontein. The next person that I met after Frans and Meriam was <u>Ruthie,</u> their 18-year-old granddaughter. Ruthie's mother died several years ago due to medical neglect and/or malpractice (Ruthie's terms). Her father is not in the picture at this time. She has lived with her grandparents for several years. She has an older sister who is living in another house with two small children and her husband-to-be (they did get married Sept. 13, 2001). Ruthie also has a younger brother, Naughty Boy, who lives with a great uncle (I think). Ruthie is beautiful, extremely intelligent (wants to be an engineer), and wonderful with the little kids and me. Although she is patient and hard-working, she tells me how bored she is with her existing life. She loves a young man who is not in the least trustworthy (again her words, not mine). Note: she did leave, after I was there about 6 weeks to try and find a job in Pretoria as a model. According to her, this is the position for young beautiful women because they make the most money. I have not heard from her since. I hope and pray that she is safe (as does Meriam, every single day), and that the opportunities she so desperately seeks present themselves sooner than later. She truly deserves the best and I know she will work very hard, if only given the chance.

<u>Wilhemina and Pete.</u> Wilhemina (35) is the oldest daughter of Frans and Meriam and is married to Pete. Both asked many questions and were very interested in HIV/AIDS. Of course, they, along with everyone else, asked question after question about America. She checked on me almost daily and set me straight (in a polite way) when I made mistakes (like forgetting my cell phone number). She also entrusted her privacy with me when she told me only weeks after conception about her pregnancy. (I say it will be a boy. We'll see). She is the mother of Philippine and Mary...more later about them. Wilhemina drives a combi part-time for her uncle and Pete works in the platinum mines. They have their own home but came to her parents' house almost daily.

<u>Hermina.</u> Hermina is the second daughter of Frans and Meriam. She is the mother of Ledia. Very pretty when she smiles but this is seldom. She may have lupus or some type of arthritis (her words). She apparently does have constant pain in her hands and fingers. She is a nurse and comes on her days off especially to see her daughter. She hurt so much the first few times she came that I saw very little of her. But after her physician did further testing and changed her medicine, she was a different person. I never did become as close to her as with the others, but believe this was because time ran out. She came to both the family party (families gave the first) and to the Peace Corps party that we gave. More about Ledia later!

<u>Paulina.</u> Paulina is the next daughter of Frans and Meriam. What can I say about Paulina that could possibly do her justice? She not only seemed like a daughter to me, she taught me so very much. Patiently, she helped me with the languages and shared her children, Kagiso and Frans. She also took care of me and became my SA confidante. Our cultures are different but our hearts are not. She is a good mother (as they all are in this family) and never did I hear her scream or threaten or ever lose control, and there was a crisis for someone in the family at least once every day. She is lovely and intelligent (as they all are). I truly see this whole family as similar to that of my mother's and grandmother's. Retrospectively, of course, and as I remember. AND some day, provided there is a someday, the Paulinas of SA will be the Sues (my own daughter) of America.

<u>Aggie.</u> 17 years old, Aggie is the youngest daughter and child of Frans and Meriam. She is high-spirited, a good sport, a tease, and an all-around great kid. Cute and little and soon to be the NEW African woman: she does not plan on following "age-old" traditions. Does not always "like" her Aunt Ruthie (only a year older) but certainly attempts to follow her very footsteps. Aggie is tired of school. She attends a boarding school in Rustenburg and comes to Sandfontein only on weekends. She is quite talkative and speaks English fluently. She wanted me included with any and all "happenings."

<u>Philipine.</u> Philipine is Wilhelmina's older daughter (13). What can anyone say about her? She is unbelievably charming, at the same time independent,

self-assured, funny, friendly, beautiful and a delight. Loves me as I do her. Were that all adolescents and young teens were such as she! And she has already called Siyabuswa 3 times to check on me.

Mary. Mary is Philippine's younger sister (10 yrs.). Beautiful, quiet, fair and down-right nice. The right stuff runs through the genes of this whole family!

Ledia. Ledia is Hermina's only child (8 yrs.) She is quiet but feisty and I'm quite sure she will also be Africa's new woman. Took a while to get used to me but when she did, could not do enough to keep me happy.

Frans. (7 yrs.) Nor could he. He is the older son of Paulina and has the brightest, most intelligent eyes in all of South Africa. He also loved me and his desire to learn was only outdone, just maybe, by his desire to teach. And this he did...not only with new words, but how to share and still look out for himself.

Must tell this story about Ledia and Frans: One day when she was supposed to be in school and I was walking to my training session, we met on the road. I asked her what she was doing out all by herself. She spoke very little English so could not tell me but shortly, here comes Frans after her. He tries to drag (literally) her back to school; she will NOT go and I offer to go with them. Into the school we go (my first time) and my appearance disrupts the whole place. Ledia's teacher (also Frans') comes to see what is going on and why all the ruckus. She finally is able to tell me that Ledia has been a "naughty" girl and punched another little boy very hard. She had sent Ledia home but Frans had said that no one was home (rarely was no one at the house) and ran after her. The teacher allowed her back in class and that night she is not allowed to play because she is a "naughty" girl. I asked her why she had punched the boy and I was able to understand that he had hit her first. I said, "Go for it, Ledia, I would have done the same thing." After this, we were good friends and everyone started asking, "Who hit first?" Of course, they didn't hear when I tried to say it is wrong to hit in the first place.

Kagiso. (6 mos.) Kagiso is Paulina's baby and Frans' younger brother. I watched him develop and sit by himself from one day to the next! I wondered how he would ever learn to walk because Paulina carried him in a backpack almost all the time. He rarely was allowed to crawl or even to cry. He, without a doubt, is and will be loved by a wonderful family. Oh, if only, we could just keep the beautiful and peaceful times that remind me of America at an earlier time. South Africa won't stay the same after technology hits anymore than any other place in the world has.

New Family. Have not been here long enough to really know, but in a week's time, all three have been good to me. I'm not myself: new job, new family, new language(s), a solitary figure...and America has been attacked. I want out and am churning up inside. Soon I will be sick. More about Rabie, Christine and Thobi later.

No, will start now and give first impressions. We are in a semblance of a routine now. Believe me, we are spoiled at home (America), whether rich or poor! The women here work, work, and relax by working some more!

Rabie. (56) is head of this household, an apostolic lay pastor, very heavy, tall and generally big all over including his heart. But also very chauvinistic and never, ever, picks up after himself. He is served on a tray. Everything, just as he tells us, must be exactly how he wants it. But, he does the outside yard work (all of the back is concrete that Christine scrubs) and takes care of the chicks, pigeons, geese, ducks and varmints he calls "ventures". What are they?? We would call them "rats". I have yet to see him angry. Worried and tired all the time but not angry.

Christine. (55) It is the same with her. She is plump, short and very much the home- maker. Works all the time: up at 4:00AM Monday through Friday...goes to pray and sing at different homes until 5:00AM and then fixes us all coffee and the day begins. For me, it is coffee in bed and for Rabie also, but not for Christine. Then she starts washing: from clothes to dishes to windows to rugs to floors to outside concrete, then cooks from scratch. No vacuum cleaner, no hose but a scrub brush and sometimes a mop (even for shoes which need to be brushed all the time). Carries water because many times "alright, water is going." "Alright," they have a certain way of saying this word and I like it. I also like Christine; she is a "nice" person and I do believe, lives very much as she preaches: "good." Never have seen her angry but does try to discipline and teach Thobi.

Thobi One could talk about this 9-year-old fairy of a girl child all day every day, and still be at a loss for words. She sparkles, is bright, chipper, a breath of fresh air, giving, loving, egotistic, spoiled, fresh, smart, busy, helpful, lazy, craves chocolate, hates cabbage, clean, covered with dirt, intelligent, plays dumb, energetic, tired, a cutie full of charm. Can wiggle with the best, graceful, awkward, neat, a twelve-year-old, a two –year-old. She is a nine-year-old.

September 17, 2001

When dreams take flight...follow them. Look at the sky, watch the animals, breath the air, hold the babies, love the life, see the sunrise, see the sunset, listen, listen more, come home.

(Instructions from daughter Sue)

Monday

Today, my first day at work, was the day we were all waiting for!! And never could there have been a more boring...troublesome...anxious day in the life of one Sydney! As bad, maybe, but this was one of the above...in spades. Awakened @ 4:30AM when 30 women converged in this house to pray and sing for 45 minutes. Could not let this bother me because Christine brings me coffee by 5:30AM every day.

Walked to work for the 8:00AM starting time and you guessed it: no one there. Finally, after I had meandered to the Post Office (not open) and back again, someone had come. David came about 8:30AM and we chatted for a bit. Then we walked to the District Office and back. He tried to find a ride to Pretoria...did not succeed. I don't understand when they converse, but it seems I am to come up with a monthly report of activities, give a little talk next Thursday or Friday (on what?). The rest of the time I was in the way. But I am aware that this is the first day. Tomorrow I am to go with Vusi to a new office and maybe, just maybe, will be able to work on a monthly report or something. David sent me home at 3:30PM and just like always, the less you have to do, the less you want to do.

2nd day Not much better but not quite so long. Walked with Oupa and Vusi to the technical school...over hill and dale and forever gone...long way, at least four miles round trip. One of our group of PCVs is heading back home. She is not happy with her assignment or her host home, and misses her friends in the States. I want to go, too! Especially since South Africa is a half century behind the United States. But the young men in the office are treating me well so far (there are no women) and the plans they want to put into action are right up my alley. Tomorrow I'm having my first real meeting with the staff and then we or I will know. I hope to become a "new hero" to many families in Siyabuswa by taking an active and vital role as a Peace Corps Volunteer (Ugh). With the help of all the others, we can make a difference.

Wednesday

Who said this time would go fast...each hour is 60 long minutes. It is not easy being new, an outsider, a stranger, and American. It's hard to know what to say to anyone! Finally found a CNN-TV station at the medical clinic and they will let me watch the 8:00AM news before the soaps come on. I can check on our status...which is terrible right now.

Work! David and I facilitated a staff meeting (in-service) this morning. The meeting was supposed to start at 9:00AM, started at 10:30AM but went well. I, of course, could do NO facilitation but they all loved that word so pretended that I had something to say. Later I went with Njongo and Oupa to a school where they observed another NGO give an HIV/AIDS presentation to three hundred 7th, 8th, and 9th graders. Much to be desired. Also a negative was that all 600 eyes were on me most of the time. Supposed to start at 12:30PM, started at 1:30PM and then no ride back to office. Naturally, after some time, the principal came back and offered us a lift back to the office.

Am slowly immersing myself, but it is not easy. Was so busy during training that I do welcome a little downtime...am not getting paid so should not feel guilty but it is hard. Actually it was beautiful that at the end of today's two hour presentation, the students themselves closed with the Lord's Prayer in English for my benefit. The whole program had been in Northern Sesotho and I'm supposedly learning Ndebele...another challenge among maybe two dozen.

Everyday I walk through the marketplace...am beginning to recognize many faces and a few by name. Hopefully, because of my age, they are sincere in caring for me. Someone tells me how to carry my purse, where to find different items and the boys offered me breakfast this morning. A whole loaf of bread was torn apart by pieces and dipped in soup (bean, I think). But we were served on the floor with everyone sitting in a cluster and breaking and dipping from one loaf and one pot. Smelled good, but I was thankful that I had already eaten breakfast. Good thing 'cause there is no such thing as lunch and a long time 'till dinner.

Tomorrow I'm to observe a presentation that ASHYO gives and figure out how I fit in. Only positive is that I am not the least bit nervous. Found a tutor today so the language will either be learned or break me.

Is it the TV that is making me think this may be the END for all of us?

Thursday

David and his troop did a presentation at Vezilwazi High School…standard 10 (probably equivalent to our grade 11). He did an excellent job. Now I am going to have to bite the bullet and speak with 45 learners (students) with Vusi as a translator. I must do this soon. Found out on our walk to the school that David has a son and Vusi has a daughter and neither young man is married. Both do call the mothers of their children "my wife" and treat these young women as such (to me). Hope they are practicing what they are preaching in these classes.

I did my first one-on-one counseling today with a young man from the community. We talked about the consequences of HIV positive clients becoming parents. Went fairly well but this is a "deadly" issue. Met with several home-care volunteers this afternoon and will meet with them again next week in earnest. They want a train-the-trainer session and I don't know if I am qualified. Now I'm home and have been requested to make potato salad. AGAIN!

I came to Peace Corps when much of this work to fight HIV was in its infancy. But it was started in the right direction, that of prevention (for the most part). So I can only say, I am blessed to be a small part in this huge endeavor and with the help of God and the many, many who are working here to beat out this disease, I may be of some help. I see this in my first week here.

Friday

Saw "culture" in many different aspects today. And was overwhelmed once again with so much going into my head and not necessarily into my brain.

ASHYO Members

Was to meet David at 7:40AM for transport to Kragge. By now I am welcome at the clinic and go there to wait for David and to watch the news about my country. They air CNN but of course are 6 or 7 hours ahead of American time. David shows at 8:00AM but transport does not "show" and we wait till after 9:00AM before it is realized that there will be no transport...just sitting.

Others of the staff drift in to see me. Every time I try to start working on something, some person feels sorry for me and comes in to chat. Then, out of the blue, David decides to take me to Siyabuswa B so the women there can teach me broom making, mat weaving, and bead work. (I decline to learn...too hard and tedious). The mat making is not so hard and would do this but I know me: I would last about 3 minutes and then lose interest, not in the product but in the work producing it. The bead work is absolutely beautiful and I do want to learn how they do this. We stayed about 1 ? hours doing nothing...and then we walked back.

We stopped by his uncle's and he asked me to review a community-based organization (CBO) proposal on the spot. Both were accepting to my comments and we walked back to the complex to the computer center, and redid the proposal (or the men in there did it).

It is 1:00PM by this time and David tells me I am released. I head for home with the thought in my mind to draft a monthly report but end up with David and Freddy in tow and they visit here for over an hour. We sit again. I don't know how: the ASHYO staff gets through the days with so much waiting and unknown and/or disorderly agendas; the women work so hard doing the same sweeping, scrubbing, tedious chores over and over all day every day...day in and day out; I never see them do anything just for fun except for celebrations and even then the women work, work, work. How the men just sit,sit,sit; do their jobs, if they have one (most don't), but never ever cook, clean, wash, serve or perform any "female" work. I wonder how the older generation can blame the younger for spreading AIDS. In their eyes, the young are "too much bad" and yet those older did the same activities when younger. It is just as it was 40 years ago in the States: sex was there, just not discussed openly. I have many unanswered questions. Maybe they are unanswerable.

I did read for fun later today, did the dishes and watched the sunset. Terrorists can not ruin the sunrise or sunset. Or maybe they can. I am sitting out on the back stoop and thinking. What do I hope will happen someday? I hope that everyone here will be proud to know me as a type of "hero," (Miranda's words) and this for many years to come. But tonight I cannot even fathom how this could ever be in the realm of possibilities.

I questioned why I was entering the Peace Corps. Did I think for one minute that I could make a difference? I must have. It is now my dream that many of the initiatives in which these young men are working so hard will become realities. That they will always see that the best work that anyone can do is to instigate new actions that reach not only as far across South Africa to the United States but even farther...to the countries that have been left behind in this global fight. Perhaps I will continue this work. I will pray to do so.

Now America has been attacked and I feel very strongly that I want to go home. I question over and over...why oh, why...am I here? But I know that we will recover and if I go home, would that do any good? The answer will come.

Saturday

Up all night, for one reason or another. Then coffee at 6:00AM. Seems Rabie went to church last night at 10:30PM and came back at 5:00AM. Chistine and Rabie leave to attend a funeral at 7:00AM and Thobi and I are here until about 10:30AM. All through the night, people from a shebeen down the road have been carousing at the top of their lungs. I call this the night of "no sleep." Later I do get to do my wash, clean my room, go to the store and take a bath. I am able to wash my hair and clean my shoes but Rabie is comfortable with me now so he comes home, takes a nap and tells me: "You cook today" (he's hungry); then watches TV with belly wide open but he is very nice to me and Christine is, too. No way can I complain. Just not used to this waiting-on-men thing. Rest of day is very quiet...able to read, take a nap, listen to music and cook spaghetti. Talked to Mary Jo and America is in such a turmoil...we both want HOME! Hopefully, one of my kids will call tonight.

Sunday

How many times (cannot possibly count) in the past 3 months or throughout my life have I yearned for a day like today? Up at 6:00AM and found I had been alone (all by myself in this house) all night. Made a cup of coffee, read the Bible, ate a bite, took a "splash," read some work papers, wrote letters, walked to buy newspaper, sat outside with paper, family in and out, had lunch (late), took nap, wrote in journal. And now I am outside and the family is asleep. I'm munching on a biscuit. Weather is great, sun is beautiful and I'm going to watch it set. In fact, will fix a cup of coffee and watch the world go by. May have few chances to do this. Ducks and chickens are turning in, children are playing, young people are strolling, as are the old people.

Am really up in the air or way far down. I don't know which best describes the horribly mixed feelings I have. And in the year since I started this process, this is the first time that I am sick to my stomach about making the decision either way. I want to be at home and have guilty feelings about being here. But also know I knew when I signed up, it would be for two long years. That was before this war situation. Both Mary Jo and Mae (PCVs) are unhappy for several reasons, (not necessarily the same) and about to go stateside. I don't know what to do.

September 24, 2001

In the Constitution it is stated that the Republic of South Africa is a sovereign democratic state founded on the following values: Human dignity, Non-racialism, Supremacy of the constution and the rule of law; and Universal adult suffrage. These values are expressed in South Africa's National Flag, National Anthem, and National Coat-

*of-Arms. National symbols are those official visual and verbal marks
that identify a people as a nation.*

(Excerpt from a Program "Celebrating Our National Symbols")

<u>Monday</u>

Today, even though it was supposed to start at 9:00AM and last until
about 5:00Pm, even I knew it would not start on time. South African time (there
is such a thing!) is new to me but I am learning. The event did kick off at
11:00AM. By this time there were a thousand (s) of people, from all eleven
tribes I'm sure. As far as one can see, there is every color of dress imaginable
and every dance is more beautiful and exotic than the next. Food was everywhere, very much like a large state fair. And imagine if you will, at least 30-40
dance styles and dress out on the same field at once. By the way, people came
by bus, taxis, bicycle, walking, private car and, of course, by combi. It was truly
a spectacular outing.

The program began with the arrival of dignitaries, a prayer and the
National Anthem. It continued with a speech, followed by a cultural activity,
either song, dance or skit followed again by a speech. And the day progressed
like this until the program was completed. Very moving and also very, very long
in the heat. We were in the shade. Almost all the women in the area have very
large backsides (genetic) and believe it or not, you become so used to this, that
the few small women look odd and not classy, or for that matter, sexy. All were
covered from head to foot; some had on running shoes instead of bare feet and
some had baseball caps instead of traditional head gear. The beads had to number in the millions, all colors, shapes and sizes. They wore them up to knees,
elbows and 12-15 inches around chest and neck (not throat), down the back and
on the head. I have no idea how they could walk with the additional weight. It
was this day that I had my first confrontation with the young men. They had
insisted that I go and made arrangements for me to ride with them. By now, I
was becoming used to being by myself with several young men. Becoming, I
say, but not completely comfortable. We arrive and David takes off. I do not
know where. The rest of us are sitting in the bleachers waiting for our table to
arrive. The boys are laughing and talking and now, one by one, they all leave. I
do not know where. Nor do I know anyone else there. Nor do I even know
where I am or how to go back home. They are all gone for about 30 minutes
which feels like hours to me and I am about to cry. They come back; I say
"NEVER leave me alone again!" They are truly apologetic and I swear that for
the rest of the day, they did not let me even breathe by myself. But I am no
longer afraid and feel I can trust them now. I realize it must be very difficult to
be responsible for an old woman to whom one owes no allegiance and for the
most part, (at these celebrations) is in the way. How in the world are they to
cavort around and party with an albatross such as me around all the time?! Am
going to talk about the weather soon.

Tuesday and Wednesday

Went (walked) to the District office both days. David spent all day trying to find a ride to Nelspruit (ended up borrowing the money from me). We shall see if he repays it...it is very different to get across that we do not get paid. Anyway, I have made up my mind to stay here; amazingly, my stomach ache is gone. Thought, thought, thought, more even than when I was deciding to join in the first place. Finally it hit me. Maybe, just maybe, I can be one of the Americans here and tell the truth about our wonderful country. I will have access to more and more people so who knows. And the Government of South Africa is paying my expenses for Train the Trainer so will hang in there...here. Bought a short wave radio and it works. Now I can hear the news on my own. But spent 1 hour 20 minutes at the bank today to just ask one question. Will talk about "sour milk" later.

Thursday

Mary Jo leaves tonight, Joyce left last Tuesday and now I am ALONE here. Not just in Siyabuswa, but these were my American friends in South Africa. Must be out of my mind! I am! Will give it my best for one more month and then see. I didn't know either of these women 3 months ago so can't use their leaving as an excuse. Have to make up my own mind. But today, I did work all day from 8:00AM until 6:00PM, with long periods of waiting, in order to write (yes, write) a proposal to be in by tomorrow (yes, tomorrow). I am back doing what I most disliked about my last job before retirement (yes, writing proposals). This proposal is asking for funding to provide home-based care and long-term support for AIDS affected families. This is much needed and IF awarded would provide a small incentive to stay...but governments are very much the same all over when it comes to money or funding for social services.

Friday

I fear today was a taste of what is to come with my job. David, Njongo, Oupa and I were to meet with a social worker from the District Social Services at her office. David, Oupa and I left our office at 8:15AM and Njongo had already arrived. He had called to find out where we were but when we arrived, he had gone (somewhere). While we are waiting on him, the social worker arrives. It is now 9:00AM and she takes off (somewhere). Oupa is not sure if he wants to turn over our work (which we have not even started) to this group. Patience, Sydney! 10:00AM and David is back (oh yes, he had also taken off somewhere), with the intent to write a second proposal. He sat down and started. Gave no apologies for interruping the work flow that we (Oupa and I) were doing. I am requested to write his objectives for involving the civil society (WHAAAAT?) After getting mixed messages across the table, we all settle down. Oupa and I stick with our plan and the social worker, who has returned, is a big help. David finally stays in place and Njongo is in and out but attempts to keep us all on track. He apparently has a good grasp of the problems. We took a very short lunch break and finished David's proposal by 2:00PM. He left and and I helped Oupa complete his. We turned in the two proposals and in my opinion, neither are written well but apparently meet the requirements they think they will need. What they want to accomplish is commendable and I am willing to help: first, their wish to provide home-based care in seven communities and second, to provide AIDS awareness and mobilization of the civil societies in the fight against HIV/AIDS (what does this mean?). We finally went back to the office at 3:00PM and I came on home.

Christine took me to a dressmaker (another Elizabeth) who will make two skirts (maybe slacks) for me. Guess I'm taking baby steps in this township.

Saturday

Quiet day: washed, ironed, shopped, spent time with Thobi (she wrote a letter to Devan), cooked spaghetti for the family and took a bath. Am looking forward to tomorrow because the family will go to Middleburg for the day. Best thing that happened is that Mindy called and we had a nice visit. She sounded a little better.

Sunday

Family stayed home after all. That is one of the hardest things for me. All meetings, plans, etc. are not taken seriously. Tomorrow we are to have an 8:00AM meeting at the District office but we are not even leaving the ASHYO office until 8:00AM and it is at least a 30 minute walk. But back to today...family went to church and Thobi to her father's afterwards. I missed her and also didn't get the right newspaper. Instead I picked up a South African gossip paper similar to our National Enquirer. But did wash my hair, listened to music, and cooked dinner, (tuna casserole and potatoes O'Brien). Hope son David calls. He does not.

Monday

Supposed to meet David at 7:15AM to go to an 8:00AM meeting at the District office. He showed up at 8:30AM. While waiting, I talked with Cam (APCD) about the upcoming Peace Corps workshop. Seems that all of the workshops that I thought I knew about have either been cancelled, dates changed or whatever. To top this off, some strange man comes in and wants ASHYO to do a Train-the-Trainer workshop. He talks, talks, talks and finally David arrives and tells him, yes, we will do the workshop on Wed., Thurs., Fri., and Sat. Sydney will do it. I said no, I would help, but had no idea what exactly he wanted. In fact, I did not even know remotely what he wanted. Mind you, I have not even sat in on a Train-the-Trainer workshop.

We do go to the District office and arrive for the last 5 minutes of the meeting. David leaves but I am told to stay and help write the proposal (where are all these proposals going?) Okay. We work 2 hours on a calendar of sorts, break for lunch, then do a hit-or-miss budget (for what?) and still no proposal. We break and maybe will meet tomorrow afternoon.

I go back to the office and ask Njongo about the workshop that is to start on Wednesday. He says he doesn't know what they will do. David is gone. I continue to tell myself that this is how So. Africa works. Oh yes, my tutor won't be here this week and I called her rather than she calling me...to find this out. Also went to get a voice link for my cell phone and emergencies. Absolutely no one knew what I was talking about and neither did I. We were just told by the PC office that this was an absolute necessity. Will wait and if reminded again will try later somewhere else.

Tuesday

Went to the District Office once again. Typed a business proposal for David. Waited around and finally went back to office. Tried to work on a quarterly report format (yes, quarterly and not monthly). Very, very confusing day. Go to workshop...don't go...go...don't go. Yes, do go to workshop on home care...but don't go. Do go to workshop on peer education...don't go (it is tomorrow). Will go but it is cancelled and David calls at 10:00PM to tell me. In between all this, I am told to write another proposal (to whom and for what?) don't write...do this PM...no show...do in AM. We shall see in AM but I'm not betting on it.

Tonight Jeanne (PCV) called me and this was wonderful. Am touching more bases with the other volunteers. Thank the powers that be for text messages. To my knowledge, we don't even have these in the United States as yet. Also received my first letters in three weeks This is toooooo long! Now for a period of time we have to wait for Peace Corps to forward out here so it is a long wait again. At least until everyone is aware of our new addresses.

Wednesday

Guess this is what you would call a typical day. We attempted to rewrite the ASHYO proposal (no workshop at all). It took me until 7:00PM to finish because of all the down time, slow time, and interruptions. Seems they never set their minds on a course and complete any project. David's mind is going in many directions at once. If he could focus for ten minutes, he would probably be a genius. It is amazing how much he accomplishes but even more amazing how much he could if he only would.

He has a working staff and for the first time in my presence, they got into a heated discussion. Both David and Freddy stomped out and not together. I left and by the time I came back, every one had cooled down. Guess they didn't mind me hearing because they argued in a combination of languages. I understood more than usual.

A group of seven kids (late teens) came by and a meeting was called on the spot...this to discuss a five-day workshop. They (the kids) were very confused and it seems that their director (a youth organization) lied to them which made David look bad. Come to find out, their director was the man who had been in a few days ago and I HEARD David promise him a workshop. But we know what happened with that! Lucky, I can remain mute through all this. After an hour, David dismissed them to draft a request. He is phenomenal at turning situations around and getting people to do his bidding.

This staff then had a fiscal meeting (what to do with the little money they do have).

I was told to write the objectives for one of the proposals. Immediately, the discussion switched to the issue about transport for tomorrow. Whose responsibility is it to get us to another workshop (which one?). Back come the kids, David shoos them out, calls a woman in the Provincial Government office about the proposal, doesn't get her, calls Cam about another workshop, doesn't get her either. He almost goes to the District office regarding another proposal but back come the kids. We listen to them. David and Freddy go to the bank. Home-care proposal (not the one above) is dragged out and finally at 2:30PM, I start to work in earnest on what I had started at 9:00AM. At 2:31PM, Jennifer, PCV from another site, and her Director come to visit me. No more work. They leave at 4:30PM. I'm tired and decide to bring the objectives home. David had finally decided to help and neither of us could remember what was to go where. He was anxious to get them done and we ended up only with one big mess. Probably still is, but I did clean the objectives up a bit and Oupa is to write and mail them in tomorrow.

GREAT NEWS. Both Dorothy and Mary N. called me tonight from the States and we talked and talked and talked some more. First call from friends since I left. I can't begin to tell how good it made me feel. But now I may be home sooner than any of us thought...IF we end up in war. I pray not.

Thursday

Did something today that never,never, ever in my wildest dreams ever hoped to do. Met David at 7:30AM on the dot and an Environmental Health friend of his drove us to Kwaggafontein. I thought it was to meet with Ruth and wondered why, since we were not attending her workshop. But no, we arrived at Lassie's (Environmental Health Inspector) office about 8:30AM and David was on the phone to everyone he could think of...for over an hour.

We left there at 10:00AM to check about a domestic violence incident (whaaat?). I met more people and someday, somewhere and somehow, I am to meet with them to discuss HIV/AIDS. Since none spoke English, this will never happen. I'm beginning to go with the flow (very slowly) and about to go nuts (very rapidly).

After this meeting, Lassie (pronounced as z) said he had a meat inspection to do. David and I must, of course, tag along. We travelled over an hour and ended up who-knows-where in the middle of somewhere. Very, very poor area. (No, I could not stay in the car...too dangerous). Only living creatures were the flies. And THEN we met four blood-covered men in white overalls and lab coats (no, red overalls and lab coats). They led me into this slaughter house (forget abattoir) and I was greeted by eleven beef carcasses (how in the world do you plural that word?) hung every which way: livers, lungs, hearts, and unidentifiables...oh yes, those too. Anyway, Lassie condemned a lot of the spare parts, slashed up the large trunks and David (who is he to do this?) stamped approval.

All the while they are explaining to me in minute detail why and how this meat is inspected, passed on to the butchery and ultimately to the dinner table. Yes Ma'am, No Ma'am, Thank you Ma'am Please, I don't need any of theeese! Then on to the heads...where Lassie checked for hoof and mouth disease. Me, all I could think, "How do these men do this hard, very physical, messy work all day, every day —-just to have a governmental official (and David isn't even one of these) pitch out so much of it?"

This wasn't enough. We had to inspect another place and it was just as unappealing with even more dead cows. Here the heads were hanging in a row and so help me, I know the eyes were talking straight at me. And now this meat is on to the butcheries. I hope I don't dream about being lost in an abbatoir or worse...hung up in one.

You guessed it. After this, we went to lunch.

Good news. Mail came today and I will have a wonderful bedtime treat. And yes, one of the proposals was faxed (that in itself is another story) to some higher power. Now we wait and see.

Friday

Another crazy day! Arrived at the office at 8:00AM No one there till 8:45AM. David comes a little later. He takes me to a soccer game. All his buddies are there, even though he no longer plays. This to start at 10:00AM, starts at 10:30AM. Lots and lots of beer but not for me. More than 100 young men, (I lost count) and they all treat me royally, as my African name means. It was fun but tiring. We headed back to the office and David had severe pain in left upper quadrant. Had to leave him and asked Njongo to go back and walk with him to the "doctor." He didn't go to the doctor but did go on home and I came on home, too. A nurse (from District office) had been by to see me and to ask for my help with a proposal. No luck!! Now come on. They are overusing this word proposal, are they not?

Saturday

Will talk about the weather because this is a cleaning Saturday and I am finished.

Weather

When we arrived in Sandfontein, early in July, it was winter! No snow, lots of sun but cold. My home did not have heat...none do...but my family had a little space heater and left it in my room. Believe me, I used it every night and every morning. Froze walking to and from class, froze all day long and in class was generally miserable (we all were). Still, the sun shone. The sky stayed vividly blue without a cloud. Finally, after four weeks, it started to warm up. Everything on the ground was still very brown, scrubby and sandy. Moved to Siyabuswa and it was mid- September and spring was arriving. The ground was still brown, scrubby and dusty but the sun shone every single day. Now it is October, windy, cool in the mornings but not cold. Hot by midday and always a breeze. For me, it is perfect weather but am being warned that the "heat" will be overpowering. Although I believe them, I won't complain. I promise. The trees are blooming right before my eyes and every color imaginable is popping up all over the ground. I hope to find the names of these trees and flowers. So far, many are different from what we have in Illinois.

Have been through the period in which I was cold all the time and supposedly am heading into the summer when it will be hot all the time. But of course, adjusting to the weather just impacts in its own way on all the other stresses. My hair is dry, I feel dirty, forget to wear my hat, am thirsty and have to find a bathroom...not easy most of the time. Especially when it's men I am working with and they don't have the same problems. Actually they do, but can handle it quite differently (and more openly). But so far, I am one of the few PCVs that has not been sick in any way. Guess I will weather the weather.

<u>Saturday cont.</u>

Okay, this Saturday turned into a real cultural day. At 3:00PM decided to go for a walk. When the third person told me <u>not</u> to walk by myself and when the second drunk wanted me to come live at his house, I came back. But three houses up, the music had started for the return of the traditional girls. Christine took me up there and it was amazing: four mature young ladies in full outfits of beads, beads and more beads...from head to toe, their parents and gogos (grandmas) all dancing. All the furniture in the house had been moved out in back and neighbors and town people were all over the place. <u>And</u> a cow in the front yard is tied to a tree. I watched (due to Thobi's pressure) and they stabbed her in the forehead...blood spurted and they went deeper. The poor cow finally died. Apparently, it does not take long but it certainly seemed like much longer than seconds. Then they proceded to butcher her and I <u>came</u> home. Enough is enough...especially after Thursday. They are going to have a brie (barbeque) and celebrate the girls' return.

At home, the living room is full of men and it seems the young man is here to wheel and deal for a niece's hand in marriage. All the uncles (great uncles) are involved. Women are in the back yard gossiping and try to tell me what they are talking about. They laugh but of course none of it can I understand. Except that Christine has cooked a feast sometime in between everything else she has done. Now she tells me she has the "flu." The woman is a saint! I sit and wonder why I am sitting in the middle of the 1930's by choice.

Oh, the cultural day did not end. Rabie's family had to go to church all night so in order to stay awake until 10:00PM when they were to leave, Christine decided to watch a video tape. This (only one they have) is a tape of Rabie's mother's funeral. Now I not only did not understand one word but did not know anyone. I did watch for 1 and ? hours and then fell asleep. Due to the celebration up the street, spent a noisy night by myself.

<u>Sunday</u>

It is now 7:20AM and I have finished my ironing, eaten a hot dog (never again), drunk a cup of coffee, read the Bible, and brushed my teeth. Music and whistles are still going strong. People are going past in droves and I am just waiting for time to go buy the paper and some potatoes. Oh, Oh, I opened the front door and some drunk came by and rattled the bars. Guys in the street tell him to come on and leave Gogo (me) alone. This time I have no idea who it is and don't answer but quickly shut the door.

Yesterday, before Thobi dragged me out to watch the cow, I was sitting in the house with the other gogos, surrounded by people who looked, acted and spoke differently than me. What did I do? Being here now for 3 months, I sat back and watched with pleasure (mostly). Asked questions later of this family about both events. I am learning words for myself but if they put more than two together, I do not understand.

Chapter Seven

"Dear America, All people in America, we are very sorry what happened in your land. We are praying to God day and day. We feel you come here because we are safe. We are in Grade 3B. There are 34 in our room. Our teacher's name is Mrs. Paulina Mdau. I am Thobile Mahungela and Sydney Kling is living with my family. My class and teacher want to be pen pals with you."

(Letter written by Thobi's third grade class in Siyabuswa, South Africa to Melissa Urban's third grade class in Peru, Illinois).

OCTOBER

October 8, 2001
Monday

America has declared WAR on the Taliban, Bin Laden and terrorists. This is only the beginning and truly, God only knows what will happen. Thirty strikes were successful and there will be many more. Am very scared what this may mean. Because of the wild demonstrations, the entire Islamic world may cause problems. The aim seems to be to destroy Bin Laden and the Taliban. But there will be counter attacks and we have no idea how or when. Today was quiet here. I'm anxious to hear what South Africa will do.

I finished the monthly report after the British Government representative did a site visit to ASYHO. As I was introduced to him, I found that ASHYO received its initial funding from the British Government several years ago...in 1995 to be exact (I think). I had received skewed messages regarding this funding from David as well as his staff. David has now borrowed money from me and has paid back a portion. I fear that he is using ASHYO funds to do this. Maybe this is appropriate but can not pin him down on exactly how he spends the borrowed money. Today, he spent time with two pairs of young women. The first two wish to become volunteers for ASHYO. This will be a first because as of now, only men are members. The other two want advice and funding to start their own organization (where in the world will they find money to do this?). A confusing day, but mostly because my mind could not leave the United States.

Tonight we had the first rainstorm that I have seen since I came. Of course we lost electricity for several hours. And once again I saw the male take-for-granted supremacy. It is 5:00PM and I am in my room. Rabie comes in and tells me to start cooking because he is hungry and Christine is not home. What to cook is my question? He responds by turning around and leaving. I search around and finally put rice on to boil. By some miracle, the rice gets done just when the electricity goes out (I don't know how to build a fire but will now learn). Anyway, Rabie sits down and does not do anything! Does not go to pick up Christine and finally, she arrives home like a drowned goose only to leave again to get candles from the "tuck" shop. Why didn't he do this before the storm?? He eats and does not help her in any way. She sees no problem with this but it is difficult for me to accept. Christine is tired. She is up as usual at 4:30AM and by 5:30AM is cleaning the freezer which of course is full of melted food. Because it is so early, she receives no help from any of us.

October 9, 2001
Tuesday

Happy Birthday Miranda! (eldest granddaughter in the States)!

Wonderful surprise this morning. Cam called and invited me to lunch in Marble Hall. It was wonderful! I have not been there before and it is a glorious ride through the countryside with groves of fruit trees up and down both sides of the road. I'm going to stay with her in Pretoria Saturday and then we will all go for a week in Nelspruitt (I have not been there before either). This should help our sadness. We are at WAR and it is difficult being here but probably not as bad as other places. And I <u>know</u> I personally am well off. Miranda called me at lunch so that was a major plus. Christine is cooking fish and chips tonight. Am not hungry because we ate chocolate sundaes late. It smells and looks so good that I will eat just to keep Rabie happy.

<u>Wednesday</u>

The United States is in deep trouble: this crisis seems to be escalating as we speak.

Today, I was like my old klutzy self. First I fall off a curb and barely miss being overrun by a combi. Next, I fall into a creek and cover my shoes with sandy mud. Finally, do you know it? I have the nerve to ask a young man, "What are you going to do with them?" Talking about no less than a box of condoms! Did attend a planning meeting on WORLD AIDS Day, kept my mouth shut and it went very well.

Now I'm home listening to the news and it is not good.

<u>Thursday</u>

Thobi's class wrote their letter to the class in the United States. She is very proud and so am I. I think it is beautiful and think it should be printed by their hometown paper.

Today was another heart-rending one. Only this time it took place here in South Africa. I went with David and Vusi up to the public health clinic to see what could be done for a young lady (26 yrs.) that David had seen last night. The clinic had 200 + (yes, I counted them) patients sitting there and this was 11:00AM and does not count those who had been there, nor those yet to come. They have no visiting or home health nurses so there is nothing they can do.

David informs me that the young woman, of course, is extremely weak and does not have transport to the clinic, nor could she walk the distance even if she did have the strength. We walked to her home and I had my awakening. A little boy was playing in the yard (her brother). He did not acknowledge us until he saw me and then he was very frightened. He had never seen a white person before. The family is very poor but the home is clean. The young lady was lying on a pallet on a dirt floor of a one room house. The room had very little light and that only from the single window which was closed. No air was moving. I knelt down beside her and took her hand. Her eyes focused on me but did not question what I was doing there. She felt like a burning cinder to the touch. Her pulse was racing and her respirations were too rapid and shallow to count. I understood her moans to mean she "hurt" everywhere, each cough brought tears and this she did constantly. Pneumonia versus HIV was her doctor's diagnosis.

I told her mother she must go to the hospital (finally agreed to the clinic) and David literally talked a neighbor into giving her a ride in the back of a very old pick-up. After several attempts, some kid finally got it started. Sputtered all the way to the clinic (the truck) and I had my first ride in the back.

This is a no-no for Peace Corps volunteers but exceptions must be made and I was not going to have her die by herself in the back. The pot holes were cavernous and the bumps were painful for her and my lap did not help her much.

A clinic nurse (very few real nurses and those are paid very little) did greet us and put her in a treatment room. Her temperature was 106 degrees and he (nurse) started IV fluids and she (young woman) smiled at me. This truly broke my heart: she has been sick for two years, is close to dying and smiles at me, a stranger.

We left her at the clinic and returned to our office and Kediboni (tutor) came by for a language lesson. I AM learning! Took lots of still photos today and came on home. David told me to stay home tomorrow and prepare for next week's workshop in White River. Will believe it takes place when I have returned so what's to prepare? The guys said they would miss me...aha...I don't believe it but it's nice to hear.

Will start a new journal with my first workshop as a volunteer. I did tell of my feelings when I started this "trek" (never ever snow-capped) so will close with some feelings I have as I face the next two years of my life. I will add more about the "food." We have "pap" most every day and always with RICE too! I can't eat both and have learned to like the pap. It is similar to what grits must be if cooked and cooked and then cooked more, has little taste, is eaten with one's fingers and used as a pusher or fork. Luckily I don't cook it. It takes an enormous amount of labor, easy to mix with the water but then one must stir as it thickens, add more mealy meal (ground corn), change utensil to a long handled wooden spoon and with two hands, stir for what seems a long time. I told them up front that it is just too much work and that my arms are not strong enough. But it is the staple for everyone here. And never have I seen so many people eat so much...people have very little cash but lots of fresh foods and pap...at least in this township. This family cooks with few spices. I have always cooked with many spices but now I know to eat what is provided or I will not eat at all. I'm having cabbage, spinach, beets, carrots 4-5-6-7 times a week, always cooked deader than any meat. But have NOT gotten sick so surely will not complain. (I actually have come closer to getting sick on the few occasions that I'm able to eat like I used to do).

I am becoming adjusted to the waiting 30 minutes to an hour to buy stamps, 1 ? hours for a combi to fill up, 20 minutes in a grocery line and forever for a meeting to start! Or not to start! But the worst feelings I have are those of always being on the outside and not understanding when others are carrying on a discussion. I find myself talking non-stop to myself and answering! I'm becoming quite good at it! Not knowing anyone, I feel as if am in a cocoon and one that will never open...and yet everyone is trying to help me...more than I ever thought possible. I wish I knew even more English words, now that my constant companion is myself. Some day I will describe my new forever-lasting friend, me!

October 12, 2001

Lotjhani!	*Hallo*
Akwande/Yebo	*Let it be/Yes*
Ninjani?	*You how?*
Sikhona	*We here*
Nami ngikhona	*Me I am here*

(General Greetings)

Columbus Day in America! David gave me the day off; not because of the holiday, but instead to prepare for next week. But as with all plans, it turned out that Mary S. (teacher I had met in Kameelrivier) and her son came to visit. I was able to introduce her to the staff and offer tea and biscuits at my new home. Both a first and both felt "good." David told me that the young lady we had seen was feeling better and was going to receive "home care." This I realize is home care provided by the volunteers and not nursing home care. But at least someone will be there with her in the coming days. She will be bathed, changed, and given fluids as well as her medicine. Her mother will also be helped with the housework, cooking and child care. Most importantly, the volunteer will pray and sing with/for her and her family.

The rest of the day I did pack and prepare. Am nervous about making it to Pretoria and on to Cam's by myself but must do it sometime. And I will!

<u>Saturday</u>

Up at crack of dawn and to the bus by 6:45AM. Pranced back and forth between one corner and another, a block away. The bus was over an hour late. Never was sure where to wait. Thobi and three of her friends went with me (yes, that early) and also pranced back and forth until I was gone. Must have been some sight! The girls did keep track of my bag <u>and</u> me! I was proud. Bus ride was uneventful and I sat beside a friend of Judas (language teacher) who got off with me and took me to catch a taxi to the Peace Corps office. Cam arrived to "fetch" me. We chased around doing errands and picked up several of the others. Went to the mall, saw a movie and to an Indian restaurant for dinner. The day was very American and wonderful. Cam has a beautiful home and we all had a relaxing fun day.

<u>Sunday</u>

Jen and I went to an outdoor bazaar. I bought a mother and baby giraffe statuette. Pretoria is unbelievably beautiful this time of year. The Jacaranda trees are in full lavender bloom. There are more than 60,000 of these trees in the city and line every street and avenue, from downtown out into the suburbs. I took many pictures.

We left the city and arrived in White River (approx. 4-5 hours ride to the east of Siyabuswa) late in the afternoon. The resort is elegant and we felt as if we were on vacation. It was good to see everyone again, although Mary Jo is gone. I am becoming somewhat closer friends to the teacher group although they are located in another province. Did meet many "nationals" who will be working with and for us...this was the most important.

Monday, Tuesday and Wednesday

The work shop was facilitated by a Peace Corps full-time employee who had been a previous volunteer. We took part in many group activities and began to really "know" a few more people. Thursday and Friday we had more of the same but with a different facilitator.

The surrounding area and landscape are awesome. I only took short walks but several did get up early in the morning and hike into the foothills. It is now springtime and flowers are beginning to blossom and here the terrain is much more wooded and greener than in Siyabuswa.

Friday afternoon we headed home but arrived in Pretoria too late to catch a combi to Siyabuswa. Jen and I spent the night in Pretoria. Forgot to mention that I took two full baths almost every day that we were at the workshop. We each had suites and our own room and a bath. Plan to take Mindy and Mallory there. A wonderful week and am now ready to head back out to my new home.

EXCEPT...now America has had an anthrax outbreak and we are still at War so don't know what will happen.

Saturday

Up at 6:00AM and started reading about the Reconciliation Act for South Africa. It is very interesting but a heartbreaking study in trust and betrayal, at least in my opinion.

I left for Siyabuswa at 8:45AM: first to the Peace Corps office to pick up the books I had left there; then took an American-type taxi to a new combi rank and then on home. Arrived here at 3:00PM after waiting in each rank at least an hour. No problems though and Thobi was surprised and happy with her book and sweets; a nice evening.

Sunday

Very much like a day at home (my real home). Up at 6:00AM with coffee, went to the complex at 7:30AM for a paper, bought the wrong one (young lady agrees to save me the right one from now on), and returned home with ingredients for spaghetti. Could not wash clothes because it threatened to rain. Family left for church and the rain came and the wind blew and the cold and the water made it to every nook and cranny and there are many. It went into seven different pots and in the windows, fast and furious, before I could close them. Stood in the kitchen and tried to decide: do I put out pots, close the windows, or run out the door and join the ducks? I had just put clean linen on my bed and it is soaked before I could get back there. But electricity never went off so I cooked dinner, cleaned up water, talked to the ducks (yes, they came in...babies that is), cleaned up more water, and gently put the little ones back out where they belonged. Family came home, we ate, took a nap (all of us) and now I am listening to Andre Bocelli and will write a letter. Notice the difference between the here and now and the past. Not once did I get upset. Any time today, yesterday or last week for that matter. Just go with the tide. Now my kids will be afraid I am going to live forever, because I'm so very mellow. Oh yes, remashed my toe and it is painful but not a big deal. Tomorrow, I may or may not talk with David about re-assessing my job and/or his/mine expectations.

Monday

I am at the office by 8:00AM. Told to go to Kameelrivier by Klaas (young man working for the doctor), but not where or why. Njongo comes in and has more details about the trip but wrong reasons. Called David, took a taxi to the Methodist Church in Kameelrivier B. Walk in on a workshop (now I am the one late) that David is facilitating regarding capacity building. He talked about violence in the home and on the streets. He did an exemplary job on subjects that only related on the periphery to his own organization's mission. We then waited for over two hours for a free ride back to Siyabuswa.

I waited another hour at the post office to pick up a package from Mindy. She had sent written material on HIV and other related public health concerns, making it worth the wait. Now I'm home and I have fallen into the habit of reading a short while to Thobi and then playing cards with her. At least it's a social life.

Tuesday

Everyone wants to know about my everyday life style here and how the hours go by. This is probably as good a time as any to start because today I feel good, but it may take the rest of the book to say all I want to say. First, I must preface this long day's journey by stating, in no way, am I living as one would anticipate one would do as a Peace Corps volunteer. The material things I lack are just minor inconveniences. And there is no lack of most support systems. The only serious lack and this is a major wearing, draining, and very, very difficult lack, is that of peer conversational exchanges of thoughts and feelings.

But on to a regular day. Tuesday is a good place in the week. Went to sleep approx. 9:45 PM Monday evening. Woke at 2:15AM...to bathroom. The hallway is very dark because the only light in the window is from a porch light several houses away. I don't want to wake anyone so feel my way in the dark. I also know that if I turn on the light in the bathroom, all the little creatures race around the room. I see them but have not stepped on them so the lights stay off. Back to bed and to sleep. I always dream a lot and now, even about the people I have met here.

I awaken, for the first of a series of awakenings, when Christine leaves for her prayer group; back to sleep; awaken once more when she come in at 5:15 AM; fall back asleep again and then she greets me for good at 5:30AM with coffee(instant with powdered cream.) It's a nice way to wake up and I'm used to the taste of the coffee now. My sleep is fragmented but I'm relaxed and rested. It has never bothered me to wake up through the night and 99% of the time, I thoroughly enjoy my dreams.

Between 5:30AM and 6:15AM, I read the Bible (really read it) and pray...not a bad habit to fall into and now a difficult one to break. By 6:15AM, I'm up and have breakfast with Thobi. Today she had a sore mouth and didn't eat with me. Usually I eat peanut butter on bread but sometimes a bowl of corn-flakes, (if the milk is cold). Today, Christine had made fat cakes (flour, sugar, yeast and water, shaped into balls and deep fried). I could easily become addict-ed. I wish she would make them every day but only does so when other food is not available. I ate two, plus the peanut butter and a small tomato. I have to eat because never know when or if there will be lunch anywhere.

After eating, it is my turn in the bathroom. I heat the coffee pot of water (when there is electricity) and put my medium-sized blue tub in the bathtub. Wet my hair down in cold water and wash my body down with warm. Have found that I can pour this water over me by standing in the tub and it feels wonder-ful and almost as refreshing as a shower. Thobi calls good-bye as she leaves for school.

I return to my room and listen to the radio and dress for work. It is 7:40 AM and I leave the house with intentions to drop my stuff at the office and walk through the complex to mail two letters. I reach the clinic and David is already there (not typical). We chat a little and I take a couple more "photos" of the clin-ic staff and walk to mail the letters. Oh yes, on the way to work, stopped by the "creche" (day care) and left the picture I had taken of Betty and her kids.

As I passed through the complex, another Betty stopped me and asked if I would come back and have a picture taken of her and me together. I agreed and later Vusi went with me and we took more pictures. Three girls, unknown girls, asked to have their picture taken but I said no. Every single person wants a photo. But later in the day, I relented and went back and took the pictures.

For the first hour at work, I struggle on my language. Then David could not locate his proposal which "had to be" faxed to the National Office TODAY. All of us searched, high and low (there is no high), and after many (when I say many I mean more than a few) interruptions, Njongo found the papers in David's top drawer (most used drawer in the desk). I took one look at it and felt sick. It was handwritten and very confusing. I asked David (insisted) that it be typed and I said I would give the typist directions. He agreed. We went to a typist and about 3:15 PM, it was done. In the meantime, I came back to the office and talked about AIDS for an hour to the two new FEMALE volunteers for ASHYO. We were interrupted over and over. David and I are to go to a committee meeting at the District office tomorrow and David is also to go to Groblestahl (a trip that could take an hour away but will more than likely be an all-day sojourn). Today, then, we must walk to the District Office for a preliminary meeting and we head out with new staff in tow. David has chest pains and returns to the office. Whaaaaaat, whose meeting is this anyway??? Not mine. All this while trying to find the proposal (think this may have something to do with the chest pains?). The women and I proceed to the District Office but since David is not there, no meeting is held and back to the office we traipse.

I checked for mail...there is none. Gave out a bag of gummy bears, eat an apple and no lunch. Betty from the creche comes by, chews David out for ignoring her request to write a business plan (for creche?) and the day drones on. 3:30PM and the proposal is done. David and I go to the clinic and fax it to the powers that be. I am not in the least impressed with it but the rest are agreed that it is perfect. I pray it passes muster and we can get on with whatever. Where did those chest pains go?

Now I'm at the clinic and watch for news. Know that I have missed it and will listen tonight (Rabie can translate from Zulu). It's 4:00PM and I am released to go home. Am feeling at ease with ALL the staff at this point and they still are in awe of me and the United States.

It is very hot today and everyone forewarns me that summer is on the way and will be miserable. So far the bugs are bearable but they will be worse also. I walk the 2 ? blocks home...a sandy, deeply rutted road. Seven kids and five adults greet me and four by name. This feels good and the day itself is beautiful.

I arrive home and my room has been aired and the curtains washed. Christine makes coffee for Rabie and me. Supper is on the stove. Christine is tired but still singing. I drink coffee with Rabie and he tells me about the upcoming wedding which is to be held in this house. No, I will not be in the way. Yes, I am to always keep my room locked. Yes, I am to eat anything I want without asking and most of all, I am to "feel free" and have a good time.

We eat supper at 5:30 PM: cabbage, chicken, pap, beets, tomatoes. We all watch the soap opera on TV (never do remember which one), while we eat. Thobi and I do the dishes because Christine has literally worked all day (why is today different?). After dishes, Thobi goes through a list of Ndebele words with me, and I spend a short time teaching her to read English words. Then we play 3 card games, one gin rummy (our version), one Old Maid (her version) and one solitaire (rules change with every game).

Now it is about 7:30PM and I watch the news in Zulu or maybe Afrikaner and then go to my room and listen to the BBC news. Read and/or write 1-2 letters until at least 9:30PM. Then start over. Nothing the remotest exciting. As I write, the "ventures" (rats) are roaming across my tin roof, which I will never get used to! But haven't seen one as yet. I tell myself they are really just field mice. Am writing this to let everyone know that, although the country is extremely poor and millions are living very close together in tin or concrete one room shacks, with no water, no electricity, little food and very sick with family members dying every single minute, I am not one of these people. We may be without water for 2-3 days (if a pipe breaks) but possibly Rabie will be warned (how...if a pipe breaks?) and they will fill barrels, bath tub, pots etc.

My room has a bed, wardrobe, large table, kitchen chairs, a lamp, radio, my CD player, plenty of reading material, many letters and pictures from home, a dying potted plant (my fault), and a large first aid and medicine kit. There is no room left for me! Except for living single in another family's home, it's a-ok or kushli (well).

Oh yes, forgot to say, our office also has no (I mean no) modern conveniences. No phone, (personal cell phones are a status symbol to hang on one's belt but have no time left on the card), no computer or even a typewriter, no fax, no book shelves, no pen, pencil or scratch paper. Drives me nuts because all seven of the staff beg or borrow everything from anyone he/she can. They did have a car (once) but wrecked it, had a computer (once) but no one knows where it is now, and each cell phone has been stolen at least once. No one has any money for coffee, cream, or lunch. But everyone is clean, well dressed, and professional in appearance. Amazing! No wonder they think Americans are rich. If they knew all the drawer space I waste with extra pencils, they would never let up on the "please, borrow me."!

October 24, 2001
"I am, because we are"

(South African Proverb)

Wednesday

Another meeting at the District Office re: World AIDS Day. Walked there and rode back. Silvia went but Alfeena didn't make it (two new volunteers).

Have read a paragraph about culture that fits me exactly and makes me feel better. To quote from "The Art of Crossing Cultures," page 76: *"What is different about being overseas, the reason we cannot continue to rely on the adjustment process, is not that this process suddenly stops or that we encounter any different kind of new situation, but that we encounter new situations on a scale we have never known before. The nearly continuous barrage of new experiences served up by the unfamiliar country and culture during our early months overseas triggers an intense wave of reaction and anxiety and an unusually strong urge to withdraw. This difference in scale might be compared to the difference between how we feel meeting one new person and meeting an entire room of people, over and over and who speak what one cannot understand."* End of quote. This is to say nothing of tackling a new job, a new community and a new family. And I must get to know and remember each individual quickly. After all, they know and remember me. The War in America compounds all this. It amazes me...how much I can observe but do not "see." Even shaking hands is a ceremony here done by three shakes and done with each greeting to each person. A habit.

Came home early today and washed and hung out two weeks of laundry. Felt good but I'm too old to start this washing routine again...another obstacle, even if a small one. Tonight we are having fish and chips, my kind of unhealthy greasy food.

News about anthrax is mixed: some warnings are bogus, others are too real. Palestine and Israel are at it again and this is not good! Bombing raids are becoming more difficult but have not slowed.

<u>Thursday</u>

Today should have been a perfect day at the office. Instead, I did my own brand of procrastinating and wasted almost the whole day. David left me alone (unusual) and I worked for a total of 1-1/2 hours. Studied a short time on the language, walked to mail my letters, walked back to apply for e-mail (back to the post office). Remembered that after applying, I not only do not have a telephone line available, also do not have a computer compatible to e-mail. Went by grocery for a few items, did not have money with me so back to the office. Worked a short time on planning (what?), walked back for groceries and <u>still</u> did not have my money, had to walk home for the second time and then back to pay for what I had selected. Walked over to the neighbors to pay a down payment on dresses and home again to cook. Now I am exhausted, don't know why and it is my own darn fault.

<u>Friday</u>

Today was another kind of day! No, it wasn't. But it was a day that many times I have wished I were a writer so that I might describe exactly what is transpiring, a painter to illustrate these people, a psychologist to get inside their heads, and on and on. But will just have to do with the pictures in my memories and the "photos."

First, I was told to be at the office at five to seven SHARP! So everyone in this family shifted schedules and I was there at five to seven SHARP! Vusi arrived at the same time. Soon came Lucas and then Freddy and Njongo. By 7:15 AM Alfeena is there and we play the waiting game: sitting and watching the road intently for any sign of our transport. Finally at five <u>after</u> eight, our driver arrives with a friend. No apologies and off we go to Wvaalbank.

Again, not one lion in sight. We pass a squatter's camp (their term) and this is another impression that I cannot adequately describe. Just suffice it to say, I could not live like these hundreds of people do for ten minutes. Maybe not even for one, and this is their life. Many tin or cardboard, haphazardly-shaped shacks with as many holes as parts. All are of variegated colors and appear disreputable, but not by choice. There are no trash containers (what is trash is usable in some way). Throngs of people of all ages, as far as one can see, are milling around, either playing (if young enough) or just sitting if too old to play. There is no employment for pay; hence, no money and no way out.

We travel on into the township and it is stunningly beautiful. We arrive at the community center in which the program is to be held. The center is very large, like a gymnasium. The high windows are barred. The room is empty except for a few rickety chairs and a couple of tables. The electricity has not been turned on and there is no water in the single bathroom. In short, nothing is ready for this huge program, hosted by the Department of Social Services of the Dr. J.S. Moroka Jurisdiction.

We wait and by 9:30AM, people are slowly, ever so slowly, starting to put this program in order. The program is to start at 10:00AM but the planners are now waiting on a generator. Our (ASHYO) posters are up but there is still nothing else in place. By 10:30AM, hundreds of chairs have arrived and many vendors, who have their own tables, are set up. We are told that the generator, speakers, and audio visuals (?) are on the way. In the meantime, many women are in the back and starting to cook huge amounts of food. I wonder <u>why</u> since very few participants have arrived. I think it must be for some other group.

It is 12 Noon and there are crowds of people converging on the center. And yes, we are about to start. NO! NO! NO! I must be at the Head Table so I can be introduced. I have no choice but to agree and ask to sit close to the end (a huge mistake). I am placed less than a foot directly ahead of the amplifiers. Thus begins more than 3 and ? hours of nonstop blaring speeches and loud music. <u>All</u> the speeches are given three times...in two languages I do not understand and English when they remember. There were 14 speakers and each outyelled the previous one. But I must say that the enthusiasm of everyone was a sight to behold.

By now there are more than 350 people present and about 100 more grade school children, and still they keep coming. Between each speech, a group of young people performed. There were 8 items (musical and/or drama productions). After the concluding speech, the music continued but I was allowed to go outside. By now it did not matter to me that the bathroom was really intolerable because I was seriously in pain (from 7:45 AM until late afternoon). But it mattered to the ladies in the back and they would not let me use the place. However, a lady next to me came to my rescue and told me about an outside toilet down the road. She went with me and asked permission of the people in the house. This crisis was handled and my white skin came to my rescue.

We were finished at 4:00PM and then the food was served...more than I would have thought possible (but remembered that these women had been working all day). Every single person could have all that they could eat. Then they (women) cleaned up and washed dishes, pots, glasses (no paper plates here).

Finally at 5:10PM I was offered a ride home (my original ride had to stay). By pure chance, the girl who brought me back just lives around the corner from where I live.

Home again...jiggety jog. Did spend a lot of time today observing people and trying to sort out my perceptions. I was the only white. I am used to this now and no, none of the others look alike. Most have vivid expressions, sparkling eyes, and white straight teeth. This makes their smiles light up a dark face. If any of them have a sullen unhappy grimace at first, and there are some, this expression changes before you can blink ...when you smile and say hallo or lentjani.

The program was given in honor of the volunteers (yes, in the hundreds). And these volunteers are not the wealthy or even the middle class. They are peers of the people they are assisting. It truly makes me wonder: When I have run into so many high- spirited, God and people-loving persons, why there is so much hate and crime in this world?

Today was not a good day for Thobi. Her mother lives in Pretoria and seldom comes to Siyabuswa. But she was to come and spend the weekend and Thobi was very excited. She did not show. I don't know what to say or how to help this little girl. In this respect, feelings of young children are the same the world over. But we did our usual cards routine. Maybe she feels better. I'll know tomorrow. I'm exhausted from working so hard today. No, I am exhausted but it is from not working at all today.

Sunday

Up very early because the family went to church in Middleburg which is a long way, especially with a car that may stop at any time. I drank a cup of coffee, went to get the paper and ingredients for supper. Washed my hair, ate a bite, and organized my room (again). Read my novel and will wright (spelling has got to go, or has it gone) Miranda. Then probably will take another nap. This anthrax situation is making the terrorist crisis even worse, if possible. No one is certain just what will happen or where it will happen. A QUAKE in New York City??

Well, I've done it now. It is 6:15PM, almost dark and the family has not returned. I think, maybe I should be nice and feed these poor little chicks, ducks, and the others; they have made a constant racket all day, non-stop. I go outside, have no idea how to do this or even where the feed is kept. Steven (a young man down the way) just happens to come by to see Rabie. He unlocks the garage and feeds the poultry. Good. But now he atempts to lock up the garage and the key has broken off in the lock. Rabie will be very upset and Lord knows how he will be able to fix it. I have been told over and over how cars are stolen. I should not have even thought to feed his stock. Did though, so will just have to wait and take the consequences (Steven's word, not mine). Yeah, he can say this, because he will be long gone and it is me who is left to face whatever the consequences.

Mindy and John called tonight. It is the first time I have talked with John. He sounds good and so does she. John said that I'll be getting a letter from Cherie (his fiancé) soon and that she is living at my house too. I am not surprised.

Rabie took the broken key incident better than I had anticipated. He was able to get the piece out and he has another key. All's well that ends well. Nobody was hungry for my dinner but ate the ice cream...of courrrrse!

Monday

I am confused. This has become the norm. Before I thought to ask Rabie and Christine what language they use to speak with each other, I assumed it was Ndebele. But when I did ask, I found that it was Zulu. And David speaks most of the time in Ndebele, as do the others in the office. I had attempted Seswanee in Sandfontein. This confusion is compounded because everyone MUST also speak Afrikaans. I happened to meet Judas on way to work and told him of my language problems. He said yes, this is a dilemma, but what did he mean by that? So I talked with David and his boys and they all also agreed, (with what?). The only true answer was to have another of my little talks with myself. Because many of the Ndebele words are similar to Zulu and all here can speak both, I decided to concentrate on Zulu. Told myself, it is still early in the game so I can do this. But I must speak with Cam and Kediboni first. They will undoubtedly say yes. Cam does, Kedi does not. Freddy will be my new tutor and it will be Isidebele with a mixture of Zulu.

Did corral David (that is the proper term) and we had a ten minute discussion about my job duties and we are in agreement (I think).

Now I must add more about this family. Tonight, Christine does not feel well. I cannot tell if it is her high blood pressure or high blood sugar acting up. I fear it is both. No matter how tired, she never stops working. The only way I knew that she wasn't feeling well was in her loss of appetite and because no tea was prepared for Rabie. I told her I was going to learn Zulu and she did not respond, but about 30 seconds later, she admitted that she was not feeling well. After supper tonight, she asked that I go to a friend's house with her to tell her friend that she (Christine) is going to the clinic tomorrow.

I sit in this home in the midst of a sea of faces. Many I have seen before but do not know any by name. I thought, "Why am I here when I could be back home visiting with my own friends?" Will I ever know or is it only God's will? If so, surely I'll see the reasons some day. Perhaps not.

Tuesday

It has been a very long time (childhood) since I have lived in a male chauvinistic and domineering world! My patience is tried and my ire is raised when Rabie refuses to assist Christine in any way. She has not felt well since I arrived, and according to her records, for a long time before that. Today she walked to the clinic which is a good three kilos. away and waited more than three hours sitting on the floor for a doctor (who doesn't show) to see her. I know this, because I have walked four kilos. for a home visit which took me past the clinic. On the way back I checked to see if she was there. Oh yes, there in a mob of people, sat she in a corner and on the floor. She promises to take a taxi home and I come on back. I arrive home a little after 4:00PM and Rabie is having his tea, fixed and served by Thobi. I see red, but can't change anything at this point. I head into the kitchen and start supper. Christine does take a combi home, did not see the doctor, and is now so tired that she cannot function. BUT she does proceed to fix tea and then to help me. Rabie does not move. I give up and come on back to my room to write it out of my system.

Perhaps this is the more unsettling because today I made two home visits to dying patients and in the homes were two men (one in each) just sitting. I thought to myself that our visits were probably reprieves for them and gave each the benefit of nice thoughts. Now I know this behavior is typical of the men in this age and area.

Daily the news from the United States is not good. Afghanistan may attack by the end of the week. I need to walk around the block to clear my head. However, last Saturday afternoon, a man was murdered on his front stoop just three houses down the block from us. I have been ordered to go nowhere alone. Guess this is one entry that I won't send home.

I will write more about the office tomorrow because I can send that home. Thobi just came in and kissed the back of my neck. The evening is much better than this long full emotional day has been.

Chapter Eight

Travel patiently. It takes time to understand others, especially when there are barriers of language and custom, keep flexible and adaptable to all situations.

(The Art of Living)

OCTOBER 2001

October 31, 2001
<u>Wednesday</u>
        Today is Halloween! No one so far, and it is 5:00PM, has even heard of it. It has been raining, dark and dreary all day. I had arrived at the office early...Njongo was already there and the day starts well. Soon in comes Oupa; the two of them talk over and around me and they leave. I work; feel good; back they come. I try to ask them if there is a possibility of setting up a hospice for the families of AIDS victims. They listen for approximately 20 seconds and tune me out. They converse over and around me and leave again! It is now 9:30AM. I think maybe Kedi can come early for my last language lesson with her. I call her and she tells me that she'll come right on over. I work on the language but mostly waste time, thinking she soon will come. About 11:45AM, Alfeena (new ASHYO volunteer) shows up and we stare at each other for an hour, drinking a cup of coffee. The men are in and out and the day darkens with a storm looming. Kedi finally arrives at 2:30PM with two friends in tow. Has not called nor does she apologize. We spent a non-productive hour and I find she and her friends are only waiting for a ride to their homes. Alfeena (new ASHYO volunteer)does go home at 3:00PM and Kedi's ride does not come. The rain is pouring now and they talk over and round me and I do nothing until after 4:00PM when the transport finally arrives. I lock up and they graciously (her apology) give me a ride home.
        It is still Halloween weather. Christine is chopping cabbage very fine, almost piece by piece with a knife. Jane (who is she?) is sitting. Christine tells me Rabie is asleep and has the "flu". Everyone who sleeps in the daytime has the "flu". Why do I not feel sorry for him? Christine, Thobi and Jane talk over and round me and I'm down at the moment, and this is why I am writing now. This, too, shall pass. Tonight I will tell Thobi about Halloween. I will see if she listens past 10 seconds. If she does, I will give her a Halloween treat! I am doing my own talking over and around me!

NOVEMBER, 2001

November 1, 2001
        Happy Birthday Rick (son-in-law) in America! Hopefully you have received my letter.
        Another day. Njongo and I talked in depth this morning because he was by himself. He told me his view of the problems ASHYO is having and there are many. Believe it, I listened. Mainly because I <u>don't</u> know what to do. Perhaps, I will have a talk with David (about what?). Will think on it. I left the office at 9:15AM and walked to the District Office <u>by</u> myself and then headed into another SA day. Meeting was to start at 10:00AM, started at 10:30AM and was promptly canceled. I was asked to stay and join the ICS (Integrated Children System). I tried to find Alfeena but she was nowhere to be found. I returned to

the room and it seems our meeting is back on but there has been a change of venue. We did have a productive hour-long meeting somewhere. As I was preparing to leave, a nurse from the District Nursing staff asked me to ride with her group to a town close by. I agreed (had no choice) and we rode what seemed a long way over sandy, bumpy, water-jammed roads. There were five of us...three of us very large...jammed into a compact car! But we made it. We met with the mayor, his assistant and a couple of others re: World AIDS Day and the menu. This menu includes every type of food available in SA. Meeting was to start as soon as we arrived but, of course the mayor had not shown as yet. We started 45 minutes later. Did get cold drinks and cookies. Left at 3:00PM and came back to Siyabuswa via another direction but still across the same type of bumpy roads.

She dropped me off at the office and I came home at 4:15PM to have juice and cookies waiting for me. It's feast or famine around here. I am to leave for Pretoria at 6:50AM tomorrow with David and Njongo so they can defend one of the proposals. It will be a difficult day for David...AND the wedding festivities start here at 6:00PM tomorrow evening.

The news from home is not good.

Friday

I don't even know how to begin. I would like to write a short story but all the events are so disjointed and happening at opposing speeds that this is not possible. I was up at 4:30AM with singing and praying in this home. Decided to stay awake and listen. I don't need to repeat that I do not understand the words, but the rhythms, tones, and structures of both the prayers and hymns are beautiful. You can tell that everyone is talking to God and singing his praises.

Am up to prepare for the day at 5:30AM and leave for the bus at 6:45AM. Njongo walked with me from my house and David met us at the office corner. We played tag with the two bus stops. Missed the first bus and barely made the second. The timing here is not a standard time; instead it is called "South African Time". And these young men are just as unpredictable. They can sit and wait and do nothing for hours, but the next time, they cannot sit still for five minutes. Hence, the jumping back and forth between bus stops.

The bus ride was fine, and we actually arrived at the National Office 40 minutes early. David barreled on into the Director's office and tried to start the meeting. But here, he was not in control and yes, we must wait until the designated time.

We did have the meeting, it started on time, and was exactly like a 100% of the grant meetings back in Illinois...the ending note being that David must rewrite his proposal and a quick rewrite it must be. This will not be easy for him so we shall see. Hopefully, he'll now listen to me because I had given him, in writing, what to expect and what questions possibly would be asked. The Director did exactly as I had written but undoubtedly neither David nor Njongo had bothered to read my notes. Once again Njongo seemed to pick up on the hidden nuances from all parties.

We left there and went to the Department of Health warehouse. The boys gathered together a big box of written materials. We then walked, walked, walked though some very rough areas. Finally wandered through a taxi rank and I thought we were at the bus depot. But no, we continued our walking through even scarier and very crowded areas. The two of them moving fast (almost running), while lugging the box, and me hopping along behind like one of Rabie's "varmints". We finally arrived at the bus stop. We looked like we were vendors and right at home in a place jammed with people, wares, and belongings. We wait in the wrong place and the bus we should have been on leaves. We change to another place, and when we should have been the first in line, we were the last. This meant we had to stand for the ride home. But by the outskirts of town, an old man gave me his seat and the boys sat on the box of materials in the aisle up by the driver.

We did make it home in a decent time, but every person, including myself, was loaded down with blankets and groceries...even people in the aisle. This meant that no one could see even where to get off. Luckily, by the time it was our turn, the aisle had thinned and I now recognize landmarks. We made it without mishap and also without the hoped-for funding.

I had mail and came on back to the house. O yes, in the middle of the Pretoria bus terminal, I had to beg to use a toilet in a private shop owned by a family from the Middle East. They made an exception of me with the permission of the owner. I think it was my age and my color. Because the mother of the man who ran the shop recognized my "need," she told him to let me use their private facilities. Takes one old woman to recognize another. It was a good thing because we had a long wait, even a bumpier ride, and a long walk back from the bus to the office.

Now it is 4:15PM and a completely different set of experiences will take charge of my life for the next two days. I hope some way, somehow, I can do justice and retell how wonderful, and at the same time, horrific, this weekend was for me.

The upcoming 24 hours proved to be almost more than one person can handle. It was truly a lesson in virtually every value and emotion that I can call to mind. I reached home Friday afternoon and there were people in the front, side, back and in between yards (proof is in the pictures)! Rabie introduces me to several, Christine to more and Thobi to even more. These introductions are to continue again and again. I am consciously trying to remember some and many, especially kids and men I will know the next time we meet. Many are from out of town and from the groom's family.

It is here that I must explain, "Who is Jane?" Jane arrived last Monday and stayed the week with Rabie and Christine. She is a niece of Rabie's and to be married on Saturday. The wedding is to be here so I thought she had come early to help with the preparations. She stayed very quiet when I was present. For some reason she did not appear to me as a happy prospective bride, nor did she seem eager to help with the upcoming festivities. I attributed this to my being a stranger and of course, I was not around during the day to see what her activities actually were.

During the first introductions, Christine offers me pap and spinach. I have not eaten since early AM and that meal was one slice of bread with peanut butter, so I accept. It is 4:30PM. Soon after this the real food preparations begin. I am taken by surprise by this because Christine and her friends have been preparing food every day this past week. But this afternoon everyone has a job (if they are at least 7 or 8 years of age). Everyone except me! I offer over and over again but this is where the fun begins. No one, no one at all, speaks English well enough to translate, either for me or to me. I wander to the kitchen where it is crowded with girls doing dishes.

Rabie calls me and I am told to start "photos". I have 36 on a new roll and am thinking about the ceremony in the morning. I want to be selective but I had promised him and he knows better than I which ones are important. Besides, I am very, very happy to have a job. This photo shooting becomes extremely difficult however, because each wants his/her/theirs/ours/its/ or any ole photo at all taken.

I wander into one of the in-between yards where a fire is being set and big pots are carried in by the young men, wander into the garage and the home-made beer is in progress. Rabie is directing "my photos"!

By 5:30PM I know that I must have more film. By now there are eighteen children here from ages 1 to 12 years of age and do you think even the one-year-old is around to run to the complex? No, all have gone with someone to somewhere. I go to the complex. Realize when I'm almost there that this is a terrible idea. At this time and on a Friday, it's jammed with people leaving to go home for the weekend. I walk directly into many, many groups of men with quart beer bottles in hand and open. Think to myself, "I should not be here" but am past the point of no return. Lots of calls to me and not all the usual friendly ones. But did buy the film and returned through the throng, only to receive a lecture from the men at the house. Do NOT do that again! But do take photo after photo! Rabie is chasing around calling, "The sheep, the sheep, the sheep!" " Photo the sheep."

I wander to the front yard and the canopy is being erected for later tonight and tomorrow. The adult women are preparing food for tomorrow: dicing cabbage, slicing beets, grating carrots, peeling potatoes, boiling pap, cleaning chicken, and washing onions. Large quantities of each and yes, this is just for tonight! Tomatoes, spinach, fruit juice, cookies, pudding, custard, fruit, and candies. Don't forget the coffee, tea, and beer. On and on and they are doing it all with only sharp knives. No fancy blenders or food processors here. Not even can openers (what's in a can?). Christine manages very well and asks me to put some furniture in my room with strict orders to lock!

I want to help but there are too many people everywhere and of course Rabie is after me with his constant, "Photo, Sydney, photo."

Oh, Oh, here comes the COW! In a pick up. The men get her unloaded and away she runs (smart). The chase is on and so are the photos. She literally ran up the street, started around a corner and ended in a fenced yard. I screamed, "Go cow go!" They, I could tell, were hollering absolutely the opposite. But you would have thought her a bull, she was so strong and feisty. They did get her caught and tied up. Miracles of miracles, Rabie had forgotten to yell "photos" when they had butchered the sheep. He did not forget now. He and the other men insisted that photos be taken from start to finish. I took the first set, those of the pickup, the cow and the young men chasing her, but balked at the stabbing death and slaughtering. Did me no good at all to tell them that I just couldn't watch, let alone take pictures. I did it.

I have listened all day to another language and continue to do so from 4:15PM until 800PM nonstop to several others. I'm becoming more and more confused, extremely overwhelmed and very, very tired. Something has happened that no one could have foreseen or forewarned me. Not only did no one understand me, nor I them but each age group treated me differently and none the age that I am. First, the kids wanted me to romp with them while their own great gogos sat and visited. The young adults treated me as their mother instead of gogo, expecting me to keep up with them, drink the beer, stir the pap and the list goes on. The women Christine's age treated me as a peer and the ones my own age treated me as much younger. You would think this would make me feel good. And it does at first, but only at first because I am older and I was tired and I was in the way or out of place and even out of sorts.

By now it is 9:30PM and time for an attitude adjustment. I'm becoming angry again at Rabie and hurt by Christine, when she leaves me on my own. I am downright miserable because I'm not comfortable in any space and don't know what I do want. You might think, my gosh, she is acting almost like a two-year-old about to have a tantrum. I decide to take the bull (or is it cow?) by the horn and to do something to keep from crying in front of some group. I go sit with the really old gogos...there are only four of us. I tell them I am just going to listen. I do for awhile and then move on to the other ages and do the same thing. I tell each group that I am older, have never had animals killed in my sight before and that I'm staying out of the men's way. This worked. I still was lost but felt better...and then my enormous gaffe happened.

All week, I had seen Jane, the bride, but never had I seen the young man she was to marry. Now I was sitting beside Leah, one of the gogos, and asked very innocently which of the young men was the groom? She stood up and laughed and laughed and soon, everyone in the room started laughing. She said he was dead (just like that) and then I really didn't understand. I had been to a traditional wedding in Sandfontein (I thought) and there had been a breathing groom. But it seems Jane was to marry this man and he had died before the ceremony. This was several years ago (eight) and his family has now paid the lobola (the cow) for his bride. The cow has been sacrificed and the spirits of the ancestors will be called to approve the marriage. I guess she is now married even though there is not to be a ceremony. Salome (neighbor) had to explain all this to me because she is the only one fluent in English. I'm still not clear on details but will learn more about this as time goes on. But it did answer very definitely why he isn't around! And why Jane hasn't acted at all like a bride to be. She is older, friendly, speaks very little English, has two young children, who also haven't been here these past few days. They all (even the men) had a good laugh at my expense and this time it was at and not with me.

By this time, it is close to 10:00PM and we are to eat again. No one offers me anything...remember, I am to be free. But still I am feeling left out. Finally I fix a plate and eat with Thobi and her gang. It's past ten now and I'm so tired and despondent that I decided to chuck it all and go to bed. Had tried the homemade beer, did not like it at all, made my excuses and went to my room. Had mail to read and this perked up my spirits on one level and reinforced my homesickness on another. Fell asleep even with the music, but was awakened in a few minutes by the singing and dancing.

Now the fun was to begin. Being afraid that I would miss out on something, I returned to the other room. Men are outside drinking but all the women are now in the living area. Some are drinking the homemade beer but all are high in spirit...dancing, singing, playing the hollow horns, clapping and laughing huge belly laughs...when I joined in. By 1:30AM everyone had wound down and a few had taken off. However, most found a blanket (there were at least 30-40 around) and were lying down and maybe they did sleep (a little). I went back to my room, keyed up now but fell asleep and by 4:00AM, everyone was back up and that included the kids and me.

It doesn't take long before the tea, coffee and biscuits were ready and we start all over again. Fires are lit, pots are filled, the pap is started and I'm getting this feeling of claustrophobia. Can you believe it! I'm feeling smothered and deserted at the same time. I now have an inkling inside of me of what it truly feels like to be schizophrenic. I really am at a loss on where to turn or where to be. About 9:30AM, they start feeding and this is where I do lose it.

Unbeknownst to me, Christine had told everyone not to fix me a plate because I like to fix my own. All the food is out and they tell me to eat. I try to tell them that I don't want to eat alone or to be the first in line and will wait on them. Everyone is in separate circles once again. Finally it is just too much. I can't communicate adequately with them and they can't with me. Tears that may just overflow like a young child's come to my eyes. But just about the time I desperately want to retreat and can't and am afraid I will cry, it dawns on me just what Christine has done. And this shows me that she does understand and is trying to get to know me, too.

I do fix my plate and make it to a circle...they accept me and it starts to go better. For awhile! We eat the sheep (they do) and the cow is slaughtered. PHOTO time again and again. Rabie is giving orders and I am getting frustrated because it is absolutely not my affair. One minute I am treated as a guest and the next as the busy photographer but never as the gogo that I am. In some ways, this culture is extremely polite, although some actions in my own culture would be considered rude, such as breaking in line for a drink, using the last glass or cup, serving yourself (or men) first, and taking ALL the cold drink, even though everyone has not had the first drink. Same with cookies, candy and all else. First person may take six cookies (truth), half a loaf of bread and not care if someone down the line will be left out. Anyway, by now it is finally 11:00AM and I'm listening to the chatter and fall asleep with my head on the lap of a gracious gogo. BUT ten minutes later here comes David and I must wake up to visit with him. At least I'm in a decent frame of mind.

The day moves on and food is started all over again and now the meat is beef. They are eating whenever and wherever the notion strikes. Kids have treats and adults beer. Those that are drinking have never stopped. But now I know from whom to stay away.

It is early afternoon and everyone gathers in the front yard and gifts are given by the groom's family to everyone in the bride's family. Blankets, tea sets, dishes, shirts, dresses, mats, utensils, and aprons are distributed one by one to at least 100 people! The front yard is overtaken and then each person brings all the "stuff" inside and four of the women re-divide it. This I think I understand but no, I do not. After the gifts are separated into approximately 25 new sets, with at least one of each item included, all are carried back outside and the groom's family repack it and carry it away. Didn't find anyone who could explain this to me.

Now that the weekend is coming to a close, I must say it was fun and beautiful. And the kids! Child abuse is a very serious issue in South Africa, but it certainly isn't in this family or their friends. Kids were all over the place at all hours, broke into the dishwashing often for a drink, food was spilled by accident over and over, the refrigerator door constantly was left open for several minutes at a time. Never did anyone holler or even get upset. There was a minimum of 16 kids here at all times, sometimes many, many more. Rarely did the baby, or even the couple of toddlers roaming around, cry! If they did, a mother was right there to hold, feed or play with each of them. It was amazing.

There never was a wedding ceremony and finally about 5:30PM, people slowly headed out, though some stayed overnight. But the bride, her new official family and her friends left to go to the groom's home in Vaalbank.

I came in and did the dishes from most of the day. And Rabie (yes) cleaned out some of the pots and took the scraps to the chicks. Because I know I can soon go to bed, I'm feeling much better. Will be adding information about this wedding as snatches come to mind. I did receive a phone call tonight from Jeanne (PCV) and they are willing for me to tag along over Christmas. For that I am thankful.

Okay, did find out a little more about traditions (what I wouldn't give for an icy cold Coca-Cola). That is just the thought that went through my mind. But they kill the sheep for the evening before the wedding and the cow for the day of the wedding as part of the lobola (payment for the bride). But the HEAD of the cow goes to the father of the bride. If no father, as was this case, than the head goes to the uncle. If more than one uncle, then should be more than one cow. Have to find out more about this!

Sunday

Will leave the previous pages and come back when I remember more. And more is to come today! Up at 5:00AM and the house is already a bustle, sisters-in -law, older kids (6 and up), a couple of men...all busy cleaning and cooking. Again, I am in the way and again, I do the dishes. Many of the dishes were left outside last night until it was too dark to see. No soap, no towels and many hands in and out of the dishwater. Finally I say I can do no more till we at least have soap and/or hot water. Kids are sent by Rabie to the complex to buy soap and bread. They buy the bread but no soap. They are not happy when they are told to go back. I decide to tag along to buy a paper and to make sure they do get soap. The women are out washing the big pots with cold water. I go get the paper and have to insist the kids buy soap and this did take persistence on my part. Return home and I continue with the dishes. But by now they have eaten three large loaves of bread and butter, had coffee, tea (this includes the kids) and every last dish is dirty again.

More tables have been set up outside and pap, meat and vegetables (the same as yesterday) are prepared. We eat at 10:30AM...another feast. Me, I have finally found my niche and stay in the kitchen with the dishes. Have taken 130 photos so even Rabie is happy. I'm in...out...clean my room, the refrigerator and roam. It is 2:00PM and all the young people that had gone are back and the music, singing and dancing begins anew. Only today they are drunk and for me, it's not funny any more. When one young man said to me that AIDS is from the white man because he has sex with animals, I went to the kitchen and stayed. The young women and the other men told him to "behave" and both of us ignored each other the rest of the day.

4:30PM came and we ate again: a feast, same as yesterday, only today we had the meat from the hooves of the cow. And yes, the women did the cleaning and scraping and a soup was made. It boiled for a couple of hours and the meat was still tough (meat on hooves??). Cannot say if it was good but did swallow one bite of the soup and everyone else was raving. To each his own.

Oh yes, Christine's room was full of the gifts I thought the family had taken home. Yes, the family had taken those and these were new gifts...all for the bride. In truth, it has been a long, tiring, beautiful, emotional, heartrending, angry, harassing, defensive, lonesome, wonderful, compassionate, understanding, and patient weekend on both sides of the picture. I have the PICTURES. I did miss photos of the bride leaving with all the pomp, marching and singing and also all the people asleep on the floor.

By 6:15PM, Rabie has informed me that it is time for people to take their leave. They have spent 2 full days, or 48 hours eating his food and drinking his homemade beer (he does not drink anything alcoholic). Dishes are done outside tonight in cold water but with soap. No towels but flies. Could have been worse. I washed and the others cleaned up and with all the big pots, this was truly a massive joint effort. By now, I have joined in with the bantering and the little guys are quite happy with me. Balloons are always a hit.

Philipine (Meriam's granddaughter), from Sandfontein called and that put me back in a very good mood.

Most of all, the sunset tonight provides me the impetus to be a painter. Whaaaat? That lucky ole' sun is definitely a "photo." Pink, blue, red, purple, orange, gold and that was a Freudian slip. It truly is God's handiwork. Now I am watching out my window and it is purple, indigo, coral, rose and yes, just a small touch of a white cloud against sky blue against lavender. To me, it almost looks as if I should be able to hear, as well as see, a sunset. Perhaps a true artist does.

Monday

It is a "Blue Monday." It is in South Africa anyway. I am exhausted from this cultural experience and didn't sleep all night. I was too busy working in my dreams. I am all set to go this morning but wouldn't you know it? David doesn't show until 9:00AM. He is upset with his girlfriend and cannot sit still for one prime minute. I am unable to do anything on the "urgent" proposal till after 3:00PM. David returns for the 6th or 7th time with Njongo and Oupa in tow. They want my input. They do listen to my comments but all three take a different view. David takes off and at 5:00 PM, Njongo also disappears. By half past, Oupa and I also leave.

Tonight everyone in this home has gone to bed by 7:00PM due to being veeeeeeery tired.

Tuesday

Today, I did not lose my cool till 4:00PM and this, believe me, had been a very trying day! Walked to the District Office for the meeting on the World AIDS Day Program and I was the only one from ASHYO. Back to the office at 11:30AM and worked next to nonstop till 5:30PM on David's proposal. Decided to take it page by page and do it quickly and better, I hoped. Told all the guys over and over that this had to be in by deadline and that I could not, would not, do the budget. Up to 5:00 PM, no one took me seriously. I decided to do the narrative (without a budget, this is very difficult) and be done with what I could do.

David had been running around and today he looks foolish, and is, because he is reacting constantly and accomplishing nothing. When he started to take my phone apart after using it many times, I caved in. I said, "NO, NO, NO, don't take it apart! That phone is my lifeline back to America and my kids." Everyone looked at me like I was nuts but I didn't back down this time. Neither he, nor anyone else but me, has worked on this proposal and if ASHYO does not receive the funding now, it will be my fault! The Home Based Care Health Organization (HBCHO) has received notification of a minimal amount of funding. I helped a good bit on that request and do feel good about that.

Tonight my PC friends called and will travel as far as Cape Town with me for Christmas. Guess that is a wonderful ending to another confusing or is it frustrating day.

Wednesday

Aha! I did much better today! That is, I did not let David's wild antics and procrastination get the best of me. I have rewritten the entire proposal including the objectives and the budget. David and I went to the complex to have it typed and the line waiting to have work done was way too long. We hiked to David's brother's (owner of a PC) home but no one was there. Finally, we headed back to the Dr.'s office (near the ASHYO office). Now, after all this time, I find out that he, the doctor, has a working computer and will let us use it. I am growing even more frustrated (flexible), am I not, when I realize we actually could have typed all the proposals there WEEKS ago. I attempt to tell each of them once again that 1) I cannot write their objectives because I know not want they want to do; 2) I cannot figure their budget because I know not the price expected on any item let alone the cost of services; and 3) I do not know the intricacies of word processing. These excuses do not matter. I did all three.

Later I find that David has had an ideal opportunity to put into motion a request for funding from the Ford Foundation. His excuse? The usual...no transport. Now he plans to go to Witbank tomorrow (transportation?) and 5 will get you 20, that everyone there will be at the Ford Foundation meeting. Don't really know how long or if, I'll be able to handle this: this being the pace or the cyclic progress made or not made in fighting this severe crisis of HIV and AIDS. And now Meg is leaving the Peace Corps to return to America and her fiancé. I had only seen her a couple of times because she has been gone on leave but she was a normal link to my thought processes.

One wonderful and enlightening thing did take place today. As David and I were returning from his brother's, we passed by Rachel's (home-based care volunteer) home. Her home is beautiful and hand-painted in the bright colors and geometric designs of the Ndebele culture. A tour group from France was having lunch there. Of course, we barged right in and of course, Rachel invited us to join the group. I declined but after the group finished eating, we were seated and fed the same meal and served in the same style. It was wonderful even though no one spoke English. Nice to know this area is part of a tourist trip. And the meal was definitely South African. Rachel's home is large and very nice. She and her family served forty people, two large tables of ten each and two sittings. Every bit as elegant as dinner parties back in the States. To add to the ambiance, there were about twenty little (2-4 years) children roaming and playing around. Of course, the French tourists wondered what I, the American, was doing there...especially, when 3 or 4 of the women helping knew me and welcomed me very warmly, meaning with lots of hugs and kisses.

Thursday

It was not an easy day. It poured down rain continuously all night and all day. It is still raining tonight. Did make it to the office and finished the proposal. I did absolutely the whole shebang, including the budget. The social worker, who was to come at 9:00AM and transport us to Witbank to print the proposal, was nowhere in sight. Finally at 11:15AM, here she comes...and David has been flying here…there...and back again. We had an hour's drive to Witbank and I wondered how he could ride so long. Shouldn't have because he didn't. We stopped twice going and twice coming back. I stayed in the car for 1/1/2 hours while they picked up some stationery for her, and another 20 minutes while she did business at the bank. Finally at 3:30PM we reached Monica (PCV in

Witbank) and she printed out the proposal. We went on to ATTIC, (another non-profit agency), and after a 30 minute wait, we picked up the certificates of attendance for the workshop, given by ASHYO more than 2 months ago. We gave Monica a ride to her house and we were on our way home. Arrived back in Siyabuswa at 6:45PM and I'm so tired. But Thobi helps me unwind now by singing to me. She sings beautifully and loves "Playmates,"(favorite song from my childhood and now hers). Have plans for Thanksgiving and Christmas.

Tomorrow should be easy. Am to go to an elementary school at 1:30PM for Meg's goodbyes. But never know what the day will bring.

Friday

Ignore that last comment. Nothing, absolutely nothing, in this place goes as planned. Meg called at 6:55AM. She will be here at 7:00AM to borrow my camera. She leaves next Wednesday...as does Robin and Melissa (all three are 1 year veteran teacher PCVs). Meg's party at the school is scheduled for 10:00AM. The invitation said 1:00PM. We arrive at 10:20AM and wait for it to begin at 11:20AM. I have to sit in front AGAIN. This is not only a party for Meg but Parents Day. The children are unbelievably polite and at the same time so bright-eyed, energetic and proud. They ask me to say a few words. I do (a few)! We (Njongo and I) must leave at 12:30PM. We do start to make our apologies at 12:40PM but no...now we must eat. Fried chicken and all the trimmings (here, that is every known vegetable, it seems). We literally had to wolf this down and run through the rain to the District Chambers, 3 kilometers across hill and dale. I had to go to the bathroom so bad that I was having bladder spasms. We finally arrived, wet, bedraggled and greasy.

There are 22 government counselors for the District Wards. Appeared to me similar to our county officials meetings. I was asked, no told, to talk about HIV/AIDS. Cold turkey...no preparation...no notes...no language (except my hands). I have a runny nose and generally not feeling too hot. I start and words just came. I then answer questions and the night came! No, that is Judy Collins, isn't it? Time did go and I was on the stand for more than 2 hours. But these are exactly the people I should be talking with and this helps me. I do not feel the least retired!

On the way home, I stop at the complex and buy a birthday cake for Christina. It is very dark and dreary now. Soon I will be at the house waiting for Thobi to brighten another day.

Chapter Nine

"To be a friend a man should be sensitively responsive to the dreams and aims of others and should show sincere appreciation for the contributions others make to the enrichment of his life."

(The Art of Living)

NOVEMBER 2001

November 10, 2001
<u>Saturday</u>

HAPPY BIRTHDAY DAVID (this David being my son)! Christina wishes you Happy Birthday! Rabie requests that you send him an "America" tee shirt. Thobi wishes you to eat lots of sweet cake (but not too much)! It has been a good day today. I washed clothes, cleaned my room, cooked spaghetti <u>and</u> potato salad. The day went by. Christina hasn't felt well and won't be going to the church for an all-night session. Rabie will. Rabie's aunt (84) has been here all week since the wedding. She speaks nary a word of English. She and I just smile at each other. She sits all day and talks in her sleep all night. She has been through so much and I would like to talk with her about her dreams and personal history. She does speak Afrikaans and Ndebele but by the time she understands my Ndebele, hopefully I will be HOME...HOME!

The Old Lady Sleeps

Eighty-four years are inscribed on her brain. How far back can she go? How far forward can she move? (Oh so very, very slowly) Can she tolerate changes, even those that make ordinary daily tasks simpler and easier? Why does she sleep on a mat on the concrete floor beside an empty bed? Why does she use an old bucket when a bathroom with flush toilet is directly across from her doorway? Why does she eat porridge, rice, chicken heads and feet...when a whole cow has been butchered and fresh beef is on hand? Why does she eat vegetables that have all the taste and nutrients boiled into the air? Why does she "splash" with only one quart of cold water from a basin when a tub and hot water are available? Why does she wear the same dress day after day and shoes only rarely? And why does she brush her teeth with cold ashes?

She is tiny, shrunken, hunched, extremely thin, very crinkled, lifts herself from the floor on all fours, and walks with a cane. Her head is constantly bowed, her hands and feet are as gnarled as the trees. BUT, when her eyes sparkle and she laughs with joy at the antics of the young, she is so unalterably beautiful that it brings tears to your eyes.

What is she thinking as she sits on the back stoop hour after hour, and day after day? She has seen the same scene change seasons, year after year. She has watched over and over (or has she?) the sky and the sun change colors throughout the days. When the rain comes, and it does, even in the midst of the sun, and the stars, lightning, thunder, flash or splash off the sun, all at the same time, does she sit in awe of her God? Does she see today, or does she sleep and remember a lifetime only in her dreams?

Does she see the avocado tree change leaves? Does she see the ventures devour the grapes before the green has had a chance to change to purple? Does she realize that the arbor that spreads across the top of cement pillars and a concrete yard houses the ventures and the pigeons? As she uses the outside toilet, does she listen to the cacophony or pure noise of the geese, ducks, hens and roosters? Has she seen the rooster hop the hen closest and then strut his stuff as the three left behind rush to him, the cock of the walk? Does she think to herself, "Now isn't that just like a man?" Can she dodge all the wet duck droppings on the buffed, painted stoop?

Does she see the wire fence with locked gates and think, "We didn't have to pen ourselves in when I was young" or "We did not have to bar our windows or pad lock the door"? But does she smile when she waves to the passersby, who, although she cannot lift her head very high, never fail to greet her? You bet she does. She has seen, heard, and felt so much...this frail, tough old lady. She fought for freedom, gained it and now does she know the free families are fighting another deadly foe? This, an incurable disease with a stigma attached that in the eyes of many, is much worse than discrimination.

Finally, what does she think of this elderly, very white woman, who is a stranger from thousands of miles away, coming into her family's life? What does this grand lady think as the hours pass into days and these flow from one year into the next Is it possibly impossible to know or is it impossibly possible to know?

November 12, 2001

Resolve to be: tender with the young, compassionate with the aged, sympathetic with the striving, and tolerant of the weak and the wrong. There will be times in your life when you will have been all of these.

(Anonymous)

Monday

David is tired today and does not focus. The proposal has been left on the desk and not faxed to the National Office. I ask him why he is so despondent and he takes me to Kaille's (home-based care volunteer) home. I was to find out when we arrived that her mother had died last week. It was an uncomfortable situation because no one had told the young men; therefore no one from ASHYO had been by her home to offer condolences. This was my first visit in the home of the bereaved and I did not know what to do. Kaille was very gracious. She offered us tea and cookies, David said a prayer, we visited for a short time, and returned to the office.

At noon, David went home and I also left for home around 2:00PM. Kedi was to come by and try once again for a language class. If I don't make progress soon, I'll call it quits. I tried to take a nap, was interrupted twice and gave that up too. Kedi did not come. I'm tired...tired of all this language...jibber-jabber and cabbage!

Tuesday

Will be brutally honest (will I be?). Today was a lousy day! Kevin was supposed to show, he did not, and my telephone was completely out of time and I was completely out of money to buy time. Meg walked by, not planning to stop but David hailed her and she and I had a cup of tea. She plans on leaving in the morning. Cam is to come by for a site visit but Meg's leaving changes that, too.

I did type an agenda for the crew today after being given the order by David. He has set up individual interview meetings for me on Thursday and Friday. We shall see. If they happen at all, it will take the next two years to complete them. I left early for another language class and then took Thobi and Mary to Meg's (for the cup of tea that we had drunk in the AM). Of course she wasn't there and her family had no idea when she would return. I couldn't fault her because we had said our good-byes but the girls were disappointed. Tomorrow will be better. It usually is.

Wednesday

Another lousy day. You would think that I would be used to mixed messages by now. I was to attend a meeting with the home health volunteers (women) at 8:00AM, no, 9:00AM, no, 9:30AM. David rushes out of the office. Njongo and Oupa do not show until 9:45AM and a few of the women come in then, too. Meeting is over shortly after it has begun because David calls and requests my presence stat at the District Office. I do catch a ride there...no one there. I walk back to the office. Come to find out, he and Cam have met for the past 2 hours and she has already left with Robin and Meg. I'm to call her. I do call her...she knows I'm upset. Yes, I am. But I am even more disappointed, in everyone, and as usual I look like the bad guy. Communications the past two weeks have been a nightmare. Cam invites me to spend the weekend in Pretoria. I'm tempted. but will be gone the following week so will hold on 'till then. Anyway, I came home early to cool down, both because of the temperature and my anger. Christine tells me (doesn't ask) to cook. I ask her "What?" I don't have the rand to buy more food. This has become the truth with all the "photo" and telephone time everyone "borrows" and never pays back. Kevin calls and that is nice. He is coming in on Tuesday to go to Witbank with me.

Thursday

Today was much better! Did have private meetings with David, Freddie, Vusi, Lucas and Oupa. Will do Njongo and Silver (finally a female on staff of ASHYO) tomorrow. Each went better than expected and I came home at 3:00PM. Can't get my CD to play even with new batteries but did not get upset. Instead I will address a question or two that I have been asked from friends in the States. All comments will be from my perceptions only...I cannot or will not respond other than that.

BUSINESS

Am not in business for myself, of course. Therefore, I will have to discuss how different people in different affairs have responded to my questions and give my own viewpoint on those responses.

Peace Corps is an American organization, extremely organized and didactic. Even when discussing culture and traditions, the leaders remained true to the major goals of the organization and provided reams of instructional materials. However, the sections operated by personnel native to South Africa operated of course on "South African" time. Schedules...for travel, language classes, technical training, or even meals served...weren't ever followed on a timely basis on any given day. And not ONCE, were we behind, ahead, or off...but every single day! If we were picked up on time, then the language instructor was late. If both the driver and instructor were on schedule, then the planned meal was late and threw off the rest of the day. By the end of training, many volunteers chose to join (SA time) as oppose it; consequently, they themselves threw the rest of the group askew and asunder.

Shopping is not difficult if in a westernized mall, (this is a kids' treat), except that one never knows if a credit card or bank card can be used. It is good to ask before and to ask someone who knows. Most of the time, people are very helpful. But sizes...from shoes to clothes...are very different and trying on either is difficult due to safety on both sides. Even the clerks do not like to be by themselves in an empty cranny.

Purchasing items in a township, such as where I am, is easier in some respects and more difficult in others. Film is old, batteries are old, and developing film cannot be done. There is one copy machine which is out of order most of the time or when it is working, the line for usage is very long. The radios have been in stock so long that the boxes are crushed and dirty (really), blankets smell moldy, no sheets are available and the towels are very thin. Pens run out of ink and WHO buys safety pins or hangers? The shampoo is for black hair (didn't know there was a difference). But there is a supermarket and most of the above is available after all. Shopping becomes easier and better as time goes by and you become friends with everyone. After you see the security guard more than 5 times, he or she will let you out the door; but only after the guard has matched your receipt with your purchases. The fresh foods are fresh but it is much better to buy from the local vendors and stay friends with each of them. There is peanut butter but only two brands and in fact, this is the case of everything of this nature: pasta, soap, shampoo etc. Meat appears unappetizing to me and I don't buy. However, I see them packaging it fresh and the cases appear clean. Service is available and the bread is fresh every 2 hours. Smells great and the odor permeates throughout the town. The loaves are put out on racks unwrapped and everyone, after waiting in a mob, runs as a mob, grabs a loaf and bags it after they have dug into it to make sure it is fresh. This, even if they see the loaves arrive from the back and are still very hot. Even seeing all this, it is fine with me because the bread tastes wonderful. I eat a lot of bread, peanut butter, and tomatoes. Not having a huge selection of brands is also okay by me. Much less confusing and each product is tasty in its own way. Actually the main brand of soap used for washing clothes is much better than any I have found back home.

Prices are reasonable in my opinion but not, it seems, to the locals. I think the ice cream and candy are quite expensive but a loaf of bread is only 2-4 rand which today is approximately 30 cents in US money. The supermarts are very busy and run similarly to those in the states. At least for me. This view changes completely when you're buying on the "square." These squares are in close proximity and make up the complex. Within these squares are located the post office, bank, copying machine kiosk, offices for municipal workers, dentists, druggist, clothing stores, all-purpose shops, and the list continues.

In between the stores and up and down the streets are the local venders. Many in a neighborhood have a small stand out in front of their home. Someday I will attempt to count but for right now, I'd be very safe in saying there are more than 300 vendors just within my walk to the post office and bank. Many are stocked by old women, but there are also young men. Every single day they unload at 7:30AM until 8:00AM and pack back up from 5:30PM until 6:00PM. Huge and heavy crates of produce, some brought by pick-up truck, some by wheelbarrow, some on top of the head, some on bikes, and some just carried; everything including buckets of cookies and chips (our French fries). The snacks such as Fritos and corn curls are brought in very large bags, counted out (some weighed) and then placed in very small plastic bags and knotted shut. All this very tedious and time-consuming. The small bags are sold at about 10 cents US money. In the US, each bag would be sold for at least 79 cents or a dollar. There are fat cakes, deep fried on the spot and to these, I have become addicted. Very tiny candies, juice, popcorn (popped on the spot), oranges, apples, bananas, peaches, squash, potatoes, corn, peppers, avocados, onions, shoes, purses, tapes, pencils, pens, and on and on...all are for sale somewhere. Each vendor sits all day...every day and many even on Sunday.

Me, I think, why do they worry about selling? They don't have any spare time to spend any profit they might make. They do have to pay bills. Very few are working for a reliable wage, but still must pay for the services they received without cost...prior to their freedom from apartheid. But ABSOLUTELY NO ONE would return to those years. I will say that from 3:00PM on Friday afternoon and on through Saturday until about 3:00PM Sunday afternoon, the music on every conceivable spot is constant and everyone is laughing, singing, dancing, drinking, and playing. Appears to my eyes as wonderful but very unsafe. Every weekend, someone is robbed, raped or killed. Sometimes, all three and sometimes it happens to more than one person. I'm not allowed out without my young men as bodyguards. This is somewhat exaggerated because they do not follow me around during the weekend but I take them seriously and rarely go anywhere without at least Thobi, who would be, of course, very little protection. Does leave one with very little social life...none in my case.

Petrol stations Do not drive and do not plan to while here, but there are several petrol stations in the area and I have become familiar with each of them. Think this is because there are so many combis. The stations are not self-service and the petrol is considered expensive. Everyone seems to buy only as needed instead of filling the tank; therefore, even if going a short distance, we must stop for gas. Each station does have convenience items such as various types of food handy. Most are a hanging-out place for the young people much of the time. Few people in this township own their own auto. Rabie does, but as yet has not offered to provide me with a ride anywhere. He only drives to save himself a walk and this not often. He has run out of gas and had a flat tire since my arrival. The cars are hijacked often and the roads are rutted and narrow. I do miss just jumping in the car and going, but I also enjoy walking and meet many more people because of this. The people who do have cars take great pride in ownership. They may drive precariously and tear up the engine and tires but, believe me, that car is washed many times a week.

Friday

Melissa left today and now I literally am out of range of any Americans or Caucasians for that matter. Except for two priests (think they are Italian and Irish) somewhere, I am the only one. I keep telling myself, I did not expect to live with such a nice family, and instead, could have been in a hut in the middle of nowhere. Except for the language difficulties, since I don't see myself, I do not realize that I am white. Am doing okay. I am lonesome but not lonely. The day was okay and it is 4:00PM. Rabie and Christina just left and won't be back until sometime tomorrow. Thobi and Elizabeth will be here with me.

Saturday

Nice day. Thobi and I spent last night by ourselves and it was just nice. She slept on a pallet in my room and both of us slept very well. Without my asking, she brought me coffee at 5:00AM. I washed, fixed us scrambled eggs (she had never eaten eggs mixed up), went to the complex, cleaned my room, and napped. I cook tonight. Rabie and Christine made it back early. Martha (19) came by to visit and we made plans for me to attend church with her. A group of little kids, whom I didn't know but who knew me, brought me a bag of tiny peaches. I thought they were still green but they were ripe and delicious.

Sunday

Today was so nice, quiet and relaxing that I wasn't even going to write in here. But this peace of heart, soul and mind lasted only until 5:15PM when this all shattered. I couldn't sit still and Rabie said I was thinking "too much." Christine said, "Come, let us go see Thobi." She was at a dance class. But this class was over before we arrived and we walked back.

Anna, a neighbor and also a home health volunteer, was outside her home chopping mangoes for achaar, (the tastiest relish in the whole wide world). We stopped to visit and she started to cry. I asked what was wrong and she said, "Amy is dead." That is exactly how she first told us. I thought it was another of my misunderstandings and asked her to repeat. She said it again, "Amy is dead." I said, "How can this be? I just saw her this past Thursday. Did she have a heart attack or an accident?" No. She had been on her way to church, yesterday at 1:00PM. A man attempted to rape her; she fought him and he stabbed her many times. Others came by and stopped and then ran for help. She was able to say her name but died before medical help had time to arrive. This is the first person that I knew personally in South Africa who has died. Hers was also the first atrocity to happen in which I knew the person. Amy was one of the homecare volunteers and although she spoke little English, she was my friend. I had had lunch at her home and she would hug me when greeting me. She opened up her home to all and was truly a beautiful and caring soul.

Monday

Today was a heartrending day for all of us and this entry will not be sent home. For me, and I hope the others, this was the first murder of this type in which I would become involved. As the details were described, it was an extremely brutal but random killing. Multiple stabs (as high as 18 were reported) and even her eyes were cut to ensure blindness. She was not raped but her clothes were torn to shreds as if the act was intended. She was left naked.

The office staff, even though suffering their own heartaches, was very kind to me. Evelina, Linah, Silvia, Njongo, and Oupa took me to Amy's home and explained very clearly what was expected of me. The men were in the front yard and the women were sitting on the floor all around the wall of the living room in which the furniture had been removed. Each woman had a head covering on and a shawl about her shoulders. Silvia had brought me a head covering and shawl. She had also told me to be sure and wear proper clothes out of respect for the family. People visit in a continuous stream all day and all night. Refreshments are also served continuously. We sat in silence for about 20 minutes, spoke our condolences, gave an offering and then we left. Similar to our visitations but with no respite for close family members. The experience for me was heart-wrenching and yet so very beautiful. Her mother said to me, "I was so scared when they told me she was dead but God is using her now." Njongo stayed by my side throughout the visit and translated everything.

Tuesday

It will be Saturday night before I write again. But have so much to say, it will be next week sometime before I catch up. But back to Tuesday. Another day of hurry up and wait, wait, wait. Expected Kevin sometime during the morning because he has promised to travel to Witbank with me. Planned on having a free afternoon and then dinner and a movie. But none of this happened. The office was chaos because everyone wanted to do their condolences to Amy's family, plus plan what the office should do as a unit. I am out of this loop because in this case, it is not only a language issue but for me it is now cultural crisis. The funeral is to be next Saturday.

While I am waiting for Kevin, he is waiting at his own taxi rank, but he does make it by 2:00PM. We say a quick good-bye to the others and then sit from 2:30PM until 5:00PM for our combi to fill. We finally arrive in Witbank at 7:00PM and take a private taxi to a restaurant. There we meet the rest of our PCVs who will travel to Barberton for Thanksgiving. After dinner Kevin and Elizabeth (PCVs) track down a ride to her house where we are to spend the night. Never in my wildest dreams, out of our whole group, did I dream I would be looking for a ride late at night in a town in South Africa. They do find someone and we are transported to her host home.

<u>Wednesday</u>

A driver from Peace Corps gave us a ride on to Barberton. We were supposed to leave at 9:00AM and do leave at 11:15AM, but are we not old soldiers by now? We arrive in Barberton around 3:00PM and it is all fantastic for the next 36 hours. The wine starts to flow, food starts to show, dinner has been arranged. My timing is way off, that 3 should have been a 5. We honestly arrived in Barberton at the hospital at 2:00PM and had an American Thanksgiving party for 50-plus orphans from throughout the area. We did the traditional activities such as making paper Indian hats, painting Pilgrim faces, hand-cutting wild turkeys, and playing games. Our meal was corn bread and milk. It was truly beautiful and set the tone for the evening and day ahead.

We stayed (all of us) at Vilma's, (Cecelia's host home). Vilma's home is a storybook enchanted cottage, including live monkeys playing in the trees. Vilma herself is like the fairy godmother. I felt as if I were back in another time and place. We did go out for dinner and shortly after arriving back, I went to bed...earlier than the rest. I was also up and out for a walk much earlier. Ed and Bev went with me and when the hike started to get steeper, I did not last long and came back. I went on my own to a historical site of old homes. It was too early to tour but the gardens within eyesight were exquisite.

By ten, everyone was up and ready to cook, walk, talk and play. We did. Everyone jumped right in and not one person did more than the next except for Cecelia. This is her homestay so she was busy, busy, busy. She did not complain, nor did anyone else. Later I sat and reflected on each in the group. I thought, if I had to go on Big Brother (TV show) who would I expect to like best, kick out first, change my mind about, or miss the most? I concluded: not any one of them for any category. No one yet has been my confidante nor is there anyone I would ask to leave. All in all, it was a most pleasant day. Both Mindy and Susie (daughters) called and that was my first Thanksgiving Day here. We watched videos, drank champagne, ate like kings and I went to bed smiling.

<u>Friday</u>

Up at 5:00AM and ready to go by 6:00AM and Vilma provided transport for several of us to our bus station or combi rank. She took Jen to her combi rank first. We were there by 6:45AM and they did not anticipate leaving until at least 8:30AM so she took us on over to the bus which had left at 7:30AM. Missing this, we scampered back to the combi rank and waited until 10:00AM for the combi to Witbank. I waited another 1 ? hours for the combi on to Siyabuswa. Arrived back home by 4:00PM and must say was relieved to be here. Although it seemed a long day, did not run into any serious problems and supper was ready early.

Saturday began at approximately 8:30PM Friday night and did not end until Monday morning. Blaring music (noise) once started did not stop and continued throughout every single hour. Each of us had very little, if any sleep. Christine and I were up at 4:30AM to attend Amy's funeral at 5:30AM.

People were already there, singing, praying and talking. Hundreds of seats had been set up and were already filled. The lawn, where people sat on blankets or the ground, was filling fast. Someone found me, as well as Christine, chairs.

People kept coming and the service kept progressing. All the staff were there and at 6:10AM, all sang and three of the young men gave eulogies for Amy. It was beautiful and I was very proud of them and her. By 7:00AM the whole place was full, by 8:00AM the whole neighborhood, by 9:00AM the street for over 2 blocks was completely jammed with people. I have never been to a funeral with so many people...and again the men were separated for the most part from the women. They took turns singing and giving eulogies. One more eloquent than the next...or so it seemed. They did not scream, shout or cry loudly, but instead were very somber, respectful and believing. There must have been 3,000 people or more. I thanked God for Christine. She literally took me by the hand ...especially when it was time to go to the cemetery. Every single combi in Siyabuswa was donated as transport to the cemetery for the townspeople. Each was filled with 16-18 people and the procession was three deep as far as I could see ahead and behind.

At the grave site, there were many tents set up and many people standing or sitting on the ground. Music was soft and beautiful, and even though I did not understand the words, I was made to feel welcome and part of the group. I was very sad and thought about my own mother often. I was asked if I wanted to see Amy. I did not but knew the others thought I should. Just as David walked with me, other young men approached the casket and closed it.

I asked, "Do this many people attend every funeral?" I was told that yes, there are always a lot of people, but this was more than anyone had expected...partly because she lived in the center of town and many knew her, and partly because of the way she had died.

After the grave site services, everyone was transported back to town. Food had been prepared at her home for anyone and all. Again the people were lined up all the way back to the complex, a stretch of at least 7-8 blocks. Would have been the ideal "photo" shoot but just couldn't.

November 24, 2001

> *I am very young*
> *I have 42 children.*
> *When I call them all*
> *I called them STDS*
> *I am AIDS.*
>
> *I am as strong as an ox*
> *I stand the test of time*
> *I am as unshakeable as mountains*
> *I am AIDS*

I am a killer
To those who don't believe
I hate those who have sex with condoms
I am AIDS
I am very friendly
I set my friends free as birds
I like those who said
They can't eat sweet with some plastics
I like those who have six girl friends
I am AIDS

I am as strong as an ox
I stand the test of time
I am as unshakeablee as mountains
I am AIDS

I am free of charge
I am not sold as a product
No price can afford me
I am AIDS

I enter to every one
President, Doctors, Policeman every person
I like those who said
They can't eat one thing every day
I am alway happy
If someone die because of me
They don't say is killed by AIDS
They always hide me
I am AIDS

I am honoured and suspected
I am not afraid to befriend dignitaries
HIV is my grandson
Drop is my granddaughter
I am AIDS

If you are affected person in HIV?AIDS don't afraid. To come out.
Come out! So that those people think AIDS is American ideas to destroy
can believe that AIDS is alive and is the killer. Youth stop doing the wrong
things, let us focus to our dream.

Good luck   Good luck   Good luck
(Written by a young man for the ASHYO training classes)

<u>Saturday</u>

As usual I'm unsure of where to be when, and we are to leave now for Tambani (village) for the first of a five-day workshop to train the trainers. Everyone (staff) comes up to me, leaves, comes, leaves and no one, least of all the leaders of the workshop, has an idea what to do next. Finally, David talks a lady he knows into providing us with transport. Seems no one is going after all, except he, Njongo and me (I had thought all the staff would be there). She stops for gas and David jumps out, not to return. It is now only Njongo and me. It is only a 20 minute ride and we arrive at 10:30AM.

Thirty young men and women are all set to go and have been since 8:00AM. Supposedly, they were told about why we would be late but this tardiness was mentioned over and over in the day's evaluation, so I am not at all sure.

Njongo does a fantastic job by himself and the group is certainly attentive.

Me, I'm in agonizing misery. I had not eaten and by 2:00PM, my stomach aches. I don't know if the pain is from hunger pangs or bladder spasms. Both, I believe. There is no key to the locked bathroom. At 2:15PM, I'm afraid because I am really hurting, have not gone since 4:30AM and for me, that is much too long. Finally, I told one of girls and she took me to a house and after much discussion, the owner let me use a concrete outside toilet. Now mind you, the concrete was very hot and the hole was way too far back for my legs. I could not stand because of that, could not sit (tried to and leaped immediately and painfully back up because of the hot concrete). I'm next to tears because my abdomen is really hurting. I am unable to relieve myself due to the environment and also cannot do this physically because I have waited too long. Finally, I climbed onto the concrete and dribbled for what seemed forever. I was scared my head was showing over the top (it was open air), also scared to death I was going to fall into the hole, because, although I had shoes on, my skirt was straight and I had to use my hands to climb up on the ledge. Not a good scene at all. Would have given my soul for a pit spot (again, losing my own language).

The workshop went well. David was to pick us up at 4:00PM. You know what? He did not come. We finally hitched a ride (my second in a lifetime) to the complex. I am to be at the office at 7:20AM tomorrow for second day of the workshop.

<u>Sunday</u>

Njongo is at the office before me, but no one else has arrived. He and I waited till 8:00AM and David came. Soooo tired...did not sleep etc. (this is now getting old). I climbed into the back of the truck that brought him, but no, this is not the transport. We are to be picked up by someone else. No show. Njongo and I take a combi. We are 30 minutes late already and the young people have changed venues on us. We walk there, making us even later. But me, I am happy. There is a bathroom (unlocked).

For today's session, there is only Njongo, (I'm learning to love this young man). <u>Until</u> 4:00PM that is, and this when he tells the group he, "won't be here tomorrow but Sydney will." Now come on...is this fair, to anyone? I literally begged him to at least be at the office so that if no one else shows, I don't go by myself. He agreed, but will see what tomorrow brings. I am home by 5:00PM today and all is well here and I DO love Thobi!

<u>Monday</u>

Okay, so what else is new? Bought the wrong telephone card and threw away the number! But on to today. No, David was not there...Njongo was. We took a combi. I paid today, arrived late anyway and were certainly reprimanded for it. <u>And</u> neither of us blamed them. David showed at 9:00AM and off and on, it was chaotic. Njongo left and David managed most of the day. When he was talking, he knew his material, but of course, he was pretty rattled at the start. And shades of the States, the VCR was next to inoperable. But who shows up in the nick of time? Vusi (another ASHYO volunteer), and he took charge of the electronics, at least long enough to show a video. Which reminds me, the news I get from BBC sounds okay one minute and mighty scary the next. I fear we are in for the long haul.

The day went by and the group is becoming used to me and are exceptionally committed to fighting HIV and AIDS. I like them. By 3:00PM I want out but the session is to last till 4:00PM and then the rain commences. And no ride! Our man, who was to give us a ride back to Siyabuswa, went somewhere. At noon, David was supposed to contact him about the change of venue. I did not know this and he had no telephone time so instead, we walked in on two different homes of his friends. Turned down tea at the first but had apples, peaches, and a coke at the second. I counted 9 times during the course of the day that he found excuses to go outside and leave the young people in my hands. Don't know how to handle this, or if I even want to...probably not. Instead, perhaps will have to change my own work ethic. Imagine I will ultimately accomplish more by staying low-key. Will think on it.

<u>Tuesday</u>

Am going to write about an exceptional group of young people. There are 30 in the class: 14 girls and 16 boys with an age range between 18-24 years. Everyone is unique and beautiful in a special way...each personality comes out as the hours go by. They may not be the best group of participants (I am not a teacher), but surely they rank in the top one percent. A couple like to talk about every issue, but everyone listens to them and they to everyone else. All are on time, do not get up and down, cause distractions, complain, act defensively, or even chew gum. And all this takes place in a garage in which they are touching side by side on benches for several hours at a time. Although the space in which they meet is not conducive to break-out groups, they do this. I am impressed by the open, apparently honest and yet personally revealing discussions which takes place in these small groups. Each is neat, respectful, and never surly. Each day is opened and closed with a prayer and a hymn. This group of young people and these past few days are providing me with the first answers to the question: "Why am I here in South Africa?" These kids are committed to fighting AIDS by any means they find available and if I can help them one tiny bit, it makes me feel better (why do I need to feel better)?

Wednesday

Last day of workshop. Waited once again but am slowly learning to take these waits in stride. Each day a different person from the office shows. But you know, an awfully lot of information was shared with this group. Seeing the leaders/facilitators from the hearts of these young people, I can see why each member of ASHYO is revered. One of the young men, wrote the poem quoted earlier.

Thursday

Jeepers! Today was the first big District World AIDS Day. And I had helped, believe it or not, in the planning. I was even looking forward to it. We were to be at the office at 8:00AM, (again, sharp). By 8:20AM everyone is there, except David. He shows at 9:30AM and with no transport. He said Oneah had told him this AM (whaaat?) that there was a free bus but he would have to make the arrangements. He's cross and will not do it; therefore, none of us are able to go. Nor are the members of several other NGOs who were to travel with us.

We are to go to Denilton Saturday for another WAD and there is another on the 6th right here in Siyabuswa. To my knowledge, we have not been in on the planning of either of these, so we shall see. Today was the kick-off for a series. I fear relations will be be strained between the government and ASHYO for the moment. But I have come to the realization that no person stays upset for long because each must continue to rely daily on another. No matter how frustrated one may become, he/she never ever turns down an appeal for assistance from another. I may think that this transport issue is ridiculous but must continue to remind myself that David himself is a volunteer. No funding for transport is available. Who loses out here? The communities!

Friday

In many ways today was a good day. Did not go as planned, of course, but have been here long enough to feel much more comfortable. Worked on my language early, my cell phone is fixed and the trip to Cape Town is planned.

David informs us at 10:45AM that in 15 minutes we must go to Kameelrivier to help with an AIDS prevention (I add this word) event there. We do have transport and are able to go. I meet many more new people. We sit in the rain but only for a few minutes. Njongo takes me to another stand and here we sit in the hot sun. We stay there about 30 minutes and then we leave for another; this continues until well into the afternoon.

For the very first time, the day passed without seeming so slow or that I was in the way. The staff is beginning to talk in their own language. When appropriate, they include me and translate if necessary. It does not seem such an enormous obstacle any longer. Today, David, Njongo and Oupa, each told me, separately, that they thought my presence was beginning to show in the community and they want and need my help. For me, my job is becoming more what I anticipated. I will be interviewing the home health volunteers, setting up training for them and providing scheduled (hah) in-services for all. I'm excited now and tomorrow is World AIDS Day. We are to go to Denilton but probably won't have transport so will have to remember that I felt <u>good</u> today!

<u>Saturday</u>

WORLD AIDS DAY!   "I CARE, DO YOU?"

Must back track a little: last night at 6:45PM Thobi came in and I thought it was for our nightly get-together. I said "Hi, Little Bit, how are you?" She said, "I'm not good." We chatted a little but she had a very sad face-. We sat on the bed for 40 minutes. She would cry softly; she did not tell me the problem. Hopefully, it is 9-year old's hurt feelings and not something even more serious. Again language was a barrier. Perhaps not, maybe just feeling with her and letting her know she didn't have to say anything is just what she needed for tonight. We'll see tomorrow.

World AIDS Day is probably celebrated (wrong choice of word I say) here very similar to the USA. Except here it gets started much later. Programs are printed, but not followed (never are). Everyone is fed free. It does not matter that there are hundreds and hundreds of people at each venue; each is fed the pap, meat, squash, green beans, beets, cookies and so on, that the women have been preparing for hours.

The program opened with a group of drum majoretttes from a local primary school. This was followed by the opening prayer and hymn (every program and meeting is opened in this manner). Many speeches were heard from local, district, regional and provincial government dignataries. After each speech, a musical "item" or skit was presented by several different cultural groups. There were tables placed strategically around the entire venue. From these, volunteers distributed written information on health issues and thousands of free condoms.

Everyone was laughing. The weather was perfect, the rain had stopped, the sun was out and a breeze wafted through the crowd. For me, it was a long, long day because it seemed I was one of the displays. Once again, I was told to sit at the head table, to say a few words and to light the center candle for the candlelight ceremony. Each is an honor and I was appreciative but certainly did not wish to be in such high profile. I kept asking myself, "What else would I be doing?" This helped a little but by the time the program started, I was already quite frustrated, exhausted, angry, close to tears, heart pounding, smiling, and again smiling. Don't know how long I can keep these mood changes going without cracking.

My day: up to pouring-down rain, no food in house, have a small cup of tea, rain stops. Reach office at 7:45AM in order to leave at 8:00AM and finally do leave at 9:15AM. David had had to get transport from Kameelrivier. We were loaded into small combis and then spend 30 more minutes for him to do "whatever." Lunga, his 2-year-old son, is with him. Made not a sound. We make it to Denilton a little after 10:00AM and everyone takes off without a word...I know not where. Lunga is left with me. David comes back, collects

Lunga, tells me he is going to release the driver and will be back. He is gone the rest of the day.

Oneah, (nurse from a governmental office), who is sitting with me when David comes back, says she'll give me a job hanging posters and takes off to find stickum. There I sit, sit, sit. No one comes back. Finally some strange man comes and he, with a bunch of kids, put up the posters. I make friends with two women sitting close by me who are from the "Women in Poverty Agency." The three of us sit, sit, sit. It is now 12:00 Noon. I have been left for almost 2 hours and am beginning to think: "I better take this seriously." I am 40-50 minutes from Siyabuswa and have no idea where to find transport. It is several miles to the nearest taxi rank. Then I catch sight across the way of Freddie, Njongo, Lucas, and Vusi. Lorraine had been with them but she has gone off with some other friends. No David. These young men thought I was with David. David thought I was with them or Oneah. Oneah did not think anything because I was not with her in the first place. I found out that she had gone home to rest. Anyway, they did not leave me again!!

The program started at 12:15PM and went on-on-on. This will become my 8th full day of non-stop listening to loud music and speeches in languages other than English. And meeting more and more and more people. Forget learning new words...my energy is going to be directed at remembering people.

The boys are getting upset, use my phone, do not reach David who I understood to say would be back at 4:00PM. Program is to be over at 3:30PM but no one thinks this will happen. No matter, by 5:00PM they are angry. I'm close to tears and here comes David. Lo, he must eat and is visibly under the weather. But of course, must run, run (where?)...leaves Lunga with the driver and everyone is gone again except the driver, Lucas (at least one has stayed with me), Lunga and me. We wait until 5 minutes past 6:00PM and here they all come and after much hassle, we do take off. Several have elected to stay for the evening dances. David is mad at someone (I don't know with whom, perhaps himself?) for leaving me. Lunga is sound asleep.

We finally arrive home. I am the last one dropped off and walk through the complex at 6:45PM on a Friday night. Not a good idea but I do get home. Not a soul here. This is a first. I come in, change my clothes and they come shortly. I go to my room after watching TV and the AIDS telecast. Eat three turtles! It has started to rain again and the drops on the tin roof are mesmerizing and lull me to sleep.

Sunday

Skies are clear. I wash, iron and cook macaroni and cheese that no one likes, sloppy joes that no one likes, canned pork and beans that everyone likes except me (unless doctored up). I'm not happy because everyone came in from church wanting the meal on the table, It's okay for me but not for them to wait. These mixed messages are driving me to the brink of craziness or tears...which ever comes first!!

<u>Monday</u>

We plan for our own Siyabuswa AIDS Day to be held on the 6th. Today is the 3rd. Need I say more?

<u>Tuesday</u>

Another chasing day: David and I walked to the township offices and begged for assistance for Thursday. No one is willing to fund, but someone did agree to help arrange the sound system and to transport the chairs and tent. We went to the complex shops and after much discussion, the SPAR grocery will provide 15 plates of food and the Confectionary 100 little cartons of juice. By three other merchants we are told to come back tomorrow.

Later we went to visit a friend of David's and watched a video of his 5-year-old's birthday party...never did figure this one, so will go on with my first impressions.

<u>*Ethics/Values*</u>

Am not quite sure if this is the time to get into what the value system is here. The family I live with seems to value very highly the same concepts as I do. Family, honesty, fairness, love, friendship, a nonjudgmental attitude...but the household is still male- dominated and without question, Rabie is head. Both Christine and Rabie take great pride in the fact that they are married, legally, spiritually, and traditionally. No matter how hard Christine tries, the extended family from each side has multiple broken strands. Her attempts to mend these are futile. All who are living in this home are spiritual and are not self-conscious in their open worship of God and Jesus. They do, however, follow the traditional beliefs that make sense to them such as calling up for help from ancestors.

They will state that they have no rand and will ask friends and me for whatever they desire, (pencils, sweets, food, coffee or whatever) but will also play the lotto every week. Bear in mind: Chistine is 55 years of age, Rabie, 56 years and Thobi only 9 years. Both Rabie and Christine lived under apartheid. Democracy and capitalism are still mysteries to them. I am finding that, as with every human being, regardless of race, ethnicity, or religion, the more one becomes involved, the more one recognizes similar or even like intrinsic values to one's own.

It is quite the same at the office. Ages here range between 21 to 34 years of age. Five of the young men each have one child, one has two and only one has none. All are unmarried and never have been. They value children (obviously) and will say they value women. How can they? They preach to their peers to have only one partner but do not deny multiple loves. It seems the more lovers one has, the more he is a man. In whose eyes? Certainly not the women, you would say. Not true: many women are proud that their young lovers also have someone else. This means they are worth having. Go figure! But I find this out only <u>because</u> of my age. They don't mind discussing these issues with me because when they were teens, they were also in the middle of apartheid and other concerns were much more important. No one had time to just listen. Is not this need to communicate and to be understood another value? Perhaps the world over.

When discussing value systems, we must consider the sheer numbers living in or near poverty as well as the horrific numbers of very, very sick families. We are viewed as "rich Americans." Why would they have no qualms about asking for items they need? They realize to borrow is to be given something to use but do not know it also means to return that item.

Wednesday
Did not realize that this journal is my sole companion and that the poor thing is taking on a "life." If I make it through this next weekend and if Cam comes for a site visit on Tuesday, I think I might make it. As it is, this afternoon I came very close to losing whatever it is and just may yet. It is only 6:20PM and this also is part of the "bad" days. But let's start with yesterday.

At 9:00AM Senna and Thambi (social workers) arrive to work on our World AIDS Day for tomorrow. David wants me to go back to the complex with him, but the program for tomorrow must be planned. Thambi wants me at a home-care meeting and Senna wants me to meet with Oneah from the District Office.

David asks me at 9:30AM to be the guest speaker and he promises to translate. I agree...first mistake...then I elect to go to the District office with Senna...second mistake. We do go and Thambi does also; only they both leave me in an office by myself. Senna came back and after 1 ? hours, I am told to "poke" my head in the door and get Oneah out of a different meeting. It works but she cross-questions us and is quite cross because everything is still up in air about tomorrow. She and David are at odds and we are caught in the middle. Oneah also wants me to speak and says she will translate but no program is finalized. In fact, a number of the people have not even been notified.

We go back to the office and I am told to type a sheet of the program and Oneah has said she will translate so it can be done in both languages (which will be the other)? I'm staying very calm and Oneah has graciously asked me to go back with her to work on my talk...no way! I do not want to sit and sit. I ask David if I can go home and do it there. No problem! Christine and Rabie are to be gone. I will have the place to myself. Who says so? Not only is Christine home but she has company! So much for me planning anything.

I do get my little spiel written out twice in longhand. One for me and one very tediously done for the translator (my handwriting leaves much to be desired). The day moves on. I'm tired but a little proud that I have kept the faith.

It is after midnight and the noise in the street outside my window commences. Voices loud, but after 2:00AM, they move on. I lie there thinking how close it is to 4:30AM but finally do doze off.

I am awake at 4:30AM for good and walk to the combi rank. David comes on time! We arrive at the clinic by 7:15 AM and the long day's journey into night starts. A preacher is shrieking in the clinic...which is jammed with about 150 people. David and I walk right on in and soon the church service breaks rank. All these women are pregnant and move to an adjacent clinic room.

I count 144 women there by 7:30AM and the room that they have just exited begins to fill with general patients, all ages and diseases, even leprosy.

David and I have moved outside by now and he chases around and I sit and walk around, sit and walk around. Program is to start at nine. It is nine and zero is done. Finally, some help does show and David himself takes off. By 11:45AM, we are ready to start but there is no MC. Oneah has said she cannot translate and David is gone. Back he comes and he has talked the preacher into being the MC. The program we had written means nothing. Every single item has changed, but each is truly beautiful and wonderful. It amazes me that no matter the chaos prior to these events, each turns out better than the last. I think it is because there are many talented people of all ages available. None of them seems to worry (like I do) whether he/she will do well. They just naturally are top- notch, even when called upon on the spot.

Now it is time for my guest slot and David tells me he must go to the SPAR for the bread and takes my notes with him. Of course, now there is no translator. I'm literally up in front wondering how I can run (anywhere). A <u>nurse</u> comes to my rescue (don't they always) and translates as I speak. Sentence by sentence. People start to leave but that is par for the course. I am not nervous because it really doesn't matter what I say. They only want my AIDS pin and their photo taken. Oh, yes, I am shaky because haven't eaten anything today and it is now 2:00PM.

Finally it is over and we are given bread, butter and juice. However, the crowd is unhappy because the usual feast has not been provided. At 3:30PM we (David and I) hitch a ride to the complex and I walk on home.

Rabie is home and I tell him I am tired enough to take a nap. He says okay, but then he tells me that Christine is gone. He does not tell me where or when she will return. I do fall asleep and at 4:20PM, he hollers through my door, "Are you sleeping? Did Christine not tell you to cook tonight?" No, she did not. I get up to go ask him if he would like tea (see how nice I am). A hen skitters into my room, up on the bed and glares, ready to attack (do hens attack)? I think so and beg Rabie to come get her out and he picks her up, the three of us squawk-ing all the time, (me, the hen and Rabie)!

I do cook rice, potatoes, scrambled eggs, fried bologna (?) and coleslaw. I had told him that I had had only two slices of bread all day. <u>After</u> waking me up, telling me to start cooking, and drinking coffee, I think he is ready to eat. But alas, at 5:30PM, <u>HE SAYS NO!</u> He will eat later. I almost took a pot and threw it at him or rather wanted to throw him in a pot. Did break a cup but it was truly an accident. We did eat at 7:00PM and all of the above was cold and greasy. The dishwater was cold, too. Good thing I have visions of "Snickers" in my head!

Ethics continued:

It doesn't seem to bother anyone to tell me to do something or that they are going to do something at the last second, never taking into consideration that in my culture we also have norms of good behavior. For instance, we would inform each other when leaving, not just get up and depart with no discussion as to when he/she will return. To me, it is common courtesy to let someone rest and not wake them up unless it has been requested. It doesn't matter if this family or the staff eat the last of my cereal, peanut butter or coffee, but I don't dare do the same. I'm quite sure this is not a belief but rather a state of the community itself being very poor and getting or taking what is there "now." Tomorrow there may be nothing.

This whole area apparently has a strong belief in God. I also feel (and it is just a feeling) that this faith gives them hope. Somewhere...some day...life will be better. But the greatest concern and one that everyone questions is: why are so many small babies and very young girls brutally raped? And this, it is reported, is occurring every single day and sometimes more than once per day. Some are saying it is because sex with a baby or a virgin will prevent/cure AIDS. Where, oh where, could this have possibly been derived, let alone believed by so many?

Saturday and Sunday

Pleasant day. Talked with Mae (PCV teacher in Northwest Province). She is trying very hard to last one year; she feels very much as I do. She too would like to be home having a good time with her own family. Why am I here? Re-organized my room again!

Jeanne called and we are all set for the Cape. Also had a very nice phone visit with David, Sangita and the kids.

This family went to an all-weekend wedding. I've had the day to myself with the geese, ducks, and chicks. Do I or do I not take care of them? Sure I do and this means doing Rabie's job. He lets them free in the morning and returns them to the pens in the evening. They know him. The geese parade up and down the road but will follow him home. Okay, today, and without him, they still wander up and down the road but do not wish to follow me home. But they did return, mostly on their own but now I had to guide each into its own pen. Yes, the geese have a fenced-in area, as do the hens and chicks. But where do the ducks go? Where they want to! And this is not where I want them to go. When some are guided in, others run out and the little bitty ones are all over, even go through the holes (or get caught) in the fence wire. All are making a racket (me included) almost as loud as the language becomes at the end of my day. Just call me the "Goose Old GoGo." Just call me anything, but please don't ask me to care for these fowl anymore. The green wet droppings are worse than cow pies. Who says one pile isn't worse than another? That's why a cow has such soulful eyes. She knows "hers" does not smell or look worse! But now I know why I am in So. Africa. It is so I can learn to chase geese, ducks and chicks before I die. Am sure in some past life I prayed for this! Needless to say I was scared. Scared of Rabie, scared of the geese, the hens, the roosters, and the drunks passing by seeing me make a "goose" of myself. And oh yes, I was scared that I would step on or strangle some tiny little chick or duck. And did I get a thank you? Nary a word, nor could they even understand when I tried to tell anyone about my silly goose tales (no pun intended).

Monday

We were on TV today. Since I was the only white person in the cast of thousands, I stood out and got told about it over and over. We were part of a community "March Against Violence." It was very long but also impressive. Hundreds received a T shirt and another lunch. Somewhere enroute, I was told to give a short talk in Kwaggefontein with Christine on Thursday (whaaaat?).

In many ways I am beginning to feel useful. So why am I so down tonight? Am in a foul mood, snapping at Thobi, angry at Rabie and homesick. Could be for starters that last night I slept with my window open. This morning, Rabie informs me that a rat could come through the window frame and bit me. Then Christine says she'll be at the office at 8:30AM. At 9:00AM, we decide to come down here and pick her up. She is doing dishes and cooking. We are to be at the march by now and still have several kilometers to walk to even get to the starting point. Then, when I thought she was asking David for permission for me to go with her, he tells me, "No, she is asking if you will speak at her church group." She needs David's permission for me to speak??

We do make it to the march but on the way, David unloads all his sorrows on me. Of course, I have no answers for him. We finish the march and I am left alone but every time I try to go back to the office I get told to stay. Once again, I feel very much in the way. Finally we head back to the office and David releases me to come home.

It is dark, about to storm, I am working on the site visit agenda and get asked by Rabie why the light is on. Then it's time to fix supper which I had all ready from last night. No, they want rice, not spaghetti. Thobi has eaten all the achaar, my green beans have been recooked to mush, the corn on the cob is tough as bone, and Thobi and Christine have eaten all the ice cream. It seems I'm to be polite but they don't have to be. Anyway, each situation is so minimal and trite that I'm feeling about an inch tall. Thobi comes in with a balloon and wants to play. I say no balloon-throwing in my room and I'm going for a walk. Have already marched 4-5 kilometers. It is 6:00PM and I do go for a walk. Naturally I missed the news. So who loses through all this?

Tuesday

Site visit today. It went as expected: lots of everyone saying what they want others to think. That's right...and not necessarily the truth. Tried to tell Cam my concerns but when spoken aloud and one at time, each seems trivial. I ended up being the bad guy, or weak, whichever. I probably have the best situation of all the PCVs. Must remember that!

Not 20 minutes later I soon forget that. Rabie told me not to use hot water to do the dishes and I lost it! Enough said. Of course, I apologized but am seriously going to re-negotiate when I get back from vacation. Maybe.

Wednesday

These newspaper horoscopes Mary (friend from States) sent...she thinks each is right on target. I'm not the least bit sure. Today was my first day all by myself at the office and it was wonderful. <u>But</u> tonight, I'm to be by myself with Rabie and hard telling what he will order me to do. The day isn't over yet!

<u>Thursday</u>

It is 6:00AM. Christine came in with the coffee and wanted to talk. She said that when I am cross, it makes her heart heavy. As it does mine. We both tried to say how we felt and I think I understood her but I doubt she understood me. She told me that this month, there is no money. What they do have is my payment to her and with this, she will buy what Rabie and Thobi want. I told her that resentment (hard to find a better word) was growing inside me because I do give them a monthly stipend and also buy some of the food. That when I buy cereal, milk, bread, and other items, much of it is eaten and none left for me. I want to pay my way and help where I can, but actually according to our agreement, I do not have to pay for all the extras. That is the reason that when I buy 2 loaves of bread in 3 days and get 2 slices, if any, and it's this way with everything, I become cross. I showed this anger when Rabie told me not to use hot water to wash <u>his</u> dishes and not to turn on the lights. I don't think she understood any of this but both she and I have agreed to talk when we are upset. She sings when she is happy, she sings when she is sad. I walk when I am happy and I walk when I am sad. I think the coming break will help. This isolation in a crowd of people and living in someone else's home is about to do me in. And how hard it must be for Rabie and Christine to give up a large slice of their home and life to a stranger. Today I am supposed to have a language class and tomorrow I am to give a talk to Christine's church group. We shall see.

PM: No, we did not have a language class. Will try again after the first of the year.

<u>Thursday</u>

Went with Christine and the women she prays with to the Community Center. They prayed and sang; it was lovely and inspirational. We moved on to the large combi rank. There were 300-plus people present and it was here that I gave a 15 minute spiel on HIV and AIDS (mostly answered questions about me).

Jen (PCV) came and spent the night at the Catholic Mission. She took me and I met two of the priests. One is from Ireland, the other from Italy. We had a short visit and they showed me around. The Mission is beautiful and hopefully I'll be invited again. Christine does not feel well. Will finalize plans for Cape Town this weekend and hopefully we can all start afresh when I return.

> Talks given so far:
> Middle and High School
> Government District Office
> Siyabuswa Health Center
> Elderly Women's group
> Community Taxi Rank
> Train the Trainer-assisted.

<u>Friday</u>
END OF THREE MONTH ORIENTATION

Good day. Home by myself, washed, ironed, ate a cheese sandwich and snacky (they are the best).

The three-month orientation period at my work site has now been completed. I want to write a little more about my perceptions of life here. It has not all been upward and fulfilling, nor has it all been downward and distressing. Like me, in general, it has been down the middle and as I have said: life in moderation.

If I could use many words to describe this place, these people, and my feelings, they truly would use all the adjectives defined in any dictionary. But if I had to use only one at this place in time and in me alone, it would be "noisy." Let me explain.

4:30AM: the day is breaking and Christine is up and out the door. The first sound I hear is the toilet flushing and soon the bolt on the front door is unlocked. Voices greet her (many) and down the way they go. Two mornings a month they are here...thirty women who sing and pray for 45 minutes. 5:00AM: back they come and voices are loud now. She unlocks the door, runs water for coffee, and turns the radio on to a preacher who gives it his all. The rest of us are up by 5:45AM and water to wash in is heated. My radio is on at 7:00AM for BBC News.

I leave the house at 7:30AM and there are all kinds of people meeting people ...from babes in arms to old gogos (that includes me). I arrive at the office which is centered between the small combi rank on one side and the small medical centre on the other. Everyone arrives at different times at each place and the conversations go on and on and on and on until it's time to go home. More people are up and down the streets now and a myriad of school children are screaming, squealing, yelling, laughing (rarely crying) and singing. No matter the time, Moses, at the small combi rank, greets me by whistling "Titanic" and Betty, vender, greets me "my mangani" (friend) and every single day, someone asks me to take him with me to AMERICA.

On the way home, I am greeted by the cows mooing and the sheep bleating...each a group of which is also being herded back to wherever they left from in the morning. Home again with the geese honking, chicks peeping, ducks quacking, pigeons cooing, hens clucking, and roosters, crowing (who says they only crow in the morning?). This cacophony of poultry sounds never ever stops while I am awake.

On Fridays at 5:00PM the music up and down the road and around the neighborhood starts and does not stop till 10:00PM Sunday night. This does not count the church bells, vehicle beeps, sirens, my own CD, nor does it count the ventures out during the night on a tin roof or the rain or the wind. I do believe the sounds of silence would hurt my ears. As it is, I'm getting claustrophobic in the center of all the activity because I do not understand. Oh yes, must not forget the many melodies of hundreds of cell phones. <u>PS:</u> I played Goose Gogo again, only this time <u>they</u> guided <u>me</u> home and we had no problems. We do learn, don't we?

Mindy called and for her and Mallory's sake, I wish her divorce would be over soon. Now Mindy must go to court. She is by herself also. Only in a much worse situation. I am going to call her tomorrow. Betty D. called as did Susie and Miranda. Wonderful presents!

Tuesday

Today was good except the package from Mindy is held up in Pretoria. For some reason, it did not make it through customs. I had to go to the police station and sign a form, have it witnessed by an officer and send it on to the post office in Pretoria. Luckily, Happy (young entrepreneur) went with me to explain the situation. When we came back, he and I had a meeting about setting up a nursing home. We shall see. He seems on the up-and-up but is only 28 years of age and very much a go-getter like David.

Today we had a mini-Christmas party and most were there. We had tea, biscuits, and bread with jam. They were very happy with my gift, a teapot. Judy (friend from States who collects teapots) would be proud of me! Now I'm trying to plan my packing for the Cape Town adventure!

Wednesday

Quiet day at the office: helped handle a communication problem concerning the office Christmas party to be held on Friday. We had a family Christmas party tonight back at the house. I gave them the photographs from the wedding in an album. They were very surprised and appreciative. We had all the snacks, drink and candy we wanted and Thobi is smitten with her harmonica. It was a good scene and I feel good about Christmas.

Chapter Ten

Travel with the spirit of a world citizen. You'll discover that people are basically much the same the world around. Be an ambassador of good will to all people.

(The Art of Living)

DECEMBER 2001

December 19, 2001
<u>Thursday</u>
FIRST DAY OF VACATION!

I did go into the office, backpack and all, but David insisted that I leave and walked with me to the combi rank. From here I was to take a combi to Witbank to meet up with the others going on into Pretoria. I waited on the combi from 8:00AM until 10:00AM and then one of the men said that it probably wouldn't leave until after 1:00PM. That was too late for me so I hopped off and ran to catch the bus which was to leave at 10:00AM. It didn't come until 10:55AM and for once I was thankful for South African time. I made it to Pretoria and had met a young man on the bus (don't know what I would do without them now) and he got me off at the right stop and walked with me to the local taxi rank. This rank was extremely crowded but he saw to it, after three tries, that I was finally on the right local taxi (a yellow cab, no less). The driver let me off at the nearest corner and here came the PCVs from Witbank and the good times began. Jen had brought a watermelon and then we bought wine and snackies (the term used here for chips, pretzels or junk food). The rest came and we all went to a western-type restaurant for dinner with more wine (wine has become a big deal now).

<u>Friday</u>

The van from the backpacker's where we were staying in Pretoria took us to the Johannesburg Airport. From there, we flew on to Cape Town with nary a hitch. A young man from the Carnaby Backpackers in which we would be staying met us at the Cape Town Airport and took us to our lodgings. These backpackers, of which there are hundreds throughout South Africa, are life-savers. Each is a hostel and caters to those of us who do not wish to spend a lot of money on lodging. At first I thought I would not like staying at these hostels because many times there are more than even two to a room and it doesn't matter the sex or age. Suffice it to say, though, that they make me feel young again and by now I realize you can ask, and usually obtain, a room that has only females.

Jeanne, Stein and I share a room. By 2:00PM, they are out for the count. I go down with my book and a cold beer to sit by the pool and pretend I am home on vacation. It's wonderful, marvelous and it's not Campbell's soup!

By 4:00PM, Stein, Jeanne and a new-to-me PCV, Betty, have rested and are set to go. We visit for a short time and then walk a couple of blocks and have dinner at an Italian place.

<u>Saturday</u>

"Up and at' em," that's me. We have breakfast and are off for a glorious day. Six of us in a van go on a day sightseeing trip to see the peninsula. First stop, the seals. There are thousands of them (not exaggerated). From there we travel on down and across the peninsula to see the penguins and again, there are thousands. We could get quite close and I swear Stein was about to join them on a private little isle.

We left there and drove across a small wine -producing area and down to the beach for a picnic lunch that proved to be more a feast rather than a picnic. It felt like a seven- course meal and included dishes specific to other countries, such as a Greek salad, and Japanese sushi.

Now came the very best...in hindsight of course! We hiked up to the Cape Point Light House...spectacular! Then we hiked back down the side to the Cape of Good Hope. Now this is normally a good thing, that is, if you are a bird. Come to find out, this is the second windiest area in the world (don't care to know where the first is). I was excited and moving right along with no thought that it might be dangerous. The wind was exhilarating and I felt as if I had wings attached. Of course I did: my windbreaker was trying to serve as a parachute and almost floated me off the high rocks and /or cliffs into the ocean. In fact, I lost my balance, went off the edge on the side toward the cliff not the ocean, and then I was made a believer. Wanted to go back but just as windy and I was at least half-way down and now I had fear to contend with. Jeanne had caught up so I hung on to her. Betty held on to me and all three of us blew or flew over the mountain and down to the Cape of Good Hope. Once again I knew why I had come to South Africa. It was to fly my way up or down off the face of the earth!! Of course we made it down and back to our spot where, wine, cheese, and fruit were set out and this made it "all better, Mommie."

<u>Sunday</u>

Today we were picked up by a local taxi and were off to the Kirstenboesch Gardens. Unbelievably beautiful day with my kind of perfect weather. We arrived before the grounds were flooded with people. I had a chocolate shake <u>and</u> an ice cream bar for lunch. I took, by myself, the trail to the section named, "Enchanted Forest," and it was just that. Not a soul (alive) around and I felt truly very close to what it must be like in Paradise. The brochure tells us that there are thousands of different species of trees and flora, but I rationalize by telling myself, I am not ready to learn more words that I cannot pronounce. Therefore, this became a day for just contemplating the beauty of a place set aside for pure enjoyment.

We came back to our hostel and met Betty's friends from the States. They are staying at the Table Bay Hotel which is very plush and we certainly did not feel like PCV. Instead, I was reminded of the trip to Florida that Mary and Holly (my friends in Springfield) took to Florida last year. Later, I went with my new friends here to dinner at Morton's, a seafood restaurant on the water side. I had salmon, a real feast. Delightful people and great to have a real honest-to - goodness visit. Even talked a little politics and as soon as we started with different opinions (maybe less than two minutes), we shifted gears and topics! Oh, that we could be this amiable on a day-to-day basis with everyone!

Monday
CHRISTMAS EVE DAY

Stein, Jeanne and I were collected very early by a Ricci Taxi and transported to Table Mountain. We all three attempted the trek to the top; none made it. I do believe Stein would have if we had been able to stay with her. Me, I gave out at the first marker. My head didn't but my legs sure did. I headed back down and even then I was nervous that my legs would buckle and I would turn into Jill with no Jack as back-up...especially since Stein was still going on up. But then the fog set in very fast and with zero visibility, she was forced back down. We all felt good that we had even made the attempt.

We returned to our room, and then because not one of us wanted to eat out, we searched the neighborhood for pizza to eat in our room. So far, it feels exactly like all vacations should.

MERRY CHRISTMAS!

We walked straight up hills (many) to the St. George Cathedral and attended a beautiful service which included music and communion. We walked down to the waterfront, had lunch and went to a movie, "Moulin Rouge." Ummm, relaxing. Later we walked along the waterfront to a grocery that was open. Now I ask myself, there are only three of us so why did we have to buy out the store as if we would never eat again? Is this another reminder of the holidays back in the States? We bought red and white wine, 3 types of cheese, 2 brands of crackers, salami, oranges, nectarines, green peppers, bananas, raisins, peanuts, lasagna (yes), yogurt, chocolate (3 kinds), cookies, and bread. As anyone can see, we are not generalists...we are specialists at pleasing ourselves.

After many telephone mishaps, call and recall, I talked with Susie, Miranda, John, David, Sangita, Divia and Devan. These were the best Christmas presents ever...and Mindy tried me and I tried her. No luck...hopefully tomorrow. All in all, a wonderful day.

HAPPY BOXER'S DAY

We were up early and took a taxi to the waterfront for a boat ride to Robben Island. It is hard to believe that most of us have led such protected and secured lives. Nelson Mandela and the people of his vintage leave us in awe and wonder. I would not survive in a cell such as he did for an hour, let alone for many years. Each day that I am in this country, I count my blessings. My room with my family feels very small and it is self-contained, different and a stress, but it is not a hardship.

Later we had lunch at the harbor and then hiked to the Museum of Natural History and the Planetarium. The day once again was perfect with novel vacation experiences. We will go out to eat tonight. And did! To a little tea room and we each had a Greek salad (again) and wine (again). Home again jiggity-jog. Missed Mindy again, I think!

Wednesday

The Baz bus, (an inexpensive way of transport to and from most areas of South Africa) picked us up a little after 8:00AM and we arrived at the George Backpackers around 3:00PM.

Cape Town is a wonderful place to visit and one cannot do it justice on a single trip. But to me, it did not feel at all like an African experience. If people come to visit me to see Africa, we will head toward Kruger Park and up North. But once again I wish I were a writer. I can only write about a small part of the reality of South Africa. In the six hours of our van ride (by a large window and watching out the right-hand side), I never closed my eyes. This was because I was sure to miss something of value. We saw the blue, blue and then blue-green ocean, large ships, tugboats, oilers, sailboats, para-sailors, bungee jumpers, swimmers, hikers, craggy mountains, gold wheat fields, green trees, blue skies, white clouds (similar to a trip from Spokane across to Coeur D'Alene, Idaho). We saw large herds of cattle, white, brown, black and spotted with both colors, deer of all sizes, cranes, many other birds, desolate areas as in lower Utah and Nevada, mountains as in the Rockies, the Smokies, the Appalachia, and green, leafy, huge oak trees of the Southern States, thousands of different shrubberies, people of every mix, little tiny villages, slums in towns, and squatters' camps on the edges of larger townships. I was amazed that if I watched from one side, on the other side the view was different. I had to give this up since a giraffe's neck does not belong to me. We all agreed that in this one stretch of approximately 300 miles, you probably could find a slice of every state in the US. We saw seals, penguins, brown sand, highways, sandy roads, combies, pick-up trucks packed with people, BMW's and Volkswagens, ethnic restaurants and ice cream. All this and we never strayed off the course to sight-see.

After arriving in George, we walked a good distance and ate fish and drank wine. It was a fantastic trip...until sometime after 11:00 PM when I started hitting the bathroom and lost most of my dinner. Hopefully, this was because I ate way too much of the oily, spicy sauce, and not a very tiny bug trying make my life miserable. I was sick until noon (diarrhea by mid-morning and exhausted by 3:00PM).

By this time I am fine and the Baz bus (van) picks us up and we drive for 30 minutes until we reach the Wilderness Backpackers. This hostel is truly a fairyland. I sat outside our room in the middle of no -where, drank Coke, ate crackers, came in, washed a few clothes, and tomorrow will be another day.

December 30, 2001
AWAY WITH THE FAIRIES

Go on, be brave, and get off the beaten track.
Come to somewhere different, we call it Hogsback.

When you get here you will find tranquility,
expression and beauty defined.

Amongst fantastic views of mountain scenery
flows wonderful waterfalls framed in forest greenery.

Climb up the ladder to our house in the tree.
Play with the fairies, there's plenty to see.

An Eden exists its hard to believe
at "Away with the Fairies."
You won't want to leave!

(Welcome poem posted in our room)

Saturday

Yes, today was another day...waded in the INDIAN OCEAN...the beaches are soft sand and long...very long! Ate lunch at a lousy (not quite) place, but dinner was at a wonderful café with a spectacular view of the ocean on three sides. The backpacker itself is very much a fairyland, even to the unicorn (white horse), pet pig, painted outhouse (inside and out with pictures all in primary colors), and the multitude of blooming flowers with tiny little figurines are all over under and about.

Sunday

We hiked part of the Kingfisher Trail (very difficult) and after 40 minutes had to come back down. I cannot describe the beauty and the hundreds of flowers we did see, nor the more than hundreds we did not see but knew were there for the viewing.

The Baz Bus arrived this afternoon to take us to Knysna and the other teacher PCVs had already arrived. We all ate at a Mexican (yes) restaurant and we are staying at yet another backpackers. It is very nice to see everyone and now I plan to bungee jump on 1-1-02. Can anyone believe it?! NO! But I will. Another day in South Africa...a place which is fast becoming a wonder spot in my world. Tomorrow, we see elephants!

NEW YEAR'S EVE

Monday

We are now at a backpackers in Storms River. The cross-country ride to get here was extraordinary. Canyons, cliffs, forest, orchards, seas, rivers, all intermingled within foggy and sunny areas that looked like moors, oh, so very green. But I cannot go bungee-jumping tomorrow because they are closed for the holiday. Perhaps the next day. We shall see. The three of us listened to a Kenny G New Year's tape, ate all the food we wanted and went to bed. Earlier today, we had wandered around the town of Knysna which is definitely touristy. But we did make it to see the elephants, all three of them: Sally, Harry and Company. Pleasant trip but no big deal. Not a safari and not even a zoo but as Stein is happy to say, she made friends with Sally. We agree the visit was a success.

HAPPY NEW YEAR 2002!

<u>Tuesday</u>

Wally, from Rainbow Backpackers, drove us to the entry and we walked the trail on into Tsitsikamma National Park. This trail was only medium in difficulty and by now, medium is not a problem. We had lunch and then hiked to the boat. We went via this boat on to Storms River and rode within the gorge to where the river meets the bay. We were all speechless. Every minute of this day passed as if we had entered a very special place. Thousands of types of plants, rocks, flowers...all meeting sky, land, water at the same time. I was left once again to wonder, with all this beauty at our fingertips, why aren't we sharing instead of grabbing? It was a day to start a new year and I wonder how long this magic will surround and enchant us.

SILVER SANDS CHARDONNAY
(Produced and bottled in South Africa)

The pansy shell which is found on the eastern shores of Southern Africa is
reputed to bring the finder good fortune.
Within the shell should it be broke five doves of peace are found.
(Written on label of bottle)

I bought this wine because the description seemed fitting to start a new year in a new country.

<u>Wednesday</u>

I LEFT MY FRIENDS AND NOW AM ON MY OWN TO TRAVEL. I will be going from Storms River back to Cape Town and on up to Siyabuswa. The Baz bus driver did pick me up at 10:45AM and I had the front seat all the way. Seheko was the perfect driver, talked some, but not for long periods of time. We listened to music and stopped for exactly 20 minutes twice. We arrived back at the Carnaby Backpackers at 9:45 PM, exactly on schedule. I was the last to be let off and was able to see Cape Town with all its lights and glitter. The main streets were very festive with actual pictures in neon all across the corner of each and every block. Certainly did remind me of our Disney parks at certain times. "Welcome to South Africa," "See the Big Five, "and the flowers, flags, and trees festooned with leftover holiday spirit. All of this in lights and after the dark of night in Siyabuswa, I could not believe I was in the same country.

The hostel was ready for me and with another cheese sandwich and glass of wine, I slept well. Beautiful trip and I appreciated it even more now that I knew a little of what to expect. Still feel guilty that I cannot do justice in describing the sheer beauty that surrounds me.

Thursday

6:00AM: the driver is on time to transport me to the airport. I found my way easily to the check-in counter; was allowed on an earlier flight to Johannesburg; my luggage was right there to greet me; a young woman at the transport desk sold me a shuttle ticket to Pretoria and told the young man to make sure the shuttle driver knew to take me the bus station in Pretoria. He did just that, took me to the "shuttle" which was a private taxi, gave the driver exact instructions, and you and I are both thinking, this has all been way...way...too easy. And we are right!

Now every little detail ended up in chaos. First: the vehicle was not a van, but instead a regular (very old model) taxi and I was the sole occupant. The driver, who was much older than most (even than me) and an Afrikaner, speaking very little English, is quick to tell me that he has never been out of the Johannesburg area except to Pretoria. He was visibly shaking. At first, I thought it was because he had some physical malady but then it became apparent that he was a long-term drinker. He did not drink on this trip but in the course of the conversations we had, he told me of his past problems, which were many, and drinking only one of them. He admitted to being a chain smoker, asked if I minded, and after I said no (a mistake), he would pull over abruptly to light up... this, with fast flying traffic whizzing past and he talking incessantly about one topic after another! I thought he was a PCV let loose to speak to one of his own!

Anyway, we finally made it to the outskirts of Pretoria. Now he informs me that he doesn't know for sure where the bus depot is. I tell him, that I don't know the address but have gotten off at the Probst Street and Hamilton corners. He says he know both of these. But I am not sure if he knows in which city he knows these streets! Finally we reach the Arcadia area and I know we should be close but now he asks directions (so where am I?) While he is receiving directions, he is talking more than listening and we head the exact opposite direction that I understood and go down a one-way street the wrong way! We miss...by inches...hitting a bus and instead of following it to the terminal, he stops and again asks directions. This time we make it to the station... TRAIN that is. He asks two people here and of course, gets two different answers and we end up doing his take on both. We continue to wander around in a really bleak and spooky neighborhood and here, he is even afraid to get out. By now, I'm a little apprehensive about his driving, because he is getting frustrated. But, always he is nice to me and tells me not to worry; he will see that I get on the right bus. I do believe he was ready to take off for Siyabuswa!

Finally, after driving through the Asian market which was an experience I had already had, we do stop and ask the right person and he said that we were on the right trail, finally. That's right, a "trail," but still ended up wrong and with the buses in sight but no street to reach them, we pulled into an office of some security type. Someone there, I know not whom, pointed us in the right area. Pointing was fine but there was no way to drive there and my driver tells everyone that he will walk me over. I have a heavy suit case and don't relish walking through this maze and doubt if he understands where to go. He is speaking in

Afrikaaner now and the security manager tells him she will escort me. I am relieved. The driver is relieved. Now he wants to go with us to make sure I will be safe. By now there are several people watching and a couple say they will also go with us. But the manager says, (I think) that she will handle it. She and I go alone and walk through a rather large, very crowded market to where the ticket office is. She takes me directly there and is about to leave when she decides to see that I get on the right bus. Would you believe, a bus to Siyabuswa (it is 12:50 PM) is just pulling out and she stops the driver by literally standing in front of the moving bus and waving her arms??! She picks me up (truth) and puts me on and then throws my suitcase after. I scream back at her, "What is your name?" She says, "Monica." I do believe in ANGELS.

Now I am on my way. But no! Out in the middle of nowhere, we meet up with another bus and I am told to switch. Do so (have no choice) and we are on our way again. This bus does go to Siyabuswa A but not the way I have traveled before. Instead we go through both Siyabuswa C and Siyabuswa D. I have now had a grand bumpy ride across the township, never knowing when I should get off. I am so lucky, because enough people recognize me and tell me when I will be reaching the right destination. Mind you, these buses stop whenever and wherever. I do make it back and as everyone knows, I truly do enjoy riding and watching the scenery. I will never complain because I had a night drive through Cape Town, an inner-city tour of Pretoria, and a drive to where it's (that word "it" again) at in Siyabuswa.

The whole vacation was grand and this family was sincerely happy to see me and I them. Mindy and I finally had a good long talk. She says she is doing just fine and I will have to believe her.

Chapter Eleven

If I could catch a rainbow, I would do it just for you
And share with you its beauty on the days you're feeling blue.
If I could build a mountain you could call your very own
A place to find serenity, a place to be alone.
If I could take your troubles, I would toss them in the sea.
But all these things I'm finding are impossible for me.
I cannot build a mountain, or catch a rainbow fair
But let me be what I know best, a friend that's always there.

(Sent to me by Dorothy Wallace, a good friend)

JANUARY 2002

HAPPY NEW YEAR TO EVERYONE NEAR AND FAR!

January 5, 2002
Friday

Home again...home again, this time jaggity jig. Not my home but it will have to do for what seems a very long time to come. The mail helps. Other people are talented and patient enough to do handwork or paint. Me, I write letters, and this only to receive them. Nice day though: washed, shopped, and redid my books (again), am becoming anal-retentive on these minute details.

Another clumsy-umsy day (Sydney-type actually). Changed my books around (yes, again) and the large bottle of sand (kids in Sandfontein had given me) fell and broke to smithereens: glass and sand scattered throughout the room. (sand is everywhere every day but not the glass). Patiently, I cleaned it up and put in all in a cereal box and took it outside. Bent over the waste can and decided someone could get hurt, raised up and cracked my head on the open window, saw stars, raised a knot on my forehead and at the same time, the concrete of the stoops, being very, very hot to bare feet ...decided to come up and meet me. I commence to hop around, still seeing stars and looking like an idiot. Oh yes, also am about to lose my jeans because they no long fit. The ducks had another good quack!

Monday and Tuesday

Quiet day at the office. Will write soon about procedures because today will be (maybe) an ASHYO staff meeting and we are to outline procedures we should be doing. Everyone has been invited and it has been planned (by me) for some time, but put off...put off (not by me). Now it is Tuesday night and we did have a very productive meeting and a lot was accomplished by two of the ten who attended. Today, for the first time (the very first), I felt as if there may be a reason, no, there is a reason why I am here and may be able to help these people who are suffering from HIV and AIDS. Let you know later. Their assignments now include:

1. Move beyond awareness into action
2. Delineate a time frame for activities to accomplish #1.
3. Finalize a funding proposal that may allow implementation of #1 and #2.

Wednesday

Today we had a meeting with the Regional Health Department. Seems there is a conflict with personnel and the conversation was strained. The home visit reports for patients diagnosed with tuberculosis are not completed by the volunteers and this is not acceptable to the Health Department nursing staff. Hey, have we heard all this before? Tomorrow, a staff meeting of the Home-Based Care Volunteers is scheduled and we shall see if it goes as well as on Tuesday.

JANUARY 10, 2002

It is time to write about home...real home! Life goes on without me. Is that possible? It certainly is! But in some cases, perhaps I can be a confidante from a distance. In these instances, I am left extremely frustrated because of distance and little or no verbal communication. At the same time or rather at some times, I feel a little like Ben Franklin or Mark Twain must have. Not as a writer, but as a mutual friend. As my friends rally to offset my lonesomeness, I recognize how important I, too, may be to them. I cannot bear to think what my psyche would be if friends were not writing and if this writing were tokens instead of sharing of feelings and problems. It proves that having a friend listen or by being that friend, we each are receiving one of life's greatest gifts. Oh, that we would recognize this. Even though I do not have the words to respond to each problem in writing, I do have the instinctive feeling that by writing me, the letters have a purging effect. Very much as this journal is doing for me.

Thursday

Will not get upset! Will not get upset! Will not get upset! Arrived home at 3:30PM and Christine is not in sight. I decide that if she is not home by 4:30PM, I will cook rice and whatever else I can find. I boiled potatoes with onions and green beans and the rice. She returns at 5:45PM but stays outside. When she does come in at 6:00PM, she tells me that they will have pap and sausage (Thobi has gone to the store) so my food is wasted. Rabie always eats rice at night. Not tonight, he says he wants pap. I'm hungry because the milk (sour and did not drink) for breakfast and a ? slice of bread had done me for all day. I had eaten a banana at the complex but given my apple away. Now I'm shaky and scared that I'll scream again. I go to my room and tell myself that this, too, shall pass. I will be leaving in a few days to attend a PCV workshop. I just never do the right thing. I realize I am about the only one who has not either moved to another organization or another host home, so these concerns must be very small potatoes. Will see. I still seem to have the best situation of my PCV group.

Friday

Pretty good day all around. I met, by myself, with the women from the Home-Based Care Organization and they seem more accepting of me. I met also with the boys of ASHYO and we talked seriously about how we would approach "beyond awareness." We decided to concentrate primarily on the support groups and counseling training that we wish to implement (I do).

The family was also less agitated tonight, or I was. They had spent all day redoing the electrical switches and everything was still in a mess. This meant Thobi and Christine were still busy sweeping up and I was able to escape and clean my own room. I am glad I didn't show to anyone but Christine how ruffled my feathers were from yesterday.

<u>Saturday</u>

I sit at the taxi rank from 8:00AM until 1:00PM waiting for a combi to Witbank. Did eat a fat cake but no coffee was available. But the place is buzzing, stalls with food opening up one after the other, but not as many as before the holidays. Again, the chatter is loud, and the music is blaring from the complex a couple of blocks away. Now I want my own kids to come visit me. They would enjoy the communion of spirit and would be willing to stomp, clap, and sing with the best of them. Surely the expense would be worth it! Countdown! Only 19 months to go.

<u>Sunday</u>

Kevin and Elizabeth (PCVs) had met me at Monica's (PCV) last night and we went for breakfast this morning. Cam (APCD) picked us up and we were on our way to Malaga Hotel located in White River. This is a beautiful and <u>quiet</u> place...only the birds are singing. We have a late luncheon buffet and a lovely sit-down dinner at which Cam gave us all Christmas and New Year gifts. Great fun with champagne as a celebration to the new year. We then had to write an affirming statement about Peace Corps. This, of course, after we received a note from President and Mrs. Bush!

<u>Monday</u>

We meet for our first full day of a workshop which will help us to set future objectives with our agencies. During the AM, we, the PCVs, drafted our quarterly reports. Our individual directors arrived after noon and together, we shared a little about each of our agencies. David and Oupa from ASHYO put up a large poster they had drawn of the sun partially shining and then next to that, they had drawn another with the sun out in full force with my arrival. A positive Peace Corps moment for me was that they did all this without my knowledge and then shared with the full group.

Another lovely dinner and now I am in bed to read Dean Koontz and sleep. I am very tired for some reason and of course, I ate entirely too much!

<u>Tuesday</u>

Today and tonight were American Peace Corps moments in South Africa. We had the usual conference day, some lectures, some fun, part interesting, part very boring, lots of good food and ice cream. Last night, we had had no water and today, the electricity went off and on. My roommate and I had a long conversation in which she confided "a bunch of stuff" to me. Confided is definitely the wrong word, because all that she told is common knowledge and the details change in the telling. What is nice, is that I feel as if I am making American friends in this country.

<u>Wednesday</u>

Once again, our conference opened with everyone in a proper mood. There were twenty of us participating. This included the ten PCV left in our

NGO group, and six directors with their guests. All got along very nicely on the surface, but as the days passed, little by little and reading all the different innuendos, crooked grins and body language, this facade started to fade. Having no water one morning and having no electricity for two evenings did make it a little difficult for even the free-flowing wine and good food to appease the underlying tensions...from what I did not know. Did find out in the middle of the night when my roommate became violently ill. We find out in the morning that half the group has come down with food poisoning. The remaining sessions were cancelled and we were sent home.

Thursday

Today was a productive day at the ASHYO office...these are rare and very far between. This would be a good time to write about "procedures" and "working environments." Again, from my perception, and only about the teams and organizations with whom I am working, and at this time (in the moment)

I will start with AIDS Sexuality and Health Youth Organization or ASHYO and move on to Tshwaranang Home Based Health Care Organization or THBCHO. ASHYO is a non-profit organization started in 1994 by a young man yet in his early twenties (21 to be exact). The building is square and constructed of square concrete blocks. The room for the office is approximately 9'x 6'... and a storeroom beside it is also this size. Although in the same building, both rooms have a front entrance. There are also two rooms to the back with separate entries that are toilets, only one of which is usable.

The store room is a jumble of educational materials, most very old but mixed with a few new pamphlets. Cartons of condoms abound and there is a small supply of tea, coffee and sugar (when money to buy is handy and this is not often). Only the ants seem to have enough of the perishable items. A double-deep sink is along one wall; however, there is no soap, no dishrag, no broom but there is an old mop, older feather duster and a few old, cracked for the most part, coffee cups. Five chairs fill the rest of the space. We do have electricity most of the time. This is because it is linked with the private medical clinic located on the same lot.

The office room has one large desk which takes the space across the back wall. There is a wooden case with 18 small shelves and four chairs. There is no space for people unless they are occupying the chairs. There is no telephone and no clerical supplies. Additional old information fills the shelves. The walls are covered with invitations the young men have received. Most are written requests for training courses regarding HIV and AIDS.. There is no calendar, no vehicle for transportation, (did have but have not had for the past few years). They also have had a telephone, a computer and a printer, but lack of funding to operate have seemed to cause the disappearance of each. Do I know where they are? I don't even want to go there! Are there policies and procedures in place? Depends on whom you may ask? If you ask me...no!

These are my perceptions and have been made after only four months on the scene. It is here, then, that I must describe in part each of the men with whom I am working

Njongo (34), the oldest of the group, appears very strong, healthy, handsome, articulate (speaks English very well), knows his culture and is willing to learn, learn, and continue learning. Periodically, he attends or takes by correspondence, courses from the University of South Africa. Very likely, he is the one in the group who understands best the subtleties and unwritten meaning behind many experiences. He can stay focused and is quite dependable. However, he will take off in what I think is the middle of a discussion. They tell me that this is a South African behavior (they call it "culture"). Njongo has recently become officially a co-director of THBCHO of which I have become a recent member (upon request, mine). Will discuss this organization later.

Moving on: next would be Oupa; tall, beautiful smile, good looking, and very self-effacing. He listens, thinks, and then responds. He also can take an issue to its core and determine the best course of action. He stays focused but he also can wander off without ending a discussion. He understands English very well but I have a little trouble understanding his speech. But this is coming, especially if I listen intently from the start. He is the other co-director of THBCHO and both he and Njongo take this very seriously. Yet they remain committed to ASHYO. The others will be described later.

January 19, 2002
HAPPY BIRTHDAY DIVIA!

Did get to speak with you for a short time and you sound very excited. I am glad. I certainly do miss you and Devan. I hope you get the little zebra magnet soon.

<u>Friday</u>

Today I washed all my clothes, cleaned my room, went to the complex, and struggled to keep my cool with Rabie. I keep reminding myself that it is his home, but I am slowly getting exhausted from the small (and they are small) struggles. Did talk to both Stein and Jeanne and Stein is definitely ready to try a Kruger safari. These calls really help me.

I am also going to write these little things down and then I will realize myself how petty each is.

<u>Sunday and Monday</u>
For instance:

1. Language misunderstanding, <u>Pudding</u> here is cake <u>Custard</u> is pudding <u>Both</u> are made with water. Bought Sprite for Christine and she tells me I should have bought butter. What does this have to do with pudding?

2. Made macaroni and cheese They did not eat. I ate a normal portion but the next night when going to eat the leftovers, all was gone.

3. Always cook on Sundays. Yesterday, Christine was fixing dinner before church. She prepares the chicken, rice, cabbage, potato salad, and then told me to make the macaroni and cheese which they did not eat on Sunday or Monday but ate all on Tuesday.

4. Christine had an upset stomach and took one of my anti-acid pills. I came home with Sprite for her and she told me she wished I had bought Coke for the pudding (?) instead, but drank most of the Sprite (or maybe Rabie did).

5. I made the potato salad but did not put in enough salad dressing. She added more, but never ever do they change any of their cooking to suit my tastes. I just don't eat it...like raw sausage (only thing undercooked yet).

This all happened on Sunday. Monday was not much better.

6. Gave Rabie a pain pill (Tylenol) for shoulder pain and another a day later for epigastric pain. Gave a pain pill to Christine for shoulder pain and a day later for epigastric pain. I told them that I could not give them any more medicine until both saw a doctor. Now both are sour on me. I'm supposed to be their private "doc." Rabie truly believes this.

7. If I close my window, "Why? It is hot." If I don't close my window, "Why? The rain is coming."

Yep, these are minor and I can rise above.

8. Until! Peaches (small) to peel (several bushel baskets full). I'm told to help, which I do gladly, and then spend two hours while the others (several neighbors are included) all laugh, talk, which is as it should be but never once do they explain what they are talking about. And to top it off, someone re-peels my peaches (each and every one without telling me what I am doing wrong)

So now I must try again...as the ants in my room crawl across my glasses.

Thank God (and I do) for my CD player and the letters from home.

<u>Next day</u>

My first true in-service for the group was scheduled for today and it did take place today. This in-service was to deal with writing proposals. There were 20 people in attendance. Progress was fair in my opinion, but the plus was that the women in THBCO came to just visit and I was able to cover the material all over again. It was a good personal day for me and I will need to remember this when things fall apart at the office or here at the house. Did I ever even in my wildest nightmares think I would be doing a workshop on grant writing? No, no, a thousand times no. The next in-service is to be on tuberculosis (I think) and will be next week (I think).

9. When I arrive home from the office, Christine is very quiet, as she was when I left this morning. Does not speak a word to me.

10. Thobi comes in, also does not speak to me. This is a first Rabie does speak by ordering me to fill the water jug. I say, "No water," but it came on right that very minute.

Something is going on but I know not what.

11. Christine made potato salad and fixed supper ahead of time. Salad dressing (lots) and potatoes...that is all. She knows I don't eat rice and there is no bread. Something is going on. Guess it is my turn to bring it up. Oh, Oh! Thobi just came in to play with my hair. Will see how Christine acts later.

Dorothy, a friend from the States called and it was WONDERFUL. We chatted for a long time.

Wednesday

Today was a good day at the office. Even David started on a proposal and I started language classes once again. Freddy has offered to tutor me and we are to meet once a week.

This evening, I did ask Christine if she was angry...mad...unhappy with me. Finally, she understood that I was asking if she was "cross" with me. She said, "No, why?" I could not explain but think the air was cleared

Thursday

Today was better all-around. Christine is acting as Christine usually does, as is Thobi. I was busy all day at the office, although at times, it was very sad. I visited for a long time with Michael, a young man who has been diagnosed with AIDS and has gone public. He would like to organize a peer group of affected young people, but no one else has offered to come forward to help.

Later, David and I worked seriously on the proposal. During the late afternoon, a young woman from the area where I stay came in to tell me about her daughter (9 years old). She told me that the 18-year-old neighbor boy had tried to molest her. She (the daughter) ran into her own house, locked the doors and hid under the bed until her mother arrived. This boy lives directly across from her and the parents are friends. This type of incident is not unique but it is very difficult to handle because everyone (literally) knows everyone and there is no mechanism for reporting such molestation attempts to the authorities. I fear for Thobi. I am again frustrated by my inability to help.

JANUARY 26, 2002

The mantra to help you make it through: "Need to, can do, Have to, will do."

(Douglas Pagels)

Thought yesterday went well. And it did. David's group met and then he had a site visit by a representative from the British Government, (I find out that this is the funding source of the initial development of ASHYO ten years ago). The site visit went fairly well but they will not be providing any more funding. I do not find out the reason for this and dare not ask.

At home, all went okay. Christine and Rabie went to church for an all-night session. She did not tell me they were going for all night and to a funeral early in the morning, also did not tell me that Brenda and Nqbile from next door would be staying with me. It did not matter, but would like to know whom and when, someone other than the family, is to be here.

Early this morning all ....broke loose. I thought (should not think), that I would get up early, wash clothes, my hair, put on coffee, and do the usual morning chores. Did these. Now it is 6:00AM and I have just wet my hair in the kitchen sink. There has been no water all week and the bathtub has been full, brought in for emergency use from a supply that is outside in a couple of barrels. No one told me to empty the tub. I think I am supposed to use the sink in the kitchen. Rabie comes in from church, sees me and yells, "NO! NO! Do NOT wash hair in sink." No matter that creepy crawlers are all over because food is all over, no matter that we eat with hands without washing, no matter that we wash dishes in plain cold water and wipe the same with used towels, etc. I am wrong and say okay. He tells me to call David. He wants to see him. I ask Christine if she wants me to move. If so, I will call Cam. She says no, "Rabie thinks you do not understand his English." I do. He was very clear. Now he has gone back to the church. I promise to never, ever wash my hair in the sink. In fact, I promise to be a good little girl (old lady) from now on. And then she says, "Only dirty people wash hair in sink." Now come on, who is judgmental here? As one would say, you win some, you lose some, others get rained out.

Yesterday, the young men from Tambanani told me that I was a friendly person and liked everyone and was just "very nice." I think I am, (oh no, can't think or I'll be wrong). Do I sound petty? Yes, and hate it...hate...hate it. But I'm tired of this feeling as if I'm not wanted except for my money and the food I buy. Now, and this I forgot: have been here more than four months and they will not show me how to turn the TV on or off because they don't want me to waste electricity when they are not home (who pays for this electricity?). Okay, when Rabie came back, I asked him when he wanted David to come. He tells me that I am a grown wife (?) and if I say I am sorry and promise never to do such a wrong thing again, I don't have to call David. He hates this "fight fight" every day and I must make this "my" home and do things as I wish and on and on. It doesn't take even as many brains as I have to know that Christine needs my rand to get her new teeth. Anyway, we have called a truce for now. I never dreamed that the reason I wouldn't last in the Peace Corps is because of the male chauvinism of one man.

But here I go again. It is 11:30AM on 1-26-02 and we will see how long we last. It's been a very long tiring week. Okay, 10 minutes have gone by. Do we now do this day-by-day or minute-by-minute?

It is 7:00PM and I just arrived home from an awards ceremony for the Tabanani Youth Group. It was beautiful and I had a good time and understood more than at the previous ceremonies. I received my very first South African Attendance Certificate and am pleased. Christine and Rabie are asleep. A little of the macaroni (made by request), has been eaten but that is okay. I now know that it will be gone sometime tomorrow.

January is almost over and my Christmas cards are almost written and somebody should be calling me!

Chapter Twelve

It's always easy to find a reason not to help another. This is perhaps the hardest part about learning compassion—fighting to overcome our own excuses when they are merely selfish

(Florence Holbrook)

JANUARY 2002

January 27, 2002
<u>Sunday</u>

An odd, wonderful, amazing, God given happening...yes, that is what it turned out to be! Friday afternoon, a man came by the office looking for " Sydney." First surprise: he is white and in his early forties (I thought he was a PCV from somewhere else). Second surprise: he is Dutch but not Afrikaner. Third surprise: he has received my mail by mistake and thought I was a man. His wife, who usually picks up the mail, saw the stamp was from the US and thought she had seen an American in the complex. He will go home and return the letter to me tomorrow. Fourth surprise: when he does come back with the letter, we chat and he is a minister. Yes, they do have a Dutch Protestant Church here. No one that I had talked to had any idea where it was located. (No surprise there)!

Pastor Willem came this morning to take me to services at one of his churches. He is from the Netherlands and into his fourth year of a seven-year mission. The church in which he preaches today is in a very tiny village. The services are in a small one-room building and only about 15'wide and 25' long. There are three wooden benches and a table. Four adults, three women and one man, six little kids and three teenagers are present. All sang their hearts out in Northern Sotho. But it felt and sounded beautiful to me.

After the service, he took me to his home, located in Siyabuswa, and here, the other end of the spectrum appeared. It was very large and nice. His wife, Dorothee is delightful and they have 4 children and each is a part of Mandela's rainbow. All are adopted. We visited for a couple of hours and she brought me home. She drove past the church here which is another tin shack out in the middle of a sandy field...a long walk but I can do it. The pastor has a translator (English) when he preaches in this church. I find out that this will be about once every two months. He is the head pastor for 32 small churches. He has three assistant pastors and several lay pastors to help him. At home, Christine has prepared a feast and Rabie is happy that I am going to church. She tells me she will go to Denilton next week because of a death in the family. I must psyche myself up to spend this time with Rabie. Well, God came through on Friday and he will again!

January 25, 2002
HAPPY BIRTHDAY SANGITA (Daughter-in-law)!

Talked with Sangita and Divia and all is well with them. Betty (friend in the States) called. Therefore, all is well this weekend. Found out Christine does not leave till Tuesday morning. That is one day less she will be gone!

<u>Monday</u>

Worked on the proposal most of the day. Emma (friend of Christine's), came in and I ordered several pieces of beadwork that she has meticulously made. I plan to take this home (18 months??) and give as gifts.

It is becoming very wearing and tonight I am close to tears. Christine does not feel well. I do not debone (I am losing my English) the fish to please her, never did for my father, either. She does not offer me the salad they are having and a whole brain (true) is simmering on the stove. They do not wish me to partake of this delicacy. I thank God for small favors.

Christine is to go to Denilton tomorrow and spend the week. Rabie is to join her on Friday. I ask how about Thobi? Don't worry about her. The neighbors will be around and so will her cousins up the street. What will we eat? Don't worry, Rabie will help. Says who? I am not going to worry, I promise to myself. One more day has passed. Maybe I should count down days instead of months.

Wednesday

Today was okay at the office. I spent all day fighting the word processor in the doctor's office. Came home and if I can pinch myself and not wake up, Rabie is gone for the evening and I am here all by my lonesome. It is powerful, as strong as any pills or liquor.

Will write now about the excitement we had Monday night. I was settled in and Christine came for me after Thobi hollered for her to come quick. She wanted me to go with her to Boy's house because he was throwing up...I thought he must have eaten something or had a flu bug. He lives only a few houses away but by the time we arrived, he had already gone to the clinic. And yes, he had eaten some seeds off a tree (no one knew the name). I tried to ask if others had also eaten them because this is the area where 18 boys (I've counted them) all aged 8-10 years, gather every night to play in the street. No one understood my question and just kept saying no. We came home and shortly, here came the ambulance and four more boys are loaded into it.

Morning arrives and I tell David about the excitement and he says these are truly poisonous seeds and several kids had died in previous years from eating them. The Health Department and Township had mandated that all these trees be cut down. He immediately called someone in the municipal office and the tree was taken out that day.

Now, of course, I am extremely worried and go to the doctor's office next to us. I ask him to call the hospital. He does. He turns to me laughing and says, "Ten boys are running up and down the halls and driving the staff crazy. They are okay." They will go home this evening after 24 hours of observation. Hundreds turned out to greet them. Boy came running to me and said "Thank you, Gogo, for saving my life." ???. It has been a very long time since I have been so frightened about my own actions (I did nothing but could I have?) I WILL learn this language.

Friday

Okay, it is late Friday afternoon, and I am once again on the back stoop with the whip, the geese, the ducks, and the rest of the creatures surrounding me...except this afternoon there is a real "goose girl." She is another 9 year-old who is a cousin of Thobi's named Togo. She is running about with the whip and herding all the little ones into the pen. She squeals, they make their own noises, and the cacophony of sounds is sheer chaos but it is delightful at the same time. She runs, they run. Little ducks are in and out of the wire fence. She is up, she is down, she is all over in seconds. But I am out of film.

Believe me, I am not wasting one second of tonight. If all goes as planned, it will be my first night since leaving my own real home that I will spend all by myself. Rabie left today to meet Christine for the funeral. Thobi is supposed to spend the night with Martha...we shall see. I have already washed out a few clothes, cleaned my floor, drank a Coke, ate some chips and will treat myself to something from the mart to eat later when I know Thobi is where she is supposed to be. Oh, oh! here come the goats. So help me, I am about to answer all these kids...no matter what the age or the species with my own shouting or bleating...Why? Just so I can answer and they will answer back in the same language!

Now my story of the night before last: Rabie, as he leaves for church, tells me that Thobi may spend the night next door. "May" does not mean she has permission...it means he is not sure. He should be back around 8:00PM and he will eat then. He tells me this after I've prepared the rice but luckily that is all. He leaves at 6:30PM. Thobi is nowhere around. I eat and write a letter. Lock up the house and then think: "I had better find Thobi because it is dark and I am not sure just what she will do." She is next door and will stay there. I put on the outside light and hall light for Rabie, go to my room and think he'll be home any moment. I do not lock the dead bold or back door. I fall asleep. He does not come home 'till close to ten. I hear him come in very quietly and am amazed because he never ever seems to be concerned about my comfort. I hear my door open and shut very softly and I think, "My gosh, he is checking on me." He roams around the rest of the house and I'm wondering what I forgot. Fall asleep and morning does come.

"Nomhlakambo. Why you not lock up the house? Back door open, lights on. I thought criminal got Nomhlakambo. So I took the ax from behind stove and walked very softly through the whole place and you were safe!!" And I was also lucky. Can you imagine the heart attack I would have had if I had gotten up and seen this big, big man coming toward me with an ax? Needless to say, he was rightfully very "cross" with me. And trying to explain that I was really thinking of him and then accidentally fell asleep just did not justify my actions. This morning when Rabie told me good-bye, he said, "If you don't lock the house properly when you leave Saturday (I am going on the 7:00AM bus to Pretoria), I will chase you all the way to Pretoria with the ax!" His idea of a joke. And life goes on!

FEBRUARY 2002

Be grateful for freedom to see other dreams. Bless your loneliness as much as you drank of your former companionships. All that you are experiencing now will become moods of future joys. So bless it all.

(Ben Okri)

<u>Friday</u>

Now it will go as I've planned! Yes! Yes! Rabie is to leave at 2:00PM and won't be back until some time tomorrow. Christine is already gone. Thobi is to stay all night at Martha's. And me, this is my first complete weekend or even Friday night or even any full night to myself. So, what to eat? Will decide on my way home from the office. Have cooked all week for Rabie and this makes me decide on a fake pizza and I buy extra cheese and two Cokes, some Pringles and home I go.

No, No, No! Thobi and three of her friends are there to greet me. I do manage to hide the Cokes and the little pizza but the cheese and chips are spotted and gone while I am hiding the important stash. Thobi, of course, wants to eat but there isn't anything. She eats the rest of the bread while I fry her a couple of eggs. She has already eaten the cheese and now decides she'll stay next door. Here I put my foot down and say "No, Thobi, you will stay at Martha's." Okay, she will. At 8:00PM, I wander down to Martha's and yes, they are planning on her and will watch her till Rabie returns. They think I am nuts for being concerned but this time, I don't care. After all, I too, will be leaving in the AM and want to know she is safe. And now I do have the place to myself: food is half gone, water ALL gone so can't have a "splash" (bath). But do have one of the Cokes and take an hour to eat the pizza (and it was good). I am in bed pretty close to the usual time and surprisingly, the quiet does not frighten me. Even more surprising, the music down the street also does not frighten me.

Up at 5:00AM, still no water and must be to the bus by 6:30AM, so brush my teeth with Coke and hope to find a bottle of water at the complex, knowing nothing will be open. I am to have the rest of today and part of Sunday to myself. Bus trip was uneventful (really), and the walk to the Holiday Inn to catch a taxi to the backpackers was quite pleasant. Cam will come by for me for a movie and dinner later. Yes, yes, yes...but no, no, no! She calls and says she will pick me up immediately and we will go directly to the mall. This is okay because she is going to take me to a travel agent. We do this and then have a quick lunch, run chores, see a movie and I am back to the hostel at 4:45PM. She picked me up again and we had a fantastic dinner that covered the whole nine yards. I even had lobster. The whole day was wonderful.

What I have learned here in South Africa, if anything, is that by the age 70 one must take every little pleasure and milk it for what it's worth. My mother told me time and time again: "Don't plan too big and you can't be too disappointed." Well, of course, you can be heartbroken and despondent, but you cannot be disappointed!

Sunday was perfect and Rabie surprised me by having dinner all cooked and "COCA COLA" just for me. Christine arrived home later and Sunday and Monday were PEACE!

<u>Monday</u>

We are to have a meeting with Peace Corps and the CDC from the US. No show! Am not disappointed, because I am learning to live by what everyone here calls South African time. Mindy and Mallory <u>are</u> coming over for a visit. What do they say? "When one door closes, another opens"? And because I am not famous, I must be setting a record with the number of letters I receive.

Now I must write about the beauty surrounding me at this very moment in time. It is close to 5:00PM and I am out in the backyard. The sun is a mass of bright red, shades of yellow and blue and it appears as a huge ball in the center of lined black, gray and purple clouds. It is thundering like what must be a herd of elephants. Lightning is streaking across the sky in front of the sun. I swear I have seen the jagged edges touch one another...the sun and the lightning. Though the rain is pouring very noisily on the tin roof, the sun continues to shine from my side of the house. Three little girls (Thobi and friends) are creeping around the corner and trying to make me think the ventures are attacking. Now the rain is easing, the sun is setting, the girls are giggling and all is proper at this moment. REMEMBER THAT!

This very moment the sky is changing before my eyes as I write: there are layers that are several shades of purple, the sky above this layer is vividly blue, and there are white and black clouds forming designs as if made with a magic marker. The rain is still falling but quietly. The woman across the way is singing and dancing in the rain with a huge tin tub on her head; her toddler is jumping and skipping with nothing on his head or anywhere else. The girls by me are on their hands (literally) walking through the puddles with the geese. Another woman across the fence is swinging a wet mop in rhythm with the rain. The rain stops, all is quiet and oh, so peaceful. This on the evening of the morning that our neighbor was locked in her bathroom and a man robbed her. There were no storms then or people to hear her screams. Now I am told once again to please lock the doors when home alone. I will!

Wednesday

We have completed the hardest parts of the proposal; therefore, this day was good. In fact, last night's gift from the Sunday School class back home has made me feel exceptionally blessed. They sent several books of all types and I will read them all...after I get all my Christmas cards out and letters answered.

Thursday and Friday

Good days. Christine received her teeth today. The proposal draft is complete <u>and</u> in the computer <u>and</u> saved. I am in language class with Freddy again and am feeling much more at home here at the office. Now, I do have to list some activities that I never thought about before, but feel amazingly good...clear down to my toes (Charlie Brown?).

1. A warm (hot) first touch of a washcloth against your face in the morning.

2. A drink of (cold) water at 5:00 PM after a long boring day.

3. The first 2 minutes in bed at night, turning on the lamp and it works and turning the pages in a good book

4.   One bite (and only the first) of a bite-sized Snicker bar

5.   Letting the chocolate of a turtle melt in your mouth, then the caramel, and saving the nuts for the very last taste before falling asleep.

Saturday

Good day today. Won't mention that Christine told me how to hang my sheets, how to make spaghetti sauce, how to fix my bedspread, and also to go to the complex to buy Rabie's lottery ticket. I agreed to all except when Rabie told me to take one rand and bring home a live chicken, I balked. Felt like a heel and a little foolish but they laughed when I told them I was afraid the chicken would cry for help before I could.

Sunday

My first excursion to the church and all on my own. The family has already left for their church and I have ironed, washed my hair (not in the sink), and eaten cereal. I am nervous because I hope not to get lost while I try to remember just where the church is located.

I think now would be a place to insert a little about the attitudes of the people surrounding me. For a long time, in fact, most of my life since I started to ponder on such things, I had thought of attitudes, beliefs, and values as all pretty much in the same category. But as in so many areas, I was mistaken. When one really thinks about it, we can believe or accept as truth any one tradition that has been passed down generation after generation. I bring to my mind the calling up of the spirit of a dead loved one. I may want to believe this is possible but my upbringing and the behavior of my own extended family does not lend itself to actually believe this. But if my mind had been programmed (such as in this family) to believe the spirits may be recalled, and that this recall of a spirit actually protects me, will it make a difference in my life or how I live it? I find the people here speak of their confusion when professing Christianity and yet at the same time are afraid to let go of long-held beliefs and traditions.

I did make it to the church and once again I was in the midst of a room full of strangers but each one greeted me with open smiles and actually with song. It is a Protestant church and the service was very much like those at home. The difference here is that any one person, young or old, or even a group will start singing at any time no matter that a prayer or sermon is in progress. It was beautiful and I will return.

Any day

On to Tshwaranang Home Based Health Care Organization or THB-CHO. This is a newly funded NGO to which I also have been assigned. This assignment came upon my request and only after much pleading and dealing with the Peace Corps staff in Pretoria. THBCHO thus far has only a few members. Njongo and Oupa have agreed to co-manage the operations and eight women have offered to volunteer their services. Up until now, each has helped (albeit sporadically), but they're not nurses nor aides, nor have they had even minimal home health training. So now what? I now have a purpose, even if it is only me who thinks this is real. I hope to help them establish a volunteer training program, similar to that of Hospice Volunteers and Home Aides in the United States. The intent is to enable these volunteers to provide quality personal services and support to the terminally ill, orphans, patients living HIV-positive, family members and friends affected by this or related diseases. In this area, this equates to 100% of the community members. We hope to erase the stigma of traditional myths (which in my mind do not make sense) that are holding back any progress that could be made in the fight against this disease.

I have given thumbnail description of Njongo and Oupa. Now I would like to provide a sketch of these women who are willing to dedicate a portion of themselves to these families. All are between 23 and 35 years of age, all are attractive and two are beautiful. Each has worked hard, had babies; a couple have husbands, one has a fiancé and the others are single parents. All are putting in personal time with absolutely no incentive, other than her love for her friends, neighbors and family. Consequently, they come and go, go and come...depending on the individual situation.

They tell me that they, too, have new-found freedom...Hah. Not as I see it. They continue to do all the work. They are the ones to do the cleaning of the office, make the coffee and serve it. The men are still sitting, hours at a time. I do observe though, that the little girls and young-teenaged girls are balking at these roles. As I recall, these roles are similar to those of women in the US about 50 years ago and before the women's movement.

These volunteers will offer the in-home care, support and respite for families. They will work in tandem with ASHYO to set up appropriate age and situational support groups. I can help them accomplish these services and that's why I have come. At least I hope so.

Monday and Tuesday

These two days were awful, both at the office and at the house. David and all were back. The 1st draft of the proposal is not done well. David, however, thinks it is beautiful because it is clean. Both days were wasted and he left this afternoon for Nelspruitt...making tomorrow a wasted day also. HBCHO is going well but I felt confused again regarding all the different proposals and which goes to which funding source.

I took food home to cook and come to find out, this was a good thing. Christine had gone to Denilton and was not yet home. Rabie told me he cannot eat my spaghetti sauce. I made sloppy joes, so mild they were tasteless to me. He ate and he ate and he ate. I think his heartburn comes because he eats so much at one time. When Christine arrives, she is sick, looks very pale and worn out. But she insisted she had to cook the pap even after Rabie has eaten. She also watched while I fried chicken...not like she does, boiled potatoes...not like she does, and finally, she realizes Rabie has eaten and she gives up by going to bed. Me, too (go to bed). Every single day, I am making too much of the little things and continue to pray for strength to not be so petty.

<u>Wednesday</u>
Today was better: in fact, it went quite well. Christine is still sick and I helped by getting her medicine for her from the clinic. A niece or somebody came by and cooked. They tell me that pap is not good the next day. Christine did not feel like eating and finally ate some very old dry corn flakes with sugar and water added. It is now 6:30 PM. We have eaten. She has fixed chips...greasy, greasy...but delicious to me. She rarely eats many chips, but now when she has an upset stomach, they sound good to her. I ask if she wants me to go get her some Sprite. She tells me no, her stomach hurts. Go figure.

The last PCV living approximately an hour from me has been moved to the Kruger Park area. This is where he wanted to go eight months ago. He will go to the same place that Mary Jo left! Now the closest PCVs to me are the two in Witbank and that trip is a minimum of 3-4 hours travel time IF the combi leaves within a reasonable time. This is becoming a true stress test and for all reasons I had never thought of. But like I said, as has everyone else, tomorrow will be better!

February 14, 2002
HAPPY VALENTINE'S DAY

<u>Monday</u>-boring

<u>Tuesday</u>-more boring

<u>Wednesday</u>-most boring

<u>Thursday</u>-the mostest boring (I told you I was losing my own language).

Tonight the radio is blaring as high as it will go because Rabie is outside and must hear it. Never mind that it may give those of us in the house a headache. I think I am homesick!

Well, now I have lost it and for the umpteenth time am planning how I can go home! I had told Christine that after supper I had a surprise for each of them. She said she had to go to a church meeting. I said okay but when she came home could I meet her, Rabie and Thobi in the living room? I thought she said yes. I had received the T shirts and pictures of Thobi from America (that I had wanted to give them for Christmas). I had been waiting for the right time and Valentine's seemed appropriate.

Thobi came into my room while I was working on my albums. I asked her not to mess them up and she immediately did and then whined because I would not let her have the ones I was planning to give her as part of the surprise. Rabie and Christine came home from church. It is 8:00PM and I ask them to call me when they are ready. They don't call for 10 to 15 minutes so I go ask them if they are ready. Thobi is outside and they don't want to call her in yet. They keep on watching a soap opera in Zulu and Thobi takes off for the store. I finally went out and said, "In America, we would not do this. If someone tells us they have a gift, we accept it, we do not turn off lights, keep on the TV and ignore the giver."

Christine then goes to find Thobi and all ask me where the presents are. I go get them and the TV is turned up louder and Rabie goes outside. I am almost in tears and just hand the packages of American T -shirts and the pictures to Christine and tell her to please give them to Rabie and Thobi when she can catch them. I am disappointed, angry and hurt because they are constantly teaching me about good manners in their "culture" but do not make any attempt to learn any of mine. I am tired, lonesome and have no peer with whom to discuss my miseries. This, too, shall pass but truly don't know how long it is going to take. Pray every day for help in overcoming this feeling.

Friday

I am rational now. Gave everyone at the office the American flag T shirts; this minor project is finally over and off my mind. The proposal came back (from somewhere) printed but with many errors and no objectives. Oh,Oh! I've lost it again. We had two meetings today and at both, David informed everyone that we MUST have this proposal done by the 26th of the month. Impossible. I call Cam to tell her not to come for her planned site visit on Monday but she is coming anyhow. Elizabeth (PCV) calls and she wants to come visit me tomorrow. This could be a problem because she will have to spend the night and how will Rabie respond? Tonight when I asked, he said "That is fine."

Saturday

Campaign to start at 9:00AM and does get started at 12:15PM. We left at 1:00PM but I had to talk extemporaneously once again. Actually, I am used to this now and it is fine. Elizabeth and I met up and had a wonderful afternoon and evening. This family was nice to her and she was a big help to me. She gave me the same advice that my daughter Susie had during our last phone call. Per their tips I am going to:

1. Not cook anymore
2. Raise my monthly stipend to them
3. Keep some food separately in my room
4. Invite David to meet with the family and interpret our concerns to both sides
5. Move if this does not work
6. Do all this as soon as possible.

Sunday

Am going to church in a few minutes to pray. Pray for guidance on how to handle this mess I seem to be making. Rabie is "cross" with me but I know not why? Both Christine and Thobi are very quiet.

<u>Monday</u>

Another mixed-up day and I don't even know why? Should be used to it by now. No food, go to the office, plan on coffee and a fat cake, no coffee, no available pot, and no cups. There is no key to the other office in which any of the above might be found and there is not one single person outside of me anywhere in the area. David does come in shortly and then Njongo arrives. They go to get coffee and I go to buy fat cakes. When I get back, Njongo asks me why I didn't tell him I wanted fat cakes. Mpumi, another NGO director who did have a PCV for a time but does not now, arrives and then there is truly bedlam. None of us can get David to settle down: he is up, down and comes, goes hither and yon (yes, we could easily write nursery rhymes about his antics.)

David asks me to go the District Office and print the proposal with its recent revisions. I do walk out there because I think he has called to tell them I am on the way. I get all the way only to find that the printer is not working and they did not know I was coming. I went to another office to use the printer and it was not available. I decided to treat myself to a cup of coffee with Dorothee, the minister's wife, who lives a short distance away. She offers their computer but I am afraid that I may cause a virus or some such thing. I walk back to the office and cannot get David to take me seriously. He and Mpumi leave and it is the last I see of either of them. It is 2:00 PM and I call Willem, the minister, and ask if he will help me print out this dratted proposal. Of course, he agrees and I walk back out there and it does get printed.

When I return to the office, a councilman and a young lady from the shops visit with me about the risks of HIV in this community. Why does it make me feel better to be talking with someone about this horrible disease?

I am a little tired and arrive home well after 5:00PM. I do not see Rachel, a new friend of mine from the neighborhood, standing there. Rabie is talking to a friend and does not see me. I find out later that I have missed a friendly visit of my very own.

Christine is on her way to church and tells us that supper is cooked. I don't see any evidence but for the first time, it is all outside in the garage. She also tells me that Thobi is going with them. I think good, good. I will drink a glass of Coke that Elizabeth (PCV) had brought. I pour it but before I can take a sip, Brenda comes in to tell me that Thobi is at the corner. I call her in and tell her never ever to not let me know she is here. Now she is pouting and I am angry again. This has just got to stop. I do not know where that child is most of the time but worse is that I do not know when I should be the responsible adult. I can tell when I am writing while upset because even I cannot read my words.

<u>Wednesday</u>

Today was good. We all worked on the proposal. Late in the morning, I accompanied one of the volunteers while she made a home visit to a very sick young lady. It was extremely difficult and very sad. She, only 19 years of age, was lying on a mat on the floor in a corner of a very dark, stifling hot room. Her skin was cool and dry to my touch. She appeared extremely emaciated and weak.

Her pulse was too rapid to count, and her respirations were very shallow at a rate of 50-60 per minute. Her lips were parched and blistered. She nodded when asked if she hurt but was too lethargic to describe the pain. I understood it to be everywhere. She did not say a word but her eyes showed fear and aching. She held my hand and did not let go. When I asked if she wanted me to come back, she nodded yes. She has no diagnosis officially. I will ask the home volunteer to visit again tomorrow and I will return on Friday. Later I was told that she had delivered a baby about 5 months ago and this baby had died at 3 months of age. We shall see if this is an AIDS-related illness and exacerbated by depression. Then what will we do?

David could not visit with my host family this week so instead Njongo agreed to help me out. He came over tonight to translate for the family and me...in order to renegotiate my living arrangements. Christine and Rabie agreed and said they understood. Of course their take on the situation was different than mine but that was okay. This confusion was the reason we had to settle the issues as we both see them. Rabie said he did like my food but I didn't cook enough at a time. They wanted to make sure that I had enough! I say I would like to cook for myself. Rabie says absolutely not. I cannot cook for myself alone and we are at it again. Then Christine offers to do all the cooking. I say, that would be wonderful and if she did this, then I would do all the dishes and cleaning up after the meals. If I could believe it, we all agreed to this arrangement. In this case, both Rabie and Christine were trying to be nice to me. He also tells me the reason he was very cross with me when Elizabeth came to visit was because we did not eat with them. I told them that I thought I was making it easier on Christine. She understood and so did I. Next time I have visitors, we will eat with the family. These communication gaps, half understood, are worse than not understanding at all. Njongo was a great help and we are now agreed on the following:

1.   Christine will do the cooking

2.   I will do the clean up

3.   I will give them an increase in monthly rands

4.   I will also share in the cost of supplies (dishwashing soap, coffee, cereal, peanut butter and other items that they do not normally buy). They will continue to provide the meat, pap, eggs that they do normally buy.

We were all laughing (yes) when Rabie says, "You do not feed me enough because it takes more to fill my stomach than it does to fill yours." This is true and understood.

<u>Saturday</u>

Best day at home (here) since I arrived. Good, good and better and best. And last night was the very best night yet. Now I can stop feeling sorry for myself and get on with why I am here...to help fight this catastrophic and deadly disease!

<u>Monday</u>

Isn't it odd? How the little things get you down and then a little thing can pick you back up. It has been very nice at the house now that I am not cooking and don't have the guilt attached. Today the guys gave me 500 rand out of their funds (yes, one of the myriad of proposals did get awarded minimal funding) to pay me back for some of the things I have done and bought for them. Cannot keep it because of PC policies and will give it back by buying what I know they need (transport for instance). But for me, it is still a wonderful, meaningful thing for them to think of doing.

Tonight we celebrate Rabie's birthday. This should go well after the Christmas and Valentine debacles.

<u>Tuesday, Wednesday and Thursday</u>

Very good days at work and very good days at home. Tuesday I went to Witbank and met with Pastor Hendrik, the Chair of the Regional Forum of Ministers and Director of Hope for Africa. We hit it off from the start and plan to work together on setting up free counseling and later on support groups. This contact was made on my own. Njongo was impressed.

I must tell you, though, the guys and I met yesterday (Wednesday) with more than 40 male heads of churches at the old Parliament building...all ages and all very interested in fighting AIDS and learning about America. Again, I had to speak off-the-cuff and with an interpreter. But must have done okay because the Executive Committee met this morning and laid the groundwork for a "forum" to <u>really</u> do something. We shall see! But at least by making this contact with the pastor, I now use the computer in his office at HOPE and that's a major plus for ASHYHO.

Back at home, I did remind Christine this morning that if she remembered our conversation of last week I would not be cooking tonight or on the weekends. She did need reminding but then did the cooking and I did the clean-up chores. She is happy with this because now she can "rest" after supper. I am happy because she "needs" the rest.

Chapter Thirteen

Look your troubles in the eye. Problems not faced do not go away. Life is a roller coaster of ups and downs. Anticipate each dip, and prepare for it.

(Anonymous)

MARCH 2002

March 3, 2002
<u>Sunday</u>

It is Sunday night, the 3rd of March and tomorrow is John's (my son) birthday.

HAPPY BIRTHDAY JOHN!

It will take the rest of this book to write about these past three days. DO not even know how to start but will say this I was on sensory overload. These did not include either the sixth or the seventh senses, even though I firmly believe both do exist. It just may be difficult to find the proper words to describe all the events and feelings that took place, many all at once.

Let me begin. Friday early AM, I was packed and ready to leave for Sandfontein, even though I thought the bus was to leave at 1:00PM. But no, on Fridays the last bus leaves at 10AM. I have paid Christine rand 300 but she is not happy with this and asks why it is not the 400 on which we had agreed. I ask her to remember that Rabie had not agreed to the renegotiated price. She accepts the money but I can see she does not like it. I tell myself that a deal is a deal and I am not going to spend all weekend worrying about what will happen when I return. I seek her out and tell her the deal with Njongo and before Rabie intervened was, rand 400, so rand 400 it is. She perks up and states, "You and I will share the coffee expenses" (this, even with the increase?). I said fine and we hugged as we said good-bye. I did not think about it any more. Good.

I arrive at the office and all three groups are requesting help, as well as Silvia. It is Thambi's birthday (nurse at the clinic). I am to leave the office promptly at 9:45AM Therefore, after drinking coffee with Thambi, no time was left to provide assistance. But my spirits were soaring because it felt good to know I had real work to do when next Monday arrives.

I did make it to the bus on time; I waited. The bus pulled in at 10:45AM and it is overloaded. In fact, so crowded that after an hour's ride and when out in the middle of the wide open spaces, it overheats and stops, never to start again (at least not today). Now the sitting, standing, lying, walking, jumping, prancing, talking, singing, screaming, cussing (I think) commences and continues for 2 hours. Few have any food, (where are all the bus vendors?), fewer have water bottles, all are hot with overloaded bladders. Once again, the men are in control. They just pop it out, spray a prickly bush or a tire, shove it back in and the heat goes on. Many women wander across the field, stand and let gravity take its course straight down. Me, I stay on the bus (am told to do this), sit on my foot and survive, barely.

Finally at 2:30PM another bus arrives and we reloaded (that is the correct word) and continue on our way to Pretoria. We do head across the city to the depot but everyone is anxious for my welfare and I am told to get off a block sooner than usual. I, of course, cannot see, so do as I am told and am off at a corner I do not recognize. Know this is not right but what is? Should I go up a block or back down a block? Finally, I just start walking and after 3 or 4 blocks, I step into a small corner shop and am told I'm heading in the right direction but need to move over a block to the left.

Upon arrival at the Holiday Inn, I'm able to catch a cab to the Hatfield Backpackers. I tell the driver it is a hotel but it is actually a guest house…my mistake and he makes a couple of wrong turns and ends up at the mall. This turns out just fine because now I can give him the correct directions. We finally arrive at 5:00PM. They don't have my reservation but do have a room and next to the BATHROOM. I have not gone since 8:15AM this morning and now cannot, but at least I know where it is. After gulping down 2 glasses of water, bingo, I hit the (jack) pot.

Most of the shops in the mall close at 5:30PM and I still had to buy a baby gift for the new little guy in Sandfontein. But for now, I am weak because I had one fat cake at 7:30AM, ? apple, and 2 glasses of water that provided little or no energy. First place I spy is a restaurant that has wine and cheesecake (exactly what an empty, inexperienced stomach needs). This, of course was my eighth sense kicking in before the other seven. The cheesecake left much of its flavor in the refrigerator but the wine was fine. Relaxed, then found the baby gift, bought batteries and salami, cheese, chips, books and I am set.

I return to the backpackers and Cam has sent a message that she's late and won't be back in town tonight. I text her back that everything is A-OK and I plan a bath, my book, etc. Tub has no plug or hot water and there is no shower. I do wash from the spigot right outside the back door and it felt just fine. I slept well and the day and night had passed.

Where do all my senses kick in? First I had to use my brain in the early AM: saw men and women urinating up and down the road, felt hot, crowded, pain in bladder, abdomen, and back; smelled food shortly after departing the bus; tasted wine; sensed confusion when I was almost lost not once but twice and on foot with a backpack; saw me as the only white in an ocean of black; heard no one speak English but instead heard 5 or 6 other languages including French. Who knows what the sixth sense could be? But it is possibly that I accidentally took the bus on Friday instead of Saturday. If I had waited until Saturday as on previous trips, perhaps we would not have been as crowded and probably would not have broken down. But neither would I have built confidence in both the people caring for me and my own developing survival skills. The seventh sense, without doubt, is the return of my angel who was with me all the way. Never, ever was I frightened or even stressed. Did what had to be done and enjoyed the private moments.

Saturday

Bathed in cool water but it felt good. Walked over and had a banana flipper (pancake) and real coffee. Taste sensory nerve kicked into action and it started my day just right. No problem with the taxi to the combi rank, no problem with the combi into the Rustenburg combi rank. Called Berthold (Meriam's son) and he arrived in less than 5 minutes to take me to meet Franz and Meriam. The three of us went directly to the hospital to visit with their daughter, Hermina.

This was my first visit to a large hospital/medical center and was pleasantly surprised to find it very nice, bright, and clean. Hermina is apparently given good care. Must backtrack a little here and explain why I am making this visit. I left Sandfontein in September and have been invited back periodically but always by one of the young children. I had not as yet accepted the invitations until Meriam called earlier this week. She told me with a tear-choked voice that Hermina was in the hospital and "Oh, so bad sick." Could I please come for a visit because this would make her feel better? Of Course!

I expected to find Hermina very ill but not as low as she appeared. She does not speak and cannot move her limbs on her left side. She is fed via a feeding tube. I think it was possible that she knew me but only in the first instant. She definitely responds the best she can, with eye blinks and slight squeezes of her right hand to her mother. I am not sure if it wouldn't be better to be in a coma than in the frustrating circumstances in which she finds herself. She wants very badly to respond appropriately but cannot and cannot even communicate these agonies except through her eyes. She has been like this since before Christmas. No one knows how she will progress or what her prognosis is. Meriam stays with her every single day and does passive range of motion exercises to her arms and legs, and gives her frequent skin and mouth care. But she is worried and close to collapse herself. Both she and Franz were visibly happy that I had come. When I told Meriam how much she was doing and that her care was vital to Hermina, she started to cry and said she was so scared that she was not doing enough. My support for her was genuinely appreciated.

Meriam, Franz and I left the hospital. I was to find out on the ride to Sanfontein that this was the first Meriam had been to her own home in 5 or 6 weeks. We went into a shopping area and never have I been in the midst of such a mass. There were thousands of people of all ages, all black. Meriam wanted me to accompany her into the shops but held my hand very tightly so I would not lose her. We got in and out of the car three times and always it was into chaos. Would like to know if they save any rand by coming here. It seems it is the bazaar area for the locals.

Franz stopped once more and this time neither would let me out of the car nor would they leave me alone. Franz brought back a yogurt, cold drink and sandwich (we shared the sandwich but Meriam insisted that the yogurt was for me). For some distance there continued to be people, people as far as one's eyes could see.

Hospital smells had given away to an abundance of other smells: food cooking, fresh bread, rotting fruit, beer, trash and people. The quiet sounds of the hospital gave way to a cacophony of loud music of all types and voices talking, laughing, singing in God alone knows the languages. Hearing should be the first sense and not the last to go. Hermina had felt warm, moist and normal to the touch. After we arrived at their home, even Franz hugged me hello, as did each and everyone in the family. Except for Kagiso...he was afraid of me.

We visited under the tree and had tea. My room had been prepared for me with a fancy spread and fresh flowers. Aggie cooked a feast and the little ones made sure I had ice cream. Little Franz and Philipine went for a walk with me and we saw a part of Sandfontein that I had never seen. It was a cemetery where the graves are outlined with stone walls until such time that enough money has been saved for a burial. The seventh sense or spiritual sense was with me the entire day. Later, about 8:00PM, Thomas (another son) called to say Hermina had pulled out her feeding tube and eaten some yogurt. Meriam and I looked at each other because that is what she had given me (for energy). But only I know that I never eat yogurt but I had done so today for Meriam's sake. Today was overwhelming.

Hermina has been diagnosed with Lupus officially. Her nurse told me that physically she was slowly progressing but the doctor is sorely afraid that there has been so much brain damage, it is doubtful that her speech will return.

Later in the evening the family told me a few of the details of the tragedy that had befallen Hermina. She had left her boyfriend and moved back with Meriam for what was to be a short stay. One weekend this man had come to town, broke into her locked bedroom and knocked her around. He supposedly had wanted Ledia (their little girl). She told her family that after he left, she fell and cracked her head (?). She has been in this condition since before Christmas. Now the final prognosis is in God's hands and this family requests my prayers for her. Will be back.

Am back. Took a hot bath, went to bed, slept well and all the kids were in on the foot of my bed by 6:00AM. Coffee and eggs for breakfast were prepared by Philipine. Peter stopped by, Thomas called again and now I have visited with everyone. Amazing!

We left for Rustenburg, stopped by Berthold's, drank a Coke and went to the hospital. It seemed unbelievable to all of us, but Hermina said her first real word to her mother since she has been there: "full." Today, I am not sure she recognizes me but her eyes are open and she tracks her mother very well. I am so glad I visited her again. Yesterday, I did not think she could pull through but today I know it will be a very long hard road but she may just do it. Little Ledia is quite stoic for her age, but I am not sure just how she is feeling.

Meriam stayed at the hospital and Franz dropped me off at the combi rank and I do reach Pretoria without mishap. But here, the driver lets (no, strongly urges) me out in the middle of some stricken, crowded neighborhood, points a finger and drives away. I start to walk through some ethnic neighborhood, in what I hope is the right direction and soon sight a mass of combis. It was here that the sixth, seventh, and eighth senses kicked in because the combi to Siyabuswa was the first in the line. Once again, the heavens were on my side. Because this was unfamiliar territory, I do admit to a little apprehension when they said this combi went to Siyabuswa. But had to take their word because what else could I do?

Made it back home (note the word "home") and never even had a racing pulse. But the weekend was far from over. My whole block was celebrating something. It is 3:30PM and now I remember Christine telling me that I had been invited to her friend's celebration. I dropped my bag and wandered on up the street. Still know only a few by name but recognize hundreds of faces. They all made me welcome. Fed me, fed me more, and then some more. All the women were dressed in bright, vividly colored dresses covered in pink, white and blue beads and then many were also wrapped in vividly colored blankets of the Ndebele culture. Anna, Christine's closest friend, is being installed as the new Gogo Queen. In the midst of all her hoopla, she presented ME with an Ndebele blanket. They joined together in traditional dance and made me an honorary member of the Gogos. TV cameras were all over. Of course I was overcome and I was asked to speak. I declined for the cameras and before anyone could insist, the music started. I have not a doubt that this whole township would have ostracized me if I had not accepted the invitation (forgetting is NO excuse). It is that eighth sense or an angel.

I came on home about 5:30PM and had literally passed out by 8:00PM. Good-bad-sad-happy-peaceful-chaotic-quiet-loud-private-public-crowded-elegant-impoverished-rich-clean-filthy-hungry-satiated-understood-misunderstood-beautifully-ugly-committed-energized-exhausted-laughing-tearful-and through all of this, my prayers were always foremost. I won't forget these past three days for a very long time. I hope never!

March 4, 2002
Did get to talk to John on his birthday and he sounded just wonderful. I couldn't ask for more!

Monday and Tuesday
Work days and all went well. I did not get to complete the proposal because, as usual, all the boys are procrastinating but the days passed without incident. The celebration from Sunday was not on TV but that was fine with me.

Wednesday
My heart broke today. Michael died yesterday and none of us was prepared. He is the young man that was living with AIDS, apparently doing well, and helping his peers set up a support group. All of us had a hard time facing this tragedy so unexpectedly. It was exceptionally hard for these young people because he was as young and beautiful as each of them. It was hard for me because I find myself feeling as if these young men and women are my children and he was no exception. Today, none of us know the details or direct cause of his death. To our knowledge, he had not been ill. He was very proud of the work he was doing and we were all very proud of him. David is taking it very hard because he and Michael have been friends as well as colleagues for many years.

Thursday
What can I say about today? It was very much like last weekend: all the senses kicking into a jet stream very fast and all at once. Arrived at the office, budget not yet done. I walked all the way out to HOPE for Africa thinking I have everything done correctly. Instead I mess it up and lose all the work Elizabeth

(PCV in Witbank) has done. Then Albert (Pastor Hendrik's right hand man) tries to help and we lose it with no retrieval possible. It was not his fault...truly it was not. Now I have no one except myself to blame. I am mad, very angry, irate, cross at myself! Seems like I have been cross with everyone else and now me... it is my turn. It is almost as if the "I" is another person and not "me." Will give both the "me" and the "I" an attitude adjustment on the way back to the office. I return to the office, re-enter the complete proposal in the computer and take it to the professionals for printing.

Once again I return to the office and it is at this time that Kale (home-care volunteer) tells me to close my eyes and hold out my hand, (my game). She places in my hand a "very much beautiful" black and gold beaded necklace. Now I truly am in tears and my thoughts go immediately to Michael.

All of us leave at 4:00PM to go to Michael's home to give our condolences. This time I am able to say a few words to his mother. She did not understand my words but did know my feelings for her son and had Njongo translate for her that Michael had loved me, too. This was also, "very much beautiful."

Tonight Rabie and Christine are at church. I did not have to cook and Thobi has been visiting with me. For the past few nights, she has come in just before she "splashes" and prepares for bed. She sits on the foot of my bed and practices her English while I practice Ndebele. It is now 8:00PM and a stray uncle has just wandered in. Made me a bit nervous but left in 30 seconds after Thobi hollered, "Go!" And another day, no, almost another week, has passed. Does it really take very close to 70 years to know oneself? Tomorrow I will finish what I can and then am off for two weeks. Michael's funeral is Sunday and I have been asked to say a few words. God will put the words in my mouth.

Friday

Good day. Traipsed out to a meeting at the District Office and my part of the current proposal is completed. Home this evening has gone well.

Will take this time and continue the short descriptions of the young people with whom I am working. Next would be Freddy. He is the Chairperson of ASHYO (each young man is an officer). He is also my tutor and very patient with me. He is tall, thin, movie-star handsome and somber. But must say my first impressions of him on Day One were way off the mark. The day that I met him, he showed up with an earring or rings (I cannot remember now); head shaved and seemed surly and angry. He no longer has the rings and never has he been surly or angry in my presence. He is extremely intelligent and I am beginning to rely on him for some purpose every day. And when he (so far) says he will do something, he does! He will listen and observe quietly, making substantial contributions to a discussion only if he sees fit.

Next is Vusi who is the treasurer of ASHYO. He is overly energetic, charismatic and hard to hold in one place longer than 30 seconds. He is 28 years of age but looks all of fifteen. He is the "cutest" one of the bunch. He wants me to learn the language and thereby insists I speak Ndebele often (this is yet to be). Although he is fun loving, he is serious and enthusiastic in his love for Lorraine, who is the mother of his little girl. And for me personally, he has been a mainstay and cannot do enough to teach and protect me. I enjoy his company very much.

Last, but definitely not least is Lucas. I first met this young guy with long dred-locks, dark sun glasses and all the rest of the garb...my preconceived ideas of how a guy from the streets would appear. In the US, he would have perhaps frightened me. Time has passed and now he has cut off his hair a time or two, has his shades off and on (as do I), is extremely polite, always nice to me and apparently to everyone else. He is as handsome as the rest and a talented artist. But again, his demeanor certainly does not match my preconceived views of an artistic temperament. Instead he is very patient and always a gentleman when around me. He also has a little girl and loves her mother with "much heart" but as is the case with the others, has no money to marry.

Aside: the women here are in a no-win situation (so are the men). A young lady would like to still be a virgin when she marries, at the same time she usually wants to prove she can have a child. Her future husband seldom has the money to marry before a baby arrives. He would like to marry a virgin, wants to know his future wife can have children, and has no money to pay for a marriage ceremony. To compound the problems, neither has the money to care for a child regardless of the marital status.

Sunday
The Next Room
Death is nothing at all...I have only slipped away into the next room. I am I, and you are you. Whatever we were to each other, that we still are. Call me by familiar name, speak to me in the easy way which you always used. Put no deference in your tone, wear no forced air of solemnity of sorrow. Laugh as we always laughed at the little jokes we enjoyed together. Pray, smile, think of me- let my name be every the household word that it always was.

Let it be spoken without effect, without the trace of the shadow on it.

Life means all that it ever meant. It is the same as it ever was, there is unbroken continuity. Why should I be out of mind because I am out of sight? I am waiting for you, for an interval, some where very near, just around the corner. All is well.

(Canon Henry Holland Scott)
Poem read by a friend at Michael's funeral service.

Remind me (talking to myself), that today, many times and out of nowhere, a shudder passed through me and I knew without doubt, that this place and this time were right for me. There have been other times, but they did not seem more than just glimpses and disappeared within fractions of seconds. Instead today, I had no choice. Each time I was almost physically stopped and made to listen to me. No longer was I justifying why I was here. The thoughts came and did not leave until promising to return and each time with a stronger impact. The first time this feeling of enlightenment came was as I awakened in the early hours and it has returned over and over all day.

Throughout the day I have felt out of place, in place, wrong, right, energetic, weary, a stranger, a friend, but most of all, today is the very first time I have said to me and listened to me, (not just being polite to me). In fact, a few of the times when this feeling overcame me, I was by myself (but not every time.) What is this I am trying to say? I AM GLAD to be here.

We are told over and over that everyone we encounter will touch our lives in a way. I believe this, but as many others must, I only consider these encounters during my own personal moments. Today I attended the funeral of Michael. He, a patient living with AIDS, who died in his sleep last Tuesday. I only knew him a few months but today he feels very close to me. For the past few days I have wished that we had known each other better. Today, I know we did reach each other sincerely and as closely as if we had. He was only 31 years of age and had been living positively with this disease for almost three years. His eyes said it all: so beautiful with his pain hidden very deeply within them. He was proud to be embracing his friends into the fold of the diagnosis. He and I had discussed it at length and made plans to develop support groups, but he was truly a one-man mission. I kept my distance. Not because of his diagnosis but rather because of his age. I did not know what to do to help him. Michael is teaching me so much and it has nothing to do with age. He shared totally of himself and did not voice resentment that his gifts to give, direct results of his illness, were ones no one wished to accept. I have many friends and all of them would be closer to me than I had thought Michael, but this is not true. I have never had any one person impact on my own self in such a short time as this young man.

We are all wondering (no, I am) why, when he appeared to be so positively living with AIDS, did he die? He was such a strong force. I do not know why but do know that for those of us left here, his leaving will make us work all the harder so others with AIDS can keep their friends, lives, and families intact regardless of the diagnosis. I know I will. Hundreds of people attended his services today and if each of them think and feel as I do, Siyabuswa will fight and win. I am very proud that he considered me a friend and hope that someday he will be proud of me. He already knows why I am here. Though I don't know just how yet, I do know... that by helping, in Michael's memory...one, a few or even many people, I will make a difference. I am glad to be in Siyabuswa and Michael's funeral must have been an epiphany for me. Please, God, let me help in some way. I do know why I am here. It is not because someone else could not do it and perhaps do it better; it is because it is a gift given to me to do. Now it is up to me to do whatever "it' turns out to be.

Will finish this particular journal by discussing or describing the young women in THBCHO...a different situation from ASHYO exists with this group. You would think I would feel at home with the women. This was not so... at least in the beginning. The young men accepted me very early, the women were wary. Perhaps this was the case because they do not understand English as well as most of the men. Also they are actually doing patient care in the homes. I am a nurse and perhaps a little intimidating to them, although I voice no disapproval, regardless of procedure. The first to accept me was Anna and the others followed suit in short order. I do think my attendance at Amy's funeral service, in which I could in no way suppress my feelings, brought to them the realization that I do care for the people here in Siyabuswa. Each of them now offers me genuine respect. They give much of themselves and ask very little in return. I thought they would not want me to go with them on home visits but instead they ask often. I never say anything when in the home but they know they have my support. Guess this helps them, in turn, provide support to these tragic families.

And just like the boys, each home volunteer has her own unique personality. Most are serious most of the time; one is playful but quick to shed tears for those hurting. All except one are mothers. Few have husbands, none have money, a few are educated, none have a paying job, and all are concerned about where their children are heading in the future. All are torn between the old patriarchy system and the new progress of technology. Shades of the US fifty years ago. They worry about their kids running loose in the streets but then leave these children alone for full days at a time. All say they want to learn but some work harder at this than others.

I am not going to describe each one individually because I want to get to know them better. Suffice it to say that I love each person in each organization and each day, I feel less and less like a retired nurse. I am thankful for the chance to assist them in learning a few of the nursing arts.

Will continue another day with more perceptions. Now have a crossword puzzle to do!

<u>Monday</u>

Today went very well, so to speak. Thobi was to sing today. That is what she told me. She is to go to a music contest at 7:00AM. She will sing at 9:00AM. I ask Christine if I can go with her and at first, she says yes. Later she tells us that she does not plan to go because she doesn't have money for a combi. Seems the contest is an annual event for all the schools in the District. The venue will be a large gymnasium in Siyabuswa C. This is too far for Christine to walk.

In the morning, it is raining steadily but Rabie decides I must go and "photo." He will give Christine and me a ride out. He does and we arrive at 10:00AM (because Christine said 9, we are able to make it by 10).

Come to find out, the competition starts at grade 3A and moves on through the rest of the grades in the primary schools. There were approximately 1500 little moppets all over the grounds...all about the same size and all dressed in their school's uniforms. I do have one roll of film with me but no more. I hear (I am not exaggerating) "photo" at least once from each and every one of these thousand and some kids.

We had to pay admission to get into the gym and listen to each age group sing the exact same song three times (native tongue, English and Afrikaner). Each child marched in and each of the 50-60 kids had to be arranged on the stage. Of course, I had a front row seat because these were "photo" minutes. Finally at 1:30PM, Thobi's class marches in. Now I must go to the stage to get pictures. No one else has a camera with them. All the schools want me (next year)?

We leave the hall after Thobi's group finishes (they receive 7th place out of about 25 schools). I think good, now we can go home. No, kids must eat and do...all over the playground and in a few of the surrounding homes. The rain is still falling steadily and the soggy trash makes a dump out of the area. Christine shares a banana with me while the kids eat, eat, eat. Finally this group is finished and I think, good, now we can go home. No, now Christine helps two other women sweep and scrub the house, garage and yard (all is sand and very wet). Yes, it is swept even though the rain is still coming. We are all soaked and cold, but finally all is cleared.

Kids are all wet through and through but turning cartwheels and walking on their hands. From my viewpoint, it is a beautiful spectacle. Hundreds of legs whirling, heads bobbing, arms swinging, and all this within inches of the next limb flying through the air. By now I am sitting on a stool and pondering, with this many laughing, singing, playing 8-11 year olds, why are we at war anywhere in the world? These kids were well-behaved and singing with all their hearts.

Finally Thobi's teacher comes to us and offers us a ride home because, of course, Rabie does not come back. Home we go, but not before we stop for the teacher to pick up something in the complex. We arrive home at 4:30PM and here I am. Not Christine though...she has started supper.

Chapter Fourteen

As we head further into the world, and gain more experience, we lose some of the fixtures of our childhood. But we also learn there are more things in life than we can see.

(Francis P. Church)

MARCH 2002

March 12, 2002
Monday

Can you believe I have started my fourth journal? Me, who does not like to write. We are attending a large PCV seminar concerning the writing of funding proposals. Our whole group is here and also includes the NGO and teacher representatives or directors for each of the volunteers. We are, of course, minus many with whom I was becoming good friends, namely; Mary Jo, Starlee, Mae, Catilla and Jennifer. We are soon to lose Alice (Aida) who will marry and move to Zanzibar. The others had varied reasons for leaving. Me, I have turned the corner and plan to be here for the duration of my contract. Believe me, it feels good to finally be over the resenting, wondering, and questioning, as well as the strangeness, aloneness, and downright frightening emotions. I now know these are feelings for which I must be thankful.

Today was the first day of the seminar. Yesterday was quite long. I left the house at 6:45AM. The bus was to leave at 7:00AM and did leave at 7:45AM. David shows at 7:15AM and Oupa not at all. Bus ride was uneventful but because we arrived late in Pretoria, we had lost our transport to the workshop at the Sparkling Waters Convention Center. David phoned Cam with the expectation that she would arrange our ride. Cam, instead, leaves the responsibility to us as it should be, but does tell us that if we go straight to the PC office, we can hitch a ride with one of the drivers (if he is around). David and I are on our own and end up with a private PC driver all the way to the resort. David's charm wins out once again.

Tuesday

Today, we discussed updated material on the AIDS crisis. This included the legal ramifications of leaking confidential test and counseling results. Although the death of Michael has made me even more anxious to help develop peer support groups for those infected and affected by HIV, I recognize the difficult barriers this law places on everyone. Once again, the lack of understanding is the major barrier, and not the law itself.

It is odd that now, when I am satisfied with my position in South Africa and when the night should be restful, tonight I provided my own crisis. At 3:00 AM, I arise to go to the bathroom. As I go to sit down, I trip on the door stop and topple backwards, striking my head twice on the concrete tile on the way down. I find myself wedged between the toilet and the tub. It hurt. I was very, very frightened that I had seriously injured myself. Elizabeth came to my rescue upon hearing my cries of "Ooooh, oooh, oooh." She helped me back to bed and I lay awake for most of the rest of the night. I knew I had bruised my left arm and leg but by morning, the only soreness apparent to me was in my left ribs.

Along with the stars I was seeing from the bump on my head, every thought went through my mind. Did I sustain a serious head injury? Will I sink into or am I in a coma? Did I break bones? How do I get medical help?

Elizabeth gave me two Tylenol. I took them, thinking, "Perhaps I shouldn't take these." But then I rationalized, "If I am going to be in a coma, I might as well be in a relaxed state." I did doze off and on and this was a good thing. By morning, I was in no pain but by 10:00AM, my ribs were very sore.

Wednesday and Thursday

There is little to write. By now, all of us are comfortable with each other and it is a beautiful resort with absolutely everything to do.

Friday

Today was a good day, as each has been lately. See how my handwriting changes with my mood! This workshop was on grant (proposal) writing and although boring, it did reinforce the grant application that ASHYO is submitting to the National Health Department. I was also able to voice my hopes to start the development of peer support groups. A few more of the NGOs are accepting me and for the time being, I am comfortable with my ideas.

For the most part, this meeting went very well. Alas, though, by the end of the week, escalating tensions and tempers were on the verge of erupting and causing a collapse of morale both with the PCVs and the NGO directors. Will not write about the others but will point out my own personal experience. I enjoyed and learned a great deal from the presentation on the medical aspects of AIDS and the review of the current laws. I was bored when attending the sessions on monitoring and evaluating of program activities. At times, I was a little embarrassed at how childish, petty, and negative that we, as individuals and as a group, acted. Then I remembered how petty I have been with my host family and realized we never do outgrow our own personal hurts. Maybe one just handles these better at one time or another.

The final session does arrive and tomorrow Stein (PCV that I traveled with over the Christmas break), and I leave for my first SAFARI! Dinner tonight will be in Pretoria at a French restaurant. Can anyone ask for more?

Saturday

Stein and I left early this morning on the Baz bus. We had a long ride to Nelspruit, but I enjoyed riding across country so much that it did not seem long. Tonight we are in the town of Hazyview at a backpackers and tomorrow we go on safari into Kruger National Park. It will be my first safari and I know how inadequate my words will be when describing the beauty of this place. My attempts leave me frustrated but for some reason, I continue to try.

Sunday
1st day

We are awakened by 4:00AM and must leave in thirty minutes. Loyd, who will be our guide, "collects" (his word) us at the gate. There are only four of us: Stein, a young couple and me. This is fortunate because we each have our own window and spectacular views surround us for the three days we are to be here.

The elephant is the first large mammal we see and very soon, we see many more. Some are very old and a few appear to be playing. They are big, bigger and biggest. Loyd is an interesting guide, does not bombard us with information but tells us a lot. He is soft-spoken, patient, and hard-working. He sees things (before my recognition) or movements like an eagle and knows not only animals but birds, trees, and flowers. He, of course, does not know my love of short stories and fables but tells us many along the way. He does take us not only on the usual beaten path but also sometimes away from these areas. This morning we saw much and I was wrong when I said we saw the elephant first (he was only the largest and the first of the big five). Instead we saw the Bush Buck, the Gnu, Impala and then "Dumbo!"

We continued to see all of these throughout the three days we were here and the impala, numbering in the thousands I am sure, were all over the place. There were many small babies, mamas and bucks, each beautiful, sleek, shiny, appearing like toys. We watched them eating, sleeping, darting, playing, watching. We even saw one poor dear (correct) hit by a maniac (we saw these too), in the road.

Later during a break (for Loyd) we saw monkeys. Monkeys here, there, everywhere. They were very small, gray and wanted to jump on us, very much like a puppy would. At this small rest stop, there were big signs posted, "Do not feed animals." But maniacs #2 do.

And now Loyd spots HIM! A big dark rock with hair! I see a rock; Loyd sees a LION. Lo, he is right. The rock is a lion! And a lioness is very near. He is partly behind a bush so we do see him but not very well. But we are patient and eventually up he rises as does she and quickly they move deeper into the bush. I have now seen a real lion and my heart and brain are calmed.

Now my eyes and ears are working, working, wanting so badly to see more...and I do, (but I'm never the first). By noon, we have seen giraffes. Let me tell you. I was looking so very hard and Michael, who was sitting in the seat directly in front of me yells, "GIRAFFE!" The biggest, tallest animal I have ever seen was directly in front of my eyes. I see his legs and look up, up into his eyes. Right on the side of the road, so close, I swear he winked at me. His coat was brown and black...an animal so unique that Loyd had to tell us details to make us believe that he was real. Eyes as soft as a dairy cow, ears white with a brown pattern, chewing a cud while still reaching for leaves, belly appeared so heavy, legs ramrod straight while the back slanted at a distinctive angle. I could have watched him all day but we moved on and we were fortunate to see many more. But he was RIGHT there and I did not see him first!

We stop for brunch which Loyd prepares. Stein and I rest; the young ones swim and we are on our way again. This afternoon we see dikors, crocodiles, and leopards. A friendly chameleon comes to visit us and I did see him first because he landed on my shoulder.

We call it a day at 6:00PM and proceed to the campsite. Stein and I share a small pup tent with no amenities. Our rest (maybe sleep) will be on small pads. The toilet is a four minute walk but inside...clean and well-lit. Loyd cooks dinner, which is steak, sausage, potatoes, and more, similar to a gourmet cook-out in the United States.

2nd day

Oh yes, yesterday, just as we were quitting for the day, Loyd took us to where a mother hyena happened to be with her little playful cubs. In my opinion, hyenas are not one of the most beautiful animals but must say when as little as these, they are also cute, beautiful and unique (when quiet). They had gone by the next day and we did not see them again.

Today, we are to see more warthogs, wildebeests, white rhinos, leopards, giraffes, and elephants. We would ride for about 1 ? hours and then have a sighting. I found each more awe-inspiring than the last. To think that we could travel these vast and wild areas over and over, maybe forever, and as long as we did not disturb or frighten any animals, they would also not disturb or frighten us. Oh, that humans could behave half as civilized.

But...now get this. Loyd again was the first to sight the lions. Much closer this time and the male was mating his lioness. Loyd tells us that this happens approximately every 20 minutes for 7 days and is done to ensure a pregnancy. The male would rise from a lying position; the female would rise from a lying position; they would frolic for seconds; he would leap upon her; when finished, he would give a giant roar and both would lie down until time to proceed again. We watched this process at least 6-7 times before moving on. It was so awesome that each of the five of us was mesmerized while waiting between the couplings. Both the male and the female are majestic and rightfully seem to be King and Queen.

We have sighted the big five, except for the buffalo. We return to the camp site at 6:00PM and have another feast. Too tired for the night ride, we are in our tents early and tonight we are able to sleep. Loyd arouses us at 5:00AM and we are on the road. Today we do see the buffalo and again all the rest, including more birds than I would have thought possible.

But most amazing! About 10:00AM here comes King and Queen straight toward us in the middle of the road. The other lions in the pride are following behind. Unbelievable! Soon other vehicles have stopped and we are all watching intently, knowing we will not see this again. We recognize it as an experience of a lifetime. Maniac #3 arrives (only this guy is an idiot), honks a horn (the first and only one heard in our three days), and ruins the show for us. The lions run quickly into the savannah. Needless to say, everyone was angry and several people missed the sighting all together.

The rest of the day we saw several zebra, giraffes, elephants, hippos, rhinos, but no more buffaloes.

My thoughts: lions are majestic, truly beautiful in every way, rhinos are huge and very dangerous, hippos are sorrowfully ugly, giraffes are unique and spectacular, zebras are a work of geometric and questionable design, wildebeest-...the name fits and is an enigma to me, buffalo are amazing, perhaps similar to the American buffalo and yet not the same at all. I will now read up on each and every one...once again. It does make a difference seeing them in their natural habitat.

<u>Thursday</u>
We headed back to Pretoria early this morning. It was a long but most pleasant ride. When we arrived at the backpackers, the teachers' group was already there. It was good to touch base with them. Stein and I had supper outside and called it a day.

<u>Friday</u>
Spent the day at Brooklyn Mall...had a huge Italian lunch and another early night. Have been playing telephone tag with Mindy (daughter).

<u>Saturday</u>
We, Stein and I, went to the new Historical and Cultural Museum today. When it is fully operational and all the exhibits are available for viewing, it will be magnificent. We were able to view an authentic Egyptian mummy. This was a first for me.
Later we went to the Hatfield Mall, attended the movie, "A Beautiful Mind." It astounded me in more ways than intended. We ordered a pizza and took it with us to the backpackers in which we were staying.

<u>Sunday</u>
Early in the morning, I headed for my home in Siyabuswa. No problems with this after a pushy Rixi (taxi company) taxi driver tried to con me into riding all the way with him. I finally did arrive home by mid-afternoon and Thobi's other family (mother and little sister) was here but no one else. Neither could speak English, making it quite strained (I was not sure just who they actually were). And so it went until Christine and the rest came in from church. Christine was very quiet, even after greeting me with open arms. Later she left without saying anything and hasn't spoken to me since.
I did talk per phone with David, Divia, Devan, Susie, Miranda and Mindy. My vacation was superb.

<u>Monday</u>
No coffee this AM. What does this mean? Hopefully, I won't become paranoid once again. But am off to the office and saying prayers all the way that some work has been done on the ASHYO proposal. It has not.

<u>Tuesday</u>
All is well. Have spent two long days working on the proposal. Should finish today and then will spend quality time on THBCHO's. No one here knows word processing and it is a cinch that I am not proficient at it, this is another reason it takes so long to finalize these proposals. Mostly though, it is because the boys lay it aside and never spend any constructive thought working on it. We shall see
Tonight Christine and Rabie hosted a big church meeting here at the house. It was very nice and with lots of food. She outdid herself and is back to

her usual singing self. It was not me that she was unhappy with; instead it had to do with the visitors. This is a big weekend for them, as it is for all of us. Easter!

Wednesday

I am proud of myself. Very, very trying day but I did not get upset. I arrived early at the office; Oupa came, Njongo came; both walk out and leave me. I take our proposal material to HOPE. Get there at 9:30AM but am told that I cannot get into the computer until 1:30PM. They need the printer because copier is down. Freddy comes by and tells me that the budget needs work and changes must be made NOW (who says so?). The HOPE staff leave at 3:00PM but now the printer is out of toner. I did not accomplish anything today. Walked over to Willem's (pastor) to deliver mail and used his printer. Walked back to the office. Arrive there by 4:30PM but it is locked tighter than a drum.

Home again, home again, jiggity jog! Both Rabie and Christine have colds. But I am almost through the month of March. It is going to be a long two years!

Thursday

Note: NALEDI is not an acronym. The word "naledi" means star.

Another day...did finish ASHYO's proposal...as much as I can do. David did nothing on it and he is back to his old tricks. He could not and did not sit still for any one five minute stretch. THBCHO's proposal demands much revamping. All, including NALEDI's are to be in by April 1. None will. All the boys left today by three. Friday and Monday are holidays here. I continue to tell them that I can only help with the writing...cannot do it all. Seems I start and finish a day with this statement. And it is a true statement although no one believes me. I do have to say that these boys are great to me personally, so I really have no complaints.

Tonight Thobi gave me a beautiful handmade card and I thought, "She does like me after all!"

GOOD FRIDAY

Today I had all to myself and it was glorious. The sunset was spectacular and sent straight from GOD. The sun itself was a red perfect circle, surrounded by clouds of every color imaginable. Just above the horizon, the little white cloud that cried was peeking, snow white with a black smear almost in the direct center. A lovely display for Good Friday and now I am excited to see the Easter sunrise and sunset.

"To Nomhlekwabo Too know you and love you is to know the fullness of life and joy and also sorrow that happened. I wish you long life so you can care of our family's the way you do know I like the way you do. So take care of your self and also enjoy your Good Friday"

(Note to me from Thobi's friend)

Saturday/Beautiful!
EASTER

Absolutely a wonderful day from start to finish! The sky was heavenly blue as I walked to the church, knowing few would be there because of the very long services for Good Friday. But never, ever did I think I would go to an Easter service and be the ONLY ONE there. Not a soul was lingering in either the church yard or the garden I entered the building and sat for almost an hour worshiping in solitude. There was no artificial lighting but the rays of the sun speckled the worn benches with a muted glow, almost eerie but in a wonderful sense. I felt very odd, even though I knew I was actually the truant because most had started worshiping Thursday night, some all day and all night until this morning. But inside of me, I was at peace and perhaps felt the meaning of Christ more than ever before on an Easter Sunday morning.

<u>Wednesday</u>

Another South African day. But now I am learning that I cannot change what will not be changed. The proposal is <u>not</u> ready... David just rewrote the beginning as an annual report. I did several firsts today. First, first: I knew no work would have been done but today I just let go of it. I had accepted the responsibility to do the narrative and this I have done, even with the multiple problems with computers, printers, copying machines and the <u>lack</u> of expertise. Today, I did prevail and took the disk to David's brother for proofing and printing (of course, the printer did not work and there was no paper anyway). Second first: proofed it myself and sat and fed a friend's printer one page at a time for a total of 24 pages. This print job took five minutes per page (not exaggerated). Oh yes! Third first: I did this at the Association for the Disabled. Fourth first: I took a combi that I stopped all by myself by signaling properly (?) and did this both to and from the Association. Fifth first: several times I started to say, "I have to get up and move" but this would be to wheelchair-bound persons, and never did slip up by putting my foot in my mouth which is the sixth first. The seventh first is that those in the wheelchair served me tea and lunch and would not allow me to serve them in any way. I returned to the office and this was the end of the firsts. David had already left for his home to "work on the report."

Tomorrow there are to be several young people from Uganda visiting us. They are an NGO on their own and are to provide us with some direction. All in all, today was a very good day.

<u>Thursday</u>

Today is the tomorrow of yesterday and three very ambitious young men did spend several hours with us. Two are from Uganda and the other is from Nigeria. They want to help us (?). Hopefully, they will. We soon find that they have their own business and as yet have no money. They want ACTION, not words. Don't we all? Suffice it to say, their visit was another empty straw.

Did I mention to the boys that in no way would I develop the budget? Of course I did, but did spend most of yesterday and this afternoon revising and recalculating figures. Now I am literally praying for these agencies and these people.

Surprise! Proposal was to be in on April 1...then no later than April 5...and now won't be until at least April 10 (maybe). But I cannot change what will not be changed. Tomorrow, tomorrow...yes,yes. I have permission to finalize everything on the doctor's computer. His computer and printer will be in working order but a patient will probably be receiving an intravenous infusion (she was). Remember, I said his equipment was in one of his treatment rooms?

I'll take a deep breath and walk out to HOPE. Yes, I can proof proposal and finalize the budget. But first, I must sit in on a meeting about home-based care and a training course. On the surface, this is all very well and a grand plan, but the meeting goes on and on, while this very nice lady tells us how essential HER course is. She has a set fee of only rand 7000 per person. Whaaaaaaat? Our volunteers don't even have a total of rand 700 among them.

Finally, it is 1:00PM and I am told the printer is out of toner (different printer). Can we print in blue ink? Will have to and I print all 24 pages. It looks nice but done in a mish mash of red and blue ink so we will make our copies with black ink and it will have to do. I meet David in the complex and I am proud that we are finished. He informs me that the auditor just asked for the last fiscal report. David has no money to take either the final report of the prior funding cycle or the future proposal to the National Office. He has promised his staff that he will handcarry to the powers that be. I don't envy him but it is out of my hands (literally). Now I must help Njongo with his home-based care proposal (THBCHO) or he will be in the same fix as ASHYO. Lucky for his group that this is the first time around for them.

Monday

Haphazard as usual...but proposal is done...not as organized as I would have liked and no excuse for it. It seems this is SA and if I want to stay in good graces with all the various groups, it is to my benefit to stay calm, cool, and collected. Tonight Christine had bought Coke to surprise Nomhlekwabo (me).

Tuesday

It has been quite awhile, but today was a beautiful cultural day. By 4:20AM, I had joined with Christine's friends in our living room to pray and sing. Thirty women were singing and praying, very loud, nonstop and out of sync with each other. No matter...each woman had a voice more beautiful than the next (my voice, of course, was silent).

I left for the office at 7:30AM and found David antsy about finding transport to Pretoria. He is to turn in the current proposal in person and he has yet to do the Annual Report for last fiscal year. This report, of course, was first requested months ago. He has given me no idea of the excuses he will use for the delay or omission, actually. I leave him to worry and walk to a meeting with the district religious leaders. Again, there is much singing, praying, and each person doing this at his/her own melody, tempo, and sound. Who am I to say, this may be in tongues? But now, all this singing, praying, talking in a mixture of languages no longer sounds like a racket.

Later, during the business portion, each was in agreement with the need for counseling clients both pre- and post-HIV testing. This is where I will fit in. They requested that I assist with the development of curricula for which the counselors will be trained. I agreed happily to help out. Perhaps this will lead to further development of the peer support groups.

I return to the office and David has gone ...but left me a note. Seems I am (must) work on (write) the monthly reports for both groups. This tells me the excuse he has in mind. Once again, I head toward whichever computer is free. I am becoming acclimated and immune to the ups, downs, and circles in which these people operate.

Tonight I broke up a fist fight between two ten-year-old children, a boy and a girl. Did not intervene at first because she was holding her own. Then he grabbed her hair. He had none and was about to smash her in the face with his other fist. She could not break free. Rabie was also watching, and this time he and I were in agreement. He took the boy and I took the girl and another day has gone by.

Wednesday

I attended a meeting held at the local public health clinic with several home-based care volunteers, clinic staff and traditional healers. I'm telling a fib; only four of our group showed, and then only two from the health department, and three traditional healers. We waited an hour and then took another 45 minutes to cancel the meeting. We will try again next week. The meeting was to organize the treatment regimen for those diagnosed with tuberculosis.

Friday

I have now been in Siyabuswa seven months. Many of my perceptions have changed drastically...some for the better and a few for the worse. Monday through Friday, when I am not attending a conference or away on a holiday, I find my day's progress exactly the same.

I awaken at 4:30AM when Christine is leaving. I awaken for real when she returns and brings me a cup of coffee at 5:45AM. I then have the bathroom for 20 minutes to prepare for the day. If bread and/or milk is available, I have a peanut butter sandwich or corn flakes, respectively. If not, I will buy a fat cake on my way to the post office and before going to the ASHYO office.

I leave the house at 7:30AM and walk the three blocks to ASHYO. There are at least thirty little ones up and down the road. Each greets me with, "Hi, I am fine, how you, Okay-Dokey?" They are so excited and so proud of learning these words that it sounds like music. There are also at least twenty adults along the way who also greet me; it doesn't matter if he/she is walking to work, sitting on the stoop, washing clothes or just sweeping designs in the sand, they pause to say some kind of "hello." The tame animals welcome me as well (there are no dogs or cats along the way), and the odd thing is, with all the cow pies, duck squirts, goat pellets, pigeon squishes and on, I have never stepped in any.

Arriving at work, if I am the first one there (which is most of the time), I continue walking on across the complex and to the post office. This walk will take me through the small combi rank where Moses will whistle for me, the theme from "Titanic." He is busy washing cars and both of us enjoy this greeting. I return to the office and Skosi, from the doctor's office, gives me the keys to open up and prepare for the day.

The rest of the staff wander in and out all day and I have grown accustomed to their habits. By now, I have become busy with my own responsibilities (I make them up as I go). Example…this week I have been to a traditional healers' meeting, a public health nurses' meeting, church leaders' meeting, to the HOPE NGO to work on the computer at least three times, and made a home visit to a client diagnosed with tuberculosis. At the same time (seems like it) I have worked in the offices of both ASHYO and HBCHO (THBCHO has now changed to HBCHO) on proposals, constitutions, budgets, monthly reports, and outlined procedures for each job description (of which there are none...meaning that before procedures can be outlined, job descriptions should be drafted). Which comes first, the job description or the procedure? According to the boys, the procedures come first. Me, I will do the job descriptions and then provide the outline for procedures. By the time they realize the need for job descriptions, I will have them in hand. The days go by.

I walk back to this home at around 4:30 or 5:00PM and even more are out and happily greet me. Christine is busy preparing supper. We eat at five in front of "Stefan" or "Days of Our Lives." We finish and I clean up in the kitchen and am in my room by 6:30PM. I now write in this journal and/or write letters. When I can corral the little girls, they help me with the language.

Note: will insert here comments on habits I have seen for myself. Must say, that I do not know if this is cultural or behavior that has just happened. 1st: Men are allowed more than one wife, but no wives may have more than one husband. 2nd If a husband cheats on his wife, it is the other woman's fault. The wife will forgive her husband but not forgive the other women, no matter that this other woman does not even know that the man is married. 3rd One must never hand an object to another or shake hands with the left hand. This is a sign of disrespect. Never mind that one may be left-handed. Seems the left hand is the toilet hand. 4th It is okay to drink out of a saucer, use your fingers to eat, (this becomes a habit and is hard to break when on holiday and utensils are used) and eat-eat-eat 'till all is gone, no matter how full you may be. 5th One does not worry if each person present does not receive an equal share: first come, first serve. In the case of a cold drink such as Coca-cola, if the large bottle is emptied before each receives a portion, this is okay. 6th Men give orders. A few may say "please," or "may I," but this is not the rule of thumb. Receiving a stated "thank you" is rare, especially to a woman from a man. 7th It takes time but you finally realize that whenever you do something and they say "you don't," they are just mixing their English words around and actually do mean "you do." 8th Pedestrians NEVER have the right away, not even toddlers who may run into the street, or old women who fall on the loose sand by the curb (that was me). 9th Traditional healers may have odd ideas but profess to be Christian and at the same time believe and follow the practices of their ancestors. Most of their work seems to me to be an art and does accomplish healing. A traditional healer ABSOLUTELY DOES NOT practice witchcraft as we think of it. If a person has a cold (they call a cold "flu"), he/she must not drink cold water. 10th It is not proper to wash your hair in kitchen sink but it is okay for a man and even sometimes a woman to relieve oneself out in front of everyone if nature calls (I never could do this). 11th Should not wear short shorts but can wear short skirts and breasts do not need to be covered, although they always are. 12th You may borrow but do not need to pay back. I think that when they use the word "borrow," (loan) they mean "give" and this is culturally appropriate. 13th Men take all the chairs and women carry all the heavy loads (on head). 14th Time means nothing. Although, without exception, when a meeting or transport is planned, the person will request that the others be on time. This request is disregarded for the most part. 15th A blanket is worn around the shoulders by the women who have husbands...even in summer. A married woman's head is also covered whenever she is outside her home.

Some of my questions regarding the above behaviors have been answered but not all. A married woman wears a full blanket wrapped around her out of respect to her husband's parents. If they have "passed on," wearing the blanket shows respect to the ancestors and when she is out in public, to the husband's family who are still alive. Having the head covered also shows respect but if a woman has very short hair (or head is shaved), she may wear a decorative band; if her hair is longer, her head is completely covered because hair is a turn-on or "enticing" to men. I received mixed messages about the length of a woman's hair. I was also told that married women have very short hair or even shave their heads because this is a turn-on to their husbands. If a woman is not married, she does not wear the blanket or need to cover her head. I will find out what the husband does to show respect to the wife's family. Perhaps it is the "lobolo" his family pays before he is allowed to marry the woman. Age makes no difference. If married very young, the woman wears a blanket; if a woman never marries, she does not need to wear the blanket.

Education also makes no difference. Even if the wife has a college degree, when in her hometown and many times even when residing out of her hometown, a woman will follow these cultural mores.

Traditional healers receive the "spirit within" to heal and are self-proclaimed. Both men and women can be traditional healers. Although they are recognized by the government, they are still paid a per-client fee. In the future, they may receive funding from the government. They treat with medicinal herbs that they find/collect/grind/mix themselves. They learn their art from another healer or Sokoma (a healer who is a leader). When dealing with a diagnosis they cannot treat, such as car accidents, severe heart attacks, and now tuberculosis, they refer to a medical doctor. When the patient is healed, the medical doctor refers them back to the traditional healer. I was fortunate to make visits with several patients to a traditional healer and was duly impressed with their knowledge of human physiology and the impact of illness on the body.

Men can have more than one wife in order to make more babies (true). I did not find out WHY they wanted to make more babies in today's world. There are times when a man may have two and even three wives (depending on IF he can care for them monetarily and few can). When a man cheats on his wife and the wife blames the other woman, this is her (wife's) decision and not a cultural tradition.

Monday

Another week starts. I had to walk forever to use a computer. Except for minor printer problems, all went well. But-but-but arrived home and Rabie is killing chickens (they are alive in his car). He is reaching in and grabbing them by the legs and quickly dipping each one in scalding water. Thobi and two of her friends are on the stoop and picking the feathers off. Christine is cleaning the feet, the heads, and the intestines in the kitchen sink (mind you, no hair). I had to admit to them that I never had to do this, even when my own mother was killing and cleaning chickens. I was too little. By the time I could help, she didn't make me and by the time I was frying chicken for my family, I bought the chicken already dressed at the store. They can buy chicken here too, but most families do it Rabie and Christine's way. They did not ask me to help (wonder why). I have not tried eating the feet, head or stuffed intestines. This is an art...the stuffing that is. (I think eating any of it is an art). I don't eat beef here because I watched them slaughter and clean poor Bessie. I seriously doubt I'll be able to face the Little Red Hen now!

Friday

I went to the complex early, bought three fat cakes and cream for both sets of workers. This cream will last for about today but lately Silvia has been hiding enough from the boys for her and me. I ate one fat cake and tried to give the others to her. She must clean first therefore hers got eaten by Njongo and Oupa. She, by habit and her nature, starts to clean first thing and waits on these guys like the maid they expect her to be. She and I later walk to HOPE to work on the computer...me to do it, her to learn, (from me?? Get real!) But it is the only way I can get her away from the chores. I am trying very hard to teach her what her role should be as a volunteer for ASHYO. I told her she must become indispensable to these guys. It will take the next 14 months to do this. While she is on my mind, I'll describe her a little. She is 28 years old, and a single parent of a 6 year-old boy. She has a serious boyfriend but is "smarter" now. She wants to learn, learn and then learn more. She is beautiful in appearance, smiles all the time, accepts criticism exceptionally well, teaches me much and does this very patiently, loves that little boy, and emanates a "goodness" that is easily visible.

This goodness, she generates just by "being." I asked her one day how her family dealt with the problems of apartheid and how she felt about "those" people today. She said, "Sydney, my father, my family and I have forgiven them." I believe this forgiveness she truly feels.

Chapter Fifteen

Travel humbly. Visit people and places with reverence and respect for their traditions and ways of life.

(The Art of Living)

APRIL 2002

April 27, 2002
A HUGE CULTURAL EVENT IS TO TAKE PLACE THIS WEEKEND!

<u>Friday Night</u>

I return to the house a little after 3:00PM Friday afternoon and Rabie leaves immediately for the "Celebration" in Pretoria. Christine, Thobi and I have time to get ready. This means we do not cook but instead, have fake cheese sandwiches and watch "Stefan." I take a bath, wash my hair and they do the same. This will be the first time that I have worn my "good dress," and we pack another nice outfit to change into tomorrow.

To backtrack: about three weeks ago, Anna, a neighbor and very close friend of Christine's, invited me to go with her and her family to this gala in Pretoria. I said yes. No one else in this family had been invited and no one anywhere could tell me what this party would be celebrating. But for some reason and for the first time, I did not worry one little bit about spending the weekend with strangers. Thank goodness I had agreed, because a couple of days later Christine walked to meet me as I was returning from the office (she had never done this). She was very excited and told me that she, Rabie, and Thobi have also been invited. Anna speaks very little English, understands less and was worried about me! Christine and I will be traveling for the first time together.

Now it is the exciting evening and Rabie has gone ahead to help prepare the sheep. None of us know what the celebration is about but Christine thinks it is the birthday of someone in Anna's family. Sometimes special birthdays or naming days are big events in the Ndebele culture (example: the 21st). Christine is not of this culture; therefore, she and Thobi will also be going as guests.

We are told that Anna will transport us to Pretoria and to plan on leaving at 9:00 PM. We are called and told to be ready by 8:00 PM and do leave at 9:45 PM. Our departure is in one of many combis hired for the occasion. This particular combi already has on board nine women dressed in full Ndebele attire, and will add Christine, Thobi, and me. We get settled...drive across town...stop to pick up some bangles...start again...pick up another lady dressed to the nines and off we go. I am seated next to the driver and he says our ETA is 11:15PM.

When we are about half way there, he worries that the other combi driver does not have the correct directions. We stop for gas and he wants to call her (yes, a woman). His phone does not work and mine has no air time. I do have a card which he tries to use but the phone is out of order. We wait 10 minutes and off we go. Do find a working phone on the outskirts of the city. He calls; she is already there. We head on into the city and to the home of the celebrants.

By now, it is after midnight and as the driver reaches the general vicinity of the celebration, he locks his horn and we make a very noisy but grand arrival. The whole block is jammed with people. TV cameras are set up in every direction and the lights are blazing. Cars, vans, animals and people are filling in all the space.

The ladies climb out of the van and meet with the others. There are 34 in full regalia and range from 25 years of age to? Each appears to be be encircled from neck to ankles in hundred of rows of pink, blue, and white beads, including for many, a beaded panel for her back and a beaded skirt/apron in front. If married, she will be also covered with a blanket and head dress. They have packed this beadwork in suitcases which are extremely heavy. Not only heavy to carry but even heavier to wear.

I am overwhelmed with the splendor and am stunned when they insist that I lead the parade to the house...for the television crews. Of course I understand none of this and am at a complete loss about what I am to do. Christine and Thobi have disappeared; a South African flag has appeared and is being held high BY ME! Lights are very bright; I cannot see and do not know where to go. As I try to fall back, somebody or bodies grab my arm, (both arms once) and force me to the front of what now is a throng of hundreds. Anna is right there just behind me and under her beads, she is wearing the T-shirt from America! It is a glorious arrival for them and after an entrance through hundreds and hundreds of people with the cameras flashing every which way, even I start to enjoy myself (after once inside the home).

Christine and Thobi have found me and will not leave my side until Sunday afternoon after the finale. Thobi is awed because this is the nicest neighborhood and most elegant home she has ever been in and of course, she thinks it is just like America. I do not think this is the time to disillusion her and just enjoy her excitement.

We now find a spot to settle down in and I attempt to count the people...cannot do this. Men are all over outside and women are all over inside and outside. There are three large bathrooms inside and each has an adjacent dressing room. There are three huge cooking areas/kitchens going full force and outside are two brie (barbeque) areas holding six spits on which slowly roasting are lamb, pork and beef. I am later told that this house has seven bedrooms, a salon, dining area, extra day room (den) and more.

Never once did I think, "Hey, it is 1:00AM in the morning." I did realize the time when I wandered around outside and the moon, which was full and very bright, shone his eyes directly on us all the way from Siyabuswa and out beyond (tonight, I believed this, too).

The Ndebele women dance, sing, and blow/toot their horns and then we are served pap and sheep. They dance, sing, and we are served tea, cookies, fat cakes and sweets. They dance and sing and we are served cold drinks, including beer. I was full and could only continue to drink tea. They dance, sing, and it is suddenly 5:00AM. Blankets have been handed out to those who don't have one (me) and Christine has made me a nest beside her. Thobi is asleep on the floor. But I am truly engaged; it no longer sounds like noise and I am not tempted to nod off. Women continue to dance, sing and at 5:00AM, here come the women with more beer, Coke, and an orange drink (this has never stopped). I drink a Coke and they serve tea, cookies, and fat cakes and then at 6:00AM, we are offered soft porridge with lots and lots of sugar and yes, more tea., fat cakes and different cookies. This porridge with the large amounts of sugar (3-4 table-spoons for each person) is offered to give us energy to last until the meal is served (whaaaaaaaaat?).

It is 9:00AM and the presents are about to be opened. I am still think-ing it is a birthday party for someone (have not been told just who). I am startled to find that several people are being honored, two older and married to each other, two younger and also married to each other. But there are also several sin-gle men and women receiving gifts. I cannot even begin to describe the presents and quickly lost count of the number that were distributed. Included in this ware-house of gifts, but not by any means the full inventory, were a full-sized mattress and matching springs, many comforters, many, many blankets, a microwave oven, full sets of dishes, glasses, towels, soap, men's shirts, women dresses and other items of clothing. As the gifts are received, the singing and dancing continues.

At 10:00AM, the full banquet is served. Everything was served to us by a group of women. This was indeed lifesaving because there was absolutely no room between people for anyone to form a serving line. No one could even get up to return the dirty or empty plates. All the while, basins of water were passed for us to wash our hands (some faces), by these same women. I was offered a chair but declined and they allowed me to bend my legs. I was as comfortable as anyone. Anyway, the food was placed family-style in many areas and the women dished up huge platters and served it full to each person. Now there was pap, rice, sweet potatoes, green beans, bean salad, beets, cole slaw, cooked cab-bage, beef stew, roast beef, more lamb, fried chicken, fat cakes and when I thought I might choke on the next bite, a pudding with cookies, jello and fruit were offered...the dessert bowl filled to the brim.

It is 10:30AM and I wander into one of the bedrooms looking for Anna and meet up with one of the young women from within the home. As good luck would have it, she and her husband are the owners of this home and this celebra-tion is for them and their in-laws. She speaks English very well and is quite happy to explain what this whole gala is all about.

Time here for me to take a break. It is 5:00PM, Sunday evening. I am back home in Siyabuswa and guess it is time for a cookie!

I can now explain a little about why the celebration took place and will then describe in more detail the women. Oh, oh, it is Tuesday and I have pro-crastinated two long evenings. Why this procrastination? First, there is so much to tell and second, I don't feel confident that I can do justice to these people or describe the event properly. But knowing this, I will make the attempt.

Culturally: when the Ndebele people marry, the father of the groom may not have a one-to-one or rather face-to-face conversation with the bride, nor can the mother of the bride have a one-to-one conversation with the groom. It is of no matter that the years go by or that the in-law becomes ill, dies, or even just wants to be a friend. If children are born, as they grow older, they become the intermediaries between the respective in-laws. This is because the in-law in ques-tion must be prevented from becoming enamored with the other. Another reason is that the younger (either wife or husband) does not become obsessed with the other's wealth (Hah). This is rarely the case except with the very young wives and the fairly young fathers-in-law.

The couple hosting and being honored at this celebration have been married for nineteen years and have two teen-aged children. To break this taboo of silence between the respective parties, the young couple must host a celebration: first to prove they are only interested in each other and second to welcome the respective in-laws into their own home. After this event, everyone may speak to anyone else, even privately. Everyone is invited to help celebrate: the extended families of both sides and their friends. If someone brings a gift...and everyone does...then the gift-sharing is reciprocal. This means that the young couple and their parents must also give a gift back to the person offering them a gift. Now I understood why it takes so long to give this party. A celebration is not held until the couple has saved enough money to host it. In this case, I was told the cost was close to rand 40,000 or approximately 4000 American dollars.

The young lady also told me that the blankets are worn by the married women in modesty and to show respect to the father-in-law who cannot speak to them, let alone touch. Seems backwards to me. The married women are taken (wed) and remain covered while the younger and single girls are running around very sexy. It is no wonder that young ladies are accused of stimulating both young and older men. It seems to me, that the men (married) would be even more stimulated because their wives are covered in public.

Now the women: each is unbelievably beaded from her head to her ankles. On the older women, the apron is squared, made of leather, and covered completely with little tiny beads worked into an intricate geometric configuration. This apron extends around the waist and is attached to a beaded leather panel draping the back. Each woman has done the tedious beadwork arranged on her own items of dress. This particular arrangement of apparel is worn by the married women during celebrations to prove or to illustrate her standing in the community, and when she does, she has also agreed to maintain her cultural/traditional observances. As another sign of respect to her husband, a married woman must always wear some form of head covering. This evening the heads of the married dancers have been shaved and a band of beads has been placed around the forehead. Some are very ornate, some simply beautiful. Dark marks (I do not know by what) have been made down the center of her forehead. Several rings of gold/brass encircle her neck. Circlets of beads go around this and on down to the shoulders. Most also have on arm and leg bands made of more beads tacked on some material (again, I do not know the material). Each woman has carried her assortment of beaded jewelry to this celebration in a large metal suitcase. I do not know how they have the strength to carry this load, let alone wear the complete outfit, all the while dancing and singing for hours on end. Now mind you, around all this is pinned a big colorful (many in the colors of the South African Flag) blanket and may be bordered with rows of black beads.

Time out. The kids in this neighborhood (Siyabuswa) are outside my window making a terrific racket. I counted 75 before they got driven away by the bigger kids. I am not exaggerating one iota when I say this place has children coming out of the woodwork like termites...no coming out of the sand like ants. They are legion!

Back to the party: In addition to this bead work told about earlier, the married women also wear neck hoops of grass twisted into a coil and covered in beads. Will quit for now because the kids are back in force. All screaming, I know not why but will find out!

Christine and Rabie have gone to a funeral. Thobi and I are home alone. She has asked (to go) and is out in this melee of kids. It is absolutely a blessing and wonderful to watch these children with their innocence in active play. And that is what the screaming is about...pure joy. When do they change? And they do, even here. Must they make the transition from child to teen to adult and lose this innocence? Or have we, as adults and surviving this process through the ages, caused this change from delight in life to fright of living?

Wednesday
MAY DAY...BASKETS Do you remember when? Long time ago!

Today was another memorable day. I stayed home with Thobi and we had eggs for breakfast. No big deal for me but she learned how to "fry" an egg. She scrubbed the floor and so did I; she fed the chicks and I washed my clothes.

Thobi and a friend of hers agreed to accompany me on a walk to David's house to take his brother Lucas a wedding gift. We met David going the other direction but he told us to go on, that Lucas was still at the house. We arrived and one of the women in the family had been in Pretoria with us last week. This meant that everyone greeted us with open arms (no strangers here)

One of the gogos was weaving a small floor mat, another very beautiful but tedious and thankless job. The bride-to-be was in the neighbor's yard, covered from head to toe and being paraded around and around by a young girl. Both were walking very slowly. They were taking "Captain, May I?" baby steps. For three days before the actual wedding, the bride stays in seclusion. The first day, she is led by a child and taken into a house vacated for this purpose and her basic needs are tended to by this young child. The second day, she stays with a young woman and the third day, she stays with the married women. All three days, they stay with her in this otherwise vacant house. All have something to teach her about her roles as a wife and mother. The night before the wedding ceremony, she stays in the house of the groom in which a "stall" has been arranged and she is hidden behind the curtains (mats). No one is to enter except an older woman and this is only to offer her nourishment. This area, although in his home, is absolutely off-limits to the groom.

Today is the first of the three days and I was allowed to watch the young girl and the bride take their exercise but was not allowed to converse with either of them. In the groom's house, young men are busy stringing wire across one end of the main room on which colorful mats will be hung. This, upon completion, becomes the "stall" where the bride will sleep the night before her wedding. Everyone, from gogos to youngsters, is very busy. David later tells me how special I am to his family and that is why they allowed me to observe the private preparations, especially those inside the home.

I have many questions, none of which will I ask. Is all of this secret preparation done because of cultural tradition or a cultural law? Why is the bride kept in seclusion, no matter that she may already have one or more children? Why will David's fiancé not be attending the wedding of her future in-laws?

I will not be attending the actual wedding ceremony because I will be in Pretoria (found out later that I could not be invited). I plan to attend David's, if by the time I leave, he is allowed...or rather if another lobolo will be available for him. By the decree of the father (in this case, the uncle) the older son must marry first if possible. This raises more questions. What if the older sons do not wish to marry or have not met the young lady they wish to make a wife? All of it is way over my head.

I think it is Friday...yes, it is! And I am on my way for a weekend in Pretoria. I was to leave at 10:00AM, was there at 9:45AM and the bus finally leaves at 11:05AM. This time, the trip is for business. I am to meet with the auditor for David and with Cam for a variety of reasons. Both cancel on me after I am already on the bus. I think, "Good, now I will have a treat of two days to myself." No way!

Bus once again has problems and we have a 2 hour and 30 minute wait before we can change to another. Do arrive in Pretoria at 3:30PM. Walk over to the mall to turn in my film, buy food for supper, have a glass of wine and am back in my room by 5:45 PM for a quiet evening. It was wonderful. Cam called and she will pick me up at noon tomorrow for lunch and a movie.

In the morning, I go retrieve the photos. Cam comes; we have Italian antipasto and go see "Monster Ball." We both enjoyed it and the evening is the same as the night before.

Oh no! The trip home! I called for a taxi (as always) to take me to the taxi rank that will have a combi to take me to Siyabuswa. First mistake...ask the name of the street and am told, "Jerusalem." Who could go wrong with that? Me, that is who. Driver insists that I get off at the Jerusalem Church! I do see combis a couple of blocks over but am not sure if they are the right ones or how to get there. I won't get out...driver gets frustrated because these are one-way streets and he has to drive by the zoo (lots of traffic) to get to the other side. He does drop me (almost literally) and I go to the first mass of combis. No, this is not right. I wander to the second, again not right. Now my backpack is very, very heavy. It is loaded with photos (27 rolls developed) and books. Why? Have not had time to be frightened but am in a frightening situation.

Finally, I allow this little kid to help me and hope what he tells me is right and all is well...oh no, it is not. We go sailing past Siyabuswa and are on our way to Marble Hall. I shout, "Let me off, let me off!" Yes, he'll let me off in the middle of nowhere and I am to hitchhike back to Siyabuswa. Now I am about to panic because today and on this combi, no one speaks English. I don't know which direction to head or for sure which vehicles are safe to board. My backpack is still heavy and in the way. But now the people, even though they don't speak English will not let the driver just drop me and insist that he gets out with me and hail a ride for me. He does and I am on my way. This driver lets me off with a long distance to walk but at least I know the way. By the time I reach the house, I am taking baby steps myself and really feeling my age.

Last week, after much finagling and negotiating, I received permission from David (ASHYO) and Cam (PC) to attend a week long conference starting tomorrow for the home-based care volunteers (HBCHO) and am excited and looking forward to the actual classes. I lie down to rest, with the plan to pack later in the evening. Second mistake: the bulb in my room has burned out and this means packing in the pitch-black. No can do. Where is my flashlight? I loaned it to someone. Christine does have a candle and I do pack and write my notes by this light. No problem, am safe at home.

All little tasks are completed and I am sitting on my bed and realize I had forgotten to pick up my phone messages. I do this and then my weekend becomes very sad. Hermione (Meriam's daughter whom I had visited in the hospital) has died on Saturday. I did not know her well but certainly do love her family and try to arrange to attend her funeral. My only means of transport into Sandfontein is with someone in Meriam's family and of course, this is not possible. Hermione had been diagnosed with lupus but the family will believe that she died of complications of the head injury she sustained several months ago. I did reach Meriam later. She is at a loss and doesn't know just how little Letha (Hermione's daughter) will handle the situation. I am at a loss because I don't know what to do or how to help in any way.

<u>Monday</u>

All of us are to meet at 7:30 AM. We do...in the rain. Everyone is very excited because this will be the first mini-course on home-based care for the volunteers. It is being held in a resort-type area, albeit quite rustic. We brought our own blankets, cookware, towels, and other necessities. Everyone is sharing a rondevaal (round, one-room cabin with thatched roof), with a roommate, except for me. I have my own room and was surprised to find that this arrangement makes the others uncomfortable. They are concerned for my safety. I tell them I am by myself all the time and will manage quite well. Must say it was wonderful, though, to have someone bring me hot water, coffee, and to keep me company until time to call it a night. Each day a different set of girls/women decided they had to entertain me. For my part, I was glad to get to know them individually and hear their stories.

Of course, on the first day we arrived approximately two hours late and this threw all the speakers off schedule. Not to worry. I was supposed to give a 5 minute introduction. In reality, this took 20 minutes and we will start fresh first thing in the morning. Oops, all of sudden I am in charge. Hah! Not only that, I now have two lectures to give, each to take about 3 hours (how did this happen)? Where are the speakers?

Guess what my two topics are? First is "Communication Skills" and the second is Stress." Hah again! But I tell them:

"Cannot speak the King's English,
"Cannot speak the Queens Isindebele"
"Cannot speak my host family's combination of Zulu-Ndebele"
"Cannot speak the office staff's mix of six languages"
"But I can speak with my hands and you can communicate with your eyes."

We do communicate!
Each participant is concerned that I will think he/she is "stupid"
I am concerned that I will appear condescending to them.

We are stressed!
I know that in this place, time means very little and I cannot change what won't be changed. I am quite comfortable with this group and know at least half of the twenty-four in attendance. I admitted I wanted a room to myself and don't feel guilty. The others are many years younger...most are between 21-26 years. They do not need me as a chaperone and one way to handle stress is to look out for one's self. I am absolutely right within myself and have only 14 months left in South Africa. I did miss Mindy's phone call but will call her later. No I won't, no phones here and mine has not been charged. We are at the SS Skosana Resort. None of the rondevals have any amenities except that each has the electricity connected and a sink (with no running water).

Tuesday
It is early and I am cold...no heat...no plug in the sink. Hark, two of the young girls bring me water but my wires are loose (no pun intended) so can-

Home Based Care Class

not heat it. Do get dressed, go over to the dining room and have a cup of coffee and prepare for the day. This ends up a futile attempt because none of the guys show up who are providing the conference, nor does the nutritionist or the social worker. They all come in at 3:30PM! None even call. I am supposed to have <u>two</u> hours and instead I have the WHOLE day. The show must go on because it is a very long walk back to Siyabuswa. By 8:30AM we have started communicating...by prancing, dancing up in front, and using every means of sign language available to my limbs. I easily gain their attention (who is this strange animal?). We play games and communicate, play more games and communicate more. We have fun. I tell myself: "All those workshops you did for the health department may not have paid off in the States, but the games certainly are doing the trick here."

The social worker walks into the room 3:30PM with the guys in tow. She is very tired and too tired to speak to the group. Who is tired??. Now come on! Everyone is young (even me today). Need I even say that she and Njongo make their apologies and leave, supposedly to return tomorrow.

It is 4:30PM and two girls, who were strangers to me this morning, are no longer strangers or uncomfortable with me. They ask if they can come by my room to just talk and of course, I am delighted. As they left later, they asked if they could come by and visit me in Siyabuswa on Mother's Day, (next Sunday). I hope they do but I don't trust any promises.

As they depart, another young woman comes to see me. She says she has big problems. And she does! Seems her boyfriend talked her into getting pregnant (they all do). She did and now she is scared because he wants nothing to do with her and has been seen around with another girl. I think he is a jerk but in this culture he is "one of the adult men." I can only listen and do. She cries, says she feels better, but I know she feels worse. I feel sad for all the women here. Again they are 40 years or maybe 50 years behind the women's movements in the United States. Suddenly it is 7:30PM and we are called for dinner.

Return to my room, add an extra quilt to my bed and sleep very well. Today is Wednesday and I am to speak on "stress" for 2 hours. I do this with much trepidation because they are each stressed and for a multitude of reasons. This is not the time to even start talking of the problems with the caterers. Okay, again no one shows to present until 2:00PM and I have spoken on the missed topics. Even I am tired and where the ideas for lecture material and games came, I will never know. Does anyone remember childhood games from years and years and years ago? I did. The topic on nutrition went well thanks to the fact that my daughter-in-law is a registered dietitian and this (?) bolstered my credibility. Next we discussed, "Care for the Caregiver" and this, as even they came to realize, is one of my sincere interests. We survive. Njongo arrives at 2:00 PM and speaks on HIV/AIDS. He did a stellar job and finally at 3:00PM, the social worker strolls in. She and Njongo hold the group mesmerized until almost 6:00PM. We all thought their talks were well worth the wait.

And now tomorrow I must speak on palliative care (a word they have just heard). Njongo and I know this topic could easily fill several days in and of itself. But the nutritionist and environmentalist are yet to speak (yes, the nutritionist). Neither Njongo, nor any of the group will be here tomorrow. Once again, I will have to facilitate the whole show. It is not fair to this group of young people to not know what the next hour may bring. I will say, they deserve an enormous amount of credit because most have overcome their shyness and will ask questions. It is not fair to me because I have to prepare at a moment's notice and do not know the health system well in this country and there are social and financial questions I cannot answer. It is not fair to HBCHO because it is paying a lot for this poorly-organized seminar. And certainly it is not fair to the patients that their volunteers are receiving only minimal training. When I try to voice my concerns, management discounts me and just says, "This is South Africa."

Tonight I find out via the grapevine that David may have a "paying job with the Government." Everyone would be happy for him but it seems he wishes to appoint an outside personal friend to his present position of Director of ASHYO. To say the others are fuming is to say that the fires that were smoldering will erupt shortly. Don't know where I want to be but do know I am glad I won't be going to Secunda tomorrow with the boys. Best I stay out of it. With the fiscal problems David is facing, I am not at all sure there is anything ethically I can do.

<u>Thursday</u>

It is early AM and today is supposed to be a very full day. The saying, "Be careful for what you ask for...you may get it," certainly applies in my own experience. I asked to come to the Peace Corps and I asked to come to this workshop. I asked permission to attend the workshop in the hopes of learning what is expected of the volunteers in the homes. I never did ask to facilitate/present the entire week, but today went extremely well. Both speakers were on time; both were well-prepared and the topics (Tuberculosis and Environmental Health) were very interesting. The food was well-prepared and delicious. The evaluations were excellent (Thank God). Most of the participants I have met with on a one-on-one basis and I know I have made several new friends.

"God is praying for the sick people. One day Father God will bless them all and all will wake up and walk."
(Note received from a participant when role playing as a patient with AIDS).

"I will always feel confused. I will loose concentration at school. I will always feel lonely to play with other kids. I will always cry when I arrive at home because of confusion at home."
(Note from a participant when role playing as a child of a parent with AIDS).

Tonight we had a brie and the boys were back to help in good time. David was in all his glory because he is now to oversee all the NGOs from the Provincial office. I do not think he knows exactly what this will mean and he admits he is somewhat confused as to his job description. Njongo is to be the liaison between the NGOs in the District and those in the Provincial offices.

Njongo says he will not be paid and David says he won't yet, either. Only I know how extremely slowly the government moves when hiring for any position in my own country. I can only think that will also be true here. But tonight, the air is fraught with confusion, desire, ambition, anger and much more. Where have I heard all this before? Surprisingly, each is telling me their take...even Oupa and Vusi. But not surprisingly, each views the situation quite differently. Of course ASHYO is David's pride and joy; he does not want to let go! In the eyes of the others, it has been a one-man operation and no one except David has received any credit for the enormous amount of work ASHYO has accomplished. Now could be their chance, but who will stand up and speak out? This is a big million-dollar question. First off, if done well, the Director should be appointed with the Board's guidance. The downside of this is that the Board is composed of relatives or friends of David whom he appointed years ago. The others seem to think that he has already promised the position to a buddy and then he can stay in control.

I fear for the organization. Do they? I realize that if they can get new blood, be it either in-house or out and if they can keep the volunteers, ASHYO could be built into what should be sustainable...and a huge resource to the community. Do they? I know personally how hard it is to let go. Does David? Letting go is hard...one of the very hardest things in management...and these guys are so very young!

<u>Saturday</u>

The workshop is over and in spite of the problems (I would be hard-pressed to say it went well), the group had a good time and learned a lot. I was accepted and will be more credible from here on out. For me, because of this workshop and the mutual trust, I became an ally and will be able to work with these volunteers from HBCHO much easier. If the speakers had all shown, and everything had gone as originally planned, I never would have gained these one-on-one relationships. I can sense that we will accomplish much more for the patients than would have been possible if we had not had this intense interaction. Now I will wait and see if anyone comes to visit me as they have promised.

But today is Saturday and right outside my window and across the road, there is a big commotion! Taking place right before my eyes, there is yelling, shrieking, all kinds of music (horns, drums, and radios), stomping, marching, dancing, and singing. laughing, and other words too! Loud and clear. Beer is flowing and tea or coffee is being served. Pickups are loaded with young men. The trucks stop and the young men (16-25 years of age at most) jump out. They take off their shirts, put them on, take them off and whatever this means, it goes on for a long time. I find out later that this commotion will last from Friday night until sometime Saturday night.

The roads and yards up and down the streets are filled with people watching the spectacle. It is quite awesome. This celebration is another very big cultural "event." These young men are off to the "mountain" where they will undergo the rites of passage from boys to men...if they survive. They will be gone for a minimum of two months, maybe longer. In this time away, each may be circumcised without any medication or deadening for pain. Just recently, they have been given the choice, but I am told that all will choose to do the procedure. This afternoon, they are leaping around and beating each other with long snapping sticks, some seriously. None dare to cry out or the beating will be worse. Already, a few have sustained bleeding wounds. For some spectators, this beating is beautiful, for others it is "crazy." For me, I am not sure. It is supposed to be a part of the preliminary preparations for the time in the mountain but I am reminded of the frat initiations in the States. Although there is lots of laughter, it is intermixed with what they call "playful" beating. And this is what we see! They are not allowed to tell anything about what goes on at the mountain. They will make up their own secret language and will not be allowed to speak anything but this language when there. I have read a little about this "mountain trip and how necessary it is for young boys. The completion of the school and the rites involved (?) give them the right to consider themselves "real" and "mature" men. I will get more details from the boys.

Sunday
MOTHER'S DAY
Today was a wonderful day. It is 6:30PM. I have talked per phone with Mindy, Sue and John. A cultural event for the United States and I made it one for the mothers I know here in Siyabuswa. Another excuse for ice cream!

Monday
Today was a good day. Yvonne Hubbard, South Africa Peace Corps Country Director, and Henry McCoy from the National Peace Corps Office in the United States came on a site visit to Siyabuswa. We were chosen as his first visit in South Africa and he is the director for all of Africa. Many volunteers showed and I am certain they were each impressed. We shall see if we get any feedback from Peace Corps. Me, I personally felt good and not the least nervous, only extremely proud of these young people. And I know all three agencies very well and could answer each of Mr. McCoy's questions. I was also impressed with Peace Corps. So another...another what? DONE!

I have questioned the boys and have a little more information regarding the Ndebele "boys to the mountain" tradition. The "beatings" I witnessed are "play" but if some one dies "accidentally," while at the mountain, the family finds out only when their son is not one of the celebrants to return. And yes, they can have sex before the "mountain" experience but not for 30 days prior to leaving. This restriction is because each must be free of any sexually transmitted disease...not that they are too young or that the girls may be too young. Yes, they do get circumcised, but the Ndebele do not die. Other cultures might because they are not fed "energy" foods from home. Now come on! It seems in truth, that the gogos take the meals to the mountains but can only see the boys. Absolutely no conversing!

David is going to take me (5:30AM) to the "Welcome Back" celebration and I will find out more then.

Tuesday and Wednesday

Typical South African days. Two steps forward and 25 steps backwards. Have entered the information into the computer but the printer is not working. (Does this sound like, went to the levee and the levee was dry?) David tells me that it is making him nervous to tell me, but he did not leave the proposal in Nelspruit. Now the rest of the gang is saying that he does not know how to spend the money if and when it has been received. I am in a quandary, could jump in but if I take sides would I not be shooting myself in the foot? If we keep on status quo, we may be hurting ASHYO and the community. We are supposed to have a meeting on Friday to work all this out. We won't but I will wait and see if and when they ever do call a meeting or if anything gets resolved. I have been here 10 months and we still have no car, no computer, no telephone, and no money. But someplace, somehow and deep inside of me, I do know we are making more people aware of the dire consequences of AIDS. It may only be on a one-on-one basis but I do know some are being tested earlier. However, obtaining the knowledge that one is HIV-positive and listening to all the counseling in the world will not make proper medications and treatment accessible to those in need in this community. The situation continues to break our hearts.

Thursday

The next South African day, and there are more and more of these: good, wonderful, simply beautiful and God-given. Pastor Hendrik, from Hope for Africa, picked me up and with two missionaries from the United Kingdom, we went to Sizanana Village.

I thought we were going to visit a hospice as did they. But we were in for an amazing tour of a complex which is sponsored and run by the Catholic Church. Yes, we started with the hospice building, which was very bright, clean, roomy and you could tell the patients were given quality care. There was space for all ages...eight beds for children and fifteen beds for adults. The reception area was large with many chairs and tables. There was also a TV room, a large dining hall, many bathrooms, and the windows were large with beautiful views of the spacious grounds.

A young lady came to show us around the rest of the complex. A school/home was available for the mentally retarded or handicapped (no definitive diagnosis except retardation) children. I am going to check out the newborn screening available in this country and what, if any services there are for serious genetic diagnoses. This building was also very large, clean and thirty children ages 1-13 years reside there. The next building is a home for orphans for whatever reasons. Note: Pastor Hendrik is in the planning phase of building such a school for orphaned children in Siyabuswa.

Not only is there the building for the special children and another for the orphans, there is also a separate shelter or home for children of the street or troubled and difficult... But of course, there was even more to see and the young person who showed us around did not want us to miss anything. She took us on a tour of the Church, the priest's home, Conference Center (with huts for visiting overnighters), a Chief's Kraal, a craft shop and yes, even a small factory where they did the pottery, painting, weaving, sewing and on and on. Each building was all brick, large, and with flowers blooming in many nooks and crannies. There were large open play areas, a tennis court, picnic areas and several gardens growing vegetables for each season. I have never seen anything quite so complete.

There is no stigma attached because there are so many different services that no one knows who belongs to what or what individual circumstances are back in their homes. Sizanana Village is supported by the church, the government, private donations and a multitude of volunteers. I couldn't help but think, if one were going to need help, this is the place. But I also realized that the people serving here must be angels on earth because the tragedy, heartbreak, and bleak future for almost all would be overwhelming at all times.

We left there, came back to Siyabuswa and I had dinner with Pastor Hendrik and his family. Oh yes, we were served tea and sandwiches at the center. Later, we went to the site in Siyabuswa C where just today, the councilmen had received a letter of approval to build a school for orphans. Everyone was elated and so am I, even though I have no direct part in this endeavor. And wouldn't you know, today I am without my camera. I thought we were going to a hospice and would not be taking patient pictures. As it is, they wanted their picture taken. It was an inspiring day and I hope I remember this day when I complain. Above all, I was totally awestruck when Pastor Hendrik asked if he could use "my expertise" when further progress of the school started to develop. Of course I said yes, I would be honored.

Friday

You will never, ever believe this! Today was a day exactly like one at home with the Dept. of Public Health Genetics Section, only it took place in South Africa! I arrived as usual at the office, with an idea that will help Silvia with the monthly report. Slovo, municipal councilman, comes and invites (tells) me to attend the Council meeting where the mayor is to reveal his budget. I plan to go that direction anyway to get the rest of the proposal reprinted, you heard me...same proposal that I started in January. Now that it has been redone and supposedly ready to submit, we are told to revise the Constitution and the Financial Policies. Because all meetings start late here and because everyone tries to be helpful, I do get everything printed and it looks nice (the print).

I am able to attend the meeting. Vusi went with me as an interpreter. After almost three hours of non-stop talk by first one councilman and then the next, of course my bladder is playing havoc with my kidneys and legs and I'm about to pop. My leg has a cramp and my seat is paralyzed. We leave...thanks to Vusi.

We arrive back at the office at 3:00PM. David is upset because I went to a meeting that he didn't assign to me, but swears he is joking. Actually, he is recovering from an all -nighter, but does have the nerve to ask me to review (write) NALEDI's proposal. Even I cannot believe that this is the very same proposal that David's uncle asked me to review the first week after my arrival in Siyabuswa. Where has it been all this time? They do not know and do not have a copy of his original business plan, nor do they have any notes. And his uncle is no longer involved. I have not worked with this particular group of young men and know next to nothing of their plans and none of their objectives. They must have it completed and in to the Provincial Office by next week. Remember this is Friday. Impossible.

These young men are far more intelligent than I, can shift back and forth in languages, have hearts as big as all South Africa but they cannot write in English and do not understand the concept of objectives. Who does? I remember going over and over and over the Year 2000 Objectives for Maternal and Child Health and there never were any two people on the various committees in complete accord. What to do? I know what. I will come home and start from scratch and write the whole darn thing. Why not? I did work from 6:30PM until midnight. It is done roughly but as good as it is going to be.

The boys are to meet me at 9:00AM. They do not show until 9:40AM and of course, I must beg them to even read it and of course, none has any idea how to continue. They must come up with the last of the objectives, (I had decided on the first four). I also told them how to proceed with the budget plan and emphatically refused to do the figures. I did agree that on Monday I will type and fight the computer once again. Truly God is on my side and these proposals will get funded. Otherwise, what in the world am I doing here? Soon, must do something nice for Silvia because she bears the brunt of my frustrations. She is the one who sees everyone pulling me in twenty directions at once. Is this not what I retired from over again? Why??

Sunday

Other wonderful, glowing, amazing things happened today. I read Matthew 20 early this morning. I also read in Max Lucado's book, "He Chose the Nails" about the crown of thorns. Every day I pass hundreds of bushes covered in thorns...but today...yes today, I punctured the bottom of my foot with one. It hurt (just one) and Jesus had a Crown! How did He survive this? This was on my way to church and yes, I remembered my camera. The man who gave the sermon (Mr. Martin, I think), spoke in three different languages but one was English. His text was taken from Matthew 20. Yes! Lucado asks us to write down all the thoughts that are mean-spirited. This could probably take a full day. Do we not find that many times our actions are nice but our thoughts are not always compatible with them? For instance:

> A very nice lady walked across the field of thorns with me...I was thinking, "What a beautiful day." She let me lean on her to get the tiny thorn out and <u>then</u> I felt as if I had been the one interrupted!

Or: Thought I would visit with Dorothee and Willem after church but they had his brother and family visiting. At first I was disappoint because I had wanted to give the kids candy as my treat to them.

Or: Arrive home. Christine is asleep so I decide to lie down...do so for 30 minutes and Rabie and Thobi come in from church as they do every Sunday at the same time. Dinner has been prepared earlier and I am disappointed because my nap was interrupted...as was Christine's...who needed it much more.

<u>Monday through Friday</u>

Busy week...have assisted with four proposals (actually wrote them). Today, (Thursday) was heart-rendering. David asked me to provide counseling to a friend of his. I was in the middle of a deadline (whose?) and did not want to take the time. But I did and now I don't know if it was the right thing to do or a big mistake. I assumed it to be an AIDS-related situation that could be handled this afternoon. Not so!

A young, attractive, sweet, woman of 32 years of age and who has been married 11 years met me in the complex. She told me that she has recently been told of her husband's sleeping with another woman. This she may have handled but just this morning, she found that this other woman has a two-week old baby and her husband is the father. What should she do? My thoughts run rampart. Leave him, divorce him, shoot him, forgive him, accept this woman as a second wife, join with the other woman and raise the two children (she has a 9-year-son). But this is SA and she "loves" him and blames the other woman. Her friends love her, her sister is her best friend, her mother understands but all also love her husband. Therefore, she cannot or will not discuss with anyone the situation because they might "hate" him and she "loves' him and he still "loves her." I listen and wonder what I can possibly do to help. How do they handle these situations in this country?

I have learned that the situation is not unique and is becoming more common every day. I also wonder, if she cannot talk any of this over with any of those close to her, how did David become involved? I find out all too soon when she drops the rest of her story. Seems on Monday she was on a chair ready to hang herself when her husband <u>and</u> David came in and stopped her. She told of a few details and then said, "They only stopped me this time." Now I do not know how to respond. Later, I gave her my phone number and requested that she call me at any time if she needed me to meet her. We made arrangements to meet at the office at 1:00PM on Saturday. In the meantime, I will find out if there is such a thing as a crisis hotline in this area. I know there are mental health workers but do not know their capabilities.

Chapter Sixteen

And Jabez called on the God of Israel saying,
"Oh, that You would bless me indeed,
And enlarge my territory,
That Your hand would be with me,
And that You would keep me from evil,
That I may not cause pain!"

(I Chronicles 4:10 (NKJV)

CHAPTER SIXTEEN

JUNE 2002

May 26, 2002
<u>Sunday</u>

A beautiful Sunday! It is exactly the right day to start a new journal. I will try to make this one more upbeat. What better way to start than with music? Right this minute, I am listening to Mozart, but in fact, several weeks ago, Lucas invited me to come and listen to his choir competition. I said I would enjoy that and amazingly, he kept reminding me and today was the day. It felt like a good thing to do. Silvia met me at the Siyabuswa Primary School where the competition was to take place. The contest today was between two choirs of fifteen singers, each composed of seven girls and eight men. In my non-professional opinion, one group was every bit as talented as the other. I recognized most of the music and about half was sung in English. The exuberance, pure joy in singing and a love for all things beautiful shone through most vividly in every one of the voices, making the afternoon truly inspiring. This,of course, is Memorial Day weekend in America so it was especially meaningful for me. Vusi, Njongo, and Freddy also sang in the group of which Lucas is the leader. They were surprised and genuinely pleased to see me. I came back home, ate the meal Christine had prepared and played cards with Thobi. The sun was a massive red ball and the horizon also a vivid red both horizontally and vertically...almost as far as one could absorb. Later the stars were so bright you could actually visualize the twinkle and see the flicker because the moon was completely full. One could imagine seeing beyond the man and looking straight into the craters.

MEMORIAL DAY IN AMERICA!

Today is Memorial Day in America! I tried to make it Memorial Day here, but it was mostly a South African Day! The difference was that today, I kept my cool...even inside of myself. And tonight that has made me feel good.

First: I had told David that I planned an American Party for 12:30PM, knowing it would be 1:00PM or even later. He suggested that everyone bring both the American flag and the ASHYO T-shirts. He's the one who forgot. He has scheduled a meeting for 9:00AM but no one arrives until 11:30AM. By this time Njongo, Oupa and David have left for a destination unknown to me. They do come back and David has his meeting at 1:00PM when everyone else is ready to party. The meeting can only last a few minutes because, of course, we have to have "photos" taken with the T-shirts. By now, the people from David's meeting are also here and are included in the party. Actually, it made it great fun because it is true: "the more the merrier." We had ice cream cones, popcorn and Coca-cola...which made them proud to be "part of America." It has become apparent to me that even though nothing ever starts on time, whatever is to take place does...in due course. It shouldn't have taken me so long to reach this conclusion because I have always advocated "moderated (my word) behaviors" and perhaps "time" should be included in the list of moderates (also my word).

Tonight, my family did put on the tee shirts without a reminder, offered to turn off TV and voiced a sincere thank-you for the ice cream. It was a far cry from the Valentine Day fiasco and this act made all the difference to me. All in all, a good day with lots of happiness shared by more than anticipated. And Mindy's call got through!!

<u>Friday</u>

Today was a very good day. Received my credit card (I had been robbed of it in Pretoria) and it worked! Talked with David and requested that Silvia be allowed to register for a computer class. He is agreeable with the idea. She is, too! Note: Friends from Chicago have offered to sponsor her and have already sent the necessary fees to me. I am getting ready for Pretoria and tonight we had fish and chips. I am happy. In fact, everyone is A-OK at this moment. And the days move on!

Actually (Divia's word), the above entry was yesterday which was Thursday. It is now Friday. Actually, it is Sunday night but I am going to write about Friday. The morning started as another wonderful day. I rode into Pretoria without a hitch, did my usual thing: walk to Holiday Inn, catch a local taxi to a backpackers, and walk to the mall. I was in the book store at approximately 5:30 PM. Was reviewing the books on one of the top shelves when suddenly became very dizzy. Thought it was because I was looking up so leaned against the book shelf and became faint. Literally felt the blood draining somewhere and my pulse start to rise...no pain, no nausea, but the vertigo became much worse. The room began to spin; I wanted to lie down but also knew I needed help before I went completely out. Did make it to the counter and a stool was there. The saleslady, of course, could not and did not help. I asked for a chair and she pointed to a bench in the mall. I staggered a few steps, fell to my knees and some gentle woman helped me to the bench, as did the little bitty child with her. Have never felt this way before so had no idea what to do.

Had not heard from Cam so knew she was not available. Wondered if the backpackers where I was to stay had a car. Needed to pick up my pictures (Why?), felt better in a few minutes and slowly walked to get the pictures. A nice young man started to wait on me, took one look and went to the back for a chair. His talking stimulated me. I did respond and in a short time, felt just fine and decided to start out for the backpackers.

By now it was dark, cold and pouring down rain. I had five blocks to go...should I? Should I not? No real option, alert, pulse now normal, no pain, no dizziness, and no nausea. Do just fine and stayed just fine. I am recording this only because if it should happen again, it will be on record. I think, "Did I have a TIA or am I anemic?" In retrospect, I believe it was a hypoglycemic reaction due to only a small intake of food all day because I thought I would be meeting Cam for an early dinner.

Saturday was just fine, except I went to see Jodie Foster in "Panic Room" and it was not a good movie. I had meant to see Denzel Washington in something but wandered into Jodie by accident. Will not recommend this movie to Marty (friend in the US). My photos are excellent and the T-shirts are beautiful.

<u>Monday through Friday</u>

Good week and it went flying by 'till Thursday. On Monday...called my own staff meeting for 1:00PM, started at 1:20PM...David was the only one late. I told all three groups that Silvia would be taking a computer class and that a telephone line would be installed in HBCHO's office. Both of the above were gifts from friends in America. The meeting went as well as could be expected. Tuesday...went to HOPE for Africa and finalized another request for funding. Wednesday...had a long talk with the boys from each agency. David may not have spent the money wisely. They are rightly very concerned about ASHYO. But so is he. Even I know we have no money with which to operate and have not had any in the ten months I have been here. This shortfall is already apparent, even with the recent receipt of rand 50,000. They are going to hold an emergency caucus with David ASAP. We shall see.

Thursday...went to Kameelrivier to meet with the home-based care volunteers there. Instead, I visited with the school authorities (teacher and principal) re: child who has been sexually abused by her grandfather. I had to tell them that I had no authority in this matter but would talk to the child if they wished.

Later, I did go with the home-based care volunteer to visit a 62-year-old man with legs covered with deep decubiti on both legs. He had recently been encouraged to seek medical attention from a physician who informed him that the only way to save his life was to amputate the right leg below the knee and quite possibly the left. He refused and stated that he had been treated for years by a traditional healer and would continue on this course rather than lose his leg. He believes that when he was twelve years of age (51 years ago), a curse was placed on him. He did not relate any details of this curse to me but I will visit him again.

Friday...Elizabeth (PCV) called and asked if I wanted to go with them to Kruger over the 4th. I said yes, but when I thought about it, decided I did not really wish to go (I said that??). Will call today and cancel.

Mindy's court date was cancelled and we all must continue to play the waiting game once again...till Aug. 15th. Is this not shades of South Africa in America?

Today is becoming the norm and I am no longer frustrated by the timing of affairs. I was met at the office by a group of young people and accompanied them to Denilton for the kick-off of Provincial Environmental Week. We were to leave at 9:00AM and believe it, we did leave at 9:15AM. That was a first. The program is to start at 10:00AM. It also starts at 10:15AM. HahdeHahHa! Did you believe that? In truth, there are several dancing teams out on the field and each is dancing to their own drum (culture). The program does start at 11:38AM precisely (just like an American). The boys do take off...and on...on and off...and off, off and off. But this time, three of the young women are also with me and they do not leave.

Njongo had told me this morning that we would be making our condolences to the family of a home-based care volunteer whose father passed away last week. We are to do this later this afternoon after we return from Denilton.

Today was the first day that I wore jeans and I could not show up at her home not dressed properly. I raced back home, grabbed my skirt, blouse and shoes and raced back to the office. He told me we would be leaving from Denilton so I carried my extra clothes with me all day. He disappeared at 12:30PM without telling me and at 3:30PM we are finished and I go back to the office, not knowing what is to happen next. I meet up with Olga and she informs me to hurry and change my clothes because Njongo is ready to leave (from where?). I hurriedly change and after he drinks a cup of coffee, the two of us are off. No, no, not that simple...we walk to the small combi rank and have to wait 50 minutes for the next to fill with the necessary quota and then we are off. We arrive at the volunteer's home and give our condolences to her family. We are served tea and cookies and everyone there looks totally exhausted. I should have been doing the serving.

As we are walking back up the road to hitch a ride back to Siyabuswa, the car with the body passes us. I thanked God that we had not stayed any longer. It is a must that the body be delivered by the funeral director to the home before sundown (they cannot be late for this). By the time we arrived back in town, only ten minutes later, the sun had completely set.

Christine is worried because I have come home after dark. It did seem much later than usual. She knew I had gone to Denilton but did not know I was going on to visit a bereaved family. Neither had I. She and Rabie are leaving at ten tonight for another all-night funeral vigil down the street. Thobi has gone to Brenda's next door and after 10:00PM, I will have the house to myself.

I would be insulting the people here if I did not tell a little of the "Programme" I was privileged to attend today. The campaign, sponsored by the Department of Agriculture, Conservation and Environment was titled appropriately, "Support is Action." Supporters included but were not limited to: South African Breweries (corporation name), Shop rite (grocery), Collect-A-Can, Blue Ribbon Bakery, Matjeni Butchery, and at least ten more. As with every campaign, it opened with a group prayer and each speech was followed by an "item" which can be a song, dance, or even a vignette performed by community members. I have yet to attend even one campaign of this nature that has not been so beautiful that tears come to my eyes more than once.

It has been quite a day!

Saturday

Tonight I am writing for me...seems I must take the Jabez Prayer seriously. Do I truly believe that there is a hand there to guide us? How will my world expand? Let me think...it already has just by attending World Environmental Week (day) for the very first time on the very first day of the month on the very first day that I finished reading Bruce Wilkinson's book, "The Prayer of Jabez." I have been given instructions to follow the prayer (by whom?). Will reread the Book of Chronicles and will focus on how this prayer relates to the other chapters. Just by thinking about "how," I tell myself that my mind expanded the second time yesterday, when I went out of town to give my condolences to a volunteer's family, and yet the third today!

Sonta, (11-year-old neighbor child and cousin of Tobie) came by the house. I told her everyone was gone but she proceeded to clean the stoop anyway. I was washing my own clothes and did not want to be bothered. But she kept coming in, saying nothing, and returning to the stoop. Finally, I gave up and asked if she would drink a cup of coffee with me (children here drink coffee). She would and when I asked if she wanted something to eat, her face came alive. I found eggs, peanut butter (no bread) and we each had scrambled eggs AND peanut butter. Amazingly, you can scramble eggs in peanut butter and it is good. Although I knew I had not been pleasant at first, we ended up by having a good laugh because I told her I had never fixed eggs in peanut butter before and she responded, "Oh, GoGo, I have never eaten eggs all beat up before." I was thankful that I had not been allowed to discount her. I am going to see if it works this way with Silvia. I believe it will!

Sunday and Monday

The weekend was exceptionally fine. It is time that I write a little more of my own thoughts. Mindy called and was very unhappy, confused, bewildered and angry. I wished I were home, knowing even as I thought this, that these difficult decisions she must make entirely herself. I know she realizes that I want to help her with all my heart. I awoke quite suddenly, somewhere after 1:00AM, thought for awhile and sat straight up in bed at 2:00AM. I knew that I must call her and must call her now. I would suggest that she call Dorothy (my friend) and Dorothy could act as my proxy. Mindy agreed and, of course, Dorothy will also. On my end, I believe talking with Dorothy will help Mindy and on their end, both will feel better: Mindy, because she needs to talk to someone who can be an objective and knowledgeable supporter and Dorothy, because one always feels good when helping out a friend.

Today, my boundaries continued to expand when I met with a small group of students from the local teachers' college to discuss the prevention of HIV and AIDS. We had met yesterday with only two but today six more arrived. I also sat in on a conference regarding a foundation that might possibly set up a trust fund for ASHYO, HBCHO, or NALEDI. Each had asked me if it was feasible to apply. I told them we must attempt to open any door available. We can only hope that one or more will respond.

Tuesday

More students arrived today. One young lady (29 years old) is not concerned about AIDS but is concerned because she cannot have a baby. She told me that one fallopian tube has been removed and the other seems to be blocked. And in this culture at this point in time, babies give young women status...and also young men. But they will "lose face" as the years pass if they do not marry. But they will lose much more if they do marry and still do not have babies. Then the men will want someone else and are at liberty to take another wife. If the husband cannot afford another wife, he may still take another woman to have his baby. The only one who does not agree to this is the wife. In my mind, this is an extreme dichotomy of values. This particular young lady has a mother-in-law who has been lucky enough (?) to have produced (?) nine children. She cannot understand why any woman cannot have at least the first. Now I realize why the language is so difficult for me to learn. It is my way of withholding comment to questions that I cannot possibly answer in any language.

The group asked me to talk to their class at the college. We shall see.

Yesterday, Leah, from Kameelrivier, brought over a very large wall hanging she had handcrafted with tiny beads. It is exquisite. My horizons are spreading and do believe everyone's would when it finally dawns on each of us that we do not need to question, only to be aware that we do believe. We must stop thinking that God doesn't know us personally, that He doesn't have time for ordinary me, or that our desires are not worth his time. He does, He does, and they are! Once we know and truly feel this knowledge, we no longer feel the need to question. We just go in the direction that seems to be there in front of us. All this takes constant practice and perseverance. We hurt...for ourselves, our loved ones and even strangers in pain, but there is definitely a peace or serenity given to us through the hands of God. We know it!

<u>Wednesday</u>

Left for Pretoria at 10:30AM, traveled with no problems, walked to the Holiday Inn, and had a delightful afternoon. Wandered into the "Curio King," an artsy shop and found a new friend in the owner named Lillian. Walked back to the backpackers, watched a little TV, ate, took a long hot bath and slept well.

Arose very early and took a real cab to the bus depot where a real bus would transport me to Vryburg. This was another first. The bus was large, clean and occupancy was as mandated, no more and no less, and it left exactly at the scheduled time. Jeanne met me at the terminal and we took a local combi to Taung Village and Stein was there to meet us.

Stein's friend, Bonnie, had arranged a ride to Kimberly (2 hours) and the driver dropped us at the door of the Gum Tree Lodge. We were at first given a very cold room with no heater. But then Dawn, who owns the place, moved us over to a nicer room and yes, Jeanne found us a heater. Each of us is looking forward to two full but relaxing days. We later met Daphne and her brother-in-law, the bartender, who told one joke after another. It was fun and reminded me of my brothers and my visits with them.

It was early morning and we were on our way to the Kimberly Diamond Mine. We managed to go underground on a guided tour and it was frightening. The guide said we would be 857 feet underground. I knew we were at least a million. The elevator was a shaft with pulleys of ropes, operated by a man. It was enclosed with some kind of wires (looked like chicken to me, but he told us it was very strong. But that didn't help when you could watch the walls of rock go on down forever to what below must be the eternal abyss. I honestly wanted to go back up before I ever went down. But of course we did reach the bottom of that particular shaft and there was much to see and learn...or rather so much that I will never learn about the industry but at least I forgot about being deep underground.

How impressed I was with the miners...each and every one...they are unsung, very strong, tireless men (no women in this mine). Once again, there were only five of us, allowing us the undivided attention of each person. One young man took me to the nurse's first aid unit and after we arrived (just the two of us through two very long tunnels with only our head lights on), he told me they cannot keep a nurse down here for long. I had the nerve to ask him, did he mean seconds (long enough for me) or as a regular job? He admitted the station was closed and had been for some time.

Janet, the tour manager of our group, gave us a lift to the Museum Park in town and we wandered through the replica of the old town of Kimberly. Appeared and felt very much like our "Old West" tourist attractions. We walked a little of the "new" and back out to the lodge for another relaxing dinner.

I cannot remember the name of the town now, but I also was driven past the hospital and old nursing school site where the very first registration of professional nurses in the world took place. Three wonderful days!!!

<u>Saturday</u>

Oh yes, on our way back up from the mine shaft, we had to go up and down in the lift several times before it became aligned. Those 15 minutes were unbearable and the longest of the full 4 ? hour tour. But no one panicked.

We caught a combi and went back to Taung Village. Stein went to her home while Jeanne and I went shopping and on to her house. Now here I am...have had a call from my friend who is really stressed in Siyabuswa (amazing that she did call). We made plans to meet Wednesday afternoon when I arrive back in Siyabuswa. Now, I will wash my hair and see what the next few days bring. Tonight Jeanne and I had homemade bean soup and a genuine grilled cheese sandwich. We talked for hours as if we were high school kids.

<u>Sunday</u>

Jeanne went to church. Me, I had a very lazy, lazy day. Did manage to scramble eggs and fixed a tasty meal for Jeanne. Will I manage another year? Sure!

HIV/AIDS AWARENESS DAY
PHUDU-IDI HALL
TAUNG VILLAGE

The program reads as above and that is right. Another workshop on AIDS Awareness will be held tomorrow at the local community center. And look, I am officially on the program. The theme is "Love Them Enough to Talk about HIV/AIDS" and is sponsored by LOVE LIFE. LOVE LIFE is a structured and financed volunteer organization composed of all young people who are valiantly fighting to lower the incidence of HIV positive people and also to provide love, treatment, and support to those who have succumbed to the virus. A possible dream but an impossible task. Once again (always), the meeting starts with prayer and music. There are speakers and believe it, I am to be the keynote speaker. What does this mean? It means I am from America, a very long way off and from another area in South Africa which is also a very long way off. If I can travel all this distance, be older than anyone they know, and if HIV has not attacked me, then I must have credibility. They do not realize how much this disease HAS AFFECTED me.

The day remained relaxing and Jeanne's cohorts (teachers) started arriving later this afternoon. They helped the young people plan a surprise birthday party for the father in Jeanne's host family. His children were also celebrating Father's Day (this, of course, was our group's doing).

Monday

The rest of the educational group came to the program that Jeanne had organized. I did give my short talk and it was okay. We had a giant slumber party at Jeanne's. The young people did all the cooking and cleaning and spoiled both of us. Jeanne had worked very hard and had done a fantastic job. They all wanted her to enjoy the evening.

Tuesday

Trish (PCV from the teacher group), and I caught the bus back to Pretoria without a hitch. She is going on a short trip and this ride gave us a chance to visit. It was our first time to spend any one-on-one time just getting to know one another. She is delightful. While at Jeanne's, I also had the chance to discuss serious subjects such as abuse and harassment with the other girls. I am pleased to know all of these young ladies a little better.

I stayed another night at the Holiday Inn. Because I was seated by myself at dinner, this couple at a table nearby invited me to join them. I know not why but I did. They live in South Africa but were born in India and both moved here when in their teens. It was an interesting conversation. I should have written in this booklet on the bus because I thought of many things I wanted to write and now have lost them. Perhaps they will return another day.

Wednesday

Another "Angel" day! This morning on the way to, or rather from breakfast, a taxi driver named "Mandla," who had taken me to the backpackers, saw me on the street, remembered me and asked where I was going? I said, "The bus station that will take me to Siyabuswa but I am not leaving for an hour." He said, "That's all right, I'll be here." I did not leave until 11:30AM and he was right there at the curb waiting. Come to find out, he had lived in Siyabuswa for eight years and knew exactly which bus I should take.

He drove to within a block of the depot, parked and walked with me over to the ticket office. This, of course, was jammed with people. Who was there but Selina who greeted me and handed me a ticket. Mandla was quite concerned about me until she came with the ticket. Selina is from Siyabuswa and today had ridden on this round trip to make sure I was there. It remains unknown what she would have done if I had not been.

It is quite a process to obtain a ticket in the townships or villages. Each day, the bus tickets are sold individually by a group of women and not by the company itself. One can buy the ticket from any of the women and Selina has taken it upon herself to be my private ticket provider. I did not know this until Thobi explained to me, but it seems the sequence goes something like the following: A person buys the ticket from whomever, wherever (on the street), and for whenever (day), shows the ticket to the driver, finds a seat, and just before arriving in Pretoria, everyone turns in his/her ticket to one of the women from Siyabuswa who accompanies the busload to and from for that particular trip. The tickets are sold for very little profit but it is a profit and an innovative way to have at least a little income. Very convenient for people like me and bet more people would ride the bus in the US if they had such individual attention.

To continue: the taxi driver left and Selina took me over to where I was to wait. When the bus came, she made sure I was on it and had a seat (there are always people who must ride crowded in the aisle). I was sure this was another Jabez Prayer incident or one of many incidents which had started all the way back to Friday and did not end until after the boys here welcomed me back.

No, actually, these incidents started back on Wednesday and must include meeting: 1) Lillian at the Curio King; 2) Joanna, the waitress who brought me a double portion of cheesecake; 3) taxi driver on time at 5:30AM to take me to a different bus station; 4) young student on bus, who has lived in SA all her life, aand told me that Cape Town is the most beautiful city in the world to take visitors (she had worked on cruise ships the world over); 5) Jeanne who was right there to greet me in a very busy combi rank when I arrive; 6) the couple who provided us with transportation in their own private car to Kimberly; 7) the owner who changed our cold room to a warm room and cooked supper for only us; 9) the tour guide who provided us with a change of clothes to descend down into the mine; 10) Janet who gave us a ride to the Museum and the Big Hole; 11) Apryl, Sarah, and Jeanne who provided American conversation Saturday night; 12) many, many people at the AIDS Awareness Day which was a total success with more 200 people attending; 13) the girls for Jeanne's slumber party and getting to know them better; 14) Trish who sat with me and kept me company on the long trip back to Pretoria (7 hours), even though her boyfriend was with her; 15) the couple from India (Miranda would love how they expedited our meal); 16) Mandla, who delivered me straight to Selina; 17) Selina who gave me my ticket, took me to the bus stop, made sure I got on and had a seat; and 18) both the boys at the office and my family who all were sincerely glad to see me. I, too, was sincerely happy to see all of them.

Isn't this a wonderful way to write a journal? I have seven letters to read, a new book to start and candy to munch on. I must remember this when I feel down at any time this week. And oh, yes, I purchased beautiful cards to send to people at home.

Thursday

Good day...went with Cam to Kameelrivier. We had a short but productive (?) meeting with the home-based care volunteers there. Later she drove us to Marble Hall for lunch and the orange groves were beyond description. Hundreds of acres of trees loaded with oranges ready to be picked. The sky was cloudless and a very deep blue, the trees are green and orange, and although the town is a mass of people, out in the orchards no one is visible for as far as the eyes can see. Unbelievably peaceful. But Freddy has a bad cold and I cannot give him any cold tablets without causing problems.

Friday and Saturday

Feel good. I am wrapping packages to ship home. But I almost lost it twice today. First, because Silvia seems to be (no, is) getting the run-around from her computer class instructor, and then David and the telephone company. This means me, because both the class and the telephone were my projects and paid for by donations from friends back home. So much for good ideas. I tell both that we will work out the kinks with time (after all, that is the SA way).

Saturday

A pleasant day at home and Thobi had received high marks on her school report (card). In my opinion, average is excellent because she does all her classes in three different languages, Ndebele, Afrikaans, and English. She also is fluent in Zulu and there may be others. No wonder some of the words are skewed and spelled wrong. I do think our working together is helping her and I know it is me.

Sunday

Today was another new and cultural experience. Christine belongs to a group entitled, "Women's Bereavement Society." I am certain that in one way or another, this type of unity must be worldwide. However, here in Siyabuswa, it is a small cluster of women (maybe 30) who have very little, if any, funds with which to bury members of their families. They meet once a month on Sunday afternoons with the primary purpose to collect fees to allay future funeral costs (informal insurance perhaps).

Today, twelve women met here in Christine's home. Each was dressed in a black skirt and an emerald green silk jacket/blouse, actually a uniform (why?). No, she is not to wear this for her burial. As each lady arrived, Christine served her a cold drink, tea or coffee, and cookies.

The meeting opened at 2:00PM (first one I have been to that started on time). Prayers were offered and songs were sung for some time. As always, when I hear this type of singing and joyousness, I am overwhelmed and wish that every household the world over could share these moments. They met seriously for a little over an hour. Money shuffled back and forth, forth and back, and back and forth, over and over. Everyone was confused and I finally decided that each put in money, change was put aside, and then the money was given back to each lady and she was then able to pay the exact amount expected. Sound mixed up? You bet it was. Three people counted and came up with three different totals. But they ended up with what they deemed correct and it's for a good cause and I am only a guest. Right? I could not understand the conversation but did get the gist of their burial insurance plan. When a family member dies, funding for the funeral is sought from this Society. The funding does not cover the total cost but does allow the family to provide food and transport for those grieving. And of course, I was the "photo" lady. Christine served more refreshments and the meeting closed with more prayer and music.

Tuesday

Spent most of the day in and out of HOPE's computer. Believe me, it feels as if I am literally inside the machine. It certainly is not inside me, or at least not my brain. It was a SA day, but now since I cannot beat them, have joined them (the days?). David and I were to meet at 8:30AM and go to Groblestal to pay the deposit on the telephone line to be installed in his office. I arrive as usual at 8:00AM, fix myself a cup of coffee with the hidden cream and start to work on my own language study. David shows at 9:15AM. We are to go by combi and soon. We race to the combi stand and we wait until 11:30AM for the next combi to leave. So much for "soon"! We are both bored, but he spends his time on and off the phone to Nelspruitt and does stay put on the combi. We do ride to Groblestahl. We find the phone company, offer a sizeable down payment and finally have what we think is the correct order to get a line placed. We have a delightful lunch _and_ hitchhike back to Siyabuswa. Through all of this, I was patient and could not believe this person was _me_. I am finding, often these days, that I am regretting that patience was not instilled in me way back when...do believe lots of things or events would have taken a different course...but doesn't everyone wish this?

Saturday

Now get this...another Skidney/space cadet (old nicknames) start, but also must be that I am not getting senile. How can I be if this is how I was even as a kid? Waited till 9:00PM last night to pack for Pretoria. For the first time, I had not received the bus ticket early. Because of this, I knew I had to be at the bus stop very early so I set the clock for around 5:00AM. Woke up, glanced at the clock, had already been up to the bathroom so saw it as ten minutes after five. Not wanting the alarm to wake the others, I turned it off, took a bath (ahhah) last night so only took enough water to wash my face and brush my teeth, turned off the heater, made bed, started to put lotion on and glanced at the clock. It is **twenty** minutes **until** 3:00AM. Now I have 3 hours to spend all dressed up and nowhere to go...awake and freezing...go back to bed...get warm but cannot sleep...read...dose off...read...dose off. Finally, it is 4:30AM and I do have another cup of hot coffee and start all over. Now it moves from old Skidney days to new SA Skidney days. The sky appears light through the window, but not after I leave the house. It is very dark (no house lights OR street lights.) I am all alone and this is very odd because usually the road is filled with children. Although I know exactly where I am going, I do want to miss all the animals and their various means of identification. The roosters are crowing, goats are bleating, cows are mooing, (but where?) and I am alone.

I walk as fast as possible to the complex and there are a few people wandering about. Is this better? I had forgotten to give Selena her rand 23 for the bus ticket and now I am at the bus stop. A fire is going a little way down the block and 3-4 people are huddled around. While I am trying to decide if I should intrude, another Christine comes up and asks for the ticket fare. She (I know her from before) can be quite assertive and has me intimidated big-time. I give it to her and she tries to explain to me that Selina has no money and that she (Christine) gave her the ticket to give to me. Selina, of course, is nowhere to be seen. What do I do? Give her the money...what else? Now it all is up hill or rather downhill because Martha (friend) asks if she can ride with me. By now, I've been on the bus many times and everyone aboard makes sure the driver stops at the right place to let me off.

I walk my usual path, go to the bathroom in the Holiday Inn, have a cup of cappuccino with whipping cream, and take a regular taxi to the backpackers. Other PCVs are there and they have decided to move to a motel. We do. They leave; no, we have lunch first. I go to the mall. Do my thing, plan on taking wine back but the store has closed at three and I don't get there until 3:15PM. Now I am here on the bed...relaxed and will go to a French restaurant tonight. Am I living right or what? Oh yes, I went shopping for warm gloves, purse, belt, took in my film and bought more <u>books</u>.

<u>Wednesday</u>

Have many things to write tonight. Will probably just get started! But first things first! Have been praying the Jabez prayer for almost three weeks and do feel "right" inside myself." Much has happened. Will write as I remember and then will try once more to keep up as time passes and incidents take place. AHA!

1. Do know I am continuing to meet people and am making a concerted effort to reach out directly to the persons I meet. A niece (?) was here visiting my family; she stayed a week. Christine instructed me to lock my door because we might not be able to trust her friends (the niece's). But! I have worn my mother's ring every day on my right hand. Phindewe, (niece) held this gold ring up and asked if it belonged to me. I thought it was an earring and said no. Thobi was behind me and said, "Yes, it is, Yes, it is," and pointed to my empty hand. It had fallen off in the dishwater and Phinde had found it. She could have taken it; it could have gone down the drain with the bath water and on and on. But it did not!

2. Caught a taxi to the taxi rank in Pretoria and the man who picked me up recognized me and screams, "Gogo, take my cab!" He takes me to the Siyabuswa combi and I ask how he knows me and he is happy to say, "I

know you very well." My trip back takes 2 hours and 20 minutes (a record) from taxi rank in Pretoria to my door at home in Siyabuswa, even waiting (no wait this time) for two combis. Is it good that the guys at Pretoria combi rank recognize me?

3. Met with the Judicial Youth Court System one day last week. This is a group out of Pretoria and one that I did not know even existed. On the same day, also had a one-on-one meeting with Mildred, the Head of Social Services. With both, I was able to broach the subject of peer support groups.

4. Christine told me that Rabie missed me...cannot quite believe this little tidbit but she was nice to say it and it was nice to hear.

Enough! Our PCV group had a wonderful trip and meeting...lots of good vibes back and forth for everyone. Saturday night we went out to eat at a Chinese restaurant and Sunday was a lazy day. Several of us walked to the Bird Sanctuary and later returned to Cam's for a true gourmet meal. I have never been to a dinner party (not even a wedding or celebration) where so much fancy food was served. Excellent and expensive wines with each course, several types of nuts, before and after the meal, many different imported cheeses, home-prepared (by Ed) sushi, seafood, pork, beef and chicken, salads, fresh veggies, pastas and more. All this was followed by a rich and creamy chocolate fondue with an assortment of berries, cheesecake, and dark chocolate cake. Cam must have been in her kitchen for hour upon hour because every single item was developed from scratch. There were ten of us present and we each knew that not only did she exert an enormous amount of time and energy but this repast must have cost her a fortune. Monday we had our meeting and she fed us once again. We did go to the French restaurant and it was anticlimactic after the meal she had prepared. Cam took the occasion of her dinner party to tell us she will be leaving for Boswana shortly. I will sorely miss her. Tuesday we sat like stuffed guinea hens through another short meeting. We all made the trip back to our respective sites without incident. My cousin Gary has died. It is hard for me to realize this. He died after only two weeks from a diagnosis of esophageal cancer with metastasis to the liver. Because I am not home and cannot attend his funeral, his passing does not seem real as yet. I remember many years ago when my own father died, I was again away and it was a very long time before I could go home and not expect to see him. Gary was one of the kindest and most sensitive men I have ever known.

JULY 4, 2002!

Thursday

Ice cream cones for everyone! Fun-Fun-Fun. Did I not ask to be "expanded"? Today, I met with the full Municipal Council but after an hour, we were asked to leave. I think we were not supposed to be there at all! Later in the afternoon, one of the young women, who had been to see me a couple of months ago and who had gone for HIV testing, returned. It was difficult for her but she told me that the test was positive. She wishes counseling. This also was not easy for either her or me because of the language barrier. I am praying and knowing that God will put the right words in my mouth. Guess He did because she is coming back tomorrow with her partner and wants me to talk with him. Now I do have to find the exact right words.

Chapter Seventeen

"Very seldom when hanging a picture can we produce an even mounting without stepping away to see its relationship to the rest of the room.

There is a great deal to be gotten from our emotions, but when possessed by such things we are often blinded and make or seek excuses (sometimes pointing the finger in order to blame). Such justice does not change that that has happened. Seeking such things only reveals an ego who's fixer is hard at work to mend an illusion...be wary of the mind. It is tricky...simply go back to the breath and relax...Let Go... It's that easy!

(Author Unknown)

JULY

July 5, 2002

Exactly one year ago, the PCVs arrived in Pretoria. It has been the longest year in my life...even longer than waiting out the last month of a pregnancy. But tonight I will celebrate that this past year has given me an armory of memories. I have survived and will complete another year. I will not wish my life away.

Today was very busy. The young lady who was to come back with her partner did not come back, nor did I expect her. I will try to find her in a few days when no one realizes why I am trying to find her.

I went with Nomsa (HBCHO volunteer) to an area in which there is an unofficial home-based care group. We delivered food parcels from NALEDI to four families. Now I know enough of the people within these small groups to ask, "Where is Linda?" I am told she resigned because she was a gossip! She resigned? Seems she had told one of the other girls that this girl's husband-to-be, who is the father of her son, is running around with another woman. Another girl told her where she should not talk (in no uncertain terms) about this, so she resigned on the spot. The man in question is very likely running around and normally, I would think that he would be deep trouble. But I have found that it really doesn't work that way here. We shall see what the outcome will be. I could be in the middle of a situation but will take the "fifth". I feel privileged that many trust me with secrets, but am quick to tell everyone that in no way will I become actively involved in their intrigues. TOO OLD! Sound like the same stories 10th or 11th chapter? Yes!

Back at the office, the men from TelKom have arrived to install the telephone lines. One man is high up on the pole when it topples with him still connected by a waist belt. Of course, he is seriously injured and everyone is screaming, screaming, and running around in circles and unable to look at him. I am sure they thought him dead and did not want to see. He is not dead and they listen to me when I say to call the doctor (remember, the clinic is within twenty steps). They do not listen to me when I say "Do not move him." It seems everyone wants to test every accessible joint. The doctor arrives within seconds and calls the ambulance which does not arrive in seconds. He also tells them not to move the injured man and this gives everyone a reason to start again with the screaming and running around. He is alert by now and moves all his extremities by himself but the doctor tells him that there is probably internal bleeding and therefore, he must remain quiet and be transported to the hospital. Come to find out, the telephone pole is almost completely rotted through in several areas. I think it is a miracle that the poor man was not killed.

I have insisted on and even paid for, from funds received from the United States, both the computer training for Silvia and the telephone lines. Both have been jinxed. Tell myself that perhaps I should keep my mouth shut and not make further costly recommendations.

On the way home, I stopped by the market and bought greasy, oily gopher guts (no, really achaar) for the family and me. Achaar is a type of relish made from mango, spices, and fish oil and I have become addicted to this treat. It is especially good if made fresh but also very tasty when made commercially and it was my contribution for the first year's anniversary dinner. Believe it! Christine bought an enormous avocado. AND I am going to drink Sprite, eat achaar and avocado, read a letter, and go to bed with a secret turtle and a Snickers. What more can one ask? Is this not the healthiest diet of all time? I am already celebrating my birthday. I have written everyone back home NOT to forget!

Sunday

Ice cream day!

Monday

Not a good day...felt down...bored...angry...sad and all the rough feelings. These down, negative feelings did pass and the up, positive feelings started to happen.

Negative

1. Jumped David about using my phone
2. Very cold
3. Cream gone (even from the secret cache)
4. Confused...did not understand where I was needed or wanted
5. Where, oh, where is Rebecca? (HIV-positive)
6. Lonesome
7. Worried about the financial status of ASHYO
8. Where is my friend who was wishing suicide? Is she still?

Positive

1. Silvia learning to do data entry
2. Rebecca met me on the walk to Hendrik's and brought people to meet me
3. Teacher came and wants to use me in her classroom
4. Requested by councilmen to attend several community meetings

Tuesday and Wednesday

Attended a workshop on the role of municipalities in fighting HIV and AIDS. The councilmen want to do everything they think ASHYO and HBCHO are doing! To make any progress though, many more volunteers are needed. David must realize he is not a one-man show and cannot be and do all things without the help of more community members. Doubt he ever will and although his heart is bigger than the township, he actually presents obstacles that may be slowing progress. Perhaps the new PCV can make a more positive impression on him and will assist him in changing his own behaviors.

Upside...Thobi is home! Am finally realizing what a positive influence this little girl has on all of us in this house. Know that is why both Christine and I are more chipper, as is Rabie.

Thursday

The boys from the "Mountain" are back! Rabie came and got me very early in the morning and told me in which house I would find them. I found my way a few blocks over and a young lady came and said, "Sydney, come with me." She was able to get us in front of the crowd already gathered, and I took some very good "photos." The young men were wearing only cloth briefs and their entire bodies were oiled to a glossy sheen. Each had his hair completely shaved off so guess the oil keeps them a little warm. I was freezing and dressed in warm clothes. All made it back. But, oh, so very young! And PROUD! The mothers and gogos were dressed in full-beaded outfits and singing loudly. Everyone, including the older men in their special clothing, was beautiful. Still odd...but beautiful.

David was not in good shape when he finally came in about 10:00AM but know he had been up all night and the excitement and celebrations of these young men are to last for many days, perhaps weeks. The rest of the day did go by. The days seem to drag but the weeks fly by. Tomorrow is Friday again. I am receiving birthday cards every day and feel pretty good. Maybe a little sad, like I do at Christmas, but come on, I will be 68 years old on Sunday. 90% of me is relieved to be so healthy at this age and 10 % of me is sad because my life is on the bumpy down-the-hill side!

Friday

Tonight, the brie in this neighborhood that is celebrating the return of the boys, is in full swing and the whooping is taking place right outside my window. Rabie has told (ordered) me to take pictures and then tells me that I should not pass them around on the street. He gives these instructions to me even though he thinks the whole idea is crazy and he has no family involved. Once again, Rabie about had me in tears but David came by (out of the blue) and I think straightened us out. He had to practically beg Rabie to apologize for talking so strictly to me. Rabie said I had misunderstood him and this is probably true.

Upside to this day: Rebecca did come back. We have had three sessions now and she has told her partner and her friend her status. She has also seen the counselor at the local health department. At least on the most important issues she understood me. The mix-up with the telephone line was also straightened out (can you straighten a collapsed pole?). Hopefully, these are all the things that can be fixed for tonight.

Saturday

Okay...everyone including Rabie has redeemed themselves. The boys from the "Mountain" continued their celebration today...starting in the early AM and going on all day in first one place and then another. They must be exhausted. But my perceptions have changed. They were very somber and not playful yesterday. Today, each gave a short testimony of which I understood very little but was still impressed with their sincerity. The older men sat-sat-sat-all day.

Mothers came later and also sat-sat-sat for the rest of the day. Both the young men and their families were waited on by friends. Christine went with me...she as a neighbor and me as the guest of David; this meant, we were also waited upon. The boys chanted and danced or pranced, changed clothes, chanted and danced or pranced every minute for several hours. It was all very colorful as were the parents and grandparents.

The host boy received many gifts, almost one of everything in a shop, and more than one of most...even a complete bedroom set (furniture). And as always at a celebration, the food started coming and was served to each of us. Last night, they killed the cow that had been tied to the tree for days and today, the brie was held. Have to say...once again I was overwhelmed with the ceremonial grace of the people who took part. I still do not know all the people by name but they know me and it makes me much less stressed. I truly am enjoying myself more each time I attend a significant celebration. Of course, they want "photos," but today Vusi has agreed to hop here and there and "shoot." He will be my "cameraman" from now on.

Sunday

My birthday is tomorrow and what does 68 mean? Not much if it's you that is that old! Or maybe it means an awfully lot. Mallory, my granddaughter will turn16 tomorrow and when I look back and reminisce, a lot also happened to me during that year. Received my driver's license, fell in love for the first time (but not he with me), moved to Idaho, knew I had (lost?) best friends and made new ones, left a small town (pop. 400) small class (12) went to a city (pop.50,000) and large class (450), left a big house and moved into a small but new house. Now it is more than fifty years later and I am living back fifty years in time, on another continent, with a new family, and experiencing a completely new (very old) culture. But these extreme changes were my calls to make and I made the decisions all by myself.

Today was a great day. Christine brought tea as usual but a birthday hug from both she and Thobi came with it. I fixed eggs for breakfast (rare), walked to church, Juan (6 yrs.) had drawn a picture for me and the rest of his family presented me with a SA painting. Arrived back home for a fried chicken dinner (we have chicken often but it is always boiled). John, David and Mindy called and I talked with Cherie, Sangita, Devan, Divia and Mallory. Sue will call any minute. Cake and cold drinks were a surprise from family and neighbors here. Can you believe this? I talked with eighteen different people per phone and received many, many cards and gifts from home.

JULY 14, 2002

All my birthdays have been great but this one in South Africa and as a vintage lady (almost), was overwhelming. Yesterday (actually, Divia) all last week was nice. But today...today was unbelievable. I went to Hope from

9:30AM to 11:30AM and David went with me (not usual). By 11:30AM he was beside himself with excitement and we just had to race (quite literally) back to the office (why?). Across the gate, a huge birthday sign was hung and everyone was already running around. Tables were set up and in the center of the largest was a huge cake with my name. They had thought of all the things that would make me feel at home and this included: peanuts, corn curls, candy, cold drinks, and of course, champagne (sparkling grape juice). There were presents and more presents. Everyone was there except Maggie who was out of town. Njongo gave a speech and I know that even the boys had tears in their eyes because of the beauty of the occasion. Vusi took pictures. Later, beer and amaretto (where in the world did they obtain this?) was served. This meant we must dance and dance we did (even me). By this time everyone in the complex could hear the noise and wandered onto the grounds. The party lasted all afternoon and ended up almost as big as one of their celebrations. Really cannot describe how I felt, but sad that I had had such misgivings for so long about these young people. Anna carried my gifts home in a box on her HEAD!

<u>Wednesday</u>

Today was another Angel Day. Went to the office and the very first thing, Freddy and I had a long, intense talk. I am concerned about ASHYO and David. So is he. David, as I have recognized has a heart that feels for absolutely everyone and a brain that thinks of much too much to do. This, of course, is wonderful for the most part but does not allow any credit to the others. They, in turn, have just as big hearts and just as active brains.

David comes in at 9:45AM, antsy, constantly on the move and then I catch on. He wants me to go to HOPE to insert some names and addresses (from?) a private business supposedly run by thirty poor people. I thought it odd because only three actual names were to be added to the list that he has, but I wasn't doing anything so I went. And then he wants me to make a copy for the hair salon. Come to find out, this is the business and he is the leader (to-be). The list is not computer-generated and must be entered. I asked him if this was one of his private deals and he said, "Yes, yes, another of mine." I did not, of course, know of any of his private businesses and told him I was sure the computer we were using should not be used for his businesses. But in the end, I said okay. But when he asked for fifty copies, I finally balked and did not agree. By this time, we had arrived (what were we there for?). He said, "Okay, fine, I will do it myself." Now I knew why he had wanted me to go: we were there and he couldn't back down but of course, he did not know word processing. Once again, he has dug himself a hole. And once again, he digs himself out. The Director of HOPE was there and lets us use the computer and I do David's business for him (Sydney, think of the poor people)

I did come out ahead, because Pastor Hendrik will help us (Stein, Jeanne and me) go to Mozambique later this year. Finally finished and was about to leave when Lester came in and asked if I would have tea with them (David long gone by now). They had been so nice that I said yes and come to find out it was lunch at Hendrik's house with Mike and Mary Thomas, missionaries from the United Kingdom. We visited for almost three hours conversing only in English. They are about my age, have lived in Tampa, FL and Modesto, CA, have a daughter named Susan and a son-in-law named David. When they are at home in England, they live close to Bristow! We became instant friends.

Thursday

Isn't it odd? I am becoming at home here and it seems that this means I have less to write. My life is expanding, but more inside me than out. God has not spoken to me in a voice but I'm hearing him within me someway and somehow.

Rebecca came back today and we are becoming friends. She is HIV-positive and if, through this friendship, I can help her deal with this treacherous diagnosis, I will. She took me this afternoon to meet her friends. All gave me gifts, a birthday gift from Rebecca, but just "goodness gifts" from the others. They are very poor. I just cannot imagine living day in and day out in such circumstances and still have such love show in their eyes.

Her close friend had a terrible toothache...she had her jaw tied up like in my childhood days (no pain medicine here) (not for her). She was in a very dark, cold kitchen. Fire had gone out in the wood burning stove. She was lying on a mat on the floor, asleep (eyes closed) when we arrived. Another friend offered me a broken straight-backed chair and then she had to sit on the floor. Rebecca sat on another broken chair and these were the only visible furniture. We talked; that is, they did; I know not what language, and then the lady with the toothache sat up and joined in with them. Right before my eyes, she changed from crone to beautiful. She has only a few teeth, appears much older than her professed fifty years, very gnarled, wrinkled, and tired, bone-weary. But her eyes sparkled and love came from within her and reached to all of us. I was mesmerized.

I left and Rebecca walked part-way home with me, thanking me profusely for stopping in with her. I was in awe of all of them and will go back. What does this mean? I do not know. But perhaps it is God's way to tell me that we do not have to know all, do all, but maybe we just have to "be all" there.

Friday and Saturday

Good Day! Family has gone...not good for them because it is another funeral to attend, but I have the house to myself and love it. Had a deli pizza with cheese and slept well. Washed and cleaned Saturday morning and the family arrived back about 2:00PM. All are exhausted but Rabie is the only one to rest. Christine cooked and did all her work and Thobi did all her playing.

I did go back to see how Rebecca's friend was feeling and I think she was much better. Know she looked twenty years younger. Does not understand English so probably won't go back unless Rebecca is with me.

Sunday

To church and the young people from Holland are working on the new church. Do believe I have been here now long enough that the thought went through my mind: the SA youth are very much attracted to the youth of Holland, regardless of gender.

But slow! It is 5:00PM and David comes by to tell me that we go to Pretoria tomorrow AM and will stay with Cam (he called her and invited us). We will ride with her to the training on Tuesday. How does he do this? How does he get away with it? In the United States, he would be the most charismatic of politicians.

Will admit, travel is much easier with someone, even David. Cam, as always, was a grand hostess and took us to a Portuguese restaurant. Tomorrow, Freddie, the PC driver, will take us to the training site where the newly-arrived PCVs are.

Tuesday

Met the new PCVs today and after a slow start, the meeting went very well. A young lady (27 years old) named Jessie will be shadowing with me. Tonight, I am very disappointed because there are several older people in the new group and I was hoping to have one of them shadow me. My hope was that the person who shadowed would be coming to my area and we would be company and support for each other. You would think by now that I would have learned to give up this second guessing. Jessie tells me there are only two people learning Ndebele and she will probably, if one comes, be the one. I liked her very much but she may find herself in a more difficult and precarious situation than I did. I doubt she will, or even, want to keep these young handsome men in control. But I have become a whiz at attitude adjustments and will hope for the best.

Wednesday

Tonight was an unbelievable "Angel in the wings night." I received a letter from Kirby. It has been 51 years since we went to school together! That was amazing enough but he told me he is now working in Sacramento, CA for Gyla who was one of my new best friends when I moved from Royal, IA to Boise, ID. Had to call Susie (daughter) on this one!

Dear Sydney,

By my nearest calculations, it's been about 51 years since I last had any contact with you. It's been much too long a time, but here I am finally writing to you about one of the most outrageous coincidences that you can imagine. I retired a few years ago and, like so many other people, I got bored very quickly so I took what was supposed to be a part-time job scoring standardized school tests in Sacramento. After I returned from attending the 50-year reunion in Royal, my longtime supervisor asked me where I had gone on my vacation. I said that I'd gone to Royal, Iowa. She said, "Royal, My best friend at Boise High School was from Royal, Iowa." I've worked under Gyla for the past three years and suddenly we've found that we have a mutual friend in you. You're going to hear from her shortly. I might add that she is one of the most respected, caring and loyal persons that I have ever met.

Best regards after a half a century.

(Excerpt from letter)

Is this not the most extraordinary happenstance?

Thursday

    Do believe something is wrong with me. So happy last night and early this morning, but then I became depressed for <u>no</u> discernible reason. Short with people at work and exhausted tonight. Why? Started at10:00AM this morning. Will see how long this mood lasts.

Friday

    Much better day...did not feel upbeat until last night with Thobi. The mood lasted approximately eight hours. And then forgot that I was feeling down. Dorothy W. called and she is trying very hard to come over to see me and now I am realizing every single day that just talking a problem over can provide an answer. Dorothy was one of the solutions last night but for me, sometimes I am my only confidante. I must accept that I am also a huge support to myself and if I expect others to take my advice, then I must be willing to advise myself.

    Today I asked Silvia how she would feel if in my position. She answered so insightfully that I was impressed and am to wonder if she is the ANGEL in my wings here on earth. Tonight will work in my room and get ready for Jessie. Whatever happens, this also will work out or pass, whichever comes first?

Saturday

    Beautiful cultural day! But first, the Jabez Prayer: enlarge my territory. Today did just that. Leave things alone and today did that, too. Jessie isn't coming until Monday instead of today as first planned. Once again I wasted time worrying.

    Okay. All about today. Two weeks ago Anna invited me to what I first thought was a birthday party for her granddaughter's 21st year celebration. Wrong. Then I thought it was a send-off party for the girls leaving for the traditional school. Wrong again...and right...at the same time. It was a celebration to send the girls off only...they had left last Wednesday! They will not be seen by us for several weeks. The girls who went last time were the ones all decked out today with the bead work. They danced and received the presents but this was all a testimony to their younger sisters, cousins and friends slowly moving toward womanhood.

    Anna had invited Christine, but last night Christine told me that she must help her friend Leah cook for the boys (they are still celebrating). I beg Thobi to go with me. We (I) went to Anna's house to check on the proper time and to get her granddaughter's name (not the one almost 21 years) who has left. I do know that she speaks no English but I understand the time as 1:00PM sharp (they all love this word but do not know its meaning).

    Thobi is anxious to go and we arrive a little before one. Would have been even earlier but Thobi doesn't know where to go either (never admit when you're nine years old that you "don't know"). Luckily, women outgrow this, don't they? Anyway, there are at least twelve older gogos and each is sitting on a mat against the wall of an empty living room. No young people are in sight as yet and this makes Thobi and her friend anxious to leave. I know it won't start on time and am not surprised that little is happening.

Oh, but it is! The young ladies are all over the back yard and have not yet donned their outfits so are naked from the waist up. The men (fathers and older) are sitting outside in the front of the house. The women in the 30-40 year age group are working. Thobi and her friend last 20 minutes and are ready to leave. They do. I sit with the gogos.

Soft porridge doused with sugar is served. Knowing much more food is coming, I eat only a little (also had had a little flour (paste) porridge for breakfast.) Wrong! We sat...did not eat again. We sat, did not eat again. 2:00PM comes but Anna has not. I have taken pictures of the girls...sat...did not eat...and finally, my bladder is the only thing talking that I can understand. Finally ask where and find that the only toilet is outside. This is fine except it is right in the middle of many, many of the younger men. The door will not close and I must hold the door with one hand and hope that I do not wet my skirt. Do handle the situation only to find that one of women was holding the door for me.

Back to sitting and by now the room is filled with 50-60 older women. I am supposed to sit on the floor with my legs straight in front ...and the others do for hours on end. I cannot. They offer me a chair because I am fidgety (my tail bone and left hip have started talking to each other and in my language). I decline the chair because I do not want to be head and shoulders over the others. Continue to sit...no food...no Anna. 3:30PM comes and by now there are 90-plus women in the house. Hark, a tent has been set up outside and out we all move. No one speaks English but they make sure I have a place and by now, there are hundreds of people all up and down the street.

It is 4:00PM and here comes Anna and now the festivities can really begin. The girls are covered in beads from the waist down and large beaded necklaces are around their throats. They start to dance and to receive the presents. The beads are more ornate today because these are fully women, although many are still quite young...beautiful and spectacular.

Soft porridge is again offered but I decline. I am offered a chair at least once every minute but continue to decline and to fidget, even though now I am allowed to bend my legs. The women, who have been cooking all day out in back, start serving the pap and beef. We eat and I am thinking that Siyabuswa is a long way from home. It is Saturday night, the sun is going down because it is almost 6:00PM., and people party thousands of miles away in very much the same way. I am in this reverie about America when Anna comes and says, "It is time to go; you must be safe." Her friends, four young men, strangers to me, give me a ride home. Am I not trusting? And here I am, safe, sound and comfortable.

Now what I have learned: you can go on a tour and see a cultural ritual performed for an hour or two and it is a beautiful show, but sitting in the midst of the players for a long time, one obtains quite different perceptions. Take these Ndebele girls and women: the young girls wear little aprons but as they grow, so does the apron. And after this initiation into womanhood, her dress will change completely. Today, when I arrived, the young women had on very short beaded aprons/skirts, no tops and just necklaces. By the time they were performing, they had long aprons and were covered in blue, pink, and white beads...legs, arms, torso and neck.

For me, it was a long day because I could not understand the gossip and joke conversations. If these women can sit still, so can I (cannot). But I was so very proud to be accepted and not once did I feel unwanted or out of place. The cacophony of sounds I am becoming accustomed to and today it did not overwhelm me. Instead I enjoyed the utter solemnity of the occasion and the beauty shining out of these people's eyes. ZeZe (the name of the young lady) is away at school knowing she is loved and soon to be considered a woman in the eyes of her people.

<u>Sunday</u>

"Oh, that you would bless me indeed...and enlarge my territory"

1 .I was offered communion for the first time since coming to SA. The service was done exactly as it is in Springfield, IL at the Methodist Church.

2. Visited the parents of a young man who committed suicide out in the lonely veldt last week. Everyone who attended church today went and offered prayers, songs and condolences to his parents.

3. His mother asked if she could meet with me privately

4. Security guard from the government buildings that I pass walking to and from church thanked me for listening to him several weeks ago. He has now seen the doctor and is taking medicine for his high blood pressure. The doctor told him he also has gallstones (the pain that took him to the doctor in the first place). He asked me many questions about "stress". Am not quite sure if this was not a word he had heard of for the first time from the doctor.

5. A friend of Christine's came by (I had not seen her for some time) and she is quite concerned about her 15-year-old daughter (normal teenager in my opinion).

GO OUT AND FACE THE DAY! WE MUST ALL BE DEFENSIVE! WHY MUST WE?

I asked Silvia to explain to me why and how, with the fast rise of worldwide communication and technology, many of the old traditions and rites continue. She told me: "Here in South Africa everyone must be defensive." I asked her to explain and I think this is what she told me.

Young: defend that they have little experience but have much to offer

Young adults: defend that they are learning from experience and should not need to be defensive

Middle-aged adults: defend that they have much knowledge, much experience and can and should still keep up with the young

Older adults: defend that they are not crazy but instead no longer care to keep up the pace of the young adult

Aged: defend the right to be calm, serene, happy and thankful that the young do take the time to listen and respect practices of forefathers

If I understood her and I think I did, my response was that in America we also have these defenses throughout the age groups and probably for the same reasons.

<u>Monday</u>
First day for Jessie to shadow and a waiting day for both of us. She was finally able to get here about 2:30PM. We met the guys and left the office. David had not come in. This did not bode well for a positive first impression of him to Jessie. We, of course, heard at least five different reasons/excuses. We went on to the house and here, she was greeted enthusiastically. Thobi was delightful and fun, as was Jessie. Everyone hit it off well, and Rabie was quite the gentleman. Jessie is very perceptive, extremely intelligent and beautiful. She is also very nice, friendly, respectful and fun. I think we will work well together. Even during these first few hours, I have the impression that she is what ASHYO needs.

<u>Tuesday</u>
The staff meeting this morning went well. David did a good job. We spent the afternoon at HOPE and Jessie was able to access e-mail. She and I went to the restaurant to eat, and being the only ones there, we were waited on royally.

DOROTHY IS COMING OCT. 11TH.

<u>Wednesday</u>
Cam came from the PC office to meet with Njongo. He did a nice job explaining HBCHO's goals and because of him, I received permission to work more with this group. She took Jessie and me in tow and we visited Kameelrivier and then went to Marble Hall for lunch. We returned to the office and all was just fine.
Then events were put in motion that threw us into a completely different set of actions and happenings than anyone could have foreseen. That's wrong. I should have known! I have been here a year now and have become spoiled with the attention and protection. Acted foolishly and let my guard down at Jessie's expense. But to start at the beginning: Jessie had at first planned to leave this afternoon for Witbank but my experience with the combis going there in the afternoon has not been good. I did not want her to travel from Witbank to Ellukwae by herself and suggested that she should go to Witbank early in the morning and ride with her friends from there. She agreed. I took her to the combi rank to find out the earliest and best time to arrive. We even went to the

combi administrative office and both she and I understood we (she) was to be there at 6:00AM. This would allow her to ride with the combi that take the workers on to Witbank. Nothing was said about coming to pick her up or leaving a phone number where the combi driver could reach us. We went on home and had a wonderful meal and pleasant evening. We all had high hopes that Jessie would be assigned here.

August 1, 2002
<u>Thursday</u>
HAPPY BIRTHDAY MINDY!

This is a day that will never ever be forgotten. Jessie and I did leave for the combi rank and arrived there about 5 minutes 'till 6. It was still dark but not so dark that we needed a flashlight. No lights were on but some combis were at the outside edge by the shops with drivers still probably asleep. We walked around to the administrative side because I thought I had seen someone walking inside. Must have been shadows because no one was there; we turned to retrace our steps to the other combis. Took a couple of steps and out of nowhere, a young man started running at us with his arm swinging back and forth. I say, "He's got a gun!" He is aiming it directly at Jessie and screaming something unintelligible. Jessie realized what was happening before I did and held her hands up saying, "It's okay, it's okay, I've got money, you can have it, don't shoot." She dropped her backpack to the ground and stooped to get out her wallet. He swipes her across her cheek, (she says later, not hard), grabs her wallet and turns to me. All I am thinking is, "Please don't shoot her because I don't know what to do."

He puts the gun to my forehead and I had to say, "I have nothing." All Jessie can think is, "Please don't shoot her because I don't know what to do." Amazingly, neither of us screamed or talked back and the other drivers had no idea anything was going on. Even more amazingly, he said what I know were a few choice words and took off at a run across the open field behind the combi stand. Neither of us could identify his face. We both remember that he had on a gray jacket, dark trousers and something on his head. He had a slight frame and looked to be in his early 20s. Our description could, of course, fit at least a thousand young people. It is even more frightening now that it is over.

We told the drivers out front and they called the police for us. However, a policeman waiting for an early combi offered to take us to the Siyabuswa Police Station and did. We filled out the report and also called the PC office and were told to come directly to Pretoria.

We went back to the house and I packed a couple of things. David and Anna came by to see why I wasn't at work. We told them. I told Rabie and Christine about the robbery but not about the gun. We went to Pretoria...filled out more forms and PC brought me back the next day. Jessie was very brave and neither of us panicked.

By now, the shock is setting in and this is the first weekend (Fri. and Sat.) that I am to be completely by myself. Wouldn't you know the lizards crawl across the floor and the ventures dance on the roof? Neither are pleasant. Three people have knocked and hollered for "Gogo," meaning Christine, but I am not answering the door for love or money, nor have I told anyone I am by myself.

David and the office gang are taking all this very seriously and want to call out the vigilantes(yes, there is such a group). I refuse to say (probably could not anyway) which man told us to come in the early AM. Everyone has decided it was a set-up...perhaps it was. But I must live here and no way am I going to take a chance, make either the right or wrong identification and become an official mark. Just hope they do send another volunteer here...or maybe it was safer when by myself. We will never know.

Saturday

Home alone but soon to be another unique day, (for me, that is)! Anna was supposed to go with me to a tombstone uncovering or placement. She was to pick me up at 12NOON. She came at 2:15PM and we walked over to another Anna's. We sit on the floor...have tea and biscuits...greet others and leave in about an hour. Anna's (2nd Anna) father died in 1999 and her mother has now bought and will place the stone. They are setting up the tent in front of her home and tonight will be the "night vigil." I was invited to stay but declined. They will pray and sing until sometime tomorrow. I will find out from Freddy more about this ceremony.

Sunday

John and Cherie called. They are to be married soon. I am very happy for them.

Went to church today and attended the reception the members held for the kids from Holland. Big event...but it will not take place while I am there. No minister arrives and after 30 minutes, I left. Had coffee with Dorothee and came home. Told Christine (who came home yesterday...funeral she was to attend will not take place until next week end), the whole episode of Thursday. She understood and now says she will NEVER let me stay alone. (What have I done to myself)? And tomorrow starts one more week.

Monday, Tuesday and Wednesday

Quiet so far but speeding up as we speak. Monday was long and slow. Tuesday: went out to HOPE and ordered air tickets to Cape Town for Dorothy and me. Pays to know Pastor Hendrik, for now I have a travel agent here via his e-mail. Wednesday: Condom Distribution Day (yes, all caps) and I stayed in the office. Made many reservations for the Baz bus and several backpackers. All went well, but for some reason, I was cross and in a bad mood. This started about 1:00PM but am better now. Same thing happened yesterday and at the same time. NO reason so better figure it out before it gets worse and I say something to hurt someone. Tomorrow we go to Denilton for a "MARCH AGAINST THE STIGMA OF AIDS" (banner). Rebecca has agreed to go. Now she is the one who should, and probably is, feeling as I do (sick about the numbers rising every single minute).

<u>Thursday</u>

Denilton today...supposed to leave at 7:45AM and did leave at 10:45AM. The actual march did not start until 12:30PM but a vigorous and loud screeching match went on outside the hospital grounds. I have no idea who was on which side nor could I tell if any in the fracas was positive for HIV. By the time the march started, at least 300 people were present. Somehow, someway, David had obtained a huge megaphone and saved the day by taking charge.

Me, I met a young woman who is living with AIDS and who is moving to our area. She promised to help me get support groups started. We shall see (I have lost count of the promises made). And no, Rebecca did not come. Very slow and difficult process, this coming out, but do feel am a little ahead of where we (they) were six months ago...even though very, very little concrete is being accomplished. Tonight we celebrated Women's Day with cake and Sprite...a surprise from Christine to all of us.

August 9, 2002
<u>Friday</u>

Women's Day: Christine has been to a funeral all night and now is ironing!! It is noon and she is still at it. Her ironing is extremely labor intensive. All the church apparel (Rabie's, Christine's, and Thobi's are heavily starched and must be ironed with a very hot flat iron. Thobi is sick and sleeping in the sun. Good-Good. I've done my Saturday chores so will do some catch-up letter-writing and work on Dorothy's itinerary...fun, fun.

But today is Women's Day here and a national holiday! For whom? An oxymoron if there ever was one! Women are still underdogs and men very much the masters and this is true from the hovels to the palaces and from the cribs to the graves. Christine worked steadily and attended church services all night for two nights in a row. Rabie slept both nights...ate...watched TV...ate...watched TV and washed his car...which he loves to do. He fed his flocks from a chair which he also loves to do. And every 30-60 minutes, he calls Thobi to do something and she comes a-running. He does NOT call me any more. This male supremacy takes place in every household except for the small percentage of women who have completed college and have high-paying jobs (none in this area). The women street venders do housework, carry their produce to market and cook after arriving home. Tea/coffee is served with saucers, spoons, sugar, and cream...as if the man is company...and upon demand as many as four to six times a day. It is amazing to me that Thobi has not rebelled. Me thinks she will before long.

<u>Saturday</u>

Attended a Parliamentary Day celebration and walked the six kilometers to do this. Each of the governmental offices was represented and yes, there was a booth for Heritable Diseases. The only written information was on Down Syndrome and Albinism, but did see several kids present with other diagnoses. I am constantly surprised that no one here has a member of the family with sickle-cell disease (at least that they know of). When questioning the nurses, they did not even know the term "newborn screening." And although there was a poster illustrating the chromosomes, no one had any idea what it was saying. I felt good at first and then despairing after visiting with them.

The day was long because for the first time at one of these community meetings, there was no entertainment prior to the start. Today's was to start at 9:00AM, we arrived about 10:30AM and the opening prayer was not until 12:45PM. Why, oh why, do they even state a designated time?

Sunday

Very pleasant day...to church...huge dinner with an even huger (told you I am losing my own language) dessert.

Tomorrow is David's (Director) Birthday!

Monday

David's birthday and of course, he only came in to get his "sweets" and then left. Long boring day.

Tuesday

Another one!

Wednesday

And another! Only today I went to HOPE for a couple of hours and then straight home for a nap. Really am going to get my blood checked...am more tired than I should be...not sick, just tired. Christine has a bad cold; Thobi just got over one. Maybe I am slated to be next.

Thursday

On the spur of the moment, David drags me to Middleburg to what I thought would be a Volunteer Counseling and Testing (VCT) conference. I was glad to go. However, instead of being on AIDS, it was on Domestic Violence. It seems that this is also a devastating problem and is exacerbated greatly by the escalating numbers of AIDS patients and the continued rise in unemployment and poverty.

David drove home (borrowed car) way, way too fast and very, very proud of his speed. I was relieved to get to Siyabuswa and out of the car. On the way, he told me that he is angry with Peace Corps because they are throwing the responsibility of Jessie's housing on both his and my shoulders. Yes, she has agreed to come and join me. It seems there are two available houses. One is right next to the combi stand where she was robbed and the other is at the home of an owner of a small business and no one knows much about him. There are pros and cons for both and while David is a big help, he doesn't understand Jessie's feelings. I don't want her in either one. Hopefully, she'll call me tonight and we can work it out. I go to Pretoria tomorrow for R and R. She will be there and we can talk the situation over privately.

CHAPTER SEVENTEEN

<u>Friday</u>

I rode back to Pretoria and linked up with Jessie. She, Kevin and I went out out for a very nice dinner and meeting (talk-talk). I did not feel so hot and returned home early. Home tonight is one of the backpackers where the PCV usually stay when in Pretoria and I am able to have a room to myself. This is fortunate because these backpacker hostels are usually full of young and loud travelers. Jessie and Kevin are also staying here.

Tonight I am outside in a separate little room with a green door; the other single room has a blue door (this is important to know). To sleep I go. But at 3:30 AM, I awake with a start and tootoot-toot and then poot all down my pant leg and all the way to the toilet which is outside and way off, at least 20 yards (more like 200). It is the middle of the night and I can wash pants in sink...rinse—but must put back on wet, of course, and must traipse back to the green door (or is it the blue?!). Two big boxers (dogs) who know me but not this smell prance all around me and commence to bark. By this time, I am all messed up again and stomach starts to cramp. Back to the john I go. After what seems like hours and after the dogs have quieted down, I slink back to blue door. Go to bed only to realize that after messing up again, I am in the wrong room! I am up at least 12 times (no exaggeration) and then go 2 hours and all is well.

To continue: mess up the shower, clean it up, steal some towels and make it to 10:00AM and feel good. The plan is to go to mall to Christmas shop, go to a movie and meet the others for dinner. Must do this. Decide I should start drinking and do stop for a Coke. All goes well. The restaurant is very crowded but have no mishap. I am by myself so feel I'm home free and the worst is over. Not so! Not by a long shot! With the street jammed with people, I decide to get their attention and start all over. Up and down my leg (yes, up...is that possible?!) Luckily, my slacks are black, my jacket long and I know where a toilet is. And there I go. Rinse my clothes in all the toilet stalls and put them back on. Am not Lady Godiva, although my hair is getting longer. Can it get worse? No I say! Oh yes, it can (I have no more clothes with me...was only to be in the city for two days...pajamas are messed up and now so are my slacks).

Who is that old lady running through the mall (not me) and I swear she could beat Mallory. I wonder "Who is she?" She runs into the department store, grabs a running suit off the rack (what else?), and races to the washroom. She has the credit card in her hand. "Poor lady," I say, "Can it get worse?" Oh yes, here it comes again. I excuse myself, beat Mallory again and go through the toilet stalls once again. Douse myself with soap and race back to the counter. This time, the very nice young man has everything ready. He is racing now, too, because the smell will drive away the customers. I want to tell him that this is just more proof that although our color may be different, we are the same on the inside the world over. He didn't want me to take the time to give him a lecture. I understand and head for the toilet.

Finally do make it the five blocks back to the green door, change into the running suit, rinse out my clothes once again and crawl into bed. Now I am sick, hurting, and I tell Jessie that I am not moving (little white lie because I make the trip to the toilet at least 25 times). I am so sore now and my whole self smells (reeks). My stomach starts to churn and to butter it tries to go, then to knot and finally to cramp. I try to figure out what to do when Peter Pain grabs hold, gives one yank that almost took me right to the sky but in reality only into oblivion, never more to dream.

For some reason, I left the old lady that could run at the mall and I am sick. There is light, am not throwing up, am in my room and can now make it everywhere barefoot and blind...cause no time for shoes or glasses. I have messed up my shoes anyway but so far not my glasses.

To bed I go and Jessie brings me more Coke and visits for awhile. I'm feeling better and finally fall asleep. But at 2:00AM, someone thought the troop of urchins in my belly should decide to party on and make me dance all night. By 7:00AM, I am exhausted and very weak. By 8:00AM, I have asked to move inside the "Big House" next to bathroom and now it gets better...yes? NO! Forgot...there is only one bathroom in here. There is no lock and these rooms (except for mine) are dorm rooms and crowded with kids. My room (the manager's) is next to the bathroom but the kitchen is on the other side. I do not have to run with the dogs but do have to share with the kids.

It is Sunday PM and the music from the bar that should shut down about 10, is still on at 11, at 12, but all is quiet at 2. I am in bed, fairly clean and my gosh, the little imps decide at 4:00AM to start hammering shoes once again.

Finally decide that this can't be food poisoning...must just have taken me a long time to catch some other bug. Also start to think that it might be serious and probably should go to the PC medical clinic tomorrow. Do this and am given a couple of antibiotics, anti-diarrhea medicine and told to do what I have been doing.

Return to the hostel and ask Mabel (maid, I think) if she will run everything through the washer. She, who of course is also tired of the smell, trundles me off to bed. I sleep from 3-5 and Jessie comes with soup (clear) and more Coke. We talk...music starts but somewhere along the way, they realized it was right out my window and turned it very low. I completely read one book, two-thirds of another and am too weak to run but truly am better.

It is Tuesday and I only have this afternoon and tomorrow left with ASHYO. Jessie will take my place and I will officially work with HBCHO. I am excited about the changes to be made and concentrate on different plans to accomplish.

It is morning. I feel like a new person and plan to catch the bus. Sorry, it has left at 8:00AM and I do not make it to the taxi rank until 8:45AM. We do leave at 11:30AM. For some reason, we are asked to change combis along the route and the new driver gets a ticket for speeding. A lady tries to tell me to get off the wrong stop and someone else says, "No, No." I do not know who is right but stay on and do make it back with no problems.

I stop by the office only to find that Jessie's housing is messed up, transport for tomorrow's meeting is messed up, and I haven't eaten since Friday night because my stomach is messed up. But yes, it could have been worse. All of the above might have happened while waiting for the combi, on the crowded bus, in the middle of downtown Pretoria, when I was sitting so my jacket would have been messed up, at a strange backpackers and the list goes on. Could have been both ends, could have had a fever, and could have needed rehydrating. As it is, Christine had a big pot of soup (bean) and fat cakes ready for me. I ate both. Hopefully, I won't wake up at 4:00AM tomorrow with my imps again... And I am so happy to be here in this bed. Oh yes, Mindy tells me she is not planning to come over. I said, "Please, oh please, come" and now think she will. She is worried (about expenses).

One will ask why I wrote all this. Let me tell you. I can count on two fingers the times I have had diarrhea in my life and never ever to this extent. And this is my first time to be sick (2nd if you count the short cold in Sanfontein) in South Africa. In retrospect, the whole scene was another new experience for me. Who knows? Maybe the little bug will tell his side of the story in the laboratory.

Chapter Eighteen

Take every day as it comes, and give it all you've got.
The thing to be afraid of is not what you fear, but let-
ting the fear keep you from going on.

(#10 of the twelve prescriptions for the millennium:
"How to win while you're losing and stay young while
you're growing old")

Author unknown

CHAPTER EIGHTEEN

AUGUST 2002

August 24, 2002

New journal...new year...last day at ASHYO...last meeting (mine) with the guys. This meeting went much better than anticipated. They took my comments in the manner each was intended.

David's and my trip to Middleburg to meet with new directors and new volunteers also progressed well. My part in the workshop for supervisors came as a surprise to everyone, and most especially to me. Because Mary, Jerry and I were the old hands, we were asked to make a few comments (we, of course, had no idea what we would or could say). We elected to answer, as a panel, the questions from the new volunteers and the new directors. But, instead, for some reason, little anecdotes came out of my mouth. According to the participants and amidst much laughter, these little stories ended up as sincere, open, genuine (their words, not mine) and <u>funny</u> episodes. Later, I was told by several that he/she would like to work with me. David said I should be on SA1 (TV); someone else said I should be a stand-up comic (tell this to my brothers). Sam said we should do a video and someone else said I should publish a book on "Mkulu Stories." Me, this was all unanticipated, unplanned and I have no idea what or why I said any of it. But so be it. Everyone had a good time and we all felt very much at home with each other and ready to move on.

David and I brought Jessie back with us and tomorrow we will all go to a Civic Forum meeting. She seems happy to be here and hopefully we will find her a good place to stay.

Saturday

Jessie came by this afternoon to visit me and she is unhappy; Cam calls...she also is unhappy. Seems Jessie wants to leave and go back to the States. I do not want Jessie to stay if she is not happy. I also do not wish to utilize and waste so much of our energies here if she would do better elsewhere. Later, I receive a text message from her and now she is unsure and says she does not want to leave. Am I or am I not getting mixed or conflicting messages here? Will bide my time and this, too, shall work itself out. In the meantime, I will start scaling my small mountain of "photos."

Sunday

A first today...was invited by Christine's friend Anna to the celebration of the girls returning from the traditional school (remember, her granddaughter left several weeks ago?) Today, I went by myself and this time I felt as if I were indeed a part of the party. Everyone treated me with respect, waited on me, and although I still could not understand the gossip or jokes, I truly laughed, visited and thoroughly enjoyed myself. It's hard to describe but I felt good-better-best.

Did worry about Jessie and how she and I would get along but did not dwell or make a problem of this thought or worry.

And then! While I am reading very comfortably in my bed, this little (GIANT) "rat," "venture," "thing," "varmint," (you name it), raced across my floor. It's the first one I have seen IN my room. I did not like it at all that it skittered right under my bed! I did not see from where (IT) came nor where (IT) went. And I do know that I would like to say, "I don't care," but guess I'll have to just call him Wilbur, and hope I never ever see him again. I especially don't want him to invite himself back! Another laugh for Rabie!

August 26, 2002
<u>Monday</u>

First things first. I have been a nurse for fifty years today. Hard for me to fathom. You would think that with all this experience behind me, I would be intimidating to Jessie as she starts her first days here. I hope not. Our first day went very well and believe we will be friends. She is in a house she likes. David can't quite let me go but this shall be overcome by Jessie. The day itself was long and I shuttled back and forth between offices but am no longer the new kid on the block. This feels very good.

I will continue now to write about my impressions of Siyabuswa after one year.

Will start with the weather because that is usually safe. This, I remind myself is Siyabuswa and by no means encompasses any other area. It is still a month until spring officially arrives. The days are 5:45AM to 6:15PM. The sun is a red ball in the morning and a red ball in the late afternoon. You can watch it set and I swear you can actually see it move, or maybe you are feeling the Earth move. The sun is NEVER directly overhead. It seems to be moving up and then immediately down, same with the clouds. The sky can be completely blue and if you watch long enough, the clouds will appear out of nowhere. Almost as if God is drawing them in and erasing those of which He doesn't approve.

When I first arrived, I did not like all the brown and dead-looking trees and shrubs. But now I have seen those dead trees/shrubs spring to colorful life. Red blossoms with no leaves, purple flowers, so abundant you cannot see the leaves, and teeny-tiny blossoms, smaller by far than periwinkles. One tiny bloom has a coat of many colors. On a Monday, Rabie can trim and on Friday, there will be thousands of blossoms again. But even though I sit and watch for long periods, I have yet to see one burst. Probably I never will.

The winter is passing and I have only had my heater on in the early AM and again for 30 minutes in the evening before retiring. Of course, Christine has me smothered in comforters. The sun warms up the day and the sky is a brilliant blue...as is the green as the trees and shrubs burst to life. Even the browns are vividly alive and of multiple tones. It is awesome to me that the ground that was ugly to me last August is beautiful or, in the case of the thorn bushes, is undeniably alive this August. I have yet to discover their purpose unless it is for land protection from scavengers. The air is dry; therefore, there is, at times, a serious lack of water.

They do have the four seasons here but none of the four is drastic. We did not have temperatures near 100 degrees F., nor did we have snow or freezing rains. We did go through a rainy season but it rained at night and the thunder-storms were the kind you can be safe inside and watch. The showers are gentle and allow the kids to play "under the sprinkles" and they do! During the dry times, there can be a serious lack of water and this places undue stress on the water systems, especially in the small outlying communities. Often the water "disappears" for several hours with no warning. Rabie and Christine keep large barrels of extra water in their garage for just such times.

Summers are hot but different plants, bushes and trees will then be in full glory. But, as with so many of us, the natives, if they know the names, can only say the word in their language. I have now lost count of the times I wish I were an artist or a professional photographer, or even a descriptive writer. As I write, the wind has come in full force so maybe it will blow Wilbur to Oz or at least to the fair!!

I don't know why I have lost so much weight. As with the weather, my perceptions of food have changed. I no longer crave or even have a real desire for ice cream, hamburgers, pizza (not so wine) and the list goes on. For instance, I had a bout with diarrhea a week ago and when I became hungry, first thing I thought of and wanted was "pap."

Tuesday

Absolutely good news has arrived from America! Miranda (MY grand-daughter) has been selected for the National Dean's List. It seems only a very small percentage of our nation's college students receive this award. Amazing, and she belongs to us!

And it hit like a bolt! Have had niggling ideas off and on but was not really sure just what my brain was trying to tell me? But yesterday and specifi-cally this morning while eating corn flakes (and not in the middle of the night when most of my ideas wake me up), my mind came alive. I know why I am here. It is to erase or at least alleviate the stigma surrounding HIV and AIDS. And I know I can do my part by working with the older population. Will start today! Not tomorrow...not some time but today, August 27, 2002.

Another Angel Day. Attended a meeting of the Community Policing Forum, (CPF). Did not want to go...did not start on time...very long and tedious and there was much I could not understand. But afterward, I did meet with a Betty who is a Police Inspector and she wants me to help her with a start-up of a home-based care agency. She, in turn, will help me in my project to work with the elderly (here the word elderly means anyone over 50 years of age).

Freddy has agreed to help me, too. He suggests we notify the schools first and work from there. Because the phone bill has not been paid, we must walk to the schools. This is good because it will prove that even though I am well over 50, one can be in good health and energetic. Note: a friend of mine from the States sent me about a hundred daily horoscopes (no dates) and periodically I pull one out for fun. Today's was: "Success is an attitude. Your creativity clicks into a magnificent production cycle. Mentally, you are astute, forceful and able to carry ideas through the planning stages to the finished product. Prepare yourself for success." The second said, "You know what is needed to get from Point A to Point B. Nobody wants to be held up, and tempers flair when others slow down the process. But try to look at the big picture. Who cares if you get there 10 minutes earlier?" Did not attempt the third.

Thursday

Big, big day for me! Farewell party from ASHYO and Welcome party from HBCHO. NALADI supplied the food! A real luncheon was served all the while David and Njongo gave speeches. All members of the three agencies were present which meant that at least 35 people were offered food, as well as those who wandered by. We were given pap, spinach, potatoes, onions, and beef. Everyone said that now, they really, really (their American word) knew me and that it seems I wanted to celebrate every holiday so they would call this exchange of agencies a holiday! Very touching and beautiful...hidden tears escaped from my eyes even though I asked them to stay put. The oldest person outside of me was only 42 years of age and the next was only 35. Now I know how my mother felt when her young students showed their love and respect for her. It is very hard to express but the love flows through from both sides at the same time. I knew that they also felt my love for them. There, I said it. A year ago, I did not think I would ever feel this way.

Friday

Want to write now about what I hope to do in the next year. What I have seen, observed, felt and realized is that one of the very serious challenges that those affected from the HIV and AIDS epidemic are facing and are not are willing to address head on...is the very poor or total lack of communication between those older than 45 years of age with those younger...especially in regard to life skills. We instruct the young, we inform the older...but we do not teach either group how to share information, concerns, issues, and needs with each other. Therefore, the support that all families need in some manner is seriously lacking. This problem has been festering in my mind for some time and now I need to focus my thoughts on providing actions that may be solutions. Let's see if I can even list the positives that are guiding me and urging me to proceed with this project.

1. The Prayer of Jabez
2. Freddy's interest in the elderly
3. Christine's (a grandmother) and Betty's (a traditional healer) willingness to help me (both over 50 years of age)
4. Jessie's placement here as a PCV and her interest in life skills
5. Peace Corps's willingness to let me move to HBCHO and to proceed with the project by approving a mini-grant for funding
6. Ideas on how to expand HBCHO services to include peer support groups keep popping into my mind
7. The first planning meeting has been arranged
8. Community leaders have voiced an interest

Saturday and Sunday

Very nice days...washed my curtains, mended them and hung them back on the windows. The darning may just last until I leave but it is doubtful if it will allow them to be washed again. Talked with Mindy and her divorce will be final once all the papers are signed. My thought is that the only one who came out ahead is her lawyer but she feels free and that is the most important to both of us.

Saturday afternoon I paid a visit to Anna, had lunch and was on my way home when I was accosted by some drunken man. I was very scared and my heart was pounding but Kathryn (her friend) and Anna had seen him approach and quickly followed after. They slung rock after rock at him but he hung on for a good 3-4 blocks (not really) with me literally hollering by now. Think he was finally surrounded by a group of young people screaming at him and at me: him to let go and me to run. He did and I did. Don't know where he went but I ran back to the complex and several people offered to walk me home. I agreed but we did not see him again. Today both Anna and Katherine stopped by the house to see me...both visits were firsts so I knew they had been fearful also.

Monday

Have written a little about the weather in this area and now will touch on the local political situation. I, of course, do not know enough to be a source of accurate information but must write what I see from an outsider's viewpoint. It seems to me that almost everyone thinks, and may even state, that the officials are corrupt (good word). I think it is probably more likely that those who are in charge and running the government (a newly-developed republic), know very little more about being in such positions than I would in the same situation. Because these are paying jobs for many who have never earned substantial wages before, he/she does not know how to manage funds for their families, let alone for the masses. It really is a catch-22 and the blind are leading the blind.

In addition to the funding issue, which provides the accusations of corruption, there is also the issue that those in charge of huge newly-developed departments have little or no experience. Where and how could they have gained experience? This is apparent throughout each governmental area, trickling down from the national to the provincial to the local and ending at the family level. But what many of the people do have, is an innate love for not only their own families, but all others and a commitment to make life better for everyone. It is stunning that at the same time as a new government was to be established, the same millions that would be "free" now face even deadlier enemies...that of HIV and AIDS. What to do? Although many in high political positions gave a huge portion of their energies to their people, lack of funding and healthy manpower continues to take its toll. What to do? A huge cry from the government officials went out for volunteers and not surprisingly, this was answered.

Volunteerism here in Siyabuswa, as it is in most communities in rural South Africa, is quite different from that in the States. In the States there are millions who volunteer energy, time, and money. But the time comes from those who have time and the money from those who have money. Most give from 2 hours to 2 days a week while others may give even more. Almost all give to a particular cause in which their energies are focused or they have a personal interest. Here, it is those who are unemployed and may need assistance themselves who volunteer and on the equivalent of a full-time basis. This can be, and most of the time is, from 8:00AM until 4:00PM every single day. Assistance is given to any family or in any area where there is a need. In this area this means everyone, and services range from medical care, food, shelter or just support to those who have lost their jobs or worse, their loved ones, for any reason. If they have energy or strength, they may work the gardens or walk to give home care. If they are willing to speak, he/she will give talks on the prevention of HIV; if not, they will lug supplies and man a booth at what has become almost weekly congregations. But what these volunteers do not want to do is to stay at home and sit and drink day in and day out. Absolutely free, they are giving of their time and the only one who is taking account of all this is God.

Tuesday-Friday

This whole week has been a mix...have officially moved to HBCHO and now am satisfied. Have completed the first steps to the project: written and submitted the funding request to Peace Corps. Many good people from a broad range of disciplines have offered to help me. The list of volunteers includes pastors, traditional healers, teachers, and people within the business community. It will work.

I have also been asked to help set up a counseling center and meet with doctors to see if they will help in a free testing and counseling clinic. It is good that I have been here a year because it gives me credibility. I can now ask for donations and put the money where it will do good that can be seen. So the week moved on. David is having a hard time of it. National does not want to fund him and he has way too many irons in the fire. The auditor will meet with us on Monday. Perhaps Jessie will be able to help more than I could. No, she won't...she has gone back to America, left last Friday. Now I am once again the lonely little petunia in the onion patch! Cam is going to try to send someone else...no, she won't. She is also leaving two weeks hence. Now I will really be out of it because she was my Peace Corps support. But hopefully this new person in Kameelrivier will be a friend...no, she won't because she is very far away as travel goes... and on the teacher team. But Jeanne, Stein and I are going somewhere in December. I hope to Zanzibar and Dorothy is coming in October. I am in a fine frame of mind because I know that the first year has passed and I survived.

Have written a little about the weather and even less about politics; therefore, that means I can literally just touch on religion. I know even less about the real feelings deep within these people than about the political unrest, but am more understanding and recognize the complexities. There are several different cultures residing in this particular area and many of the people in each of the cultures continue to follow certain of the old and handed-down traditions. However, within these cultures, most profess to be Christian as well. There are also many denominations of Christian faiths within the area. Does this lead to confusion?

I should say so. To be Ndebele, attend the traditional coming of age or rites of passage schools, open the tombstones, call back the ancestors, and also be a Catholic, Baptist, Apostolic, Reformed, Methodist, or another, is difficult for me to comprehend. But what I do see is the love shining in their eyes, the forgiveness in their souls, the anguish in their brains, the pain in their hearts, and the desperation in their day-to-day lives. And if their belief in Jesus relieves this overwhelming misery and provides the reasons to give their lives up to him, am I not doing exactly the same? I am much older than 90% of the people here and have never undergone personally the never-ending struggles to just feed, clothe, and care for my family. Nor have I ever been a child, who, when I did get fed, had to eat from the garbage in the streets with the wind, rain, sand and hot sun my only companions. But I do know that my love for Christ and his everlasting love for me has often sat me down, made me face the world head on, perhaps disciplined me and then stood me up and told me to go on, go on, go on. He will take me as far as He thinks I should go. And I see this same idealistic gut feeling in many or perhaps all, right here in Siyabuswa.

Isn't it stunning how when asked if my experiences here would enable me to grow within myself that I answered, "How could it?" But it has and maybe someday, I will be able to describe just how.

Thought I would run out of subjects to write about; instead, I find there is so much to tell that I often wish that I could tell it and someone else could do the proper writing.

Want to tell about the creches now.

First things first! Newspaper clipping with Miranda's picture arrived today. She is beautiful.

SEPTEMBER 2002

September 11, 2002

One year since the horrible terrorist attack. Am certain this has been a very painful day for every American. Even here, prayer after prayer is being raised for all of America and the whole world.

Wednesday

I personally am becoming busier and busier. But now I do feel as if the pace has also increased for those with whom I am working and even achieving the smallest objective has become a momentous accomplishment. The project has moved from mine to theirs and we are getting a lot of positive feedback.

ASHYO may receive funding from Impumalayo (a non-profit agency receiving international monies to distribute and one of many to whom we had submitted a proposal). If ASHYO does not receive funding, perhaps they will at least be awarded a written certificate of appreciation. HBCHO probably will not, but maybe they will next year if the CBBG Project (Communication Bridges Between Generations) takes off and runs.

I have started working with HOPE for Africa and will be doing the HIV and AIDS counseling at the soon-to-be-established free Testing and Counseling Center. And in all of this, I truly am taking part. Not to say that nothing would have been done without me...but maybe not...and the bottom line is...things are beginning to happen.

The weather, politics, and religion have been noted. I will now write a little about the schools and will begin with the creches or pre-schools and day cares. Creche means school for little ones. These little ones are ages birth to 4 years and they may be in the care center because both parents/guardians are working (seldom the case), both parents are gone (often the case) or because the guardians feel that day care is good for development of the youngster (rarely the case). There are many of these centers; some are nice... most are not. Some have an adequate adult staff to child ratio...most do not. Some have a play area...most do not. Some have a substantial building...most do not. Some are light and airy (only because it is a tin shack with more holes than tin)...most are not. Some provide nutritious food...most do not. Some have toys and a couple of books...most do not. Some are not heart-rending but most are! I have by no means visited all of them in this area, but I have either visited, walked by or been told about ever so many.

What I do see is tiny eager faces lit up and singing at the top of their lungs at any time of the day. The children have no conception as yet that things could be better (and they could). Many creches are located adjacent to the gardens maintained by the elderly and the camaraderie between them...the older singing the Lord's praises and the younger singing "Good Morning, Lord Jesus" is beautiful...and one must ask: "Why is the country moving so fast with its new freedom and advancing technology and just dragging the little ones along?" Someone... and not the children...should be spanked. This must change, if only because, as much as they may be singing, most will return at the end of the day to homes very much like the place they spend their days. Yes, there may be a roof overhead but many times not; yes, there may be food but most of the time, there is not enough; yes, there may be heat but most of the time, there is none; yes, there may be water but too often, there is not a trickle. Yes, they do have freedom, but all must pay to attend school, even if these schools are of poor or substandard quality. Most in the area fall into this category. The children do, however, grow and learn in spite of all the obstacles placed in their paths.

Friday

This was another South African Day. Up-down-in-out-on-off-exciting-scary-happy-sad and all in one day. True. 7:15AM: walked to the complex, mailed one letter, forgot to bring the other. Went to the SPAR (grocery), bought tomato sauce (catsup) for chips (French fries) and cookies for dessert; backtracked to the office and had a cup of coffee. Freddy is there to tutor me. We decide to work on my language for 30 minutes and are interrupted four times. I sort the pages of the current proposal, make list of things to do in Kameelrivier, and answer a couple of text messages. Njongo and I walk to the Health

Department meeting for volunteers in which we are to discuss the role of the volunteers in providing for those suffering from tuberculosis. Conversation swirled around me but by now, I know the gist of the subject and am able to understand most of the material. It did start at 10:30AM, only 30 minutes late. We walked back to the office and leave for Kameelrivier at 12:20PM. The combi is full and able to leave right away. We are to meet several volunteers at Sam's (Director of the Tantanami HBCO) office.

I find I am in Kameelrivier B and thought I would be in Kameelrivier A (where I was to meet January, a new PCV). Not so. We are to meet at the Methodist Church and although this is where I am and also where she is, it obviously is not the same Methodist Church. Seems both A and B have look-alike Methodist Churches and also look-alike roads leading to them. There are two and we each went to the opposite. Outcome is that I will not be meeting January today but will do so on Sunday.

Njongo and I walk into Sam's (another home based care director) office, and there are 5 kids (oldest 11) sitting there who have been abandoned by their mother. The oldest tells us that she is off drunk somewhere. She has been gone for two days and none has had any food or sleep. Sam asks me what to do? I can only suggest that he call someone in Social Services. He does but has to make arrangements for them himself, and therefore he must leave with them immediately. Where is he going?

Njongo and I decide to go ahead and meet with Leah because she wants to do bead work and be on the planning committee of our project. I am beginning to fear that our planning committee will be made up of more members than participants! But this is okay because they also need any information I can give them.

Matt (PCV) arrives and asks me to go to lunch with the SA9 group in Groblestahl tomorrow. I agree and make contact via text message to meet January at this lunch.

I go alone to make a home visit to Simon. Remember he is the one who the doctors wanted to remove his leg but he elected to stay with the traditional healer. He has made me a believer because his leg is completely closed and he is once again "up and at 'em." He says he feels great because of all the herbs, salves and incantations of the healer. But he reminds me that this is not just any healer but instead is a Sangoma (one who has been called).

I catch a combi back to Siyabuswa and find an apple to munch. I work on my proposal for 30 minutes and at 4:00PM head for home. Decide to drop my groceries at the house and to walk over to Anna's to tell her about Leah's offer. Take a wrong turn and become hopelessly lost. Mind you, this is 4:30PM on a Friday, the 13th evening and I have just come from observing the magic of a Sangoma! All the young men have hit the shebeens (small home bars) and the streets. There are many small groups and each is hollering at me. They can tell I am lost and want to take me home, give me a beer, walk with me, and even marry me. By now, I am becoming frightened but way too nervous to ask for help. I am very far away from the house now and know that none of these people in the street know from which house I should return. I decide to retrace my steps but this means meeting again all the groups, who are already quite drunk! It is getting late and this leaves me no choice but to turn around and believe it or not, reach my own area without problems. Am so relieved when I meet the drunken guys that I know on my street, I say to myself, "Thank you, God, for my very own friendly drunks!" Do make it home and am told that potatoes are too expensive today so we will have catsup and pap! Somewhere out there, I did find my daily penny (another story). All is well with the world tonight. I am on my way to bed with my book and my mini-candy bar.

America must not go to WAR.

Chapter Nineteen

I can still be loving, though discouraged,
Still giving, though spent,
Still patient, though exasperated,
Still sensitive, though offended,
Still hopeful, though worn down by life.

(Larry Crabb)

CHAPTER NINETEEN

SEPTEMBER 2002

September 21, 2002
<u>Saturday</u>

Have not written for a few days...really thought that since hitting the one-year mark, there would be little more to write. Not true, sometimes I wish I had never read the Prayer of Jabez...but I did, and every single day, someone or some activity expands and enhances my life. Would these events have happened anyway? I will never know, but this I do know: when I get an ache in my heart or some worry on my mind...in other words, what would have been hard to deal with...is now approachable. I still resent what I perceive as rudeness but the feeling does not last very long and I can distance myself. I no longer take every single slight as a personal assault on me.

<u>Tuesday</u>

Left early to catch the 7:00AM bus for Pretoria. It arrived at 7:15AM which is the closest to being on time that I have experienced. All went well. Walked to my usual coffee haunt and met with Lilliette (shop owner) who had voiced an interest in purchasing bead work from the Siyabuswa volunteers. I had met with seven of these women in the past few weeks. No business women these! In fact, by the time I had tried to discuss this money-making deal with a couple of the women, who understand little English, I was losing patience with the whole idea. I have nothing concrete to offer Lilliette. She, who is Afrikaan, understands and suggests that she will go to them instead and work her own deals. The women do not understand that by selling a necklace and bracelet together as a set they could make more money than by selling each item separately at a higher price per item. How could they understand, when none have had any experience in a capitalistic world?

Left Lilliette and checked in at a different backpackers...supposed to have dinner with Cam but she won't be back from Nelspruitt in time. My feelings are hurt but for only 5 short seconds. Take my photos in; go to a movie...popcorn and Coke (the first time in many years). Later I shop for a skirt, eat an ice cream cone and hole up in my room for the night. All in all, an R and R day. I sleep well.

<u>Wednesday</u>

I am here in Pretoria for my mid-service medical and, of course, I am the healthiest one around. Later, I meet with Yvonne (Country PC Director) and get this! She informs me that the Ambassador (from US to South Africa) wants me to present at a luncheon of the Regional Ambassadors (Africa). They will be holding a two-day caucus on HIV and AIDS. Seems David's charm got me into this. But it is a big honor and although officially it has not been finalized, if they do want a PCV to speak, it will be me. I am nervous just thinking about it. But will rely on the new me and it will be fine. Have been saying that I wish I could meet with someone in control and maybe this will be a foot in the door. Oh yes, the meeting will take place in Cape Town and PC will foot my part of the bill. We shall see...shall see...see what!

It was almost 4:00PM when we were finished so it was too late to return to Siyabuswa. I felt so bad about this that I had another ice cream cone and quiet evening in the room. Slept well and that was a good thing because the next two days or actually three days are once again South African big time.

Thursday

Very nice breakfast and a nice taxi ride to the combi rank with a person who has become my taxi-driver on call. Does that not make me sound like a VIP or what? Arrived at 8:45AM and sat, sat and sat. Watched and watched and watched the people and activities. A few stalls over, two young boys started horsing around, then started fighting in earnest, and then, for real started trying to hurt each other. More boys came running up and instead of trying to stop the fracas, entered in and then everyone came running and the men on my combi jumped out. It was a mob scene. The police came and guns were used as clubs and soon an ambulance arrived. I don't know why or for whom...could not see by now because of all the people. Do not even know if the ambulance left with any of the boys. The men came back on the combi and jabbered away while heartily laughing. Everything must have been settled

I started watching the people and would like to describe them and this combi rank. The men are all in slacks (some jeans), shirts (both tee and dress, a few are wearing ties, many are very neat but hundreds appear as old-time hobos (barely clad, with holes everywhere and bodies covered with caked-on dirt). There are thousands (nearly this many) of stalls set up, most covered overhead with tattered, falling-apart umbrellas. Tables are covered with cardboard and set in the sand. The food for sale is plentiful: big bananas, bigger apples, oranges, ice cream, cold drinks, chicken, beef, pap, rice, fish, chips, cabbage, beets, and the list goes on and on. Also for sale is any merchandise one might want...from batteries, cell phones, jewelry, trinkets...to all items of clothing.

The women are not to be outdone by the men. Only T. Caldwell could do justice in describing the multitude of details these women go through to appear beautiful (?). There is no rhyme or reason to the outfits. Most are in house dresses (my word) of any color. Patterns are mixed or rather may be a blend of plaids, polka dots, checks, or all of these; skirts may be long, tight or loose and some are even in trousers. The women, as opposed to the men, all appear as clean as one can get. All wear shoes of some type but the feet are so callused that soles of feet appear as soles of shoes. Most have something on her head and I do mean some thing: hats, scarves, or turbans. They may have their hair done in fancy curls, tiny braids, fluffed or even completely shaved. It is 11:45AM and we are pulling out. Away we go.

First stop: fill up with gas; second stop: driver (who looks to be all of 14 years of age) with a big grin on his face, gets a ticket for not having his seat belt fastened; third stop: driver, (who still looks all of 14 but no longer grinning) gets stopped for speeding but is not given a ticket. To him, this means he can keep on speeding and does not have to wear his seat belt! Fourth stop: combi checked for drugs under hood, in the very back, in glove compartment and I think, also some of the passengers. Driver is TOLD: "Put on your seat belt, slow down and don't get stopped again!"...this by the guys in the combi! Does he listen? NO NO! Fifth stop: lend a jack and pump to a stranded car with a flat tire; sixth stop: all of us must change to another vehicle because the passenger door won't close tight and is shaking, rattling and about to roll. We do change and the seventh stop is in Mashiding which is where we are supposed to catch another combi on into Siyabuswa. These stops don't count the times we stopped to let people on or off.

We finally make it home and it is close to 4:00PM. But now I must tell about two of the passengers, or three really. Directly behind me was a young lady with her one-month-old baby. She was on when I got on and got off at the same time as me. Neither she nor the baby let out so much of a whimper or complaint the entire time. So how could I? I couldn't, but my bladder sure did try. But I told it to be patient and that I was doing the best I could, considering the circumstances. This silent conversation was heeded and I did not damage my skirt.

I walk on home, drop off my bag and head toward the office. Am told that Leah will be in tomorrow; several letters have been given to me and I return home and am in bed early as possible. Friday comes and goes. Leah finally comes by the house at 6:00PM but still has not finished the beaded snake for a friend of mine. The whole bead business is again a mess.

Saturday

Christine came in at 6:15AM to tell me that Rabie's son, his wife and two kids are coming this afternoon. This is their first visit in more than a year and she wants to borrow a sheet (hers anyway) and rand 100 (she is visibly nervous and excited).

I leave for Groblestahl, meet Matt, we go for lunch and by 1:00PM, we are waiting for the combi so I can return to Siyabuswa. Make it home by 4:00PM and a feast is being prepared. We eat at 5:00PM and by now I am a stuffed goose. That's the way it goes: feast or famine.

Rabie's son and his family are very nice and we have a long chat. Both Peter and his wife speak English very well and we had an intense conversation about HIV and AIDS. I excused myself in order to pack for Sparkling Waters where another PC conference will be held next week. Jeanne and Stein will return here with me and that makes us all look forward to the week. Njongo is to pick me up at 5:45AM Monday. And life goes on but now at a faster pace. Will take time tonight to do a crossword puzzle which I am about to do this very minute.

Oh no, forgot to tell about the other passenger from Thursday's trip. We picked her up in some little village. She was quite pretty, tall, slim and was wearing pink shoes with 5-inch spike heels; her skirt was an open wrap-around of deep purple, blouse was filmy hot pink with ruffled scoop neckline with a black, lacy bra showing above and through. Her hair was covered with an orange turban about 12 inches straight up. No one said a word as she climbed aboard. I thought, "I wonder if she is a true lady of the night?" She seemed very sexy in my eyes. When she got off, everyone started talking and laughing. I knew without understanding a word exactly what they were saying. And in the midst of this, the young driver heads straight off the road and we are all jumbled around (is there room for such contortions?). No one was hurt and the whoops for him to pay attention to his driving and not to the woman (I think) could have been heard all the way back to Pretoria!

Now it is Sunday night. Rabie's family is staying until Tuesday and I find that even he had a life before Christine. Seems as if all the men lead double lives some where and some time in the past.

It's been a very long, boring, exhausting day. I am very glad that I am leaving early, early tomorrow! Family(all) are in and out of the house the entire day. I am in the way...want me to take photos...then don't, then do. They talk over and around me, forget me, and then wonder why I don't join them. Never tell me what is expected or why they are called together or even if they were. Missed Mindy's phone call and then when I reached her, the line was full of static. But the day (inside me) was so much better than months ago that as I lay in bed, I could not help but wonder, "Is this not a glorious place to be?" I was surprised at the thought. Rabie is much nicer now or at least I know how not to pull his chain.

Monday

Up early and Njongo is here at 5:45AM sharp and we are at the bus station at what I thought would be much too early. But for some reason, this bus leaves as scheduled and we are on our way to Pretoria by 7:00AM.

We walk to the restaurant that I usually go to and I offer to buy Njongo breakfast. He is uncomfortable with this because it is not "African" food and he is unsure about the items on the menu. We settle on a grilled cheese sandwich which he ate with a knife and fork. Me, of course, this is what I do eat with my fingers. We go to the PC office and they provide us with transport to the Sparkling Waters Resort.

I room this time with Jeanne and Stein. Very few of my own group could make it and they had already chosen roommates. We had plenty to eat and to drink the entire four days and were all contented souls.

Monday afternoon, the entire group (both directors and PCVs) discussed our morale after first coming into South Africa and how this may have changed by now. I personally have changed a million perceptions and felt good. But know there will still be moments and days that will be difficult...do know that I will be able to handle most situations from now on out.

Tuesday, we started with Life Skills and incorporated drama, safety precautions and other issues minimally. Once again, I felt as if the workshop reinforced much of what I am trying to do and gave credence to what we at ASYHO and HBCHO have already started to work on. All in all, I had a very nice week and it was wonderful to see everyone and be spoiled for almost a week.

Now the weekend has arrived and Jeanne and Stein are spending it with me and will tell about this later. So far it's been wonderful.

Friday

Njongo and I get all messed up with the travel again. First we are told that the PC driver will take us all to the bus and then that he won't. We all get the picture, on and on. Finally we do leave at 1:00PM (supposed to leave at 11AM) but absolutely must have lunch. Njongo got all four of us on the bus to Siyabuswa (PC did NOT drive). We arrived home about 6:15PM. Christine and Rabie were glad to see us and BOTH were fantastic hosts for the whole weekend. No Thobi, though, and I missed her (where was she?). Christine made a pallet for me on Thobi's floor and I slept all 3 nights with nary an ache or a pain.

Saturday morning all three of us were up very early. We went to the complex, ate what we wanted for breakfast and went to the office. I quickly showed them around and we left for Kameelrivier. Leah met us and took us to Sagoma Cultural Village, on to her aunt's house and then finally to her own home. Here she served tea, sandwiches and the others bought some of her beadwork.

Later we went to the Chief's home (really), met Matt and toured the water plant. This was amazing to all of us because it is a huge, antiquated and complex operation and apparently supplies water to hundreds of thousands of the people in a large geographic area. It is no wonder that periodically and with no warning, "the water goes."

We rode back to the complex with a friend of Matt's and visited the "Confectionary." This is what Siyabuswa considers its very own restaurant and has services only when the manager wishes to open. Today, no one was there except some strange guy whom I had never met. But he insisted on unlocking the room, told us to choose a table and he called the manager. She, yes, a woman, came in and offered to cook us a full meal on the spot but I knew Christine would also be cooking. I tried to tell her that we had not wanted to bring her in and after much confusion, finally everything was settled. We drank cold drinks and wandered home.

We were up early again Sunday morning, bathed by taking turns with my tub and in my room, drank coffee and ate peanut butter bread. Walked to Church, were invited by Dorothee to her home and there had coffee and homemade streusel (she is Dutch). We walked on back to the house and I cannot help but say how proud I was that all the children (and people) along the way knew me and were pleased to meet my friends. Christine had prepared fried chicken, rice, beets, squash, cabbage and pudding with fresh peaches. Not only this but a delicious butter/brown sugar custard which is what we would call cake. Again, I felt very proud of MY FAMILY. We all three sat out on the back stoop and visited for hours.

We went to bed early because once again we had to catch the early bus to Pretoria. It left at 7:15AM but broke down and we sat for over an hour before continuing. We finally arrived at the very busy local bus station at 11:30AM. We had lunch at my haunt and I took them to meet Lilliette. She sold them even more crafts.

We found our way to the travel agency recommended by someone? It was way out in Gezina (North Pretoria, I think) and it took us quite awhile to get there via a local cab. I was afraid I had really goofed this time because she was not there and because I did not know if she was a real person. She did come late (South African time) and had a trip to Tanzania already set for us. We shall see.

The three of us had another bed picnic and retired early.

Monday

Picked up more pictures (even the young people in the camera shop now know me and this is Pretoria), had breakfast with Jeanne and left for home via the combi. Checked in at the office and they apparently missed me. Seems some bookcases that I had ordered (unknown to them) had arrived and WHAT are they and WHAT do we do with them? Will explain and do all tomorrow!

Thobi had her first field trip today. She and her class traveled by bus to Johannesburg to visit the Gold Reef. This is a closed gold mine that has been made into an amusement park and one of the attractions is a ride down the shaft into the actual mine. Visitors can go down deep underground and watch how the miners used to find the gold veins and also how they brought gold back to the surface. Christine had told me that Thobi was almost sick with excitement. I am anxious to see her. We had dinner, watched "Stefan" and 10 more days have passed.

OCTOBER 2002

The daily confrontations often leave me less than the best
But still something ever new keeps emerging
Hope-now deeper, more enduring
Love-yes but in unsentimental dailyness
Faith-not enough to move mountains
But just enough to keep me in muffled triumph.

(Tim Hansel)

October 1, 2002
Thursday

The days are getting away from me. Must tell just everyone! There is absolutely no better way to start a day...Christine laughing and talking to her friends at 4:30AM as she passes by my window on her way to pray and sing. I doze back off and in a little while, she returns still singing. The sun is almost up and she thinks she is waking me when she gently taps on the door to bring me a very hot cup of coffee (she brings mine even before Rabie's). As I am reading the Bible, Thobi awakens and in a very short time is singing outside my room. I am only sorry it took me so long to appreciate the beauty and love with which each day is started. I do now and am thankful.

Today we had the first planning meeting for the PROJECT and even though it is being developed because of heart-breaking reasons, I was anxious to get started. Fourteen participants came straggling in and made me think that this was not a good idea after all. Once everyone settled in, even though several uttered not a word, we accomplished all we needed to at this time. Everyone appeared very interested and willing to do whatever would be requested. It was difficult for me to convey succinctly, and especially tactfully, what we hoped to accomplish within the next few months. This was especially hard to explain to those who had never ever been involved in a long-term project before (none had). I did leave, however, with a sense of anticipation that it will be a "good" endeavor. For today, I had witnessed an apparent maturity in this group of young adults.

Friday

Patsy, a young lady from PC stateside, did come out to visit us. I was called last night and told that she may come but her trip was to be very fast and again, she might not make it. I was thankful that our meeting took place and that it was mostly productive. Of course, for my part, it helped that she told me that Henry McHugh (PC office in Washington DC) had given my name to First Lady Laura Bush and that she may have used it in a speech (she did not).

David should have had his first airplane flight today. He was almost sick with excitement. I told him to enjoy every single moment and not to waste his energy on being frightened, or even to waste his brain power by taking anti-nausea pills. Am anxious to see if he fell in love with the sky (he did).

Saturday

I attended, as a guest, my first dinner party in an African home tonight (not the White American Volunteer but me!) It was given by Mary (South African) and there were six of us: two of us were PCV and the other four were Ndebele. She served a scrumptious meal, several types of wine, and the conversation flowed in both Ndebele and English. We laughingly decided to start a women's group and to meet once a month. We decided we could prod the women of South Africa to move onward (what?)? We will call ourselves WOM or Women on the Move (where)?

Sunday

Good day! Rabie told me he feels down today and doesn't know why. I know that this sounds odd but I am glad. No, not because he is down but because he told me. Maybe we are becoming friends.

Monday

I walked to HOPE for Africa to meet Aisha, a delightful young missionary from the United Kingdom. While walking back, I saw something quite spectacular. A spicy snacky (corn chip) was wobbling along on a path. To where? No one knows. I sat on the side of the road and watched it being carried by a group of ants...and so help me...there were three or four of these teeny-tiny black creatures carrying the front load...the same in the back...and a massive army surrounding them. Hundreds were scurrying, some standing (maybe sitting or lying, who could see?). And right smack before my eyes, a group broke the file and moved to carry the middle section!. Now there were 20-25 carrying the one snacky. Now who told them to do that? Perhaps I would still be watching if those on the sidelines hadn't decided to investigate my skirt (and under it!).

Tuesday

Aisha, a volunteer from England, facilitated a class on counseling skills for a group of home-based care volunteers working with HOPE for Africa. She did an excellent job. She is only 22 years of age and reminded me of Miranda. Later Togo, from the Saturday night dinner party, stopped by the office. The boys from HBCHO asked if we could use her on the project. Only ten months, 3 weeks left. Good vibes at the moment.

Wednesday

Finished in the office early and have everyone excited about my friend's visit from the States. They are looking forward to meeting Dorothy and having me shut up and gone for a week.

Thursday

I am off to the city! Hi Ho, Hi Ho! I caught the bus at 7:30AM; made it to Pretoria with no mishaps; ate a very nice breakfast; did a little shopping (specifically for a bath towel and a phone charger); called the shuttle services; was picked up by Ignatius at the Holiday Inn; rode to Johannesburg and checked in at the Birchwood Hotel. Ignatious is very nice and the Birchwood is elegant. Again, no unforeseen mishaps took place and I have found a new good friend in Ignatious.

Friday

Dorothy was right on time as was I and of course, we recognized each other (far cry from MY arrival over a year ago). Ignatious called and he also is right on time to transport us to Pretoria. Dorothy looks great, acts greater, and is the greatest! We stayed at the Protea Hotel for one night and she was able to rest from a very long flight. I woke her up in time for dinner at a *Greek restaurant* (?). Of course, we had champagne while we settled in for long talks.

Saturday

Dorothy experienced her first (and only) packed combi ride. She now knows why she was told (ordered) to jam only her necessities in a backpack. The ride was as bumpy, crowded and noisy as she had been told but she made it to Siyabuswa without complaint.

We arrived at the house and the whole family as well as neighbors welcomed her. She is fitting in much better than I did during the first hours. We helped Christine celebrate her birthday. Thobi is simply delightful and all is well.

Sunday

Off to church...long walk and quite warm. Dorothy met Dorothee who invited us to their house for coffee and cake after the service. The two of them became friends immediately and the conversation was delightful.

Dorothy and I walked to the complex to pick up a paper and on home for the Sunday dinner Christine had set for us. The family returned later, bringing friends to meet with Dorothy. They, of course, all like her very much. We played cards with Thobi and made it an early evening.

Monday

We left for the office early to beat the traffic (whaaaat?). A big meeting to plan for World AIDS DAY was to take place and wouldn't you know? After telling Dorothy that probably no one would show (Day is not until December and this is October), eighteen (right, 18) people did attend and we accomplished much more than usual.

Tuesday

South African Day! We took a combi to Kameelrivier...rode all over the place because the driver had no idea where to let us off. Tried to show off my language skills to Dorothy but this was hysterical. At first I had known where to go but by the time I had tried to tell him, we all were completely lost. He asked directions several times but no one spoke English and did not know Leah or Kenneth (whom we were to meet) by these names.

We finally drove to about a block from Leah's house and I recognized the area and asked to be dropped here. We walked over to Leah's and she served us bologna sandwiches (my first here), cold drinks and cookies. Christine had already stuffed us with fat cakes. Dorothy was so impressed with all the bead work that she impressed Leah by buying many of the items.

We returned to the office where the young people gave her a welcome party with more snackies (correct) and cold drinks. Dorothy will tell everyone back home not to believe me when I say that some days all I get is "pap" to eat. Did have one setback, though, because Christine had misunderstood me and thought Dorothy was to visit for two weeks in Siyabuswa. She was quite put out with me when I told her we were leaving in the morning. But Christine gathered everyone back together for a visit and more food. Dorothy left on a good note. Have no idea what the atmosphere will be when I return.

Wednesday

We left for Pretoria via GT and Vusi (a different one). No bus ride for my friend. Ignatious was right at the hotel to meet us and drove us on to Johannesburg. We stayed at the Birchwood and had dinner on the balcony of the Air Lounge (very posh) which overlooks the golf course and a beautiful, fully blooming, multi-colored rose garden.

NOTE: I received a text message from PC that a new PCV is coming to Siyabuswa to take Jessie's place. Hallelujah!! And good-good-good!

Thursday

We flew to Cape Town and will spend a couple days staying at the delightful backpackers named "Sunflowers" before catching the Baz bus for ports unknown. Actually, I am acting as tour guide and retracing the trip made last Christmas with Jeanne and Stein, another chance to show off for Dorothy. I hope I do a better job than in Kameelrivier. Dorothy and I (especially me) are talking nonstop but are having so much fun. She is very patient and is making these days perfect. I don't know if I can stay another 10 months after she leaves.

Friday

Baz

Tour of the Peninsula was not as absorbing as last time because of the rain and overcast skies. But the penguins were all dressed up to greet Dorothy and she almost fell in the water trying to shake their hands. It was the same trip and after the early morning rain, the day was wonderful and beautiful. We had dinner at a very nice restaurant on the wharf… steak and the whole shebang.

Saturday

Today was the long ride to George. We arrived about 3:00PM and the manager of this particular backpackers was very stoic and cynical, but the room was nice enough. We walked the town and then ate at the restaurant next to us which he had not recommended. It was one of the best meals I have ever had in any restaurant and definitely in South Africa. Also went there for lunch on Sunday and again the menu and cuisine was one of the best ever (Dutch).

Baz bus picked us up and we were on our way to Knysna.

Sunday and Monday

We arrived in Knysna in the late afternoon. We had dinner at an Italian restaurant and more good conversation. We were up early to take the ferry ride to Knysna Heads. Indescribable beauty surrounded us...the weather was perfect.

The Baz bus was late and we were very tired by the time we reached Rainbow Lodge Monday afternoon, but the trip was worth every weary second. We stayed in a rondavel which thrilled Dorothy. Had a hot shower, became warm, had wine, snackies and a good night's rest.

Tuesday

A young man drove us to the Storms River Gorge. It was the highlight of the trip last year and is again. Dorothy took what seemed like hundreds of pictures and now we are again resting. I had a few pangs when I thought she may be lost or hurt but she was taking pictures and is A-OK. I am relieved.

We are going to walk to the local hotel tonight and see what they have to offer. We did. All the tables were booked so we walked another couple of blocks into the middle of nowhere to another restaurant (there are only two here). This one did have room and we were lucky. It was a very tiny place, although quite charming. The food is home-cooked (we watched) and served family style to all patrons (there were six of us). The manager/cook/owner started with soup and ended with sherry served later in a small library.

We walked back to the hostel in the moon and starlight. Kitty, the owner of Rainbow Lodge, was as delightful as she was on my previous visit. She remembered Jeanne, Stein and me and the conversations we had had. Now she told Dorothy and me that during this past year, she had lost her husband after a long illness. She is running the hostel by herself and with the help of the young man who gave us the ride to the gorge.

We will head out tomorrow for Wilderness with its unicorn and pet pig.

Wednesday

We left at 10:00AM and traveled across country to Wilderness and arrived there by 1:30PM. The owner gave us a ride to town where we had a huge lunch of salmon and ice cream. We walked back to the lodge and talked until after ten. Susie (daughter) called and she and I also had a good chat. Now it is early AM and we are about to go down to breakfast and then maybe to the waterfall.

We do go to the waterfall for a very short time. It was spectacular and rainbows kleidescoped (is there such a word?) all over the cliffs. It will take a visit to Victoria Falls to prove to me that it is more amazing.

We hope to make it to Table Mountain tomorrow (if the fog permits) and have dinner again at the wharf.

Did leave for Cape Town and once again, it was a most pleasant trip. It is stunning to me that this short ride of about 250 miles (maybe not even that long) has the same scenery as many of the states back home. And here it can all be taken in at once. Now that is crazy: the changes in terrain take place within the blink of an eye. As one absorbs the beauty of the sea, the mountain leaps out right at eye level, but never at the same time as one's brain; or at least I cannot see the sea and the mountain at exactly the same time.

We arrived in Cape Town after dark and the lights had the city as glowing as Chicago or New York. No, Cape Town is built on many hills so it must be more like San Francisco at night. We were given our same "best room" at the Sunflower. We talked, read, and went to sleep.

Friday

We are off to Table Mountain and are driven to the proper stop to ride the cable car to the very top. The view is overwhelming and I am very sorry that Jeanne and Stein have not seen the world from this vantage. Perhaps they will when their visitors arrive. Our driver picked us up exactly as planned and we were dropped at the wharf. Dorothy did a little shopping and we had an early seafood dinner.

Saturday

We are up early and travel out to Kirstenbosch Gardens. I am once again amazed at the mass of different shrubs, flowers, and trees and because this is a different season, different plants are blooming then when I was here last year. We roamed all over but took the tour per jeep and visited truly a paradise. I will assure Divia that the gnomes are alive and well in the enchanted forest.

Our same driver, Hendrik, picked us up and took us on to the airport. With no problems, we were able to get an earlier flight back to Johannesburg and the van was already there to transport us to the Birchwood. Tomorrow we are planning on taking a city tour. The hotel arranged this for us while we were in Cape Town. Both Dorothy and I were appreciative of the young lady who did this for us. We hadn't even known she was going to and when we asked her why, she just said, "I thought you would like it and if not, I could always cancel."

New friends met this trip: GT (old but actually talked with him and learned about his family); Vusi, new young friend of David's who did the driving from Siyabuswa to Pretoria; Ignatious, who drove the van from Pretoria to Johannesburg and back; Hendrik, driver in Cape Town; Kitty, renewed relationship at Rainbow Lodge; Corey, driver of the Baz bus; and now Sara, a young lady at the Birchwood Hotel. Dorothy is usually very quiet and shy but she is open to meeting all these people.

<u>Sunday</u>

Can you believe? Yes, you can! Today we were to take the day-long tour of the city. The tour company driver did not show and even though our reservations were confirmed, it seemed to be a no-show. We sat-waited-waited-sat-waited and finally I called and the lady said the driver would be here shortly. We sat-waited-waited sat. Now to make a long morning short, the staff called and the driver is not coming. We messed around-sat-now phoned and finally switched arrangements and will go on a half- day tour (that is all that is left of the day). Oh, guess what? We will take the second half tomorrow (no, we won't). We go to the mall after sitting and waiting for that van also. Wandered a little bit, ate lunch and walked some more before we sat-waited-waited-sat-and eventually caught the van back to the hotel. I am sitting and waiting as is Dorothy. Hopefully the PM will not be a repeat of the AM.

Okay, 1:15PM finally comes. We wander out and the van is there to take us on the half-day tour. There is a lady in the front and she is visibly very angry and said they had been waiting for us. I said not near as long as we had this morning. Both Dorothy and I thought she was the tour guide, but lo and behold, she was a private customer and had every right to be upset. She had already paid big bucks for a private run and did not wish to wait for anyone. I opened my big mouth and said, "If we are all going off on this jaunt in a bad mood, then I don't even want to start." She had to laugh at this and said in turn, "Me either, let's start all over." We did and had a wonderful time and met another new friend. She is also a nurse and on contract with Physicians International and extremely interesting. By the end of the day we had exchanged addresses, and seen many areas of interest. Not the least was The Apartheid Museum (very hard to comprehend the misery and suffering the people endured while under apartheid). We went down in the Gold Mine (Thobi had visited here), and rode through Soweto and to the church where the uprising had taken place. We did not stay for long and did not leave the van.

We came on back to the hotel and had a picnic out among the roses. The city tour was costly and the most emotional leg of Dorothy's trip but I think she appreciated her visit even more.

Monday

This is the last day of Dorothy's visit. We went to the mall and she finished her shopping. We left for the airport mid-afternoon and she checked in. We ate a hamburger and fries (shades of home). I went back to the hotel and although I felt a little despondent, it was nothing like I had anticipated. I took a long walk, had a bath, watched a movie from start to finish and slept well. Moment of truth: never once thought, "I wish I were going home."

Tuesday

Ignatious is "Johnny-on-the-spot" to pick me up and drives me all the way back to Siyabuswa. This was costly but worth it. Actually more worth the money than the Sunday tour had been. We came home through Marble Hall and across a new part of the country to me. It is beautiful farm land for as far as you can see. The orange and lemon groves are vivid yellows and greens, the corn is knee high and the potatoes are bursting with flowers (yes). There were times we felt as if we were the only ones in these wide open spaces and we were!

Back to work by 12:15PM and everyone says they missed me "so much." Even Thobi came to the office after school to make sure I was back and had not gone back with Dorothy to AMERICA. I did not meet Cynthia (new PCV) but was told she has arrived. Ten months is still a long way to go!

Wednesday

First full day back at work. David and Cynthia are there to meet me...as is everyone else. Have I said a hundred times, "Silvia is an ANGEL"? She truly is! Rained most of the day and very little was accomplished. We did have a combined meeting with a youth developmental team (I knew not who they were) and HBCHO. Both were at odds with each other. It seems neither is giving enough credit to the other, sounded a lot like any meeting of more than one in a group. But the day passed. I like Cynthia very much and think she will be a positive influence...if they can listen and will try.

CHAPTER NINETEEN

Chapter Twenty

NGOs will participate in information sharing, collaboration, and coordination with other organizations and institutions, both governmental and non-governmental, documenting and sharing best practices and lessons learned, and seeking to develop healthy partnerships.

(Goal 3: Peace Corps Project Goals)

OCTOBER 2002

October 31, 2002
<u>Thursday</u>

Halloween...trick or treat! We had to cancel our project planning meeting because our attendance was needed at a big kick-off for the Dr. J.S Moroka Municipality AIDS Council. We, meaning the members of ASHYO and HBCHO, are excited about this newly-appointed council. The mayor has deemed it necessary to utilize all members of the community in the struggle against HIV and AIDS. He has appointed just about everyone of any status (he has decided just who has status) to this council. We rode over to Vaalbank in a bus because of the transport problems. Although this problem is no longer difficult for me to understand, Cynthia is at a loss. It won't take her long to get with the masses though and she will also find that most of the time, it is much easier to walk (which means 6-10 kilometers is within reason).

The meeting was fine...very long and impressive and we shall see if anything comes out of it. The program ran something like the following: opening prayer, welcome address, introduction of guests (I was one of at least fifty), speech concerning purpose of the day, music, candle lighting ceremony (to show respect for those who have died from AIDS), message of support (given by His Majesty King Makhosonke II), more music, keynote address by the Executive District Mayor, music, a reply and vote of thanks by another mayor, announcements, and closure by singing of the National Anthem.

Nkosi Sikelel,'IAfrika
Maluphakanyisw' uphondo lwayo
Yizwa imithandazo yethu
Nkosi sikelela
Thina lusapholwayo

Sound the call to come together
And united we shall stand
Let us live and strive for freedom
In South Africa our land.

As has become his custom, David again shone. He is in his element at these "status" meetings. But I fear his time is short...for some, he may no longer be the youngest or the brightest shining star.
Jeanne and Stein are investigating our Tanzania trip...many questions there.

The launching of the space shuttle with the first South African aboard has lifted. And even though everyone here wants to take me with them to many points unknown, not a one has asked me along for a shuttle ride.

NOVEMBER 2002

November 1, 2002
<u>Friday</u>

Frustrating day. Hope not for you, Rick (son-in-law) Happy Birthday! Talked privately with Njongo and Oupa. They both voiced concerns about ASHYO. They told me that although both organizations have tried to follow many of my recommendations (for more time and volunteers) for the Project, they cannot be as useful as they would like because ASHYO is in deep trouble. The phone has been turned off, the electrical bill has not been paid and on and on. Where do we go? I told them that I am supposed to meet with David on Monday and will also have Cynthia sit in. Perhaps she can help them.

Late in the afternoon, David came by the office dancing and prancing. I don't know how Cynthia will take his active behavior. Luckily she had gone for the day after agreeing to meet with him on Monday.

She and I went to dinner with Togo and Mary of the WOM group. This dinner was an eye-opener for me. I found out that women in the 45-55 year age bracket are not only assertive but also quite aggressive. Each woman, whether So. African or American, came across as strong, determined, verbal and free. I was the oldest (by at least 10-15 years) and the outsider in both groups. I could only hope that I came across to them just as strong and determined. The outcomes of tonight's dinner meeting were positive: all want to work on the Project, the group has expanded to eight, and everyone enjoys a glass (or two) of wine. Life does go on and all the plans we have should make the time pass faster. Only now I really want to make a difference and there is such a short time left to do it. Did I say THAT?

<u>Saturday</u>

Another wonderful day and am up by 6:00AM. Washed, hung out clothes, and cleaned my room. All this accomplished by noon. Tired but a good kind. Walked over to Cynthia's and we went to the complex for ice cream and shopping (hers). We came back to my house and visited. We talked about the positives in this area instead of all the negatives. It was cathartic for both of us. Hope she stays. Walked back to the shops, to her house and home again.

Had supper and then Christine asked me to go with her to a birthday party for a six- year-old (this event is rare). Was I in for a surprise! Ten little boys and ten little girls, all decked out in royal blue outfits (costumes) were already dancing (boys with girls). There were seven tables under a canopy and each had a birthday cake and a fruit bouquet. On a larger table were an enormous birthday cake and the largest fruit bouquet that I have ever seen. All the tables were covered with starched white cloths and decorated with blue ribbons and streamers. I have never been to an affair this spectacular for a 6-year-old child who is not a prince or wealthy, (if ever). The birthday boy was just a neighborhood kid and everyone was there. Again, as in every celebration here, there were hundreds of people. They danced (the kids) down the street and then disappeared.

Approximately15 minutes later, the girls came dancing from one end of the street and the boys dancing from the other. Mind you, this line was blocks apart (how did they get there?). They have changed clothes and now are not formal but instead are dressed in red shirts (not tee) and blue jeans (yes) but just as cute. They meet, pair up and dance again into the canopied area. Here they will all receive treats and he will accept his gifts. It all is absolutely stunning and again I ask: "When do they lose this innocent vitality and love for every one?" Later, (after the kids this time) the adults are fed and as it was with the kids, this is a feast. Christine and I ate and as the dancing began for everyone, we left for home. I continue to be amazed at the bounty given to everyone, at any one person's individual celebration.

Sunday

Have had a heart-stopping run-in with a bull. Yessssssssssss! It happened this afternoon when I was on my way home from a new friend's house. I was directly in front of this large brick retaining wall (yes, a lot of brick here, may not have a roof on a house but will have a brick wall). I heard this thud-thud-THUD on my heels and glance behind me. Here came Bullwinkle, (lean-mean-ugly) straight at me. I can only run into the wall and DO. This squeaky clean voice squeals YAHOO (no computer game here) and Bullwinkle veers away. This little tyke of 7 or 8 came to me and said, "Gogo, Gogo, are you okay?" I swoon, am overcome with a triple heart rate, breathe as if in Tibet and tell him I am fine…if being saved by a boy half the size of Thobi…and if except for an old lady's bruise on my arm where my irresistible force hit the immovable object of a brick wall, means I am "fine." I stand and wonder that I am still staring after a herd of cattle instead of up at the hooves of Bullwinkle. Came home and told my family and they had the NERVE to laugh and send me out to feed the geese!

Now this is the honest-to-God's truth: Have absolute proof that steers talk to geese because the geese for the first time chased me, one with his beak wide open and throat stretched to talking level. The other couldn't honk because he had ahold of my foot and holding on as if waiting for Bullwinkle's orders. I was sure he was on his way here! Again, the family laughs.

And then to have a grand finale! I am quietly writing a letter in my room and glance down. The flying termites (?) have decided to take a stand on their landing field or my floor. Hundreds are marching instead of flying to Pretoria via Siyabuswa. I call Rabie and he laughs. I say, "Is that all you can do is laugh?" He says, "Awi (no)" and then proceeds to guffaw with his belly which would put Santa's to shame and his nose is no cherry. But I am surviving, and although I'm not progressing much with the language, I can speak to the animals.

Wednesday

It is great having Cynthia here. In fact, it (did I ever define it?) is getting better and better. She will do the grant-writing (and likes to do this) and I can focus on the patients and volunteers (and like to do that). We should make a good team and the best of all worlds...IF I can let go (did I say that?). I will! For that is the only way forward.

Thursday

Baby Henry is due today. Have not yet talked with my son John, the baby's daddy, so don't think Henry has arrived yet! Today is his mama's last day at work so now it is day by day, hour by hour, minute by minute, and for her long seconds by seconds! How do I feel? He probably will be my last new grand-child, maybe not, but if he is, what does that make grandmother? Old, no... young, no...happy, yes...scared for your children...yes and no. But I'm happy that it is not me beginning this exciting venture...yes! Life does progress in a natural order, as it should. We will welcome you, little Henry, and love you and perhaps you will love your Gogo as the others do. You will...it is the way.

Thursday in South Africa. It is meeting after meeting,   including the first planning meeting of the Project (it is on schedule). This was followed by a rescheduled Advisory Board meeting of ASHYO (not on schedule). Although many problems had surfaced prior to the meeting, it did take place and do believe a few concrete solutions to the fiscal problems were broached. Cynthia is a God-send (to all of us). This is more proof to me that one should not attempt to go it alone if in over one's head.

Friday

To Groblestahl with Freddy, ASHYO member and also my illustrious tutor. Probably this was a perfect day for me but cannot say the same for Freddy. He had come with me to settle the telephone situation and after this was done, I planned to spend the weekend here and he was to return to Siyabuswa (I thought by combi). I left him to go back to Siyabuswa and later found out that it took him well over six hours, hitchhiking all the way. Me, I was staying on to meet with others from PC and we were to stay at the Lion's Inn Guest House.

The PCV, who are here for an R and R, met Hank and Dinky, the own-ers, and all of us became instant friends. This wonderful place is a retreat for us and all because of January (PCV), who had stayed with them the previous week-end. She had made all the arrangements for us. There certainly is life after retire-ment. Today: peanut butter sandwich in the room (to myself this trip), coffee in bed, chocolate sundae with extra nuts, glass of wine with several new PC vol-unteers (teacher group) from surrounding areas, beautiful inn, charismatic own-ers, pizza, more ice cream, more wine, hot shower, big bed and CONVERSA-TION by the hours (jokes, laughter, seriousness, and just plain fun). To me, "Remember this page when you hit slanted downer days and you will!" Everyone does.

Saturday

Yesterday was mixed up and not as easy as the earlier entry tells it. Once again, went to one of the banks to transfer money from my bank in the US to this bank in South Africa. I stood in line 45 minutes, sat with the consultant another 45 minutes, only to be told that I could not transfer money without my passport (it is locked in the PC office in Pretoria). It matters not a bit that I have other ID with me (PC ID card). Could not and did not transfer money. Therefore, I could not make airline reservations for our Tanzania trip. I spent the rest of the day and most of the night trying to figure just which bank to rob.

Up...breakfast at Wimpy's (a local fast food restaurant). Called Stein and she advised me to get money out of the ATM from the states and deposit the cash in the Standard Bank and purchase the ticket then. I can do this in Siyabuswa YAHOO! We shall see...will be glad when all is finalized and tickets are in hand.

Wonderful heavenly afternoon...huge rib dinner and back to the Lion's Guest House for more conversation and fellowship. I feel GOOD. And you know, no matter how crazy things are, I am much more in control of my emotions than even 2 years ago. I never truly believed PC would help me get to know myself better but it has done so. Does everyone like the word "truly?" Doubt it. Will try to stop using it all the time. Why? This journal is for me!

Sunday

Another combi day. Up early; turned down breakfast, to the grocery store, buy a cheese pie and Coke, trek to the combi rank and arrive by 9:30AM. It is now noon and we are still at the combi rank. Guess we will be here for a while! Read, eat an apple, and wait.

Will write a little about the guest house while I am sitting here. Lion's Inn is beyond belief and located in the middle of a small town (bigger than a cookie but not as big as a cake). The grounds are enclosed by a five foot high brick wall. This wall surrounds about three acres (Hank's words) of well-kept flower gardens. The home of Dinky and Hank has been turned into a bed/breakfast (and any other meal) but they also have 4-5 small cottages in a corner of the grounds. There is a large swimming pool surrounded by huge palm trees and multiple blooming flowers. The house itself is huge with a formal parlor, family room with fireplace, library, dining hall (it is), office with access to computers, and 6 bedrooms (all large and four with private baths). They have a home as posh as any in upper-class America. The kitchen is huge with every gadget and convenience imaginable. They opened up not only their home to us but their hearts, as we did to them. Both had traveled in America and get this. They did this by flying to one city, staying a few days, and going to the airport and catching the next plane with open seats to a point that could be exciting to them. They traveled six weeks by doing this and thereby knew the areas from where each of us came from. Must say, that Springfield, IL never did match their criteria for a point of interest.

It is now 3:15PM and we (Cyn and I) have given up and headed back to Hank's for another night.

Monday

Up very early and are on our way back to Siyabuswa by 6:15AM. Hank has put us in contact with Hannis Korf, the owner of "Build It," a lumber/hardware store in our town and we hitch a ride with him. He is also Afrikaner and the only one that we have met to have his business in Siyabuswa. We were glad to meet him and make the connection. I am going to recommend to Njongo that he approach him to be a member of the soon-to-be established Advisory Board for HBCHO.

David invited Cynthia to the launching and welcome of a LoveLife (NGO located in Pretoria) branch in Siyabuswa; then was a no show himself. LoveLife, which is Youth Against TB and AIDS Partnership with Love, is trying to establish groups in the smaller communities in the Province. David's positive reputation had preceded him and LoveLife members had expected him to participate in the ceremony. All of us were disappointed.

Tuesday

Everyone from ASHYO and HBCHO attended a Sister Love (another NGO being developed in several communities of South Africa) -sponsored workshop. One of the directors and/or a representative from the American CDC was also there and it was good for these young people to put a face with the group who is providing a large part of the funding for this NGO. The turnout from this area was better than anticipated (money talks) and ten smaller NGOs from surrounding communities were represented. Each participant presented the facts as honestly as they could regarding the devastation HIV and AIDS is wreaking here. One of the most frustrating concerns of mine is that the data, if collected at all, is skewed, inaccurate, or is not distributed. The number of HIV-positive people is unknown, the number of those with full-blown AIDS is unknown, the number actually practicing the ABC's of AIDS prevention is unknown, and the number of those dying from AIDS-related causes is unknown. The only known fact is that, even with all the interest generated in prevention, there is no way of knowing if any of the practices are making a difference in the actual counts of those infected. We, of course, know that 100% are affected.

Even though we had told David yesterday that we were disappointed in his behavior, he came out ahead today. He was chosen as the representative to Sister Love from our area. And his staff backed him! Hopefully, this will be a good chance for him to grow and with Cyn's help, he can.

Tonight I went to dinner at HOPE for Africa. Aisha prepared and did the whole party. We all had a delightful time and I was able to visit with Evelyn (Pastor Hendrick's wife). Do believe this second year is a "way forward".

Thursday

Very good day. We completed Aisha's sessions on counseling and each received positive comments (no evaluations here). Several volunteers voiced an interest in our HBCHO Project and will be available to not only attend but to help.

Later Njongo and I went to visit Hannis Korf. He was honored to be asked to serve on our Board and will provide business expertise for these young people. Almost missing her but not, met late in the afternoon with Mary from Love Life (Pretoria). She agreed to come in tomorrow, on her way back, to meet and discuss our Project. She is most interested because the older people in the community will be included. Too many of my thoughts and ideas hinge on "we shall see".

Kulo ma na mi dilaleli
Talk to me
I am listening

(Thobi's song)

Friday

It's becoming a normal family around here: Thobi has been invited to a party, received rand ten from Christine for transport; now needed another rand ten and this Christina did not have. As I came in the door, Thobi is not speaking and Christine is sad too. Christine tells me (I think) that Thobi should not pout (I think this, too). But we both also understand, that she (Thobi) thinks this is a dire and crucial crisis! I stay out of it. Christine asks me for rand 3...she has rand 7. I give it to her and Thobi doesn't know how to apologize for being a brat so she mopes some more. But as she leaves, she does say, " Bye-bye, Sydney, see you in the morning," and bye also to Gogo. All is well in our worlds again.

Saturday andSunday

Friday night continued: Thobi came home... she was to stay over with a friend but tapped on my window and slept in my room. This, I am sure, is her way to make amends. It certainly does.

The family left at 7:00AM and I stayed here without leaving until 10:00AM Sunday. It was very nice and I accomplished many minor tasks. Did go to church and for coffee at Dorothee's. She and her family leave for Holland at the end of the month for two months. Needless to say, they will all be missed.

Tomorrow I am to go Pretoria to check on pamphlets for the Project. Cynthia is going with me. That will also be a first. But you know, in retrospect and now that it is over, I do believe I gained from this year all by myself. Was forced to become a part of this community and have. Will never know, but it is doubtful that as many of the opportunities offered to me would have taken place, or even if I would have been as wholeheartedly accepted, if the people here had not recognized my aloneness.

Tuesday

Very nice day in Pretoria...did not find the books I was looking for but didn't really expect them to be handy. Cyn and I saw a movie, had delicious food and an easy trip back here.

As I walk in the door, Rabie (yes) is fixing pap and spinach and said very nicely, "Nomhl, are you going to eat pap with me?" Yes, I am going to do this. Now this is a message to me from me, "Sydney, let Cynthia write the new proposals. You asked for someone else to do it...now let her and don't get defensive. This will give her something concrete to do and she'll be more apt to stay. You always hated that job. Now 'fess up."

Life here in South Africa has begun to settle in. A new PCV arrived, stayed one week and left, second came 3 weeks ago and is still here, so here's hoping! She took my place in ASHYO and I have moved full time to HBCHO which is exactly where I want to be. And now I am thinking, "Only nine months left (only!) and cannot possibly accomplish what I wish!" Guess it took the first year (I must be a slow learner) to become one with the community and guess being alone kind of coerced me into knowing these people better. We shall see. Lots of things have happened to me that have had nothing to do with why I am here and makes me kind of wonder. What would I be feeling if I had not: spent so much time in the community, been chased by a bull, bit by a goose, attacked by flying termites, punctured by a thorn, stranded in the middle of nowhere, stranded in the middle of somewhere, had diarrhea in the middle of everywhere and in front of everyone, went to a matinee by myself and was the only one in the theater to watch "Panic Room," attended church completely alone in the church on Easter, been grabbed by two drunks at the same time, had credit card stolen, cell phone torn apart, scared by man in this house carrying an axe down the hall looking for the criminals, cheated out of my change, taken advantage of, made to feel like a heel, treated as a 5-year-old, suffocated because of no electricity, frozen to death for the same reason, held up at gunpoint, fallen three times in the street, cracked the back of my head very hard, scraped my arms, bruised my legs, washed my hair in freezing water, listened to rats over head, been misunderstood in some way every single day for more than 365 days, drunk too much, drunk too little, been really hungry, been way too full and this could go on and on.

BUT

Have also had the sparkle and free love shown to me by babies, toddlers, teens, young adults, moms, old people, dying people, traditional healers, professionals, evangelists, AIDS victims, and angels; the last bit of food in the house offered to me, coffee served to me in bed every morning, a young one wanting to sleep in my room on a pallet and sing me to sleep, parties given for me, invited to family celebrations as a friend, seen the sky so spectacular that it cannot be described and this list goes on and on...tipping the scales heavily to the positive side.

Chapter Twenty-One

HENRY MILLER KLING BORN 11-21-2002

Who would dare say there is no GOD? When I awaken and open the curtain, the sun is rising in the WEST. How can this be I ask? Oh, there it is in the East! It is true and I have to be one of the very few fortunate enough to recognize this. I can see the wonder of the early morning rays as they hit both sets of my corner windows at exactly the same time for a few seconds each morning. Could have missed it completely...but didn't!

(Gogo)

NOVEMBER

November 22, 2002
<u>Friday</u>

Another South African day...only today has been put aside to celebrate (?) children! We are to go to the ceremony and festivities hosted by the Social Services Department for the orphans in the area. My phone is broken and I do not know where or how baby Henry is...took the phone into some shop and the guys there will do their best to fix it. Cyn and I then walked out to the celebration. We sit...sit and kids are running all over the place. When they say orphans here, they mean orphans. There are no adults except us within shouting distance and we know not the children or whence they came. Although the program was to start at 9:00AM, it doesn't until approximately 12:30PM. The children are hot, tired and hungry, as are all the gogos and everyone in between. David is prancing around...now here, now gone. But must say all the rest of us are as jittery. We leave at 2:00PM and walk down to the shop to check on the phone. Not fixed. Walk all the way back to Cyn's house and drink a cup of tea. Call John on Cyn's phone and Henry was born yesterday at 1:00PM. He is perfect! I am truly celebrating children!

<u>Monday</u>

Am well past all the lonesomeness and crossness of the weekend. Do realize that homesickness doesn't go entirely away and having no access to a phone does not help matters, even if you don't plan to use it. But today was another day. Met everyone at the office at 6:15AM and our transport was there but left without us (why?). Bus came back and finally, we did leave at 7:30AM and made it to Moteti where we wait until we are told, "Get off." No, ordered to get off. It is cold (really) and we try to find some coffee but it is brown water with sour milk (sour is not a bad thing for those used to it, but it is bad for me). Another bus comes by at 9:30AM and a few of us are taken on into Denilton and the program is underway by 11:30AM. This program is the launching of another Municipal AIDS Council and progressed very much like the other programs.

However, the afternoon proved to be one of the best that I have attended. Deborah Frasier (whoever that might be) gave a succinct, informative speech and this was translated into English (just for Cyn and me). The other speeches were also well done and informative and we were finished by 4:00PM. I am tired of sitting though, because on Friday and Saturday worked at my desk, worked at home on Sunday and than sat most of today.

Our bus finally left at 5:30PM and we arrived in Kwaggplaza with no problems. It is dark now and we have no transport into Siyabuswa. Finally, someone's friend who has a combi arrives and 16 of us pile in. There were supposed to be three in the back, three in the middle and two in front; usually there is one extra in each seat but tonight we had six in back, six in the middle and four in front. I am all bones on top of all bones and head would touch top if sat up straight or actually go through the top if it was soft. Now get this: three young guys catch on the back and now we must go very slowly and even then one does fall off. We leave him and the other two ride all the way with us. I almost became hysterical picturing this old gogo in the midst of these bodies and couldn't stop laughing at the cartoon in my mind.

We do reach Siyabuswa and drop (literally) people off as we go. Njongo walks me home because it is pitch-black and I am afraid of the stray varmints (including drunks). We get here at 8:45PM and Christine has saved me food which I gobble.

Oh yes, Sunday or rather in the middle of the night, a man from the house across the street from us is very, very cross (their word, mine would be irate and murderous or even crazy) and giving his family big trouble out in the street. But this morning, Thobi greeted me with coffee and her singing. She informs me that the police came and took him away.

Tuesday

To Denilton with David for a Home-Based Care Research(?) Program (what?). Absolutely nothing for me to do and no reason whatever to be there but David seems to need me as a buffer (Where is Cyn?).

Wednesday

To Witbank with Njongo. We rode in five combis to get there and five more to return home. Good meeting though and the speaker explained a lot to both of us about financial strategies. I was not surprised to find that most of the small NGOs in the Province are in the same boat as ASHYO and HBCHO are ... sinking and maybe even drowning.

Took fruit and peanuts for the office and Cyn brought a cake to help us celebrate Thanksgiving back in the States. Mkulu story: my family had been invited to the party and Rabie did not get enough to eat. His comment: "Given a piece of meat that would fit up my nose!"

All four of my children called and talked with all the grandchildren (even Henry!). They tell me all is well.

Friday

I will start here for Saturday because it will probably take me to the end of the book to finish. David and Freddy came into my office (corner) and told me we had been invited to Thandi's wedding. First question: Who is Thandi? No, I don't need to go, I say. Oh, yes, you know her and she specifically said to invite you. It will be the first "white" wedding I have attended while here so am curious and decide to go. "White" here means a formal wedding with the bride wearing a white dress and most of the time, the ceremony is in a church. Silvia agrees to meet me no later than 11:00AM. It is supposed to start at 10:00AM (even weddings are late here?). I am okay with this just as long as she comes!

<u>Saturday</u>

Am up early, drink coffee, wash clothes, wax floor, clean up the kitchen and head out the door at 10:40AM. It does feel odd to deliberately be late. The event is to take place at Ketwile Park which is a twenty- minute walk and it is very hot! When I arrive, there are lots of little kids running all over, a few adults standing around and absolutely no sign of a wedding. I ask around and yes, it will be over there. "Over there" is a big covered area which appears to be a conference area of some sort but no people, no tables, instead just an "over there." I wander around and continue to ask about a "wedding" and soon there are people arriving and they start to decorate. I think, "Oh, we were invited to the reception but not the wedding. Jeepers, this could be hours from now." Soon, though, a girl from nowhere takes my arm and she is a sister of Thandi and I am at the right place. She takes my gift and takes me to a seat that has just arrived. If you can believe this, I am the very first person to arrive in what will become a very large crowd. I wander outside to pass time and soon carload after carload of people arrive and the festivities are about to begin. None of my group is here and there is no sight of Silvia. Oh my, here comes David dressed to the nines in old tee shirt and ball cap. Happy-happy (he forgot to take the Agreement to Nelspruitt and is afraid Cyn will chastise him. He needn't have worried. She did not come today. Obviously, he has never worried about me chastising him.

The ceremony starts about twenty yards outside the entrance when four young ladies about seven years of age dance ahead of the very beautiful bride and the man who is escorting her. Thandi is stunning and as soon as I see her, I remember her well. Then four women follow, carrying her train. David is hopping and dancing behind. I was embarrassed for him but no one seemed to mind and now the entire area is jammed with people. David comes back to me (insists that I join the wedding party, but this time I said NO and stuck to NO). He leaves me and I am beginning to enjoy all the pomp and soon Silvia arrives. 11:00AM Hah! But I am glad to see her.

The wedding begins and to do the couple justice, I've inserted the program here. And before I say how long-long-long it was, let me say that not only the bridal party but everyone in attendance was elegantly dressed and all in good taste. It was apparent to me that there are those even in Siyabuswa who have a lot of money.

Thandi's sister came to get me to join the front group but again I said NO and meant it. I sat with Silvia and enjoyed myself immensely. It is about 2:00PM when it becomes evident that this ceremony will go on and on and with AMEN after every word. Had a terrible time deciding whether to let my leg stay asleep or get up and stamp it. Finally, some women brought cold drinks to every-one. This time, due to the crowds, many of us had to share a glass. At 3:15PM, after the couple are pronounced man and wife, everyone took a break to eat. But no food is in sight so I begged off and came on home. Silvia was disappointed that I was leaving but I was at the end of my stamina, tired, hungry, and had been there much longer than she.

Did come back home and Christine had gone to a party of her own and that meant there was no food here either. Had peanut butter and bread (my fourth slice for today) and took a bath. It is now 7:40PM and I am going to bed. We are to go to Middleburg for World AIDS Day in the AM and should be at the office by 6:30AM. Another long day awaits us.

The following Program was written on very nice paper and distributed to the guests.

WEDDING PROGRAM OF THANDI AND JOSEPH

First Session 10AM-1PM

<u>MC:</u> A. Mr. Lucas
       B. Mr. Leshata Ledwabe

<u>Chorus Leader</u> 15-20 Minutes

<u>Opening Prayer</u>

<u>MC's Remark</u>
<u>Bride and Groom</u>
    A. Ushering of the bride to the alter
    B. Ushering of the Groom to the alter

<u>Musical Items</u>

<u>Speech</u>
    A. Victory Fellowship
    B. Seshego Assembly of God

<u>Matrimony</u>
The Word of God
    By Rev. I. Mtshweni
    Assisted by Rev. D. Makweya

<u>Speakers</u>
Bride's Family
Groom's Family
Speech
Groom's Friend
Bride's friend

Second Session 2PM-3PM

<u>MC:</u>   A. Mr. Leshata Ledwaba
        B. Mr. Lucas

<u>Choirs</u>

1.   2.   3.   4.

<u>Reply</u> Bride and Groom

<u>The Word of God</u> Rev. G. Nkomo

<u>Musical Items</u>

<u>Cutting of Cake</u>

<u>Vote of Thanks</u>

<u>Closing Prayer</u>

The bride wore a white satin and white beaded wedding gown exactly like the bride would wear at a formal wedding in the United States. Her four attendants were in matching long satin and lace dresses. The groom and his four groomsmen wore dark suits with matching colored shirts. The three flower girls were dressed identical to the attendants and the young ring bearer dressed as his daddy (one of the groomsmen).

It was hard for me to comprehend when I was told, that this young couple had already had their "traditional" wedding (months ago) which was also very expensive and extravagant.

<u>Sunday</u>
WORLD AIDS DAY

The world over they call this World AIDS Day and I hate this term. It seems that we are celebrating such a disease as AIDS as opposed to struggling against it. The semantics are not proper and should be changed.

We went to Middleburg via bus but this time transport was organized. Cynthia spent the night at my house because we had to leave early in the AM. She lives much further away from the office than I do and it is pitch-black until at least 6:30AM. We were in for a day of sitting but there were so many singing and dancing groups from all over the province and of different cultures that the day passed quickly. Again, it seemed odd to me to be singing and dancing for such an unjust cause but if this is what draws people to react and help, who am I to speak against what works?

Oh my gosh, Yvonne (PC Country Director) just called me and <u>if</u> the First Lady comes to visit South Africa and <u>if</u> she wants to meet with a PCV, Yvonne has put in <u>my</u> name. I don't care if it doesn't come to pass, but it's nice to know they put in my name. Hopefully, it won't be while I am on vacation.

Back to WAD. Program once again was nice after it got started! Waited for the Premier but he never did show.

Cynthia and I had a long discussion concerning the ups and downs of our work here. She is feeling much like I did the first months. It is extremely hard for us to understand why these young people cannot put together a proper budget and then follow it. It takes us a long time to realize that first, none have ever before had funding, not even childhood allowances, and second, that even those who are doing the funding may not be capable of providing proper oversight in grants management or even budget control. She is becoming disillusioned with the NGOs and I am having a hard time by being in the middle. If I tell the truth, and I must because she is very perceptive, I'm feeding into her dilemmas. But if I try to make it sound better, I am fooling both of us. I tell her that we can only take what we have and work with it (never will find out what it is)...

<u>Monday</u>

I seem to be very tired today and did not accomplish much.

<u>Tuesday</u>

Cyn and I went out to HOPE today and she started a draft of a new proposal for her group and helped me with our budget (HBCHO).

<u>Wednesday</u>

A wasted day, but these are further apart. Friday is to be our own WAD and will be held in Kameelrivier. Right now it is a MESS. Cyn is trying to work with Love Life...hope it works out for her.

In the meantime, Susie sent me a Christmas tree and all the decorations. Thobi and Tqobile (her friend) came to the office this afternoon and put on the ornaments. It is beautiful. I requested that Thobi and Njongo sing together and after much begging, they agreed. There were very few dry eyes because of the love and sincerity in the blend of their voices. Truly a Peace Corps moment.

Tonight Thobi stamped all my Christmas cards for me.

Another journal almost finished. Never dreamed there would be so much to say. I am lucky and blessed. Very rocky start to 2002 but the finale is just fine. Cyn and I are getting to know each other and she is saving my neck on these proposals. She is much better at writing them than I. The Project is on track and have many other ideas in mind...cannot possibly get them completed because they will be ongoing but at least the seeds will be planted.

Mary and Jerry (PCVs) came on Saturday and we all stayed at the Guest House which has recently opened here in Siyabuswa. Cyn and I will celebrate her (Cyn's) birthday.

A good friend from the states (Barb) called and we chatted for almost an hour (her nickel, actually dollars). This call was a super Christmas present.

Must write Thobi's sad news. Last Saturday morning, she and I were home alone. It was close to 7:00AM when a man came to the door and hollered through the screen, "Gogo, Gogo." I asked Thobi to see who it was and he told her that her uncle had died. Just like that...no explanation or lead-in to his news. She was already feeling somewhat sad because it is school vacation and her friends have all gone to their respective parents. She cried and tried to tell me. Almost an hour later, Christine and Rabie walked in the back door. Both were tired and had already been to two funerals (Rabie is to go to church every night next week). They were short with Thobi and she broke down and sobbed. They prepared to go to her daddy's house and I told them that I was leaving about 11:00AM and who would be here with Thobi? They told me, "She can stay by herself." I think (ask my own mind) and then say, "She is very unhappy and I hate to leave her." Christine agrees and says, "I can see that...she will go with us." I'm afraid I'll be in trouble for interfering but actually they were good with this. Her uncle was only in his early thirties. They do not know the cause of death and probably never will.

Thobi is feeling better tonight. I will try to talk to her a little later. Cannot say for sure if she is spending more time with me because she is lonely and sad or hopefully, it is because she is just a 10-year old little girl waiting for Christmas goodies.

Our WAD in Kameelrivier was a bomb that never blasted off. We think it was a dud because of the apparent friction within the troops. But after I arrived back at the house, there was another joyful little kid birthday party taking place right outside my window.

I have all my Christmas cards sent, packages wrapped and am anxious to start the Tanzania holiday. Party for the volunteers is tomorrow and the family's tomorrow night. Will pack on Friday, but will wash out some clothes and take a bath now. What more can anyone ask? It is amazing to me that I spend so much time writing about day-to-day events and back home, I never would even consider this a thing to do.

Rabie, Thobi, and Friends

As I look out my window very early each summer morning, I am reminded of mornings of almost fifty years ago. I was in San Francisco attending nursing school at the time. My roommate and I would watch the sky out one set of windows and see the Bay Bridge and then we would trade beds and look out the other set. Here we saw the Golden Gate Bridge...and all the scenes over and under and in-between. We were on the fifth floor of the eighth hill; therefore, the people appeared very tiny, the buildings very tall and we were above! We saw it all: the sun, stars, buildings, vehicles, more buildings and each was mesmerizing. It was not difficult to start the day because we were young, eager and knew that each night we would talk about everything that happened during our day and watch the night sky, all the while listening to "Ebb Tide," her favorite and "Yours," my favorite, before finally turning and saying, "Good Night."

Now all these years later, I awaken very early and the morning is as beautiful as fifty years ago. Out one set of windows the sky is very blue, the clouds white and fluffy, the rooster is saying hello (only he doodles all day and night) and Christine's friends have come to walk with her to pray. Out the other set of windows, the sun is rising and reflected in both the top panes and I am able to appreciate two sunrises simultaneously.

The geese start to answer the rooster. This is no longer noise. I anticipate all this and never do cease to wonder. But my early morning becomes more meaningful. Christine serves me a hot cup of coffee and sometimes a fat cake. A short time later, Thobi will visit, half-dressed, and sit on the foot of my bed and sing praises from her very innocence. Her eyes sparkle and we both start our day with eagerness...hers from the perspective of a 10-year-old child and so far she is able to do this and me...from 50 years living more than she. Perhaps there is no better life here on Earth than this and we don't realize that this very same scenario is taking place the world over...no matter in what culture we are participating.

Some mornings the sun is not shining in my window and instead, it is storming and there is rain thundering down. This is also a wonder, especially on a tin roof. And even though it is dreary in color, my day really starts very upbeat. The same coffee, the same singing...and the sandy roads have cooled and it is much easier to traipse or navigate the deep zig-zagged ruts.

I leave tomorrow on vacation and have received three invitations to celebrations that will take place in my absence. Toffee will welcome her in-laws, Leah's niece will celebrate her 21st birthday and Togo's nephew will also celebrate his 21st birthday.

The funeral for Thobi's uncle will take place all day tomorrow, tomorrow night and into the next day. And the odd thing is I would really like to go to all of the celebrations and even the funeral.

More about the Ndebele culture was explained to me today by Rabie. When a baby is born, the father takes him/her to his family and the grandparents take the baby to the graveyard and call up the familial ancestors. They are requested to protect the life of this newborn child. As soon as it is possible, the mother does the same...only this time the infant is taken to her parents. If the baby has been born with a noticeable defect and something is wrong, the same ceremonies take place in the hope the malady will be cured or go away. If it does not and the burden is to be carried throughout life, this is the will of GOD and His way of saying it is meant to be and is His wish. If there is something that develops as the child grows but is still very young, a sheep is sacrificed. If the child is not saved, a cow is sacrificed. Does not jibe with Christianity in the New Testament but I was told that those within the Ndebele culture do believe in a universal God. Today, as Rabie tells me, many are Christians but are unable to let go completely of many of the old traditions.

Chapter Twenty-Two

Ngorongoro Crater evokes the image of Aladdin and his magic lamp. Polish the lamp and an amazing world of riches unfolds before your eyes. The difference, however, is that you do not need a magic lamp and the world of make-believe at Ngorongoro. What you see is real.

"Ngorongoro Tanzania... Land...People...History"
Into Africa Travel Guide

DECEMBER 2002

FIRST DAY OF VACATION

Different but not really so different after all...am awake at 4:00AM, up within five minutes and repacked, drank a cup of coffee, read, tried to sleep, up to stay, left for bus at 6:40AM which is to arrive at 7:00AM. 7:30AM arrives and no bus is sight. 8:00AM: no bus, and this goes on half-hour by half-hour. In my mind, I had forgotten my airline receipt and naturally in the rest of my body, my bladder was trying to forget that it was full, my stomach that it was empty, my legs that they are both weak (very), my back that it is tired, my seat that it is not normally creased and the bus forgets to come at all! Finally at 10:00AM, Christine from the bus, no, Mary from another bus, arrives (how did she know?) to take me to the combi rank. We do leave after forty minutes with 18 (3 kids) on board and three phone calls to the shuttle (Ignatious) that I will be there some-time today! As always, I really had to go and absolutely know of no place to do this. I must have been obviously jumping around when three young teen-aged boys led me to someone's outside toilet (one way for this township to know me). I have lost count of the toilets I have tried and used. And very thankful to do just that!

We do make it to Pretoria but am left off a block from the combi rank and the place is mobbed. At least twenty people offer to take me to a combi which I do not want; instead I am trying to find a city taxi. I also don't want to wait in the midst of this crowd but no one understands me. Finally I pay rand 40 to a combi after all and he promises to get me to the Holiday Inn (I hope) where Ignatious is to meet me. He does with the aid of the other ten people all scream-ing directions.

Ignatious and his wife (who took all my phone calls) have been very patient and he is there to drive me on to Johannesburg and the Birchwood Hotel. Cyn sends a text message to me that she didn't sleep last night because of the money situation at ASHYO. She is off this afternoon on holiday, too. Maybe the time away will help both of us. Is this not shades of bringing your work home with you?

Ignatious thinks I am very brave because I told him of all the commo-tion and confusion in trying to connect with him. But I am at the Birchwood now, my airline receipt has been found, the wine for the others is chilling, have watched a stupid movie, my bath is coming next and will start Mindy's Deane Koontz novel with some Snackies soon. Will sleep well tonight. Never did have breakfast or lunch but did have cheesecake and a Coke when I got here.

The three of us leave for Tanzania early Monday and will be back some time. Oh yes, the proposal that Cyn helped me with is in the mail.

<u>Sunday</u>

Jeanne and Stein arrive late (at night) but are in good shape. We talk until much later (after 1:00AM). It is good to see them and we are excited once again about the unknown.

Monday

Up and out for a full breakfast and leave for the airport with no complications. The flight to Dar es Salaam is uneventful. We arrive at 7:15PM and although an hour ahead of schedule, it is already dark. There is only an hour's difference (ahead) in the time (of Siyabuswa). We make it through customs quickly, buy a visa, and after much hassling between taxi drivers, we are finally put into a taxi and hope to be taken to the Safari Inn. The driver tries to decide what to do with three old ladies when he must let us off a block down the street and we have no idea in which direction to proceed. It has been a long ride to downtown through not the greatest area and no women are in sight. He points in a direction and we must walk down a cluttered alleyway and still there are no women but hundreds of men milling around.

The hotel is very old and much more decrepit than we were led to believe. Although it is in a very sad state, the young men in charge (two) are very nice. We walk up four flights of stairs because the elevator is broken. We are very hot and even I am sweaty but there is a private toilet, a shower, and ceiling fans in both rooms. After our hearts calm down because of the climb and our fears have no place to take us (where can we go but here?), we find we are fine. I drew the short straw and am in a room by myself but am too tired to stay afraid for long and fall asleep very soon. Woke very early to good cooking smells and am ready way ahead of Jeanne and Stein. They forgot to set the clock ahead so I have time to write here. Have been reading about this country and as always it sounds like more than what could be true but seems lately it is. Don't know how to explain, but it seems in my eyes that these countries that are so poor have been moving ahead technologically...for those well-off or in charge of businesses...but for those who are very poor what they did have is no longer available (note the hundreds of men in the street and most look down-trodden and impoverished).

We are to take a ferry to Zanzibar and meet up with Aida (Alice, the PC trainee who shadowed with me) sometime today after we figure out how to get/or exchange money. We find that here they do want US dollars! Don't we all? Of course, now we have South African rand which they do NOT want and will not take!

Tuesday

Obviously we did not make it to the ferry. Today was a long, but not so hot (temperature) day. We were in air-conditioning most of the time (banks). The day was fine and pleasant for me, a little panicky for Stein, a little more panicky for Jeanne, and a good deal frustrating for all of us. One of the men at the desk called us a taxi and told the driver where to take us and also told us to pay x amount and no more. We arrived at the bank and faced the first problem. This bank did not accept either of their ATM cards even after multiple tries. I was guardian of the luggage (we were to be at the ferry by noon) and just had to wait out in the lobby. Learning the art of patience this past year paid off.

We walked a few blocks to another bank. I used my card here but Stein and Jeanne still did not receive any money. We did not make it to the ferry but good things also happened all day long. Security at both banks was great. People at the hotel from check-in to checkout were very nice. Think Jeanne and Stein ran into problems at the telephone center but I was the "keeper" so didn't even meet any of that personnel.

They decided that we should see if the American Embassy could be of help and again, the man at the hotel hailed a taxi for us. Although we had to wait there, everyone was extremely nice and offered to loan Jeanne and Stein money. By now Stein has realized she has been inserting the wrong PIN number and is able to receive her money, I have mine and we offer to subsidize Jeanne until we meet up with Aida who can certainly help her.

We did get our hotel room rebooked and returned there and went to find a beer. That, of course, is a joke because there are absolutely no women out and we are not about to drink with all these men. Nor would they with us! We did walk a little way down the street in search of something to eat when a young man named Frances approached us. He offered to take us to a restaurant nearby and leaving us no choice, we walked along with him. Luckily, he was on the up-and-up and did all the ordering, and also escorted us back to the hotel. He reminded me of David's crew (David himself). Now we are about to shower and hope that we make the ferry tomorrow.

Wednesday

After our long non-productive day yesterday (hey, this is vacation), today everything goes very well. We are walked to a different (the 3rd) bank by a nice young man and all three of us are successful in obtaining money. He then leads us to a taxi and gives the proper instructions to get us to the ferry. He rides with us to make sure we get tickets. We find out later from Aida that this was necessary because one never knows when tickets are authentic or as in the States, scalped. The ferry dock is a mob of people but by 10:30AM, we are on our way.

The ferry ride was utterly delightful and after the crowd at the dock had dispersed and there was breathing space, the ride itself was a pleasant two -hour interlude. I watch the different boats and the others rest.

The arrival dock, of course, is jammed as we deport but we manage to call Aida, wade through Immigration and she is right outside the gate. We meet her husband Barouk and he is just as nice as she and we are on our way. Oh yes, Aida is the PCV who did not stay in the PC after our training because she decided to marry Barouk and move to Zanzibar.

We stop for lunch which is very tasty. After all, we are now in "Spiceland." We are served large dishes of rice, chicken and bananas. Yes, banana(s)! We each try four or five different types before we leave: tiny, little, regular, and one downright fat. Some are sweet, others are not. One has the consistency of a potato. Later Aida promises she will treat us to these cooked/prepared several different ways. We also try mangos prepared differently. I have come to relish these in any shape or size or even age.

We take our first ride in a dalla dalla, an open air, very crowded public vehicle. Elbows and other bony objects constantly are jabbing other body parts (must be like chickens in a coop vying for space). We move on and out. They live near the beach in a big apartment rather like our condominiums, because it is free-standing. There is plenty of water, a bathroom, fans, and here we are to stay until Saturday (I think). Do have to say, one does learn more about the culture and the beliefs of the people if one is living in the midst of it. Aida and Barouk are teaching us a little about Islam and again, I am struck by our drive for the good life that is technologically-driven when the simple art of living in peace should suffice.

Thursday

This morning, the four of us (Jeanne elected to remain a beach bum) went to Stone Town: Aida to finish a class, Barouk to do whatever he does and Stein and me to be overcome with history, people, smells, vendors, and rain.

Stone Town is distinguished for us first because it is the city in Africa in which the first building was supplied with electricity (so they tell us). More importantly (for me) because the Cultural Center, where Aida teaches art, was a hospital when the British were here. The building is huge, though crumbling and the massive doors are intricately carved (know not the wood).

The streets of Stone Town are very narrow, room for motor bikes but not room for larger vehicles. The evidence of the scraping of the sides of the cars, buildings and even the people, is everywhere.

Women are out in the streets here but most are dressed in the Muslim custom as is Aida. Many are completely in black and the school girls also are covered but with colorful material. Stein finds cloth she likes and I find a book of "Ghost Stories of Zanzibar."

We are intermittently wet, dry, wet, dry but remain overwhelmed. We never are frightened but we do not wander by ourselves far from Aida.

Friday

I do not profess to be a writer, an artist, musician, or photographer...but do know I am blessed with a fertile mind and given the new seeds every single day with which to sow. Let's take today. It is only 9:00AM. I have walked alone to the beach by Aida's home. This morning it has already rained, and a mild breeze and a soft cloud cover encompasses me. Many men are sitting on the sand and mending the fishing nets. These nets are not for fish but rather for tiny rocks. Later the women will arrive and gather bucket after bucket of stones, rocks, shells and use the nets to filter out the tiny pieces which will be used in making cement.

A cow is grazing (yes, all alone and chewing what?) on the beach. I am sitting inside a beached water-worn dinghy or dao, as I watch the different boats: some dinghies, some daos, some sail, and others out on the sea. The sun is coming out, the sky is turning blue on the horizon and I am safe from the millions of ants on the sand, the cow, the men and the elements. The war-to-be is very far away. Also the petty worries of my day-to-day world are very far away. Still think about them but am working very hard to replace the "cannot do" with the "will do."

Two young boys just surprised me or I them. They watch me for a few minutes and without saying a word, scamper off very fast. A young boy of about 9-10 years of age has joined me on my private yacht. He speaks no English and seems impressed with my writing and cannot hide his awe at the figures I am making. Even though I realize there are millions of people in this world who are illiterate, I have never met anyone who did not recognize that written letters, even in different cultures, are symbols with which to communicate. I won't make a difference in his life but he has blessed mine.

Oh,Oh! Now a hen and her chicks are visiting us (on the beach?) and Sefe (how I understand his name) moves closer and closer to me. He notices my scratches (I think) and tells me he is sorry (I think). He puts his arm around me and hugs me; now he is kissing my scratches and wants to touch my white skin all over. Just about the time that I think, "How do I stop this?", three more boys his age approach. I realize that my wrecked ship has become an ark and decide it is time to return to Aida's house.

We meet the women in the evening when we come down to play in the water. The water is invigorating-cool-relaxing-warm-clear-dark with seaweed refreshing and as clear and blue as some spots as the sky. It is difficult to tell where the water meets the sky. The sky at dusk is unlike even the South African or Idahoan skies. The white moon rises in between large coconut trees and out on the water, the sun sets between layers of multi-colored clouds. If one could turn 180 degrees without moving, one could watch both at exactly the same time. Would like to know the ratio of time from sunset to moonrise on nights such as these. Both appear to the naked eye as the same.

Later, much later for us, we dress and take a night ride on the dala dala (taxi) to the area where we had had tea in the afternoon. During the afternoon hours, the beach area was forlorn, all tables were empty and few people were milling around. It is much different than the market or trade areas where hordes of people are congregated throughout the day. Tonight, though, these same hundreds of venders and people are on the beach and serving fish, lobster, crab, huge shrimp, all types of calamari, all types of white fish including tuna, lamb, beef, salads, chips...choices are limitless. The people are joyous and I cannot distinguish the music from the squeals of the children and laughter of the adults. Aida tells us this gathering of the masses takes place every single evening and again, the wonder of peace is over-powering. We came home in a jammed dala dala (makes a SA combi a ride in the park). Jeanne rode home with Barouk on his motorcycle: her very first cycle ride and she was exhilarated.

Three men in the bed and the middle one said "Roll over." This is true for the three of us on the 2nd night.

Talked or left messages to all four of my children last night. Wished each of them a Merry Christmas because I am not sure where we will be next Wednesday (I never ever dreamed I would be on the island of Zanzibar, let along spend Christmas in Tanzania).

Home here again. After a quiet morning and about 1:00PM, Aida and Barouk took us on an amazing spice tour. We traveled far, far out into the country in a dalla dalla. This time Barouk drove and there were only the five of us. I expected to see the spices grown in separate patches, orchards, or even farms but never did we see them like any of those. Hundreds of different types of bushes, shrubs, plants and trees were all grown among each other and all together on one site. We visited four different locations and in each, the cardamom could be growing next to lemon leaves, next to coriander, next to pepper, next to bananas of all types, next to pineapple, next to sweet lime, lemon, jack fruit, lipstick plants and over and over again. Cinnamon next to nutmeg, next to bread fruit, and then over again.

We watched as one of the men shinnied straight up a coconut tree (sometimes he does this 200 times a day) and he put on quite a show. He sang and danced all the way up and all the way down. He moved so quickly at right angles to the tree...it was as if he was ascending using no hands. We were reminded of high-wire circus acts.

Those on the ground were busy using materials such as leaves, twigs, seeds, weeds, stones, dried fruit, peels, and rinds...turning these into art. Baskets of all sizes, jewelry, footwear, edible jams, dried fruit, and candies were all available for the asking. We tried much of it until we just could not eat anymore.

We continued our ride and Barouk wanted to show us the land they have bought on which to build their house. We found it a piece of Eden. Jeanne and I wandered down to their beach for an ocean swim (wade) and watched a fiery sunset. The sun was a brilliant red beach ball being smashed between two black pieces of sky coal. It was crushed into tiny slivers before it totally was lost to us.

Aida roasted us casalva (banana dish) on the beach and we returned to their home closer to town. Our visit was wonderful from start to finish. Tomorrow we leave for Dar es Saalom and the next day for Arusha which will be a long bus ride. Hope the next week goes as well as this did. To bed! Now!

CHRISTMAS EVE 2002
Merry Merry Christmas!

Tuesday
Lake Manyara Resort

Once again I will have to work backward...so much takes place every single day...even with all the waiting periods. Today I am writing in the hotel room and trying to catch up. Yesterday afternoon somewhere around 3:00PM, I did not feel "very much" well (SA term); my stomach started churning but just a little. We had left the Tarangire National Park and driven here. After all that we have seen on this trip of the very poor, this resort is like a garden of paradise. I did not appreciate it then because I was in-out-up-down-roundabout and generally miserable and messy, messy. Missed a good meal and went to bed maybe twenty different times. Today Jeanne and Stein are off hiking and I am here trying to get well in a hurry and I will! Stein had had this 24-hour stuff on Zanzibar and she had recovered in that time.

We are up in a room on the lake side. Mountains are in the distance and flowers abound, trees, too and so many different species. Stein is our in-house botanist.

Yesterday we left Arusha after breakfast but with no tea or coffee (we are totally spoiled) and a lot of errand running. We went to a bank once more to obtain money but neither Jeanne nor Stein were successful. My card worked and now they both owe me. Shopped in the market place for a hat and flip-flops for Jeanne. Her hat had blown away on Zanzibar and her flip-flops had broken (another story). Finally we are on our way...oh, yes, confirmed our airline tickets back to South Africa, made arrangements for bus, and paid Lazaarus (first driver).

Ziggy is our present driver and guide and will remain with us for the remainder of this trip. He drove us to the national park and we saw a herd of elephants, a pride of lions, giraffes and absolutely one beautiful water color landscape after another. We had arrived in a world to be envied.

On the way here, we passed a village with people from the Maasai Tribe. We were told by Ziggy that this (may be the only one) is one of the few tribes still completely practicing their ancestral culture and traditions. But he said that even as he speaks, the conservationalists (government?) are moving them off their own lands (as they have already done with other cultures) and into the larger towns. He said this will make it extremely difficult to continue living in their old way.

There are many grass huts in circle groups and similar to what I had pictured we (PCV) would be working in when going to South Africa. Today, the young boys were dressed in black and their faces were intricately painted white. They had just returned from being circumcised. The others that we are able to see are in what Ziggy says is their native dress and not for show. We drove past many people and he suggested we not request to take photos.

Must say something about the Arusha area. If I thought the Siyabuswa markets were busy and they are, I had not seen the vendor markets of Tanzania. For many miles in several horizontal rows, there are people to people, wares to wares and animals to animals. I cannot imagine this life every day. This is the rainy season and everything within sight is wet and muddy. This goes on and on, never ceasing and then we reach the countryside. This, too, goes on for miles and miles with nary a soul (maybe souls but not visible bodies). Why??

But now I am back to Sunday when we depart Dar es Salaam and take a very long, tedious bus ride. Before leaving though, we squabbled with a taxi driver and he finally drove us to the bus station. We got on and off four different buses and then had to give up our seats (did not give up...were shoved out of). The bus was very crowded and Jeanne was shoved so hard, she fell and hurt her hip and broke her shoes. We finally arrived in Arusha in the rain and at a mobbed bus terminal. Lazaarus, our first driver, was there to greet us and took us to the cheapest place imaginable. I tell you: we go up, down, halfway up, all the way down to the worst and all the way up to the peak of the best...all on this one trip. We are very tired...no, exhausted...but we manage and settle in (whatever that means).

On Saturday, we had left with Aida and Barouk at 8:00AM for the ferry which was to leave at 10:00AM. We missed it and left on the next one at 1:00PM. The ride was glorious. Aida, Jeanne and I went to the bank and got lost. We took a taxi there but decided to walk back and of course, we had no idea how to find our way and this time no young man came to our rescue. It turns out that after going almost nine blocks in one direction, we find we are only an alley away from the hotel after all. We would have been just fine with this walk except there were no women out except two Caucasians and one Muslim (us). Aida was the one who could get into trouble. She did not. Our hotel for tonight was fair but nicer than the first. John (son) called me to wish us a Merry Christmas and baby Henry is gaining weight and doing great.

Back to Christmas Eve. I am going to venture out and hope that my anchor holds!

MERRY CHRISTMAS!

It is stunningly beautiful at this resort. I am still cramping and heading to the bathroom on the run. Consequently, I have stayed very low and in the room. Did eat last night because I could resist no longer. But even a little was too much and the sip of wine which I also did not resist aided and abetted my poor criminal innards. Today, I am missing out on another walk into a genuine native village. But all this could have happened when on the road and although this is an expensive holiday, no, an expensive malady, will not complain of the timing. I am praying that America is doing well and know my family is...a new baby is the very best gift God has to offer.

Thursday

Today we drove to Ngorongoro Crater. Wonderful! Spectacular! Awesome Day! We all felt recovered and excited. The drive down into the gorge and over and about was breathtaking. There are only the four of us in a jeep and we have our driver all to ourselves. He speaks English very well and was better than an encyclopedia. We saw zebras by the zillions (only a little exaggerated), gnu by the gnunions (new word), warthogs, elephants, flamingoes (by the thousands, a virtual sea of pinkish coral) and at least twelve lions very close. One king was down for the count (guide said this had been a "kill") and appeared very hot, exhausted and I doubted if he would live much longer.

We tried to watch gold crown birds and pelicans take off and land but there were too many to keep an eye on any few. We had no difficulty watching the hippos and jackals though. No giraffes are here. These mammals were all in large herds and the scenes over and over were what one imagines when he dreams of Africa (if he does) and safari (when he does). Wonder-inspiring! Why can these animals live and play together, and prey on others only when necessary, and yet humans who are further advanced (?) can barely agree when more than one meet for even short periods of time? We have so much to learn and don't even try. We finished the day by driving on to another elegant resort, enjoying dinner and conversation and we are ready to go toward Mt. Kilimanjaro tomorrow.

Now it is tomorrow and Oh-no- no-no-my stomach acts up all day. I only had toast and tea for supper but today I am back two days. Don't know what is causing this distress but am off food until I go a full 24 hours without mishap. Would rather go hungry than smell with no way to wash out anything except what seems to be my insides. We have a long bus ride tomorrow.

December 27, 2003
Friday continued

Today, we head back to Arusha and cannot even imagine or even want any event to top the trip of yesterday. How could it? Those memories are to pull out, cherish, and to dream on. But must admit the trip back to Arusha was exciting in itself.

As we drove off, the rain continued to pour, and filled the deep ruts. This provided a serious threat of not only stalling out the engine but getting stuck in the mud (worse than snow). Because Ziggy was responsible for seeing that we had a good trip, he elected to take us to visit friends of his in a Maasai Village instead of taking his usual route.

In this village, there were only eight huts; two were not completed. Nine women from about 16 years of age to 60 (looked 100) and ten to fourteen children of all ages, were in sight, all working at some task. Each was colorfully dressed and decorated with exquisite bead work from head to toe...but their eyes were not radiant nor when they danced (for us) was it for joy. Instead, their eyes appeared forlorn and the children's demeanor appeared to me as very sad or weakened by I know not what.

Wounded lion, Ngorangora Crater (Tanzania)

The men in this village (there are only three, we are told) have gone off to hunt. The women are left to do all the day-to-day labor. This includes the building of the homes which is done entirely by hand. The huts have dirt floors, mud walls that are reinforced with cow dung, and the roofs are thatched over mud and dung. The rooms are tiny with no furniture. Cooking is done over a pit in the floor. There are no windows and the rooms are very dark inside, even though the sun is bright outside most of the time. They sleep inside on cow hide at night and outside on the same hide during the day. Today absolutely everything is covered with mud because it has been raining quite heavily off and on.

No one spoke a single word of English but each was polite and welcoming to us. They did a short dance to show their welcome but only the teen-aged girl (even she stayed at a distance) and the children approached us (they much closer). We took no pictures.

Ziggy told us that meals consist of only meat (no fruit or vegetables) and all subsist mostly on milk. I cannot begin to understand how they manage to get through each day when tomorrow will always be more of the same. Ziggy tells us again that they are one of a very few tribes in Africa who are still resisting changes of any sort. Actually, this is what I had envisioned my tour with PC South Africa might be. Now I'm relieved it is not. I do not think I could have coped, although many PCVs have helped in these villages. Perhaps if this is the case, then the PC training is also different.

We left the village and came on back to Arusha. I am in my room...have it alone tonight and have drunk a Coke, eaten a banana and the last time my stomach spoke was at 3:30PM and it is now 5:30PM. We leave in the AM around 8:00AM for the long bus ride back to Dar es Salaam. It has been quite a trip and have done or rather have not done it justice. Both Stein and Jeanne have said the trip has been beyond description and it is that, even for my now-quiet stomach.

<u>Saturday</u>

Probably the best bus ride I have ever been on. It was long but the right temperature, stomach calm with a bathroom on board, and Tanzania is a smorgasbord of vistas (window seat). We only caught a glimpse of Mt. Kilimanjaro but had not planned to climb it and are satisfied. Most unsettling to me as I watch out the window, is that despite the wealth of the environment in which animals and flora are apparently healthy and plentiful, the people appear to live in abject, downright poverty. Perhaps this is not a truth because all the small villages appeared in the same distressed conditions. However in the larger towns and cities, there are shacks, men (outnumbering the women), women, children, babies, animals, market stalls, mud (today), hot sun (most days), vehicles (where there is space) up and down every single square inch and many times one on top of another. And although food of all types appears more than plentiful, the people and animals do not appear healthy or well-nourished.

Coming into Dar es Salaam was much better than the first night. The hotel this time is a little nicer but still a taxi ride away from the depot. Stein had made friends with a lady on the bus and she gave up her taxi space to us and also told the driver the fare we would pay. Had a nice dinner and a nicer rest. Earlier, we had met a nurse from the UK who is working in a clinic in Kenya.

Sunday

Quiet day in Dar es Salaam. We took a taxi to the shopping area and it was closed. We wandered to the Royal Palms, an elegant oasis where we had lunch. We walked to a museum but did not go in, walked on to the Lutheran Church and did go in for a few moments. Outside it started to blow dust and it looked like rain was coming. We returned to the Jambo Inn and took a nap.

December 30, 2002
Monday

Another quiet day in Dar es Salaam, but not by choice! We went to the airport for a 9:00AM flight. We took off as planned but were in the air only 10-15 minutes when we had to turn around due to technical trouble with the engine.

Once again we are waiting, this time for the entire day. We are told that a plane only flies between Dar es Salaam and Johannesburg on Monday and Wednesday. They will try very hard to bring in another plane but if they are unable to do this, we will not leave until Wednesday. It is approximately 8:15PM when the airport manager announces that a plane has been found and we will be leaving at 11:15PM. We are able to reach Ignatious (the third time today) and cancel completely and Gertie (also the third time) and ask her to meet us in the middle of the night.

All in all, it was a very good trip. We could not help all the crazy mishaps or illnesses (all three of us were sick at one time or the other), and my favorite part, Ngora Ngoro Crater, was worth all of the trouble, a once-in-a-lifetime experience. We also met many wonderful people just in the past two weeks: Aida (my PC shadow roommate), Barouk (her husband), little boy on the beach, Sally the maid, Carol the nurse from the UK, receptionist at Jambo Inn, Ziggy the guide and driver, Vickie, young lady with whom I sat on the first bus ride, taxi drivers (even though we were never sure if they were on the up-and-up), the security guard at the bank and the list could continue. Do admit I'm looking forward to returning to Siyabuswa and doing major work on the Project.

JANUARY 1, 2003
HAPPY NEW YEAR!

Wednesday

Left messages for everyone. Baby Henry is doing well. And the thought (thinking again) went through my mind: "Tomorrow I get to go home," meaning Siyabuswa. Over two weeks ago, the thought, "Tomorrow I get to go on vacation" meaning away from Siyabuswa was in my mind. Is this progress?

Now back we are in Johannesburg. We flew from the airport in Dar es Salaam and finally landed in Johannesburg at 3:00AM. Gertie was already there and took us to her lovely guest house. We were up early and Gertie took us to the mall where we ate breakfast and saw the movie, "Greek Wedding." Yes, at 10:00AM. It was a delightful movie. Later I made arrangements with Ignatious to pick me up at 9:00AM Thursday and drive me to Siyabuswa. I also talked per phone with Christine, Thobi, and Rabie (who said he missed me).

Another quiet day passed. Beth, Jeanne's daughter, is here from the States to visit her. We also met a family from Mozambique: Helen, Jade and Sean. The world is so small. Every single day we seem to be meeting new people and expanding our territories.

Thursday

Ignatious drove me back to Siyabuswa today and I was ready. Must note here that I have had many vacations in my life but do believe that with this one, I have done ...done less...had more feelings...had more exciting adventures and had more boring periods than during any other single vacation. Let me see if I can even recall the highlights of the varied activities and feelings.

1. Long wait for bus from Siyabuswa to Pretoria which did not come and had to take a combi; received my money back for the bus ticket which is not easy because it may have been spent; jumped off at the busy city taxi rank and had to get to the Holiday Inn for Ignatious to take me to Johannesburg.

2. Ignatious became my private transport to and from Johannesburg.

3. Stayed at a five-star motel and watched movies on TV.

4, Stein and Jeanne came in on Sunday and stayed at same motel.

5. Flew to Dar Es Salaam, Tanzania; arrived late, area very depressed, taxied to maybe a one-star hotel. It was very dark, dreary and raining outside and only men were on the crowded streets!

6. Jeanne and Stein had problems with money and we visited the American Embassy...my first time to visit an American Embassy.

7. Had to stay another night in the hotel, no mishaps, but did not feel entirely safe.

8. Rode on the ferry to Zanzibar...wonderful ride.

9. Aida and Barouk took us to their home...very nice.

10. Rode on a dala dala and it was even more crowded than combi!

11. Saw the sun go down on the Indian Ocean as we were playing in the water.

12. Roamed around Stone City: very poor, crowded, wet, and muddy. We were the minority but everyone was very nice to us.

13. Ate shrimp and chips on the crowded beach.

14. Spice tour: watched a native climb for coconuts all the while dancing up and down the tree. Ate five types of bananas and one had been cooked in coconut milk and another was the consistency of a potato.

15. Rode the crowded ferry back to Dar es Salaam.

16. Left very early (5:00AM) for bus to Arusha; taxi to terminal (not sure if it would take us to correct depot), took different bus than assigned; no one spoke our language...very long and uncomfortable ride-more than 12 hours.

17. Met by Lazaarus, our driver and our guide.

18. Met Ziggy, our driver for the rest of the way to and from Ngorongora Crater

19. Went to Ngorongora Crater and the number and types of animals far exceeded our expectations.

20. Visited an authentic Maasai Village by accident.

21. Had a luxury bus ride back to Dar es Salaam.

22. Stayed in slightly-nicer hotel.

23. Were in the sky 10 minutes when the pilot turned the plane around and then spent from 9:00AM until 11:30PM in a very small airport.

24. Arrived in Johannesburg at 3:00AM and were picked up by Gertie and were transported to her guest house.

25. Had my own private transport back to Siyabuswa.

Chapter Twenty-Three

Never give in! Never give in! Never, never, never,
never-in nothing great or small, large or petty-never
give in except to convictions of honor and good sense.

(Winston Churchill)

JANUARY 2003

January 4, 2003

<u>Saturday and Sunday</u>

Christine and Rabie have gone to a "party." This is the first time that I know of—not a funeral, not a wedding, just a "party." Thobi is home with me. Nqobile, Nomhlebeka, Boy, Sonta, and Togo are also here and it (it again) is a mess. They are: in-out-out-in-door wide open-locked (me in) shut-locked (me out)-open. They clean-mess up-mess-up-clean, eat...five different kids and five different times-twenty-five different times in total. Refrigerator is opened at least fifty times...is shut the same number of times...greasy bowl of tomatoes turned upside down and dripped from the top shelf to the bottom and onto the floor. The freezer accidentally turned off...Thobi is upset because I don't let her eat off the floor. The kids are noisy...quiet (worse)...play hide and seek in the house...chased in and out of Christine's room. Thobi locks Christine's door. Christine will be upset and it's CRAZY and not fun. But they bring me a beautiful tiny rock. More kids come. I fix macaroni and cheese no one eats and it is good...fix cheese sandwiches...everyone eats...have Rice Krispies and milk...no one eats...dry bread and everyone eats. Andrea's cookies which were sent by my friend in the States are shared by everyone (believe it). This includes Rabie and Christine who have returned to a spanking clean house, laughing children and fresh cookies. They believe our day has been wonderful and it has! But the best of all was when a whole gang of ten-year-olds (must have been 12 or 15 by then) called me outside and asked questions re: HIV and AIDS. I was surprised and pleased and ANSWERED while I had them corralled.

<u>Tuesday</u>

We had good meetings today. David has promised to take me with him tomorrow when he visits an authentic traditional healer. He said she will explain to me the difference between medical healing and witchcraft. I am especially interested now because I am learning about the culture from the inside and no longer from the outside.

<u>Wednesday</u>

A cultural day with Peace Corps moments! David took me to meet face-to-face a Sagoma, (David tells me she is actually one step above a Sagoma, what-ever that means). She is a young (in her early 30s) traditional healer and <u>not</u> a witch doctor. She read his bones...a conglomerate of bones, shells, dominoes, and dice in a knit bag. He blew into the bag and shook all of the items out on a mat. She then read them. She told him he has pain that comes and goes (true), that the people don't like him (they are envious) but he is strong and will over-come them. She then told him to take a stick with a very pointed end and move it up and down his arms several times a day. She mixed a packet of ten different herbs (?) which looked like ground pencil lead and ground alum and told him to mix a spoonful of this with a glass of water and drink it. She gave him enough to last five days. He is to come back in two weeks.

Then she read mine. I blew in the bag two times. She said that I was "White" (the bones placed next to the three on the dice told her this!) She also said I was "light." David interrupted and said this means "free." She went on to say that the others in the office think that David is my "favorite." She also said I was "tired." She was very nice. Today the visit reminded me much of a fortune-teller or palm reader except that she goes further. She supposedly called back David's ancestors and during this time, they both spoke in their native language and he did not tell me what was said. Because of this, he could not say good-bye to her (the healer) because that would be telling his ancestors good-bye and reverse the effects of the medicine she had given him. She did not call up mine so there was no problem with my saying "Good-bye and thank you" to her!

Her family appears very poor and she gave the readings in an extremely small and dark room. This separate room was close by what I was told was the extended family home. The room was fairly clean but with no furniture except drums and many different containers of the herbs and other equipment (I know not what). Little kids ran in and out in tatters but looked well-fed and happy. She did not ignore them but did tend to business. She charged rand 20 for David's visit and nothing for my reading. It was not what I expected...there was no evidence of bad spirits or black magic but she did tell David that someone was trying to hurt him emotionally by sneaking something evil into his beer. Me...she said, "Nothing evil is after you." I think that is why I am "light."

I hope to visit others to see if they follow the same process. I am also reading on this type of healing and can't help but agree with some of it but...

*Must insert here my perception of David after working closely with him for over a year. He is the founding Director of ASHYO. This means he started the organization when he was only 21 years of age. He is young, handsome and energetic. He must be a mix of Tom Sawyer and Jean Valjean with maybe a little Robin Hood thrown into the mix. If I asked him, "David, how do you get away with your shenanigans?" He would answer, "Why ,Gogo, everyone here knows me and loves me." If I asked his family and friends the same, they would answer, "Why, Gogo, we all know and love him." If I asked myself, I would say, "I feel exactly the same."

Other events today: Cynthia had a good strategy meeting with ASHYO and she hopes they will follow through with the plans they put on paper. Later she told me that this afternoon David had been caught in one of his made-up stories that he had apparently told the doctor who is footing many of ASHYO's operational bills. These fabrications are going to do him in. If the others weren't also wholeheartedly dedicated to ASHYO, he'd be out or they would be gone. I remind both of us that no matter how inexperienced he performs, none of his omissions are hurting anyone. In his mind, he is doing only what is best for these suffering people. He continues to give 150 % of himself and takes only verbal credit and not material or monetary reimbursement. And when he does receive wages (of a sort), he turns around and gives it to friends who are worse off than he is. How can anyone fault his commitment to his cause? Age-old dilemma: does the end justify the means?

It was a long and busy day for everyone and the others are not used to a full day of work. Tempers are flaring to say the least. Even Freddy and Silvia were at it because we never ever can find anything (from pencils to contracts) and David is given the blame. Perhaps David is sabotaging himself. Or maybe they are all sabotaging Cyn and me.

Friday

The Project is to start on Tuesday. Even after Lucas did a great job on the art work, the others have put off and put off posting the notices. Then only half were distributed. I doubt if any one shows. I have found, though, that it doesn't do one bit of good to chastise anyone because no one accepts responsibility for any errors in judgment (myself included). In my case, they can pretend to not understand (don't get away with this much anymore). In fact, if I could have moved a little slower back before my retirement, when I was working on projects like I am now, perhaps much more would have been accomplished. But better now then never. Planned on writing the new proposal for HBCHO today but there is no electricity. See what I mean? If no one else worries, maybe I would get more done if I didn't either.

Saturday

One of those moods again today...guess it started last night. I know everyone is tired again (Christine has every right to be), also know that I must listen to everyone else but no one really cares whether I am tired or not. Now come on, do I really care if they are? Yes. Christine and Rabie went to a funeral again, Rabie all night, she at 5:30AM this morning. Both came home about 9:30AM and he is "very hungaary (his word)." She does not feel well and goes immediately to her room. No rest for her though because company arrives a few minutes later. She is very quiet to me and I am feeling as if I have done something wrong, but what? You know, this is or must be the hardest part of the hardest job I will ever love...living in someone else's home.

Thobi is in and out. I couldn't survive without her but never know when she will be here or when she is my responsibility while they both are gone. And my feelings are hurt because everyone has put lip service to the "Project" but no one is really interested except maybe Maureen (volunteer from Weltevrede). Christine acts like she understands me but has not told her friends and never remembers just what we are talking about when I bring it up. Hope this feeling passes before next Tuesday because I don't want to be in tears or worse, blow up. The way I feel now it could go either way or both ways. Maybe it is just opening-night jitters. Guess I'll go to bed and finish my book.

Sunday

I cannot stand this ambivalence and feel sorry for myself so asked Christine this morning if she was cross with me. She said no-no and crossed her fingers so maybe after I go to church I will feel better.

And do.

January 14, 2003
<u>Monday</u>

We held our very first workshop of the CBBG Project. I am here to say that it bombed big time. Only two legitimate participants showed and two more came at closing (almost). What did save the day...six helpers came from other areas and three more from my own group. With the four of us working, it ended up with a presentable group (we called it a dress rehearsal). I had told them that we were going to do this even if no one came. Now I had to follow through: it was a lesson in patience, forbearance, and downright tongue-biting for me. At first I was proud because the kids at the school had swept out the classroom and cleared the tables; then angry because the teachers did not come back for the class. My team did not come until 2:49PM and we were to start at 3:00PM. We still had a tablecloth to buy and the room to arrange. Freddy and Njongo go for ice with <u>my</u> materials and I am like a snake in a hot skillet and <u>no one</u>, I mean no one, has shown for the class. Will I never learn? I could not scream because I had already bit my tongue in half and the show had to go on.

Arrived home at 5:45PM and Christine with no remorse says, "Did you have your show today?"

THE SHOW
COMMUNICATION BRIDGES BETWEEN GENERATIONS (CBBG)

HBCHO (sponsor of CBBG)

The Home Based Care Health Organization (HBCHO), located in Siyabuswa in the Mpumalanga Province, was established in 1999. HBCHO is a non-for-profit non-governmental organization that operates throughout the Dr. J.S. Moroka Municipality in the Ekangala Region.

HBCHO attempts to offer services within twelve villages. These villages each have their own volunteers (members) who deliver home-based care and support to families affected by the HIV and AIDS pandemic.

CBBG

The HIV and AIDS epidemic continues to pose serious challenges to communities as adults die in the prime of their working and parenting life. This disease compromises the work force, impoverishes families, leaves millions of children orphans or living with much older grandparents, and devastates communities. According to a document issued by the Population Unit of the Department of Social Services, Population and Development of Mpumalanga, it is estimated that more than 320,000 people are infected with HIV in the Province. This represents almost 10% of the total population. Mpumalanga, with a poverty rate of 57.3%, an antenatal HIV prevalence rate of 27.3% and 61% of the population living in rural areas, is very vulnerable to HIV/AIDS.

In many instances, people infected by the virus become so sick that they are unable to continue working. This lack of employment results in loss of income, diminished health care, depletion of household resources and adds to the poverty experienced by individuals. Even families who are not poor prior to contracting the disease can become impoverished by the loss of an adequate income.

HBCHO, as it did in the early years of operating, continues to provide home-based health care and support services to the infected and/or affected families. The number of families seeking services has raised annually from less than forty in 1999 to more than five times that many in 2002. However, as these numbers continued to escalate, volunteers voiced the desire and commitment to assist the families even more. Because of misinformation generated and believed by many, a negative attitude and stigma continued to surround the families. This negativity prevented those affected from taking the crucial forward steps that would alleviate much of the pain and heartbreak suffered by them. There were no situational or even peer support groups formed or facilitated by any NGO in the area. To address this concern, HBCHO developed plans to implement the CBBG Project. This Project would ensure that a multi-discipline and diagnostic approach would be utilized when forming peer support groups.

After intense study and direct observation of their clients, it became increasingly apparent to volunteers, that the HIV and AIDS epidemic posed many challenges to the patients living with the disease. It was determined that one of the most serious was the lack of communication of facts between persons older than the age of fifty years with those younger in age. Very few were willing to address their concerns either directly or even implicitly, especially in regard to life skills and human sexuality. The younger may have received information about the problems during school hours by a teacher, but more likely they became "aware" by peer discussions. The older may have been marginally informed. But neither had been provided with skills to help them share information, concerns, issues, or needs with each other.

THEREFORE, THE SUPPORT THAT WAS DESPERATELY NEEDED WAS NOT AVAILABLE.

This lack of communication from the older to the younger or even from the younger to the older may include any one, several, or all of the reasons listed below.

The list is not prioritized but rather is listed as reasons randomly collected from community members.

1. Lack of updated information or fear of providing wrong information.
2. Older persons unable to read or write.
3. Information not translated or available in appropriate languages.
4. Subject matter is taboo and/or does not agree with cultural beliefs.
5. Gender traditions.
6. Respect for those older in age.
7. Lack of respect for those older in age.

8. Family roles rapidly changing: partly because of advances in the status of women and partly because of necessity due to premature deaths caused by AIDS related illness.

9. Technological advances have not been available to older members (computers, television etc).

10. A stigma surrounds communicable diseases, specifically those that are sexually transmitted.

11. Personal feelings one has when dealing with people with HIV.

12. Personal feelings one has when dealing with a family member with HIV.

13. Personal feelings when one is the patient and living with HIV.

14, If the communication lines have been free prior to a positive test, a breakdown is usually inevitable due to a poor understanding of the disease and its ramifications; fear of rejection, labeling, discrimination, and/or resentment, frustration, sadness, anger, conflict or even poor medical care.

15, The times are changing and advancing very rapidly. Most of those within the older age group are not keeping abreast of these changes, either because of a lack of resources or the unwillingness to accept any change.

16. There is a vast difference in the education that was provided to the older generation and in that of the school-aged children of today.

17. Socio-economic status varies within neighborhoods.

18. Religious groups may treat the HIV-AIDS epidemic from different viewpoints, as may the medical community.

It was the intent of the CBBG Project to lay the groundwork for the implementation of age and situational support groups for families and friends affected by the HIV and AIDS epidemic. This groundwork was formalized by providing current information regarding health and life skills to older members of the community.

Was the project a success? Absolutely! A series of eight two-hour health classes were held once a week in seven different locations. This free course informed older members about diseases with which they were familiar. Each class included a discussion of the nutrition necessary regardless of the diagnosis and pointed out that all diseases also affect all ages. At the same time, each class stressed the need for support regardless of the diagnosis, and gradually the topics concerning human sexuality were introduced.

The course syllabus was as follows:

Class #1   Introduction and discussion of general health problems (headaches, backaches, arthritis). The participants were requested to list the topics they would like to discuss. More than 75 topics were questioned.

Class #2	Hypertension
Class #3	Diabetes
Class #4	Infectious diseases (tuberculosis, pneumonia, influenza and others)
Class #5	Sexually transmitted diseases
Class #6	HIV and AIDS
Class #7	Communication
Class #8	Support Groups

Classes were held once a week in the villages of Denilton (hospital), Kameelrivier (elementary school room), Kwaphaahl (school room), Siyabuswa A, (school room), Siyabuswa B (school room), Siyabuswa C (large garage) and Weltevrede (clinic area). The primary focus of the classes did not change but interest was generated by the participants and age was no longer a factor. Age of the participants ranged from 15 years to 72 years and depended on the venue or specific interests. Men and women in each age group attended at each venue. Although only two attended the first meeting, by the end of the classes more than 350 participants received a certificate of completion. More importantly, the participants felt freer to discuss many health topics and move forward with the development of situational and age appropriate support groups.

I AM VERY PROUD OF EVERYONE!

January 19, 2003
HAPPY, HAPPY BIRTHDAY DIVIA!
Saturday
One week is down and it had its ups and downs but mostly ups. We met on Tuesday and this time four participants arrived: one man and three women. Two came very late. Seven of the crew with whom I work also joined us. This was good.

Wednesday morning Njongo and I met with a group of twelve elders. I thought I was just going to meet them but no, it was to talk about the project. They are interested and want to have a class of their own. We will start next Wednesday. I felt much better.

Thursday we had the first class with the group in Weldvrede (Maureen) and seven showed, two men and five women. One mother and her daughter are affected by AIDS and are willing to start a support group. Five from HBCHO came and on time. We spent the entire two hours talking about many health issues. It is hard for me because even though we have reviewed the material, the translators do not know the words of the conditions in their own language. We don't start on time but this is the way it is.

We have booked more sessions for each week. I will be busy with a class somewhere four days of the week and on Thursday we will have a class both in the morning and in the afternoon.

I have also committed to help Njongo write another proposal, finish the Constitution, Financial Plan, Strategic Plan, the protocols for the Advisory Board...all for HBCHO. This leaves me very little time to review my own lessons but have already done that many times over. I only have eight months left and am getting nervous. It is not enough time.

Cynthia will help me and already has...but is staying clear of the project.

Friday, she and I went into Pretoria to collect public health brochures on whatever conditions they had available. We went to dinner with Matt at Carrie's (Cam's replacement) and had Mexican food.

Sunday

We arrived back in Siyabuswa with no problems and found everything quiet.

Tuesday

We were supposed to go to Sister Love for a workshop and did go to say hi to Trifinah (Director) and Monica (PCV) but did not stay for the workshop. We came back early so I could work on the class for this afternoon. Not to be.

Two men came in and the brother of one of them was told yesterday that he is HIV-positive. He asked me to visit the family and I agreed to make a home visit if Oupa would go with me. He agreed to go as a translator and the men were agreeable with this. We were told that the man affected was very angry when he heard the diagnosis and was wrecking the house and tearing up everything in it.

Actually, although he was just tested, he knows he has been positive for some time and therefore, he is very angry (at everyone but mostly himself), impatient, short of breath and yelling incoherently (even at Oupa). He is also on a lot of medicines for other problems and these he is throwing all over the room (or has thrown them). He settled down shortly after we arrived and was quite open and willing to talk to us. But this being my first visit with him, I could not offer much encouragement and offered to come back in a few days. Oupa urged the rest of the family to be tested and they agreed (they always agree but rarely do). He has a wife, six small kids and his mother living in this house.

This afternoon was the first of the 2nd sessions. We talked about hypertension and how even children (especially Black) can have high blood pressure and even strokes (they did not know about sickle cell disease). It went very well...at least twelve more people attended.

Wednesday

My stomach had been upset last night but today is just fine. Do think this stress of HIV is taking its toll even on me. My heart aches for the people affected here and that is everyone.

Today was the first session for Siyabuswa B and word of mouth has helped to increase the number of registrants. Njongo is coming into his element as a translator and doing an excellent job. He also held a strategic planning meeting that went as he wanted. David, however, has the governmental inspectors coming tomorrow and is visibly and verbally quite nervous. Something is bound to come down. Let's just hope it is the roof with only enough damage for these guys to see the light.

<u>Thursday and Friday</u>

Good days and classes are going well. On Friday, we had an incident at the office. Seems Silvia thought she was joking around and said something to Lucas that he didn't like. He was stressed (unknown reasons). When she went a step too far and continued her joking, he hit her with a stapler. When Cyn and I walked into the office, she started to cry...a long story short...I called both she and Lucas back to my place. They talked it over and he apologized; she accepted and another crisis is controlled. There is too much of this untoward behavior because stress levels are always at a precipice. Just this morning, I had lashed out at Silvia because she borrowed my phone; she was on the tail end of a series of borrowing...this was a straw that broke the back. The dominos never cease to fall. Everyone in this township...or country for that matter...is stressed (they know not this word)...each privately as well as communally.

David's father is ill and he also worries about ASHYO's finances and his loss of office esteem; Cynthia is stewing over the dinner party she is hosting for WOM tomorrow night; and Silvia's father did not receive his pension and she must take a computer test that will cost her (?) too much. Funerals are multiple and take place every single Saturday and Sunday; Vusi is getting his first pair of glasses; Lorraine is borrowing money; January is getting frustrated; Zach is upset over the denial of funds for NALEDI; Oupa is far too busy and has too many red hot irons in the fire. My room is full of flying gnats? These stresses are everyday and ongoing occurrences of one nature or another. Thank God that because they do not know the word stress, they also don't know about drugs to take to alleviate same.

<u>Saturday</u>

Cynthia's dinner party was a huge success.

<u>Sunday</u>

My normal Sunday morning: walked to church and to Dorothee's for coffee. She told me that her family will be leaving shortly after I do. I am relieved that they will be here for the rest of my stay. I was afraid that because Joanna, their daughter, will be leaving in June that they were going back early, too.

Does this all sound as if life has normalized around here? Talked with Mindy and she is over the legal wrangle of the divorce. I am glad for her.

<u>Monday</u>

Worked in the office on CBBG...then during the evening on the new proposal...productive day.

<u>Tuesday</u>

Sister Love came with representatives from the United States. They were impressed with the project but everyone is when talking directly to me.

There was a better turnout this afternoon and at least all of the members of HBCHO and most of the members of ASHYO are attending at one location or another. In fact, those assisting have grown from eight to at least twenty and include both the men and the women.

<u>Wednesday</u>

Very good session this morning. Do believe the idea is getting across. And Linah said she is learning and hopes to facilitate a class of her own one of these days. I will see that she does.

<u>Thursday</u>

Another good day and now the funny incidents are happening. Class was held in a garage with at least thirty people (including gogos with two babies). Three of these gogos pulled out their snuff boxes and asked if chewing caused high blood pressures. The groups are beginning to bond and we are having fun. Great!

<u>Friday</u>

Good day spent working on the computer with Cynthia's help. She really makes a difference.

February 1, 2003
<u>Saturday</u>

Another overwhelming day. David's father died last Sunday and his funeral was today. We were up by 5:00AM and at the family home by 6:00AM. There were already hundreds and hundreds of people there. The speakers and music were very impressive. We were finished by 9:30AM and left for the graveside ceremony which also was beautiful.

Later Njongo, Cynthia and I left and went back to the office where the first meeting of the official Advisory Board for HBCHO took place. It went very well...and better from my perspective than they could possibly know. Njongo led the meeting and he doesn't realize it but he has taken many of our suggestions to heart and slowly it is becoming natural for him to lead. I felt good knowing that our input has fallen on ears that are listening. I was very proud of him. He was credible to his Board and some of his excitement about helping affected families rubbed off. They left with the promise to start work as soon as possible.

<u>Sunday</u>

Will start...Others had told me I would grow with this Peace Corps experience in South Africa. I tried to think how at the age of 68? Before coming here, I already firmly believed in God, had received too many blessings to count, and had seen His mercy at work. After coming here, I was scared, lonely, unsure, lacked confidence and questioned the why of experiences over and over. At the same time, I felt unafraid...comfortable and secure in myself. Once in a while I even knew why I was here. It has been 19 months (a long time), and now I <u>know</u> that it does not matter your age, it does not matter your skills and how you use them, it does not matter the situations, it does not matter if you are called or not called to the front of the church, it does not matter if you are a missionary, it does not matter if you feel as if you are talking one-on-one with God. What does matter and this may be different for others, but what does matter to me is that there was a moment when the realization came to me that I have grown since coming to South Africa. I was propelled to take the plunge, I was driven to produce, but the real growth was not in swimming far or in producing observable outcomes. The real growth came within me and my relationship with God, His relationship with me and me alone. I had a hard time believing He worked on a personal basis but He has, He does and He will! It is almost too much to fathom and I am even more afraid and less assured of what the future holds. At the same time, I am more exhilarated, confident and willing to continue on this journey within myself. This path that I am just now embarking on is by far more exciting than I ever deemed possible. After 19 months, perhaps (no, I realize with certainty), I am on a sabbatical or retreat that has enlightened me and now in my last seven months, I will be given the capabilities to help the situation here (how remains to be seen).

<u>Monday through Thursday</u>

I was invited to the first workshop given by Peace Corps for the new group of volunteers. They have been here seven months and I have seven months to go. I am much more relaxed and will enjoy myself. And did. The entire workshop was A-OK. Njongo went with me and his maturity in leadership is commendable. I realize it has little to do with me but some of it certainly does.

<u>Friday</u>

Life continues very much the same on the home front, some ups and some downs almost every day. For example: Rabie and Christine leave for a funeral. I still must ask when, where and will you be gone all night? I still must ask, will Thobi stay with me or will she go with you? I ask this as she is in and out and out and in. I no longer am stressed over this, though, because this <u>is</u> the way it <u>is</u>.

Today at the office was fine. David did not feel well and is worried about a report he has due. This time we cannot help him. He is Chair of the NGO Subcommittee for the Provincial AIDS Council and doubt if he has had any concrete objectives given him. He will come through.

Rabie told me today that he was going to call President Bush and tell him to leave me here. Can you believe that?

My phone time has all been loaned (given away) out and I cannot call home (United States) this weekend. I am not upset this is the new me. At least I am going to try...will turn into Christine yet, or maybe even Silvia...patience personified.

CHAPTER TWENTY-THREE

Chapter Twenty-Four

The world will never have lasting peace so long as men reserve for war the finest human qualities. Peace, no less than war, requires idealism and self-sacrifice and a righteous and dynamic faith.

(John Foster Dulles)

FEBRUARY

February 11, 2003
<u>Tuesday</u>

Another huge problem is about to land in Siyabuswa this week. The people here will soon have to start paying for water. On one hand, the people are free but with this freedom comes personal responsibility. They may have to start paying for that which was provided previously without monetary cost. But how can they...when most do not have an income and certainly not enough to warrant new bills? On the other hand, they have wasted water because they did not realize the cost it takes their own government to pay for obtaining it. Rabie asks how we pay for water in the United States. I discuss with him our taxation process. Today there will be a town meeting and tomorrow a toi toi (demonstration or riot) will take place. I thought this at first sounded promising but Rabie informs me it is very serious and also very dangerous. Someone or perhaps many will get hurt.

At first Rabie tells me I must march because I use the water. Then he tells me that I will be locked in my room because the people will come break in if they have to and "get me." I think he is kidding in both cases and when we arrive at the office, the guys there tell both Cyn and me to stay out of town tomorrow. Because of all the violence here and just to be on the safe side, we decide to spend the two nights in Groblestahl. Come to find out, even Hannis stayed at home (Groblestahl) on Wednesday. And you know what? Just yesterday the thought went through my mind, "I like that man," Speaking of Rabie no less. Can you believe it?

<u>Thursday</u>

Tomorrow is Valentine's Day. We had a good time getting ready for our party; worked a lot, visited a lot, ate and drank a lot. Another proposal is finished and in the mail.

But today, the 13th, was heart-wrenching. I was up at 5:30AM, although I had not slept well and we were on the road from Groblestahl at 6:15AM and arrived here at 8:00AM. Cyn and I walked to my house and Christine had made and saved us fat cakes. We enjoyed these and sauntered back to the office. I collected the material for this afternoon. The bookcase had arrived, as had the file cabinet. We are now in business.

Linah met me and we rode on over to Kameelrivier and were there to meet Aletta by about 10:30AM. We waited an hour for her and then she drove us to Kenneth's home. David had told me that he (Kenneth) was very sick and he (David) wanted me to visit him. Kenneth is a friend of mine and had attended the week-long workshop for volunteers many months ago. We knew each other fairly well but I was afraid he would not want to see me. However, he did and it broke my heart. He is very thin, appears very sick, weak and tired. He has a dry, nagging cough and does not remember how long he has had it, perhaps several months. He has been to the clinic but not to the doctor. He talked openly and his biggest concern today was that his mother, who lived quite a distance away, did not know how sick he is. Could I go and tell her? Oh my, he has no definitive diagnosis and I am leery about telling her how sick he appears. We talked more and he agreed to see the doctor and be tested for tuberculosis before we go see her. I will try to set up an appointment with a doctor in Siyabuswa. I'm concerned about him. Health care in this area is abominable and of course, he has no money.

I met Linah and Aletta and we went on to our class which was on diabetes and well-attended.

Maureen asked me if I would visit one of her patients living with AIDS (PWA) on the way home. I agreed and found she was a participant in one of the other groups. Progress is in sight for the project but is also revealing one familial crisis after another in this area. It seems there is no glimmer of hope in sight.

When I arrived at home, Christine was not well.

Friday came and we are to go to dinner with the WOM group tonight but Mary and January are no-shows. Mary is on her way home from a funeral in Pretoria and January has no ride in from Kameelrivier.

Saturday

The second board meeting for HBCHO also went well. Christine, with much urging, agrees to go to the doctor's office if I will go with her. I do and he lambasts us both and home we come. I am exhausted (oh yes-walked-walked-walked on Friday). Now I am cross which I always am when someone close to me does not feel well and this time it is Christine. Thobi is scared and acts out. Rabie does nothing but then does cook supper for him and Thobi and he comes through by agreeing to sleep on the couch so Thobi can sleep with Christine.

The next morning Christine is feeling as bad as she ever has (her determination) and Rabie and Thobi are both helping out. Christine is now in the cross mood with herself for feeling tired and not well. Will see if she heard anything of what the doctor told her yesterday. She has morbidly high blood pressure and her blood sugar is also too high. She has osteoarthritis, her ankles and hands are swollen and she is generally miserable. She must pay attention to her diet.

Sunday

This is a marvelous Mkulu story. He is cooking big time: potato salad, rice, beef, chicken for me and did not want his picture taken (doing this). Christine is resting. This is the very first time I have seen him do "inside chores." Thobi will stay home from church and nurse her. I am not sure if Thobi wants me to stay with her but believe it is better if I let her "gofer" for Christine. Probably Christine will crawl out of bed and do everything anyway, but this time her family is trying to help.

Okay, remember when the days for me were so long and I wondered how each would be filled or when I would have something to do? I have had the lesson which starts, "Be careful what you ask for." Following is a synopsis of my past few days.

Thursday

6:00AM shower, ride home from Groblestahl (the demonstration did not take place), walk home and drink coffee with Cyn, walk to the office, to the complex, ride to Kameelrivier, wait for Aletta, visit Kenneth, ride to Weldvrede, hold class, walk to visit a PWA and visit her family, walk and catch a combi to Siabuswa, work on the computer until 9:30PM.

Friday

Walk to the office, walk to the public health clinic and ride back, walk to buy telephone time (out of cards), walk to Hope for Africa and work on the computer, walk back to office.

Saturday

Walk to the Advisory Board Meeting, walk with Christine to the doctor's office, walk home, wash clothes, clean room, work on computer. Note: by now I have a lap top that was left to me by one of the previous volunteers.

Sunday

Walk to church, walk home, work on computer.

Monday

Walk to Hope for Africa and work on the computer, write letters.

Tuesday

Walk to a meeting to discuss what can be done for orphans, made appointment with doctor for Kenneth, made arrangements for me to go with him (Kenneth), walk to class, walk home, write letter to John (son) ...his birthday is coming up.

Oh yes, every evening have played cards with Thobi, seen that Christine takes her medicine and does not overwork (she does take her medicine and does overwork). Believe me, it is wonderful to be busy.

Wednesday and Thursday

Classes are going well. I have not had to give myself an attitude adjustment in some time. Cyn is the one at a low point these days because in her opinion, ASHYO is making little or no progress. Christine is still ill but Rabie and Thobi are hanging in there.

Friday, Saturday, and Sunday

At the moment, I do not feel as if I am in the Peace Corps...more like a regular job...and in some ways this is good...in fact very good. I feel comfortable, am no longer resentful, am less impatient, and am more adjusted to the slow flow of the days. On Monday...no, Friday, I called Kenneth and planned to take his x-rays to him; he was gone and instead of getting upset just decided to take them on Monday. I planned to mail the proposal but it was too late to buy stamps; did not get upset, will mail it on Monday. Friday night was unusually quiet on the street. Saturday I went with Christine back to the doctor. Her blood pressure and blood sugar were both still high so the doctor told her in no uncertain terms that she had to take better care of herself. She told me later that she will NEVER go back to him so imagine she is feeling better. Sunday, Cyn went with me to church and afterward we traipsed over to Dorothee's for coffee.

Monday

I did go to Kameelrivier with Kenneth's x-rays and to the clinic with him. He *is* on treatment for tuberculosis. The proposal did not get mailed. Njongo has it so it is literally out of my hands (no pun intended).

Tuesday

Class went well and we talked quite openly about sexually-transmitted diseases. I do feel lately that this little (enormous) idea just might work. After class, I walked out to HOPE for dinner which was great. Had not wanted to go but am very glad I did. I believe Pastor Hendrik is as sincere and truly loving person as anyone I have ever been privileged to know. I made a list last night and have met more than 300 people on a one-to-one basis since arriving here in South Africa. Is that not incredible?

The stars tonight are outrageous.

Chapter Twenty-Five

We give of ourselves when we give gifts of the heart, love, kindness, joy, understanding, sympathy, tolerance, forgiveness

(The Art of Living)

FEBRUARY

February 28, 2003
<u>Friday</u>

When do they do it? When do they go from vivacious, lively, beautiful young women to tired, worn down, not-so-lovely old women? How do they skip the middle years...each looks twenty-five years of age or less, or forty-five years of age and older? None, or very few, appear young for their age; one is hard-pressed to say who is 60 or 70 years or if any are 80 years of age. You would say...well, they work very hard. They do...but not all and not always steadily, taking sometimes long rest periods. And some do the same work as others but have learned how to accomplish the same more skillfully. Why after more than fifty years of washing does Christine still bend straight down with each individual item of clothing? Why does each person wear an item a very short time and then wash it? Why wash six blankets (woolen) or more at the same time and often? Why sweep the dirt and wax the stoops every single day and then throw trash willy-nilly on the newly swept ground? Why let the fowl have the run of the place? I cannot answer. Why does each grow old prematurely? It is actually work (for me) to walk as slowly as these women do...even the little kids who run, skip, hop and jump WALK in slow motion like their mamas. What are the thoughts that go through their minds? You would think after almost two years I would know. I have often wondered how a baby's brain develops a thought process without words. And I wonder here... not because they do not have words but because life is the same...year in, day out. Gossip consists of births, illnesses, and deaths but what are the dreams, goals, and desires?

I have many things to write now...don't know where to begin...okay, will start with health care: what to do? What can do? What should do? What should leave well enough alone?

There is a local public health clinic in Siyabuswa. Clients can go there and receive free medical care. However, the clinic is severely understaffed and no professional home nursing is available. Often, even though very ill,the very young or very elderly clients must walk far distances to reach the clinic. After arriving, most must wait long periods of time only to find the doctor is not in, the medicines are depleted or it is the wrong day for laboratory tests to be performed. There are no appointments made because many clients do not have a telephone service.

At any given time, Siyabuswa also boasts (?) at least two to five private physicians, and even fewer dentists, optometrist and pharmacists. These professionals serve a minimum population of at least 20,000. There are a larger number of traditional healers. The healers and medical staff do operate on a reciprocal referral system. A hospital is located approximately 25 KM away and an ambulance service is available. Although most family practice medical services are available, access to these services remains extremely difficult and for most specialty care, clients must rely on the medical facilities located in Pretoria or Johannesburg. Much of the time, this specialty care is unobtainable or received too late.

The home health care in the area is provided mainly by community health volunteers. A few of these volunteers may have received a short training course on health care but most have not and it is only through the love for these families do these volunteers offer any services at all. Volunteers may provide a minimum of home health care and support for clients affected by AIDS, the elderly, the disabled, the abused, neglected, bereaved and/or orphaned. Cleaning, cooking, child care and transport (rarely possible) are other services provided. The list goes on.

A middle-aged lady has malignant hypertension, diabetes, kidney or bladder infection, pains in neck, shoulder, back, abdomen, and legs, mood swings, and sleep deprivation. She often sleeps for short periods during the day because she is worn out and works very hard. She finally visited the doctor who told her all these problems, including that although overweight, she is malnourished (his word which she does not understand). She will not go for regular blood pressure or blood sugar checks because she cannot pay his fee and he gives her "nothing." She will not go to the free clinic because she must wait-wait-and may or may not see the clinic doctor and the clinic is very crowded and noisy and this makes her head ache. She continues to eat, work hard, and is cross when it is not her nature. If mention is made of any changes she might make that the private doctor has recommended, she is cross. She has come to only one of the health meetings HBCHO is holding and there have been six so far. She came for the last 30 minutes of the first one. <u>What to do?</u> Her husband is helping a little but agrees with her. I am concerned that she is unwittingly killing herself.

A friend is a 30-year-old young man, finally diagnosed with tuberculosis. One lung is almost totally occluded and the other is rapidly becoming so. He is extremely intelligent but has been sick for more than three months and he has no money to see the medical doctor. When he did go to the clinic, they informed him that he had to see the medical doctor. He did not; a friend told me and I visited. He is losing weight, coughing and has all the major symptoms. I literally took him to the private doctor who diagnosed tuberculosis. No response was made because he has no money. I toted his x-rays to him and again almost carried him to the local clinic where he immediately was given free medication to take for six months. However, as contagious as this disease is, no one in his family will be tested for tuberculosis, nor has he agreed to be tested for HIV. His mother lives far away and does not know how very ill he is. <u>What to do? What can I do?</u>

Another friend is HIV-positive as is his girlfriend but not under the doctor's full care because they have no money. Although he has tested positive, he has not been checked for HIV status or stage (his girlfriend is even sicker). He is willing to try and help others but does not know exactly how far he is willing to go. <u>What do we do? What can we do? How do we do it?</u>

A little boy has developed a large fatty tumor under his arm. He is eleven years old and although he lives within a large family unit, there is no mother in the picture. There is no one to see to his medical care; however, an older sister did arrange for him to go to the free clinic. Here they told him to see the doctor and to go by himself. He, of course, would not. I interfered and said he must go and I would go with him. The doctor said the tumor is not dangerous but should be removed and because it is large, it must be removed in a surgery. Everyone is cross with me for going this far. <u>What do we do? What can we do? How do we do it? Who takes responsibility?</u>

A young lady is HIV-positive and will not go to the doctor for a status check. She is "feeling good" (her words). She has confided in only her brother. In my eyes, she is beautiful but haunted. She visits me rarely and never when she says she will. <u>How much do I interfere?</u>

The misery continues on and on and on. What can be done? I do not know but I do know that something must.

Why not try?
- Professional nursing in the homes by public health nurses?
- Free accessible clinics with adequate professional staff?
- Medical cards for those who can pay a minimal insurance fee?
- Health volunteers for home visits regardless of the diagnosis?
- Referrals made to appropriate services?
- Free <u>transport</u> to and from specific services?
- Educational classes on specific health topics every day at different locations and for the entire family regardless of age?
- Follow up on referral letters which would allow access to hospital care?
- Age and situational peer support groups?
- Appointment times at physician's office, free clinic, or in the home.

Any one or all of these could be done as a basis to start and as a show of respect to community members and their families.

MARCH 2003

<u>Tuesday, Wednesday and Thursday</u>

These have been the best three days since before and after Dorothy's visit. Took the bus to Pretoria with no problem, except that I had to run like a chicken to catch it (old hen is more like it). Ignatious was waiting for me, nice as always and drove me to the hotel in Johannesburg. He is going to set up the trip for Cynthia and me to take the train across the desert in Namibia later this year. Tuesday afternoon I scouted out the mall, watched TV, and later met personnel from this hotel who would help me with my mini-welcoming party for Gail and Marty (friends from the US). They did arrive and we talked all afternoon and then went to dinner and talked more. It was good for me psychologically to know that three of my friends have "cared enough to act." I love them.

They left early Thursday morning and Ignatious arrived with all the flyers on the Namibia trip. I spent the afternoon at the Protea Hotel in Pretoria, read my book and took a nap. I was happy.

Saturday

And here we sit like birds in the wilderness...much better weekend than last when: 1) Mindy could not get through with a phone call from the States; 2) little boy went to the doctor and it was not a satisfying experience; 3) The Advisory Board meeting for HBCHO was also unsatisfactory; and 4) Christine is about to get sick again and in a very bad mood. From her perspective, I do nothing right, first by rinsing blue jeans in the kitchen sink, next by making a track of dust on the waxed floor and ending by not buying a battery for Rabie's phone. She, on the other hand, will not take my advice (orders) to revisit the doctor and to pay attention to her dietary intake. I know her whole system is out of kilter. My break to visit my friends has been good for all of us.

Upon my return, Rabie had his phone working and called me to come pick him and a friend up in the complex at 8:00PM. I was gullible and fell for it...his idea of a joke. He was in his <u>bedroom.</u> My idea of a joke also so that eased what might have been a strain when Christine and I meet (she has not been to the doctor).

Sunday

Jeanne called and wants to meet in Pretoria next weekend. I will try to do so but don't know if I can swing it (am very busy now) (AHA!) Thobi is here alone this afternoon...no rest for the weary (meaning me). I seem to be the only one concerned when she is left alone. I tried to work on the computer, write a letter, take a nap...but accomplished absolutely none of these due to interruptions (chicken flying, YES in room, MINE).

Wednesday

NEWS...NOT NEWS! 48 hours until the war begins...hard to believe but I just don't want it and of course, no one else does. This morning I knew what I wanted to say but tonight, I am worthless. The war is supposed to start between 1:00AM and 4:00AM our time here. Thousands are trying to evacuate before their country, Iraq, becomes a war zone. I am sick to my stomach and a good bit stressed and feel guilty about it...should I go home <u>NOW</u>? Would I be in the way of more important figures? Will the answers just come to me? Should they?

Freddy explained more to me about opening the tombstone (tradition/culture). Actually, it is opening the grave site. If I understand correctly, the series of events is something like the following: when someone dies, a funeral service is held usually at the home; the person's coffin/casket is taken to a grave site and although not buried, it's covered with soil. The funeral services have been expensive and funds are not usually available to handle the additional burying charges. When enough money has been saved, (may take years), another service takes place. This time it is at the cemetery and the coffin/casket that is on top of the ground is uncovered and then buried. This memorial service may also take all night and long into the following day. Note: the term coffin is used if it is not considered expensive; the word casket is used if it is considered expensive.

Don't know if I should meet Jeanne in Pretoria or stay put.

Today was difficult. Everyone was concerned about America going to war. Everyone was also concerned about me and wanted me safe. I did not go anywhere alone (no one would let me). Walked out to the Knosi home...gave the lecture discussing infections...walked to Hope for Africa...walked back to the office...sat in on a Sister Love meeting...sat in on the beginning of an Advisory Board meeting...met with two young people who are scared to be tested for HIV...both say they will be back. The first I have talked with several times over the past few weeks, the second is an old friend who requests help for her "friend." I hope I am wrong...wrong. All this in one day leaves me feeling pitifully inept, knowing that I have no solutions to world-wide and local problems and yet personally, I have absolutely no complaints.

Do not know how to begin. We are at war very big time. I do not understand but do know I have never been in the position of the bad guy. We hear a very biased newscast here and it is definitely negative to our side. I pray it is resolved soon, as does everyone, but it continues. It will be a week tomorrow. Cynthia and I are reacting differently but both of us are stressed to the max. It is not good to be away from one's home in times such as these. If I cannot understand the why...how can they (friends here and family at home)? Please, Dear God, help us all though this horrendous time.

My classes are about to reach completion for the first set of three groups. The first finished last night, the second will finish tomorrow and the third two weeks from today. Last night's was everything I had hoped and they are putting lip service to the first planning meetings for support groups. And of course, this was or is the whole idea!

Oh, yes, just in case I could ever forget these animals! I walked through a herd of goats in the complex today...eight of them. Absolutely no one was worried about them barging into a vendor or eating the food. They were herded by a boy no older than five or six years and of course, the Gogo (this was me). Think everyone thought I was the menace. Wonders do not cease! We bleated on through the stalls with nary a mishap.

March 27, 2003

Two mini-courses finished and only two classes to go to finish the third. Next we face four new complete sets in four different locations. Thirty certificates were issued at the first, 20 at the second and all want to continue and help support their community. We shall see; at least for me, I have a goal. I was given a quart of guava, two beaded bracelets and two beaded pins for being "so nice."

I was very upset today, though. The young men in the office were very proud (at first) when they asked me to sign a petition to stop the United States war in Iraq. I could not do it. This is my country. I do not want war but neither will I go against my homeland. Once again, everyone was confused regarding communication. They were proud that they showed concern for me and I was stunned that they would even ask. I want to go home. As it turned out, when I would not sign, they took the petition, tore it in half and threw it into the waste basket. Now I was proud.

Am I once again thinking wrong? Should I stay? What am I proving? Could I be doing the same activities at home?

<u>Sunday</u>

And the war continues...I am very confused, sick at heart, worried and scared. I awoke every morning for weeks wondering if the attack had started. Now I am awaking every morning praying it has stopped and stopped completely. I have spent this weekend packing to go home in five months.

The days here are still beautiful, the air clean and the children are free...so why? I am in my room, it is 4:00PM, the sun still is bright but low on the horizon. Children, and there are many, from ages two to twelve are shouting, squealing, laughing, and playing: some handball with a collapsed bean bag, some stick ball with a stick and a large stone, some cricket with a battered bat, some house with wonderful finds from the trash, some watching it all but not for long, and some are jumping in and out of a yarn rope pulled taut. All are bare-footed on hot gravelly sand and even hotter concrete stoops. All this is accompanied by the bleat of goats, the honks of geese, the cooing of doves, the doodling of roosters and the rattle of cars as they fly by throwing dust in a storm to all in the way. I sit here in my window and watch with awe. Peace and freedom are not free but they are here on this street!

I am going to travel in my mind back to Friday and relate the conversation that took place...two of them in fact.

<u>Young man,</u>	"Gogo, do you remember when I told you I had this sore place?"
<u>Go</u>go (me)	"Am not sure."
<u>Young man,</u>	"Well, the doctor gave me more medicine. This is it." He hands over a tube of antibiotic salve to me.
<u>Go</u>go,	"Yes, I remember, I thought that you had taken care of that."
<u>Young man,</u>	"Not quite, my penis is still sore." He laughs and says he feels free to tell this to everyone and does. I don't understand why he wants to do this but he has it in his head that a "real man" is free with "everything."

Move to later in the afternoon. A group of young men from both agencies are in their normal circle just talking and from my understanding, one of the young men, whose birthday it is (#30) is going to take an enema (his new English word but the concoction is actually a laxative) tonight so his sex drive will be at its max for the fun he plans to have. His girl friend is not here. Thank goodness, because this conversation reminds me of perhaps 12 and 13 year-olds and not adult men. None of the group is showing any respect to the young lady or me for that matter. They are surprised that I understand the conversation. I said, "I doubt this works" because in my wildest dreams I never related either an enema or a laxative to an aphrodisiac. But the rest all agree with him.

<u>Monday</u>
April Fools Day!

Before I forget, we should do a new dance. Call it "The Walk," and do it to South African time. I tell you, it is work to walk slowly...and it does turn into exercise just to put one foot in front of the other. You use muscles in your feet, calves, shins, knees and hips. And don't forget your sacra-iliac. When you take a step every 5-8 seconds, you even have to <u>think</u> about it. Now I do not have much muscle left to use so this is wearing on my bones. But I pretend that each muscle has to move 200-plus pounds of female instead of only 110 pounds and then I know for which woman I feel the sorriest. Practice in this case just makes it harder.

<u>Friday</u>

I am going to ask Freddy to explain to me his thoughts on apartheid and the African National Council (ANC). As with everything, I am finding there are many gray areas.

This afternoon only <u>one</u>...that is right...only <u>one</u> person...showed up for a follow-up planning session for support groups. While waiting, Njongo (male) and Linah (female) entered into a private conversation. Each talked non-stop for more than thirty minutes discussing the government and its problems. On many issues (my take), they did <u>not</u> agree and talked right on top of each other. It is the first time one of these women (with me present) stood up to a man in a conversation and I was surprised that it was Linah. Will talk with Freddy about all this.

Insert: The horoscope (mine) drawn out of the envelope today. "Cancer: you are due for a trip back into the past. Get a look at one particular episode that is still affecting you."

I am really sorry to end this journal on a very sad note but my mind does not seem to be on anything but Rita. She died on March 10, 2003, from metastatic cancer. She and I go so very far back (childhood). For more than sixty years, our lives continued to cross, run parallel and juxtapose in oh, so many directions. And hers ended too abruptly when she made the conscious choice to accept no treatment. Our paths crossed at the very end when her hospice chaplain was Jeannie, a friend of mine from Springfield, who moved to Denver over 12 years ago.

My family was like a second family to Rita, even my aunts, uncles and cousins. When we were in our early teen years, we were together almost every day. Amazingly, both of us remember many anecdotes, good and not so good, from those days. In our early years of marriage and child-rearing, through her divorce, her second marriage, my divorce, and her husband's premature death, our friendship remained steadfast. She was undeniably one of the most vital, honest, brave, open, non-judgmental, most judgmental, delightful and loving persons I will ever have as a friend. We were never embarrassed to say we loved each other but we could also fight worse than any dog or cat. Neither of us could bear the thought that we could ever be anything but "best friends."

Chapter Twenty-Six

"Can a black person's heart be transplanted into a white person or vice versa?"
"Do black people have white blood cells?"
"Does anyone ever have black blood cells?"
"Do both black and white people have the same color of blood?"

(Questions asked of me from the people)

APRIL 2003

April 9, 2003
<u>Wednesday</u>

Very good day to start a new journal! Good from start to finish. First, first and again first! Baghdad has been taken...huge statue of Sadam Hussein toppled and in smithereens. It is not over-over or final-final as my brother David would say but hopefully, the worst is past. Cannot begin to describe how I feel and would feel very small even making the attempt. The problem may be that there are none who are totally right that are running any country in today's world...that we as humans can recognize and follow. Maybe though, we will learn yet from experience.

This day continued very "okey-dokey," or at least for me on a personal note. We held the 8<u>th</u> and final class for group #3. I arrived at 9:15AM with a fancy cake, peanuts, drinks, certificates and pins for me to give <u>them</u> a party. But instead, they gave me the party. The garage, in which we meet, was all decorated with streamers and tables were set up in the main house complete with centerpieces and china place setting (all this for a class of thirty-five participants plus the leaders). I could smell the cooking as I entered but thought it was for their lunch after class. The evaluations were wonderful, pictures were taken and the certificates presented. But before they served a large lunch of pap, chicken, and cabbage, they <u>each</u> came and presented presents to me. These included a beaded necklace, a bracelet, a decorated jewelry box, a lunch towel, two fancy glasses, rand 20 for me to drink Coca-cola on the plane home, a handmade floor mat, and Nomhlakambo #2 and Nomhlakambo #3 (small beaded dolls). They named <u>me</u> Nomhlakambo #1. It was more than overwhelming. A few even gave a speech and told me: "Even though you do not communicate totally in our language, we all know that you love us and all our sick people." Could anyone ask for a testimony better than this? No! The day ended with Rabie, Thobi and I at home and even Rabie was happy for me. Thobi spent the night in my room and slept, "very well."

<u>Thursday</u>

Will tell a little more of the heartache out here in Siyabuswa. Oupa came in early this morning and said he was "Not good." This was a different answer than usual and I asked, "Oh, Oupa, what happened?" I did not expect the answer he gave while breaking down with sobs. His very good friend, only twenty-three years of age, was shot to death last night. His car and everything on him was taken and he was left in the middle of the road for the next person coming by to find. Oupa feels very sad and when he told me that the young man's mother is a member of one of our classes and has become a friend of mine, I too joined in his sorrow. I cannot imagine but do believe that there must not be any pain worse than losing a child. All the young people here know the family so it was a very somber day.

Later in the day, Maggy, Olga and I went to Kameelrivier to start the 4th set of classes. There were 20 participants and it promises to be a productive and fun eight weeks.

Friday

I went to Pretoria with Cyn for her to take a government test for International Service, and for me to collect informational material for the upcoming classes. We split about 11:30AM and I wandered over to the PC medical office to receive the results of some blood work. All was normal so guess it is just the aging process that has me a little dizzy at times, or my imagination. I then went to the mall and met Cyn back at the Backpackers. Only four months and I will be HOME!!

Received a letter yesterday from Rita's daughter Laura. It was a beautiful note and paid tribute to the friendship Rita and I had over these, oh, so many years. And Rita you will always, always be my "Forever Friend."

I am reading "Country of My Skull" and it is truly heartbreaking and with the way democracy has progressed here, I am very fearful that similar ideas will be pushed on the Iraqi. No one or no group of people can change beliefs, cultures, politics, and religion of others overnight. No one can turn a nation to capitalism and at the same time promise to take care of all the people all the time. No one can offer billions of dollars to billions of people; this equates to a very few dollars to the masses and ultimately a lot of dollars to a few. The necessities such as health and education are left in the far wings. Why-oh-why is health care at the bottom of the needs list when if you are not healthy, all the rest is moot? You can educate but if one dies prematurely has not it been at a high cost to the family? You can provide food but if one does not receive enough to sustain ener-

CBBG Class

gy, one is not strong enough to work. You can build roads, cities, airplanes, factories, mines and if people die prematurely, who are you building these for? We talk about volunteer counseling and testing for HIV; we talk about prevention of sexually-transmitted diseases; we talk about erasing the stigma of disease. We talk, talk, talk, but we do not "walk the talk." We know people are not being tested; we know children are dropping out of school; we know friends are deserting friends; we know kids are raising kids; we know all of this. But what are we doing? Where is the vaccine, where is the treatment, where is the palliative care, where are the regular food parcels, and where is the medical advice? So now I ask: what can I do? I do not know. I would say I need to put my money where my mouth is but no, now I need to put my actions where my money is not. How many times have I said, "I do not know but I will find out"? Well, I still do not know and I have not been able to find out.

I have found that Siyabuswa and the surrounding communities are undergoing vast and multi-dimensional changes every single day. These communities are comprised of several different cultural groups. Although most are a mixture of modern and traditional cultures, some continue to adhere strictly to familial historical rites, ceremonies and beliefs. It is not unusual for families to speak a mixture of Zulu, Indebele, Afrikaans, Sotho and English. It is also not unusual for families to respect and/or celebrate multi-cultural weddings, birthdays, holidays and even funerals. When celebrating, many are in traditional dress, play traditional music and eat the food native to their own customs. But at these same celebrations, many are also following more recent and westernized behaviors.

I have found that Siyabuswa itself is a township with an approximate population of 20,000 people. Within the surrounding area and in close proximity are multiple smaller villages with populations ranging from a few hundred to more than 10,000 people. It is documented by the Department of Social Services that Mpumalanga Province has a poverty rate of more than 57.3% of a total population of more than 320,000 people. Siyabuswa with an unemployment rate of more than 65%, most certainly has a higher- than- average number of people living in or close to poverty levels.

I have found that Siyabuswa is considered rural in its landscape. There are a few small farms, those that raise grains and domestic vegetables and those that raise livestock. There are large fruit orchards owned by a few and most families have at least one or maybe two mango or avocado trees. There are many communal vegetable gardens tilled by senior volunteers. A few families, such as Rabie's, have a small private garden. However, there remain a large number of families who have no vegetation on their individual lots, and most are located in such a small space that caring for cattle or sheep is prohibited.

I have found that Siyabuswa is located in the high veldt area and surrounded by vast areas of desert-like terrain. It does have all four seasons, although each is not as highly defined as in other countries. Winters are cold, dry and windy but warm during the sunny portion of a day. Summers are hot but cool during the late night or early morning hours. Spring and autumn arrive early as opposed to a full three-month season. The weather is conducive to the growth of a vast number of floras and except during the very heart of the winter, trees, bushes and other plants are in a cycle of greenery or colorful blooms throughout the year.

I have found that small businesses are trying to sustain themselves. For example, Ndebele beadwork done by the women abounds, as does other artwork done by both men and women. However, there are rarely outside visitors and locals do not have either the money or the desire to purchase. There are no large businesses or factories in the immediate area. The shopping complex does have two moderate-sized grocery stores, and boasts at least one hardware store, furniture store, lumber store, medical clinic, a police station, the District governmental offices, schools, post office, bank, and many other small shops. At times, hundreds and hundreds of venders are lined up, down, and across using every available space in the streets. Prices of goods are increasing daily and at the same time, paying jobs remain at a minimum. Most of the social, education, recreation and health care needs for the community are provided by volunteers. Electricity, water and indoor toilet facilities are available but many cannot afford the daily and monthly payments for such amenities.

I have found that although there are many creches, primary schools, secondary schools and several technical/colleges in the area, there is an extraordinarily high student-to-teacher ratio in each of the classes. There is no central library and very few books, maps, charts or posters in the classrooms. Even so, the children and young people are bright, energetic, and eager to learn. They advance in spite of the paucity of teachers and materials. It is heart-rending that a high percentage (I do not know the exact figure) of children must leave school at an early age and before graduation. A main cause of this drop-out rate is because it has become necessary, especially for girls, to stay at home and care for an ill member of the family or even provide parental support if the children are orphaned. Boys must also leave school before completion in order to work outside the home and perhaps provide a small income.

Most importantly, I have found that each family in Siyabuswa has been affected by HIV and AIDS. It is very difficult, if not impossible, for anyone to ignore the impact that this epidemic has had on the personal life of each and every man, woman and child.

One of the lessons the people here have learned from HIV and AIDS over the years is that this disease is not only a health problem, but also a developmental problem. Teaching the ABCs of prevention has not been enough to change behaviors. Without adequate income, people engage in behaviors that put them at risk for disease. Without adequate food, diseases can progress more rapidly. Without education, social support and protection of human rights, people become open to disease, isolation and discrimination.

Easter Sunday 2003

Message on my telephone sounds as if it might be Devan and Divia but it also sounds like water. Hope it was them because they will call again. Today I am in Groblestahl at the Lion's Inn with Cyn, Jan, Pat, Bobbie, and Karen

(PCVs). At the moment I am up on a deck overlooking white cotton fields and harvested corn fields. The mountains (high hills) are on the horizon in the distance, the sky is clear, doves are cooing, birds are chirping, trees are blooming (pink cottonwoods and orange and red something-elses (my word)). We have just come from the Catholic Mass and the priest allowed all of us to take Communion. The service was in English. Hank, who drove us, also attended.

Cyn has cut my hair and wandered down to the pool where the rest are. That leaves me up here by myself and every time I look out or down, I see more flowers...purple now. I feel good, really good and can go another four months, maybe more.

Now I am becoming so immersed in the culture that it may be difficult to rejoin my own people, but then again in most ways, it will not. A couple more Mkulu stories: he left for church last Tuesday night and I said, "Be careful of the criminals," because that is what he tells me. He said, "Oh, I am a tiger and can fight them off but for you, Nomhlekwabo, I would be a LION!" Oh, how he has changed. Or is it I? Thobi crawled up beside me in the bed the other night as I was reading. She said, "Nomhlakambo, what is this in English?" and pointed to her nipple. I told her and then she asked about her breasts...why we had them and when would hers get big? I told her when she started maturing and that they filled with milk when a woman has a baby to feed. She reached over to me and said, "Nomhlakambo, you don't look like you ever had nipples big enough to feed babies!"

Life goes on. Thobi's mother is supposed be here this weekend and help Christine for two weeks. We shall see. Christine has not been back for either a blood sugar or blood pressure check. Boy has another visible lump. Rebecca has not been for a follow-up retest. She is to come to class on Tuesday with a friend and both are to come for counseling on Wednesday. I have not heard from Kenneth.

And life goes on...names change...situations change but still everyone and everything remains the same. The United States is helping Iraq (?); Israel and Palestine are fighting big time and I am sitting here worried about my own family. Each has his/her own problems and I do not know how to help. Do know that if I am supposed to step in, if I am patient and ask for help on how to do this, I will be shown the way. For the past year, this is how it has been.

<u>Monday</u>

Today is a holiday here called Freedom Day or Family Day depending on who you happen to ask. Cyn and I had an easy trip home from Groblestahl but when I walked in the back door at home, everyone was very sad. Thobi's mom did not show or call on Friday when she was supposed to come with her new baby. Thobi is very worried, but Christine and Rabie are angry because she has not kept her promise once again. Christine then tells me that the brother of one of the young men who is a good friend of mine, was stabbed to death last Friday night. He (my friend) was attacked and almost killed two weeks ago. It is dangerous in this township. His brother makes the fourteenth person that I knew (at least slightly) to be murdered since I have come and the sixth one in the immediate neighborhood. There have also been many more that I either did not know, or did not even hear about. Christine says it is devil worship and too much drinking. I am not sure if it's devil worship but I do know that the lack of work and so much idle time, day in and day out, does allow many to drink almost steadily. There are shebeens on every block and sometimes more than one. I am still not frightened because I feel quite protected. For instance, last Friday Njongo walked me home because it was 6:30PM and starting to grow dark. Rabie gives me a frequent lecture and commands me to carry very little with me at any time (cell phone, purse, etc.). I think I am conscious of these crimes because I am working within the age group in which most of them are happening. Would tell PC that there are dangers out here but Siyabuswa has become home here in SA and I would be even more leery if I had to relocate and find my way around once again.

Will do what Thobi wants tonight and maybe I can help her out a little.

<u>Tuesday and Wednesday</u>

Last weekend with PCVs in Groblestahl and this weekend in the Sabie/Glaskof region were fantastic and entirely two different types of escapades for Cyn and me. I left the house at 7:30AM Friday, waited at the taxi rank until 11:15AM, arrived in Witbank and left by combi almost immediately for Nelspruitt, arrived about 3:30PM at the Promenade Hotel, had a beer with Cyn and she left with her friends. I had a wonderful BATH, talked for 45 minutes to Cecelia (PCV friend in this area), ordered room service and could have sworn I had died and gone to the Hyatt. Saturday had breakfast with Cyn and her friends. They drove us to Sabie. We roamed around a little and they dropped the two of us off at the Green Castle Backpackers. Manda (owner) was delightful and after many, many false starts, she found us a driver for tomorrow.

In the morning, he picked us up and drove for almost three hours around the countryside. It is spectacular and a God-given natural miracle in landscaping. We surveyed, much too quickly, God's Window, the Pinnacle, Pilgrim's Rest, and the Lisbon Falls. Chris, our personal driver, agreed to drive us to the Nelspruitt taxi rank and we came on back to Witbank. Cyn stayed and I returned to Siyabuswa.

Thobi's class placed second at the Music Festival and they are off to Marble Hall next week for the regional contest.

Two classes today, back to back, but am down to only 22 left out of 58 so I am breathing now. Participants are now from ages 15 to70 and all very interested. So far, they have not established the support groups I had envisioned but perhaps these classes are of even more value at this time. If each shares what she/he is learning with one other, and so on, soon many will be reached and at least a little support will be offered to those with all sorts of existing conditions. It was most amazing to me when one of the women said to me, "Sydney, I hope this learning spreads as fast as the disease does only for the good and not for the awful."

It is turning cold now. Finished reading "Country of My Skull" and the book is tragic.

MAY 2003

May 1, 2003
<u>Thursday</u>
     May Day! All is well here but I did get attacked and it was not bad at all! By a goose no less! I was hanging clothes on the line yesterday (yes, <u>all</u> wash is done by hand, even heavy blankets and yes, I do my own, even the curtains) when I felt this sharp pinch on my calf and lo, Father Goose took a nip. I had on slacks so he did not break the skin but did give me a bruise. He's been aiming for me for quite some time but always as a frontal attack. This is the first time he did a sneak approach from the rear. And wouldn't you know it? Tonight when I went outside (after I had fed them), the rest of the family: mom, sister and three little goslings, beaks wide open and honking loud, louder and loudest, did meet me head-on but not Dad! The kids (children) are out here playing and screamed, "They are after Gogo, they are after Gogo." Out comes Mkulu and by now it is bedlam. Even the chickens or rather the rooster has joined in the melee. Now there are squeals, cooing, chirping, horse laughs (Mkulu) and giggles. I don't know whether to laugh, cry, cuss or pray but this I do know, I don't want to stand there and be eaten as a scrap. I just say, "Listen, you dumb geese, move it!" Do you think anyone wanted to help? No! All they did was laugh and say "Goose goin' to get you, goose goin' to eat you, goose goin' to beat you" and then laugh all over again. Richard Scarry has nothing on them; they had made up their own nursery rhyme. I bet you early tomorrow morning, those geese will be outside my window honking to get my attention and asking me to come out and Mkulu will have put them there!

<u>Monday</u>
     This day was one mixed-up mess. Christine has the flu with a sore throat and all that goes with it. She is cross or at odds with the world when she does not feel well. I talked her into going to the clinic with Boy (11 years of age). He has another large lump (?) under his arm. It continues growing slowly and I am concerned that he may have tuberculosis. He has no adult in his family that can take responsibility for him and have it removed. Christine, who is his great aunt, will have to give permission for any medical care. We do make it to the doctor's office and he calls the growth a lymphoma and tells us that it must come out and be tested just to make sure. Now that means a trip to the hospital which is forty minutes away even in the best of conditions (which I know not what these are). Who has the money to transport him there or the desire to do so? He does have a mother but she lives somewhere else and is very sick herself. In the meantime, Christine is miserable and Rabie (all 300 pounds of him) has a backache and thinks one Tylenol is magic. "Please, oh, please Nomhlakambo, give me a pain pill." This same day, Thobi has sores in her mouth because of too many sweets, David is told he must have a hernia repaired and is scared of the knife, and Oupa really does have the flu with a high temperature. The young man that I had been told was killed was not; instead, he is accused of doing the killing.

One of the young men who works with us was mugged over the weekend. He shows up at the office with an unstitched, unbutterflied 2 inch gash over his eyebrow, a broken nose, and lips popped up to his nose. "What do I do gogo?"

May 11, 2003
Sunday

MOTHER'S DAY and a perfect one!

Actually this weekend started on Friday when Cyn and I decided to spend the night in Witbank. Mary and Jerry (PCVs) were to pick us up on Saturday and we were to visit their PC home-based care site. All went even better than planned. We had called both Monica and Elizabeth (PCVs in Witbank) and asked them to meet us for dinner. They did. Elizabeth is very happy now and has a serious boyfriend who is very nice. She has also received an offer to extend her appointment in order to direct the opening of an orphanage in the area. This has been a dream of which she has talked many times. Monica is officially engaged to her young man but plans to move back to the States when they marry.

Mary and Jerry picked us up at ten sharp the next morning and we went to Secunda. They gave us a tour of the area and we saw the movie, "Chicago." Very fitting for Mother's Day, don't you think? We spent the night with them and Sunday, Cyn and I came on back here. All four of my kids reached me.

Monday

Good day at the office.

Tuesday

Good one-half of the day: we started to cancel the afternoon workshop and then everyone showed up after all.

Wednesday

We went to Denilton and fifty people had registered for the last set of classes.

Cyn and I leave Saturday for Namibia. We are both ready. I am anxious for time to pass although now the days are packed with tasks I want to accomplish here at the house. To list a few:

1. write the PC final reports
2. write the Impumelalo grant for HBCHO
3. update the HBCHO forms (monthly reports)
4. organize the HBCHO files
5. write one really nice letter to friends in America
6. put photos in order
7. review letters from home that I wish to keep
8. decide who gets what of the items I am leaving here
9. pack last couple of boxes and post

10.   attend PC Close of Service windup

11.   have Mary, Togo, Cyn and January to WOM dinner

12.   have HBCHO women volunteers to lunch or coffee (better not do this but will do something)

13.   finish CBBG workshops; and

14.   meet with developing support groups (at least once for each).

Boy finally made it to the hospital for the removal of his tumor and is at home now. He must go back next Wednesday. No one has any money. But he's home now and getting all the attention for a change. In the meantime, I am caught in the midst of this horrible situation right now. His (Boy's) mother is very sick. Our classes are being held at the hospital in Denilton; therefore, I was able to meet and visit with her. Her feet are red, swollen and painful. If she were little, one would think of sickle cell disease and I still do. The doctor said she probably is in congestive heart failure (only 34 years of age). They had done a chest x-ray and blood work but I do not know the results. His gogo must take charge of Boy's health. This is a given even though she knows very little about health care and has no extra money. I find out that he (Boy) stayed in the hospital for several extra days because no one had the funds to pay for his release. My heart is sore for them and the many, many others here who are in the same or even worse conditions.

Chapter Twenty-Seven

Learning how to work with others is one of the most important lessons confronting us as we make our way through life. Cooperation moves us along faster and faster.

(Paraphrase from the introduction of "The Blind Men and the Elephant" excerpted from The Moral Compass).

MAY 2003

May 17, 2003
<u>Saturday</u>

Cyn and I are on our way to a new adventure: a train ride on the Desert Express across the desert in Namibia from Windhoek to Swakopmund and back again. Our bus is to leave Siyabuswa at 8:00AM and it does! Ignatious meets us and transports us exactly as scheduled to his guest house! We stayed there the first night so he could take us to the Johannesburg airport early the next morning. I finally met Yvonne, his wife, who is just as nice as he is. Both of them took us to the Kolanada Mall and all of us had a delicious Italian dinner. This morning she served everything one could imagine for breakfast and we went on our way.

We flew to Windhoek and a driver was there to take us to the Three Gales Guest House. Here, we again are the only guests and treated royally. I have a few flu symptoms and am full of antihistamines. I feel a little under the weather but cannot complain because it is not a run-to-the-bathroom situation.

<u>Sunday</u>

Another wonderful day and another elegant dinner also served by the owner.

<u>Monday</u>

We are up early, take a warm bath, eat a sumptuous breakfast, take a leisurely walk and just generally have a relaxing morning. By 1:00PM we are boarded on the train. There are a total of eleven cars on an exotic passenger train (must be shades of the Orient Express) ...but only twelve passengers. We each had our own compartment with shower, toilet, comfortable bed, divan, and full compartment window. The others were very nice and because there were so few of us, we bonded quickly and easily. The countryside out of Windhoek was truly the bush and at PEACE! I don't know why I have been so fortunate to be able to experience this. God will have to tell me someday.

<u>Tuesday</u>

We spent the first night on the Desert Express racing across the desert. I awoke many times...afraid I was going to miss something. The moon was very bright but we were moving so fast that I could not see the stars that well. We arrived the next morning about 10:00AM at Aus. Here we transferred to a bus and rode on to Luderitz where we stayed overnight at the Nest Hotel Luderitz. The town of Luderitz is one of the very oldest seaports in the world and as colorful as a box of crayons. The houses are blue, yellow, pink, green, purple, orange and lined in row after row up and down hill after hill. We wandered down to the wharf and watched the boats. I found my book of fables.

<u>Wednesday</u>

Today we went on a guided tour to Klomanskop, a ghost town, and then visited other places in Luderitz. We left by bus to return to Aus and the train. Oh yes, we also wandered through a very old casino with a bowling alley on the lower level (now is that a thrill?). The biggest thrill, though, was to attempt to climb the dunes surrounding this dilapidated ruin. Some of us made it but others did not. I was one of the others.

We spent the night on the train but this time, it stopped mid-route and we were able to watch the sunset and again to see the moon and the stars. Nice people, nice views and a nice trip.

<u>Thursday</u>

We flew back to Johannesburg and Ignatious picked us up and took us to Pretoria where Yvonne had soup waiting for us. We stayed the night and he took us to the backpackers for PCVs where we stayed for the next two nights. I jumped on Cyn for absolutely no reason and apologized. Guess it was too much togetherness and post-vacation insanity.

May 25, 2003
<u>Sunday</u>

I am back in Siyabuswa now and also back to headaches galore. Boy did have his surgery repeated and all went well except once again, he cannot get out of the hospital...no money and NO ONE to pick him up. More pitiful Siyabuswa health care. Finally Rabie did agree and they, meaning cousins, aunts and anyone else who happened to be around went to rescue him. He is home now and feeling very well.

<u>Monday</u>

Work day and it feels good to be back, but I know now inside myself why I am always jumping Cyn. She is invading <u>my</u> territory! Can you believe I said that? How can this be at my <u>age</u>? And so close to my end of service but not hers? I get many more kudos but that is the way of it. Will try harder to act my mature age.

<u>Wednesday</u>

Quiet week here...workshops going as scheduled. Every day, the sun is very bright but it is very cold (for me). Our electricity is gone and the water goes during the nights.

More questions from the CBBG meetings.

> *If someone with AIDS gets blood on my orange and I eat it, will I get AIDS?*
> *If I have diabetes, will I lose my desire to have sex?*
> *If I have a piece of my private parts taken off, can I still have a baby?*

Boy is finally home as is his mother who is morbidly sick with kidney problems. She has many children and this is the first I have seen of her except for the brief visit in the hospital. None of the family has any money...kids are not orphans because mother is still alive and usually does not live with her family. Several are married with young children of their own. The youngest live in the same house as the father but he is out of work and has been for some time. Christine feeds any of them often or until her own food runs out. Where do they go from here? I have talked with the volunteers about this situation and they will ponder (someone's new word) on the issue and try to come up with a plan. The biggest issue as I see it is that this family is not unique. There are too many families to count who find themselves in the same dire circumstances. Is there anything I, we, PC, others can do about the health and poverty status of these townships??

One question that comes to me from the people here over and over again is, "What do you miss most about America?" After almost two years, this is not difficult to answer.

I miss:

#1   Freedom

    a)   to walk, go where I wish and not be security-conscious even though I do not go to dangerous places;

    b)   to leave the house doors unlocked when at home,

    c)   to eat what I want when I want

    d)   to be alone when I wish (although the idea of privacy in this culture is alien and they do not want me to be lonesome);

    e)   to take a bath with hot water whenever I wish;

    f)   and most importantly to have health care at the end of a phone.

#2 My Family

Each remains supportive but do not hear often enough from them. They, of course, think I do (my mother must have felt the same way).

This question, of course, follows: "What have you learned?"
I learned:

#1 Respect

    a) a healthy respect for rules; I have a hard time breaking them;

    b) respect for the young men who do not want a paying job for their own reasons;

    c) respect for the women who are culturally submissive while struggling to keep a quality of life amid the turmoil of disease;

    d) and ,of course, a guarded respect for the geese!

#2 <u>Patience:</u>

Wait-wait…move-move…then wait again. I truly have learned very little of the language and yet still become impatient when <u>they do not understand me.</u> And yet, the important tasks do get done. We will never know how much more could have been accomplished if we hurried to finish a project and moved on to another. Most likely, we would only take a nap, walk, rest or use the spare time to get into trouble.

#3 <u>Communication:</u>

I have learned to listen but also still interrupt. The "eyes" have it here…pain, anguish, guilt, happiness, and love. But oh, such mix ups…just short phrases said backwards as in, I ask, "Would you like to go to HOPE with me?" The response is "You want to go to HOPE?"

#4 <u>Fortitude:</u>

My chain is pulled when:

*a) every single item I have has been borrowed at one time or another by someone and the term does not mean lend here, it means give;

b) being cold; I have a heater but feel guilty using the electricity even though I pay for it;

c) interruptions, or even worse, when someone just walks away when they do not understand or do not wish discuss what I think is important.

*I now realize that they ask to borrow because they <u>do not have</u> and if they do have will give away to someone who does not without questions asked!

<u>Friday the 13th</u>

Njongo and I went to Alemansdrift and both of us gave a presentation on infections in the morning and HIV and AIDS in the afternoon. Seems our CBBG workshops did make a few people sit up and notice.

June 14, 2003
<u>Saturday</u>

Today was my last bus trip to Pretoria! It was wonderful…but not for the reasons you would expect. I had made arrangements with Selinah and she had told me to be at the pick-up spot at 7:00AM. She had brought my ticket to me at the house last night. I left for the bus all packed and knew exactly what to do. Christine brought the coffee early but I was smart and only drank a couple of swallows. I arrived at the stop at 6:50AM; it was cold and the bus did not come as scheduled. First, I was told it will leave at 7:30AM because it is Saturday. It was bitterly cold. 7:30AM came and went. No bus was in sight. I grew colder but others grew colder. By 8:30, I was frozen but others were solid ice. 8:45AM showed on my watch and there was still no bus. Why should there have been when it could only pick up chunks of ice, some larger than others. A cry rang out, "Hark, here comes the bus." It was now 9:00AM. Amazing: there was a straight line with no pushing or shoving because the line was now just sticks of ice with no tongs with which to lift them onto the bus. I thought to myself (told you about me and my thinking), "Aha, there will be no problem finding a seat." BUT the bus was already filled because the earlier bus had not shown and both sets of patrons were getting on this bus. Most of us were able to get on and stand the entire trip into Pretoria. This would have been much worse except that we were so packed it was like sitting on your feet. We did warm up. The venders literally went across the top (seemed like it) of the people to get from front to back. We finally arrived in Pretoria and everyone hollered at me where to get off (my corner).

Yvonne (Ignatious's wife) was already at the Holiday Inn and she and I had a pleasant lunch and visit. They really do plan on coming to the United States. She brought me out to the hotel and all was well. I left my purse outside the wrong door, spent a frantic ten minutes looking and very conveniently, the maid had it.

Now I am settled in and warm, relaxed and this is the world. I am happy to be a part of it!

More details of the last meeting of CBBG at Siyabuswa C. Once again, I must say, it was to be me giving a thank-you to the group but they did to me instead. We had our meeting as usual in the garage. As I arrived, they were cooking pap outside in the big black kettle and everyone was glowing with excitement. They came to meet me with music playing and dancing in a line. They guided me (the first in the line) into the house. Here a long dining table was decorated as if a wedding were to take place. Snackies, peanuts and candy filled several china dishes and were placed all around the room. They had a seat decorated in the center for me to sit and presented a written Program of Appreciation. I was taken by surprise because it was exactly like all the celebratory programs given by the community. There were speeches, music, more speeches, more music and gifts (I described those before). They dressed me (even remembered that blue is a favorite color of mine), took pictures of me (who hates this) individually with almost everyone. I know everyone was genuine. The idea of setting up support is a good one. I know this because of the unconditional support shown to me. I love these people and they love me.

Only have a few sessions left. I did not join PC to make an individual difference and never thought I would grow or change but I did and I have.

<u>Saturday</u>

All the SA9 PCV returned to Pretoria for our Close of Service workshop. We stayed part of the time at the Backpackers and part of the time at the Protea Hotel. Went to the Brooklyn Mall and PURCHASED MY AIRLINE TICKETS FOR HOME!

<u>Sunday</u>

Finally after two years, we, (Jeanne, Stein and I) were taken on a guided tour around Pretoria by a guide that Stein had found. The highlight for me was the Voertrekkers Monument and Fort. It was huge, stark and impressive and the history told to us was heartwrenching.

<u>Tuesday and Wednesday</u>

The COS workshop was informative and interesting, although at times several of us were close to tears. Most of us saw movies, ate out and shed tears during our spare time.

June 19, 2003
<u>Thursday</u>
Close of Service Banquet

A lovely, simply lovely, banquet was served to at least fifty people, including drivers, teachers, and other PC administrative personnel, as well as all of us. We were each awarded certificates of completion by the Country Director and other individual citations by the involved teachers. I received three if you can believe it and you can! These gems are for 1) the most imaginative use of the local language, 2) only PCV to pose with topless men and 3) the most time spent at site. I deserved every one. A style show was presented by the volunteers who strutted down a makeshift runway wearing South African cultural dress (I was a model but not the one with the mostest)!

COS ended with a fancy breakfast at Rudee Vallee (convention center in which our very first workshop was held) and good -byes all around. It just doesn't ring true. Always before, when you say good bye, you expect to see each other again. Most, if not all of these, I will probably never see again.

<u>Saturday</u>

I am back in Siyabuswa. This morning washed clothes and linen until a blister showed on my thumb...washed some more...hung all outside taking the entire clothes line...chatted with the geese while the chickens squawked (jealous?). Walked to the complex and had lunch. Washed my hair and played cards with Thobi as if we will never play again (we may not).

<u>Sunday</u>

Have fallen (quite innocently) back into the trap of thinking I must get this and this done; hence, I'm not writing in the journal to pass time anymore. How can that be? Am so excited about returning home and these journals have been such a comfort, I cannot leave out all the good happenings. But...trap it is. Today went to Church with Cyn. It was very nice with only a few people present and the message was short. I planned to work on the final CBBG class but am home now and there is no electricity. Am frustrated but have many other tasks to do that I can do without power (electrical, that is).

David was told I wanted to work at home next week so he made an appointment (a first) with me to meet his friend on Monday at 10:00AM at the house. This friend apparently has had really bad news and maybe it will help to talk it over with an outsider. Because I will soon be leaving, more young people are approaching me because they know I will not be around and will keep their news confidential. What they do not realize is that I will also not be able to help them in any way. As for David's friend, I am not too sure which of the several stories told to me to believe. The story first told: a young woman has had an affair with an official (define official) and someone (who?) took a message to the head of the agency that the person is HIV (which person?). Second story told: no affair has taken place as yet but someone who is HIV positive has fallen in love with an official and the affair is imminent (how does she/he know this?). Which story, if either, is true? What does David's friend wish me to do?

David had a hernia operation the 24th of May. His stitches are to come out Monday afternoon. He is scared and rightfully because the stitches are covered with part skin and part hair. Will not be an easy task nor will it be pain free. As you can see, I am immersed with the office affairs and family life. This is good, huh? Also makes me realize it is now time to call it quits. I really can do the same thing at home.

Monday

During the late afternoon I went to visit Boy's family and this was very sad. His mother's funeral was yesterday. She had been sick for some time and finally her kidneys shut down. I do not know what final definitive diagnosis she was given.

Tuesday

Last class at KwaPhaahla...electricity was off all day throughout the town and we were unable to buy the large celebratory cake but did have two small pretty ones. This group will meet next week for their first planning meeting for a peer support group.

Thursday

Office day...slow but nice.

Yesterday, we had the Denilton Reception for CBBG. What can I say about this wonderful, horrible, uplifting, sad, moving, standstill day? Morning: we are to leave by eleven...no transport...Maureen (different Maureen) finally picks us up at 12:30PM. We do make it to the reception and everyone is there and upset at us for being late (everyone is always late). Remember, this is the CBBG class with fifty participants. Everyone is bossing me around and ignoring me at the same time. Is this possible? Yes, it is...when communication is half understood. Actually, sometimes it is easier when not understood at all. But I hold my cool and after a late (supposed to be early) start, we are to celebrate our last class (my very last class).

Maureen, who was to translate, is busy in and out and Linah ends up doing most of it. As we start the certificate ceremony, Maureen drags in the Director of Nurses who is a young man and visibly not the least bit interested. Those who had not received a certificate were almost in tears and those who had, started to sing. I insisted that before the singing, we continue with the ceremony. They do not listen and we are sinking into chaos when Linah saves the day. She whistles for everyone's attention and states, "We will finish before any food is served." That does it and we are back on track. Then a whole roll of film is ruined by overexposure (had photos of two groups on it); therefore, we will not have any closing pictures of either group. Finally, it is over and since this was #58, guess one could expect a few snafus along the way. None were important but also none needed to have happened. Here, again, is my obsession with organization lugged along with me from stateside.

A black cat crossed directly in front of me when walking from the hospital to the car (I have seen very few cats in this area). I am not superstitious but this almost made a believer of me. Truthfully, though, at 4:00PM when we were leaving and the cat walked across my path, everything turned around. All were happy with the classes. All wished me well. The taxi was right there and every single person said over and over that it was a great party. I told you: they either bossed me to do what they wished or ignored me making, in their eyes, this day glorious. The mishaps were not even noticed by anyone but me.

June 30, 2003
Monday

Back on track: counseled, no, did not counsel...met with a new young lady (23 years of age) who is HIV-positive. She is very pretty, very healthy (she says), very intelligent (maybe). I hope she comes to me again but doubt if she will. She does not believe (so she says) in support groups and thinks, at this moment, that she is handling the positive lab result well. She does have a new twist to a serious problem, though. She presents a different scenario from others with whom I have visited. She has told her family and although they did not want her to disclose it, they have. It is her father who has told her new boy friend. He, the boyfriend, says he will stand by her but does not want to have sex. This has made it very difficult for her and I know not what to say.

The rest of the day moved along. There is no electricity in the house tonight and my visit with President Bush (yes, Leah asked me if I would represent PC) will probably be cancelled (it was).

July 1, 2003

Eight weeks from today I fly out! But today was the first planning meeting for a support group. Njongo took charge and apparently did a very good job (spoke entirely in their language). Three people plus Silvia, Njongo and I attended. That is three more people than at the first meeting (progress)!

But now, instead of helping these people let go of me, must teach myself to let go. Cyn wants to attend the support group and she should.

Thursday

Excellent meeting with HBCHO. All are willing to help me wind up my work here. Had lunch with Matt and Cyn. Everything is full steam ahead with their duties here also. Cyn is feeling better and attributes this to Leah (PC Assoc. Director) who has given her the support that I received from Cam. The three of us go to Groblestahl tomorrow which will be my last trip out of Siyabuswa. We are to celebrate the 4th of July with the others from their group.

Friday, Saturday, and Sunday

The weekend in Groblestahl was very sad. Cyn and I met David (son of owners) in the driveway and he told us that Dinky (owner of guest house) had died last Saturday. The funeral had been this past Wednesday. Hank (husband), of course, was very despondent, sad, stoic and all one expects. She had had a bad heart for about two years but was only 67 years old and was such a dynamic force in his life up to the very morning she died. It was good that we were there because he was able to talk to someone besides his family and go through all the poignant last moments with us.

Monday, Tuesday, and Wednesday

Uneventful except for when Leah (PC) came on Tuesday. She had a short but meaningful chat with Njongo about HBCHO. All of us felt good about the meeting. I am sure he would call it, "a way forward."

Thursday

The last meeting of the CBBG planning group was today. We were to have a short business meeting and a small party. I hoped that all, or at least most, would show up. I was amazed that every single one did (100% is a first). The meeting went very well indeed and all say they are committed to continue. From now on, I am literally only the consultant. I had copied the entire course outline for everyone on the committee. Now they were amazed.

Another cultural point of interest: Lorraine (ASHYO volunteer) had a stiff neck and David covered his hands with fresh ashes (from the burned garbage/trash pile), rubbed them into her neck and then proceeded to manipulate her neck. I have seen this done (manipulation) but only under anesthesia and that years and years ago.

At the moment, I have forgotten the second tidbit. Everyone is laughing about me-to me-around me-over me-but I can understand enough to know they are planning surprises for my going-away. Since I make no secret about loving parties, I'm sure that they are combining my birthday and the going-away celebration for one big event. They have asked me to be sure and stay in Siyabuswa on Friday, August 15th. All three groups are chattering like the geese. I will see later if I understood any of the above.

Six weeks from today, I leave Siyabuswa and seven weeks from today, I will be home. My family here was very quiet tonight. I don't know what is wrong. I left the light on in my room yesterday and Christine reminded me to shut it off. But doubt that could be it. Tomorrow everything will be all right but

I bet when I go home, I will have a stress ulcer just from being on such a fine line so often. I never do know if I am being paranoid or if I have really incurred some infraction that bothers or hurts them. At the same time, I am defensive because I give them so much and that I want to do but when they act out, then I am put out of sorts. Hate-hate this feeling. Did I subconsciously join the PC to prove I am a good person and then hate myself when I don't measure up to my own standards? Or do I even know if I do...or don't?

No, Christine is not upset. Don't know why she was so quiet but think it may be her concern over the care of Boy.

Saturday

There is a wedding to attend across the street. When I awoke, I was up for it and planned to enjoy it much more than the one two years ago but it is now noon and the day is going downhill fast. They have slaughtered <u>three</u> cows after throwing each of them...one at a time...into a pit, crying (I mean it) all the way. I was afraid that those poor cows would cry from their graves (what graves, they will be eaten).

The wedding was absolutely the most...several hundred people...all happy. The bride was stunning and I <u>did</u> recognize the music and even stomped in rhythm for a short time. I felt quite relaxed and had a lot of fun. But no, I could not or would not eat any part of those poor cows. I asked why there were three cows instead of just one. I was told that this shows how much the groom treasures his wife (with cows!) and proves also that his family has enough money to display their high regard for her. Seems this "lobola" also is a way to prevent divorce because should this happen, then the "lobola" must be paid back (how?).

Sunday

Attended church and then went to Dorothee's for coffee. It was a very pleasant day.

Wish now that I had written down the titles of all the books I have read during these past two years. There have been many of them.

July 14, 2003
Monday
Happy Birthday to Mallory! And to me!

It was a nice day...have talked to all of my family and believe I better get on home... ...they are forgetting me...people here say they are going to combine the going-away and birthday parties. We shall see...have received lots of mail and that is great.

I have never started a diary. No, that is not exactly true. I have started a diary, a dream journal, and have often thought that I should write my autobiography for my grandchildren to read someday, (but never really did until I decided to come here). And here I did continue to write in a journal but only to maintain some sanity. I have written about South African weather, education, health, people, culture, politics, Peace Corps, even religion...and all from <u>only</u> my perspective. But now I know that underlying every single thought and entry has been the support from my own people in the United States. Even though I have been alone over here and thought I was enduring so much, they have gone through the fear and anguish of 9-11 and the misery and love that is WAR! And never, not even once, did my family or friends forget me. With battles to wage on the home front, with fear in their hearts for our own countray, with love in their very souls for humanity, never did a single one place any guilt, doubt, anger or animosity on my shoulders. Instead, each has been there for me every step of the way. I will never forget South Africa or the people I have met and learned to love...but neither will I ever forget all my friends from home who indeed have made this journey with me.

Tuesday

Today three very good events took place. The first: the Kameelrivier group held their first support group planning meeting. Ten people attended and I only sat in and listened. The second, which is better: Rebecca invited me to her home and her friends dressed me in all the authentic Ndebele beadwork. It was very heavy and I could not even shuffle by the time they were finished. Third and the very best: Rebecca is going to meet with Amy, another HIV-positive young lady. I am certain they will become friends and help each other. With six weeks to go, finally I can see the start of the plan I had envisioned more than a year ago! They have made a start and I am sure that when two come together, four and more will follow.

Speaking of dreams: I dreamed a few nights ago that I stepped off the plane in Springfield and my family was there to meet me. They looked exactly like who they are, only each was black. I said, "My goodness, you are all black." Susie said, "Mom, we expected you to be black." Support?

Wednesday

Revisited with the group from Siyabuswa C. It was very pleasant because progress has also been made here. Before they had their regular meeting, (the seniors here have been meeting for a long time...at least twice a week), they did exercises. After they ate lunch, each was given an orange for dessert. They have added both the exercises and the fruit for dessert as a result of our CBBG classes. Mmmmmmmmmmmmgood!

Thursday

Today was the first time that I had to see the local doctor and that was because of my own clumsiness. Tripped over the telephone cord...fell flat on both knees and they hurt. The x-ray showed no damage had been done...they hurt. He gave me a salve and pain medication...both hurt...first one than the other...they hurt. I am home in bed writing all this and they still hurt. Njongo said just yesterday that he had never heard me complain or mention going to the doctor. They hurt! In spades!

I have heard from Linda (cousin) and her Don has been diagnosed with cancer (I don't know how long ago). It is difficult always, but more so for her because her mother died of cancer and Don has apparently always been healthy. I haven't met him but that is what I have been told.

Monday

Only two but it is a start: two HIV-positive clients agreed to meet with each other. I visited with them also and while both were a little awkward and shy, they did converse for a short time, exchanged phone numbers and smiles.

I worked at the office and at the house on the computer. I am starting to write my final reports for PC and they are a pain...so much to say and know so little on the "how-to-do-it."

Thursday

A group held the first CBBG meeting (or so I thought) where I was not in charge. They all did very well and traded many new ideas (or so I thought). They started laughing a lot and I started to pay closer attention and come to find out, they were planning my going-away party. It was not a CBBG meeting after all and they don't realize how disappointed I am...that it was not. I am at a loss. I am excited because they are, nervous because this may be all talk (they have no money), disappointed in myself because I want them to give a party, guilty because I don't deserve all they talk of doing.

Friday

They had a support group meeting at Weltervrede and it was exactly what I had hoped for: a small group of very committed and loving men and women. I went on a home visit to a daughter of one of the group. She is very weak but strong in spirit, as is her family. It is and will take a very long time to move the sun and erase the shadows but these people are the foundation of this movement and will build upward.

This afternoon I went to Groblestahl and we had a wonderful PC week-end. I am moving toward the end of my commitment to PC and it is becoming way too emotional. I never thought it would. January, Hank, Pat, Bobbi, Tracy, Cyn, Matt, and Karen gave me a gourmet dinner and a handmade (by Hank) silver bracelet. I will miss these young people who became my support a year ago. All are from the teacher group except Cyn and Matt.

Tuesday, Wednesday and Thursday

I spent these days having my last meetings with Patients Living with AIDS (PWAs). I hate to leave all of them because I know they will not receive the necessary care and support they must have. I also spent time holding final meetings with HBCHO.

Saturday
     Today was Lorraine's birthday party. There were four people celebrating birthdays at this party. It was huge and Cyn and I felt honored to be invited to sit in the family tent. First, each of the celebrants came in dressed in beautiful western clothes and danced in and out; much food and drink; many speeches...and then each changed to beautiful traditional clothes and danced in and out; much food and drink; many speeches! There were hundreds of people wandering all over the block. Because we were friends to many that were there, we had a wonderful time.

Sunday
Church

Monday
Lunch with Matt

Tuesday
     Today was supposed to be the last workshop that I would attend here. It was cancelled until Thursday.

Wednesday
     Dorothee and Willem invited me to their home to say good-bye. The kids were delightful. I will sorely miss each of them.

Saturday
     Cyn and I attended the wedding of Mary's daughter. This wedding was a white wedding and held in the Methodist Church. It was also quite lavish and must have been very expensive. Mary is a seamstress and had made all the dresses, even for the five bridesmaids and two flower girls. Each was exquisite with hundreds of seed pearls intricately attached.
     At the reception, we sat in the main area and once again as friends and not on display.

Sunday
     My last day to attend this church and members of the congregation had to tell both Joanna (Dorothee's daughter) and me good-bye. She leaves for Holland on Tuesday.

Monday
     A congresswoman from the States visited us today. She was impressed with the people she met and voiced genuine concern about the HIV and AIDS devastation here.

Chapter Twenty-Eight

UBUNTU CAN BE DEFINED AS A COMPREHEN-
SIVE ANCIENT African world view based on the values
of intense humanness, caring, sharing, respect, compas-
sion, and associated values, ensuring a happy and quali-
tative human community life in a spirit of family.
(UBUNTU Life Lessons from Africa)

AUGUST 2003

August 13, 2003
<u>Wednesday</u>
Radio Interview (mine with Siyabuswa station)

Question: What did you think about HIV when you first came to South Africa?
Answer: When I first came here, everyone told me that HIV was a big problem. Now I have been here two years and have seen this for myself. There remains a shadow and stigma that surrounds the very word. Because of this, people are discriminated against and do not seek testing or even medical care for other diseases.

Question: What comes to mind when you hear the words HIV and AIDS?
Answer: I think the word that first comes to my mind is "fear." Fear that one will die soon or become very sick or that they will lose friends, loved ones and close family members; also fear that one will no longer be able to care for his/her family.

Question: Do you think the oganizations that you work with are making a difference?
Answer: Absolutely! ASHYO because they are keeping the community updated on new information regarding HIV and AIDS and are training others to do the same. NALEDI, because they are providing not only work but food for those affected. HBCHO, because they are treating all those affected with courtesy and respect in the hope that all those who fear they may be at risk will be counseled and tested.

<u>Thursday</u>
  I talked with my family in Sandfontein and Meriam had very sad news to tell me. Their son, Berthold died in June. She did not tell me the reason but he is the third child she has lost within a few years. Each had been in his/her early thirties and left young children behind. I will go to see her one of the days that I am in Pretoria...before I leave.

August 15, 2003
  Last working day! Actually it is not nearly as easy as one would think.
  Last Tuesday was my family good-byes and every day since, it has been good-bye to someone. A large part of me is very happy and excited but that same part of me does not want to leave. There is so much to be done and some of "it" has a start now. I feel like I am letting the people down just as we are making these starts. Medicines will come, more people will be tested and more families and friends will care enough to act. I want to be here to see all this happen. I also am aware that it is time for someone else with a new voice and new ideas to respond.

<u>Saturday</u>
  Should not this completion of service be the beginning once again of something for me? Life is a great drama with many acts. While some acts may

only be developmental stages, some may be very long sagas, and some may be only scenes. But I am asking myself what is to come next? I do not know. Nor did I know when I first arrived in the country.

Today was my farewell party from South Africa. This party has been planned and changed often but finally takes place (with changes up to the very end.) Perhaps that is the largest breakthrough in communication that I will take back from this country: that no matter the obstacles, no matter the innuendos, no matter the misunderstandings, what needs to get done will get done and done even better than hoped.

The party was to be yesterday and to start at 10:00AM and be held at Ktweni Park. Instead it was today at 1:00PM and held at the Ekupelini Clinic or our own little compound. It did start at 2:00PM. Rabie, Christine and Thobi and the other neighborhood kids were to go with me. Rabie and Christine had been at the church all week and a funeral all night. Both are legitimately exhausted and asleep when I leave. Thobi has gone to a school function so I go by myself, all decked out in cultural dress...very nice but feel a little as if I am in costume. Many people are already there and are as impressed with the numbers as I am.

Njongo is to be in charge but David quickly takes over. This turns out just fine. I am overwhelmed with accolades and thankful that I am still unsure of the language(s). Today, as during the first days, they are speaking in four or five different languages. There are many speeches and some with translators. Each speech is followed with music of some nature.

The three groups of young people with whom I work sang for me, "We love you, Sydney." It is the very first song I have ever heard with my name in it! Others san gospel songs and what they call "jazz." Of course, each brought both goose bumps to my arms and tears to my eyes. Many, many gifts were given to me. I will not write here all the gifts but will write them down so I can write a thank-you note to each and every person (this can be my new project).

And you know what? People from all over came: nurses from the Health Department and the doctor's office, representatives from the district and the municipal offices, many vendors and shop workers, families, PWAs, and the list goes on. I must confess I know this type of farewell is given to all PCVs who leave after fulfilling a contract but it has never happened quite this extravagantly to me. Have had several overwhelming special parties including birthday, moving away, and retirement, but never where the people gave so much of themselves: a gourd (calabash) to drink fresh spring water for a healthy life, "I love you" from young, adult and old, a certificate beautifully framed from a councilman giving me a key to the city (so to speak), a hand-sewn dress, a scrapbook of heartwarming personal messages, and a special clock from Skosi...who never failed to ask, "How many seconds till you be back, Gogo?"

AND the women cooked and laughed when I could not move the iphini (wooden spoon). They gave me rands to buy soft drink and ice cream for the isiphaphamtjhini (plane). They gave me laughter, tears, happiness, and sadness. They left me to wonder, "Why me?" I have done so very little here. Americans could just as easily ask, "How are you spending our tax dollars?" I cannot answer. I could not two years ago and I still cannot. But me, I have learned that human kind can love, people are good, people are kind, people are desperate, people are sick, and people are one and the same as in all. Is this God in us?

<u>Sunday</u>

I did not go to church but absorbed the whole of Siyabuswa as my church. I went by myself and I walked: from the house across to the complex (many people) and from the complex across to the veldt (zero people); under a blue sky with not even an imaginary cloud in sight; by trees that were green against the blue, by trees that were brown against the blue, by trees that were stark, by trees that were beautiful. I heard voices singing, voices calling in greeting; I saw eyes that spoke in silence and still I walked. My head was clear, my vision sharp, my head was muddled, my vision was blurred. My feet were very tired but would not stop. My heart was joyous, my heart was aching and still I walked. I could not wait to leave this Siyabuswa and cried out that I could not leave the people. God heard. He sent me back to Christine, back to HBCHO, back to ASHYO, back to Peace Corps and back to America

August 19, 2003

Today is my last day in Siyabuswa. All the reports are done, I have given my gifts, and last night Thobi was sad but ready to move on...as are all the rest. They will miss me but I will miss them more.

But before I leave I must tell the last Mkulu anecdote. For the past year and half, I have been picking up pennies off the street and saving them. One by one, they are not worth anything at all but of course ten will buy a tiny piece of candy. I have asked Thobi to save hers but she just laughs and says the piece of candy is not even big enough to eat. But I have saved them and now have almost 1000 (947 to be exact). Thobi asked me to leave them for her and I said no, because she had not helped collect them (shades of "The Little Red Hen"). I asked her to invite her cousins over and we would share all the pennies with them. She did and the pennies were put in a pile on the kitchen table. I agreed that Thobi could count them out. She went around and around the table saying, "One for you, one for you, one for you and three for me." I stood in the doorway watching and wondering how long the others would agree to this. About four times around and one little boy said, "It is my turn to pass them out." She agreed and he started to chant, "One for you, one for you, one for me and none for Thobi because she already has too many!"

<u>Wednesday</u>

We leave Siyabuswa and it is a SA day. At 7:30AM, my phone rings, no actually, at 5:30AM, Christine and Thobi come into my room and we have fat cakes and coffee on my bed. Thobi hugs and kisses me good-bye as does Rabie. Christine is going to ride with me to Pretoria. Mary is on the phone and will be there to meet me at the office. I leave for the office and Betty (traditional healer and crèche teacher) runs to catch me and takes me to her home where she gives me a set of glasses. She was not able to attend the party but this is her gift to me from the children in her crèche.

We are to leave at 8:15AM and do leave at 9:30AM. Simon is the driver and he has David, Njongo, Linah, Christine, Evelina, Maggie, Olga, and Anna with him. The other driver, Vusi, has Lorraine, Gugu, Silvia, Oupa, Charles, Lucas, Samson, and Dinah. They had played my game and drawn straws for those that could travel with me to Pretoria. After we arrived at the regular Backpackers, I surprised them (they said they knew I would) with a mini-party. We eat and laugh. They tell me some last minute secrets and leave to go back to Siyabuswa without me. How can this be?

SOON WE HEAD FOR HOME! Will we make it? Time will tell!

Afterword

Make the most of yourself by fanning the tiny inner sparks of possibility into the flames of achievement.
(Foster C. McClelean)

AFTERWORD

This was the opening to the invitation to the Open House my children were hosting for me to be held from August 29, 2003 through September 1, 2003. Is it not beautiful?

I did make it all the way home (who says you can't go home again?) with absolutely no problems. My plane took off as scheduled. Thought I would be sick with anticipation and was overanxious, excited, nervous and oh, so happy! But never sick and truly appreciated each moment that flew me closer to home. We arrived in Springfield exactly as promised at 2:20PM. As I came down the steps of the plane, I was looking across the stairs to see if the kids were at the window. And then I looked down and who was right there but little Henry at the foot with his arms out and smiling! He let me take him. They were all there except David's family but they will be here soon. Susie and Mindy started to cry as did I...after laughing with joy. We moved into the airport and there was my old office gang...with flags, balloons, and flowers! To say I was again over-whelmed is the understatement of my life.

Everything went according to plan and allowed me Thursday and Friday to get ready for the party Open House which was exactly the thing to do. Friday evening, David came and neither Devan nor Divia had forgotten me. Divia said, "Grandma, I am never going to miss you again." Devan is so tall and handsome; Divia so petite and beautiful. Who could ask for more... and then Henry came as a precious bonus?

The party was glorious...the weather beautiful...the house even more so... and cinched it that I am not going to buy a condo in the near future. Must admit, though, that I already miss the friends I made in South Africa. It is diffi-cult to start to ask Freddy something and he is not around and won't be (the same is true for the rest). Will write more later because I am about to cry all over again. For some reason, I am very tired and exhilarated in my heart and soul. My arms and legs are also exhausted. Is it possible for this to be happening all at once?

<u>Sunday and Monday</u>

People are still coming...not as many at any given time but I continue to be at a loss as to how to accept graciously all the accolades given me. I do not deserve them. I never did suffer on the scale of those men and women in the Armed Forces or even come close to measuring up with those who volunteer in the war and disaster-torn countries.

<u>Tuesday</u>

Today is my first full day by myself and I am at a loss. It is raining, and I don't know where, when or what to start? I will take a nap.

September 3, 2003

I am home and home is good.

TODAY WAS MY FIRST TIME TO BABYSIT HENRY. He was bet-ter than perfect!

Epilogue

EPILOGUE

JANUARY 2006

January 31, 2006

I am going back!

Yes! Cannot quite believe it! We do have choices in our lives. I have recently been reading my first journals and if they are to be believed, why would I choose to return? But as one cannot read verses of the Bible and only follow one interpretation, one can not take a few months of a long life and make of it a whole of the experience. I am going back because I miss them.

I am excited (almost sick) to be returning to those friends. Dorothy, my good friend, has agreed to accompany me, even to Siyabuswa. We plan to check on our mini-business (our excuse for going). We hope to bring back here the bead work that is made by the home-based care volunteers there, sell it to friends and return the money to the volunteers. We plan to visit the HOPE Christian School and meet the students there who are sponsored by friends here. We also hope to visit the CBBG groups and see the progress they have made in providing health education to the communities. We have no specific time set for any of these (did learn from my previous sojourn!).

<u>Wednesday</u>

We arrived in Johannesburg about 1:00AM (South African time) and Gertie, the owner of the guest house where I had stayed before, was right there to meet us. We were at her home by 2:00AM and went almost immediately to sleep.

<u>Thursday</u>

We did sleep very well and were up early to prepare for Siyabuswa. David is to pick us up at noon. First it was to be 1:00PM, then switched to 12:30PM and then to 12:00PM. All these changes were made by communicating with Gertie who is arranging a meeting place. She finally decided on the Total Station and asked Maurice to drive us over.

David arrived at 1:15 PM. He was in a beat-up pickup truck with the back enclosed. You guessed it! We (Dorothy and I) are to ride in the back: a blanket has been spread across the bed for our comfort. David jumped in front with Leonard who is the driver and a cousin of his. Think Maurice was taken back (to say the least) when I hugged David and when we agreed to ride in the back, luggage and all. The almost three-hour ride was uneventful and although very hot and bumpy, Dorothy never complained. My heart was bursting with excitement.

We went first to the ASHYO office. I had worried that I would forget names...should not have been anxious because we were greeted with bubbling, sparkling juice and popcorn. The drink was shaken, popped and spewed in a spray over many of us. This was a reminder to me (and them) of the first bottle of bubbling juice they had opened in front of me. Luckily, even though there were new faces, I did remember each of those I had known. We visited the doctor's office but only the doctor and Skosi are still there.

David saw to it that our luggage was taken to Christine's and Dorothy and I walked on down to the house. Christine and Thobi were there to greet us, my room was made up for two and supper was on the stove. So far, David, his group, Christine and Rabie ...appeared as if there had been no changes in their ages. But Thobi! Thobi has grown at least four inches, is significantly taller than I am and absolutely beautiful. She is no longer a child; instead she is a young lady. Just as ASHYO had grown in numbers, so has this family. Little Ambrosia (3 years), a brother of Thobi, and Petros, Christine's father of 85 years, now also live with this family.

It was great to see them and later Boy and Togo came. We were not to see Sonta until a few minutes before we left on the following Sunday.

We relaxed and were in bed early. Because this is the hot season in Siyabuswa, Rabie had even given us a fan which we needed to blow directly on us. Oh yes, we were greeted with fat cakes (my favorite) and after the first bite, Dorothy's. Where are the geese?

<u>Wednesday</u>

We were awakened early with tea and more fat cakes. We wandered down to the office around 8:30AM where I was delighted to find that the pickup is David's and he will transport us wherever and whenever we wish. Sure beats the transport problems of my first stay.

This morning he transported us to Kameelrivier and Welterfrede to meet with the home-based care volunteers. We also met with the rest of the ASHYO team. There are now 26 members of the organization and more than half are women.

We were in town five days and met with many different groups. There was a good bit of confusion about our proposed bead project. It was difficult to stress that we wanted the home-based care volunteers and/or specific patients with AIDS to benefit from the sales of the beadwork.

<u>Wednesday, Thursday and Friday</u>

At each meeting, we attempted to explain or rather to come up with a workable game plan. We drove to several craft centers which are interested in doing the work but this is not our intent. I am sure we stepped on a few toes but in the end, we believe that at least four or five of the small HBCO organizations will be involved.

<u>Saturday</u>

David drove us to Kameelrivier where we met with representatives of three different organizations. He also explained the concept as he sees it of the plan to sell the beadwork.

A tentative plan was developed and Dorothy and I can only wait and see how it all falls out. We hope that the volunteers will purchase the beads and produce the crafts using their own designs. They will ship the finished products to Dorothy and me in the United States. We will market their work and return the money received to them. The volunteers who provide home-based care and support services to families devastated by HIV and AIDS will benefit!

One afternoon we visited Pastor Hendrik who took us to visit the Grace Christian School. I was stunned and in awe at the growth. There are more than 300 young people attending the school and 36 of these are resident students. There are seventeen teachers, the facilities are beautiful, and the grounds spacious.

Best of all, I was able to meet the young man whom I sponsor face-to-face. He is eleven years of age now and a delight. During our visit, he was very polite and introduced us to his friends. He was proud to show us his room and around the area. Later I was to meet him in the complex and he gave me a sincere hug and kiss. He said good-bye and said sincerely, "Go in peace, Gogo."

It was a productive and rewarding trip for me. I touched base with many old friends and suffice it to say, there were too many to list. But will say that a highlight was my visit with Silvia. She came to see me just before we left and we were able to have a real "talk" as we used to do. She is as self-effacing as ever and truly a kindred spirit.

Dorothy remained a real trooper through all the greetings and meetings, the rides in the back of the pickup, the walks in the hot sunshine or rain and sleeping in hot, close room. She never complained (out loud) or was unwilling to tag along.

We left Siyabuswa Sunday a little after noon and were transported to Pretoria once again in the back of David's truck with Leonard driving. This time, Dorothy was able to ride in the front and David and a friend of his rode in the back with me.

Leonard TRULY saved our lives somewhere between Siyabuswa and Pretoria. Dorothy told me that all of a sudden, a car going in the same direction as we were, made a sudden U-turn, going very fast. Leonard stomped on his brake but could not stop fast enough and swerved off and then back onto the highway, and narrowly missed hitting the crazy driver broadside. Believe it or not, that driver stopped; we backed up and he apologized. The boys were ready to fight but we (old women) probably saved a true confrontation just by our presence (or we could have been marks and this a set-up).

Angels on the highway make this a good place to end this sojourn.